The Great Power of Small Nations

EARLY AMERICAN STUDIES

Series editors: Kathleen M. Brown, Roquinaldo Ferreira, Emma Hart, and Daniel K. Richter

Exploring neglected aspects of our colonial, revolutionary, and early national history and culture, Early American Studies reinterprets familiar themes and events in fresh ways. Interdisciplinary in character, and with a special emphasis on the period from about 1600 to 1850, the series is published in partnership with the McNeil Center for Early American Studies.

A complete list of books in the series is available from the publisher.

The Great Power of Small Nations

Indigenous Diplomacy in the Gulf South

Elizabeth N. Ellis

PENN

UNIVERSITY OF PENNSYLVANIA PRESS

PHILADELPHIA

Copyright © 2023 University of Pennsylvania Press

All rights reserved. Except for brief quotations used for purposes of review or scholarly citation, none of this book may be reproduced in any form by any means without written permission from the publisher.

Published by
University of Pennsylvania Press
Philadelphia, Pennsylvania 19104-4112
www.upenn.edu/pennpress

Printed in the United States of America on acid-free paper
10 9 8 7 6 5 4 3 2 1

Library of Congress Cataloging-in-Publication Data
Names: Ellis, Elizabeth N. (Elizabeth Nicole), author.
Title: The great power of small nations : indigenous diplomacy in the Gulf South / Elizabeth N. Ellis.
Other titles: Early American studies.
Description: Philadelphia : University of Pennsylvania Press, [2022] | Series: Early American studies | Includes bibliographical references and index.
Identifiers: LCCN 2022007622 | ISBN 9781512823097 (hardcover) | ISBN 9781512823189 (ebook)
Subjects: LCSH: Indians of North America—Mississippi River Valley—Politics and government. | Indians of North America—Gulf Coast (U.S.)—Politics and government. | Indians of North America—Mississippi River Valley—History—18th century. | Indians of North America—Gulf Coast (U.S.)—History—18th century. | Mississippi River Valley—History—18th century. | Gulf Coast (U.S.)—History—18th century.
Classification: LCC E78.M75 E45 2022 | DDC 976.004/97—dc23/eng/20220225
LC record available at https://lccn.loc.gov/2022007622
Hardcover ISBN 9781512823097
eBook ISBN 9781512823189

CONTENTS

Introduction	1
Chapter 1. A World of Towns	17
Chapter 2. Establishing Relationships with the French	45
Chapter 3. Enslaved by Their Allies: Tensas and Chitimachas in French Louisiana	75
Chapter 4. Colonial Propaganda and Indigenous Defiance	108
Chapter 5. French Transgressions and Natchez Resistance	140
Chapter 6. Imperial Blunders and the Revival of Interdependency at Midcentury	172
Chapter 7. Tunica Power After the Seven Years' War	196
Chapter 8. The Beginnings of Marginalization	213
Chapter 9. Remembering, Forgetting, and Mythologizing the Petites Nations	229
Afterword	255
Notes	259
Index	319
Acknowledgments	327

INTRODUCTION

This story begins in the present-day community of the Pointe-au-Chien Indian Tribe of Louisiana. Like the community's French name, which means Oak Point or Dog Point depending on whom you ask, this Native nation carries the memories and influence of the region's colonial past. The marshy coastal lands where the present-day Pointe-au-Chien community resides are an hour and a half south and west from New Orleans by car. Driving from the Crescent City into the southern bayous leads you along a series of sun-bleached elevated roadways that curve down to the very bottom of the Mississippi River Delta. Here, the muddy waters empty into the Gulf of Mexico and alligators rest half-submerged in the murky shallows. In the spring, you can pull off along the highway and pick up flats of tiny, deep-red strawberries at roadside stands and from the backs of farmers' trucks.

The Pointe-au-Chien Indian Tribe is a small community of roughly 680 people, most of whom live along the rapidly receding Gulf shore in Terrebonne and Lafourche Parishes. There, the marshlands cut through the neighborhoods, and the environment is as much water as it is land. The last narrow strip of road that stretches into the community is flanked by a bayou and propeller boats draped with trawling nets. These waterways provide easy access to the rich Gulf waters that many Pointe-au-Chien families rely on for shrimp and catfish. At family gatherings, Pointe-au-Chien aunts and grandmothers transform the day's catch into sizzling pot-fried crabs and prepare crispy, golden soft-shell shrimp. The community's culture, foodways, and health are intimately intertwined with the welfare of the bayou.[1]

These coastal lands and waters are temperamental but fertile. At least, they used to be. For centuries, Native communities have managed the region's ecology with sustainable fishing, trapping, and caretaking of marsh grasses through controlled burns. However, in recent years, extractive industry, modern infrastructure, and ever-increasing levels of atmospheric carbon have taken a devastating toll on Louisiana's southern bayous. In the early twentieth century, the

Figure 1. Bayou Pointe-au-Chien. Photo by Laura Kelley, 2010.

strategic damming of the Mississippi to prevent flooding of riverine farmlands and homes interrupted the river's natural drainage and stopped the rich silt from washing downriver and replenishing the coastal marshes. Then, in the second half of the century, the construction of oil pipelines that bore through the mud eroded the coastline, creating deep chasms through the delicate wetlands that let saltwater seep into the soil, killing the grasses and trees. Over the past two decades, hurricanes and oil spills have exacerbated the damage. With each successive hurricane, more and more community members have been forced to elevate their houses to protect against future storm surges, and now much of the neighborhood floats twenty feet in the air. As you travel further down the bayou, you pass ghostly, desiccated white oak tree trunks that serve as stark reminders of more abundant times. This massive environmental destruction has left Pointe-au-Chien and other Gulf Coast Indigenous communities on a shrinking land base that is steadily being reclaimed by the sea.[2]

Figure 2. View from Pointe-au-Chien Community Center. Photo by Laura Kelley, 2010.

Pointe-au-Chien is one of the many Indigenous communities that have managed to remain in their southern homelands despite hundreds of years of colonial, environmental, and biological challenges. Today, the state of Louisiana recognizes fifteen Native nations within its borders whose ancestors have lived in the region for centuries. In the Mississippi Delta, Alabamas, Biloxis, Chitimachas, Choctaws, Coushattas, Houmas, Ishak/Atakapas, Tunicas, and many other Native people found ways to evade removal and preserve their communities and cultures. These Indigenous Southerners are diverse, and the people who make up these tribal nations today have a wide range of eye, skin, and hair colors, but all have Native American roots and identities. Their Gulf homelands have changed dramatically in the last three hundred years, but their peoples embody the enduring traditions, communities, and politics of a much older South.[3]

In that much older South of the seventeenth and eighteenth centuries, these Native communities' ancestors shaped European empires and forged vibrant and powerful nations. The erasure of their histories has had massive impacts not only for contemporary tribal nations but also on how we understand the historical and ongoing struggles over sovereignty in the American South. During this era, the small Native nations of the Gulf South both facilitated and strategically limited European colonization, and they developed strategies that enabled their nations to survive the onslaught of violence precipitated by European arrival. As European newcomers were dependent on these nations, Indigenous policies and visions defined the communities, economies, and conflicts of this era at least as much as imperial orders and initiatives.

In the decades after the American Revolution, the few colonists who lived in the Lower Mississippi Valley were joined by increasing numbers of non-Indigenous newcomers. During these last decades of the eighteenth century, many Native nations were pushed off their homelands near growing colonial settlements at New Orleans, Mobile, Biloxi, Natchez, and Pointe Coupée. By the early nineteenth century, European and American immigrants displaced thousands of Indigenous people and transformed their territories into cotton plantations. These dispossessions created new communities of Indigenous migrants and refugees who fled the onslaught of white settlers. For example, the Pointe-au-Chien trace their origins to the migration of small groups of Ishak/Atakapas and Biloxis who joined Chitimachas in the bayous of southern Louisiana. Similarly, the Tunica-Biloxis, who reside near Marksville, Louisiana, today, tell stories of the relocation of Choctaw, Tunica, Avoyelle, and Biloxi peoples to lands west of the Mississippi River where they would be better protected from the settler invasion. By migrating, adapting, offering refuge to others, and forming strategic alliances, their ancestors managed not only to survive for centuries but also to sustain their communities and cultures and retain portions of their homelands.[4]

So how have the many Native communities that reside in Louisiana today been able to remain in their homelands? Part of the answer to this question lies in the work of their ancestors, and in the more than three-hundred-year struggles of their peoples against colonization. Returning to this deep past and to the first century of these Native nations' fights against imperial invasion sheds light on the strategies, practices, and social norms that have enabled generations of Indigenous resilience and power.

In this book, I contend that the political systems of these nations made them strong during the seventeenth and eighteenth centuries. Chitimachas, Chakchiumas, Mobilians, Tunicas, and many other small nations steered the course of the development of the eighteenth-century Lower Mississippi Valley. Their networks and alliances protected their peoples and allowed them to exercise powerful influence with their colonial neighbors. International and cross-cultural relationships also strengthened their communities. In this era, the majority of these small nations lived in multinational settlements—meaning they resided in very close proximity to foreign peoples who lived under separate governments. By residing alongside other nations in clustered settlements, these small nations were better able to collectively defend their peoples, and their communities enjoyed the economic opportunities that came from access to international markets.

These multinational settlements helped ensure the survival of small nations during dangerous times. Multinational settlements were often not permanent, and migrants might live alongside foreign nations for short periods during times of crisis, or for multiple decades before they moved again to seek new opportunities. The partnerships and alliances that Native men and women built with their neighbors could result in the permanent incorporation of migrants or the joining of two or more nations, but often they did not. Instead, Indigenous political systems protected the rights of nations, towns, and even individual families to leave multinational settlements, and even their nations of origin, and build new communities elsewhere. Essentially, this system laid the framework for the creation of the large and powerful nations of the Southeast, and it also ensured that Native people always had the ability to break away from their nations or communities and form new political groups. Fusion and fission were both vital parts of these processes. Multinational settlements were extremely common across the Indigenous Southeast, and Native Southerners' customs of providing refuge for, living alongside, and incorporating outsiders and migrant groups help us understand both the processes of Indigenous nation-building and European colonization during the eighteenth century.

These historical patterns of settlement and political organization also suggest that, in these seventeenth- and eighteenth-century pasts, Native Southerners had capacious ideas about what it meant to be part of an Indigenous nation and to belong to a tribal community. Multinational settlements—and the mobility and relationships among polities that enabled many small nations to survive the colonial era—help explain the later emergence of American Indian communities who trace their ancestry to multiple Native nations. The incorporative frameworks that small nations used to build their nations relied on their abilities to forge new kin ties, thereby creating political communities and societies that were not restricted by racial or ethnic origins. This older Indigenous ideology of nationhood provided a model of belonging to peoples and to lands that stands in stark contrast to the later exclusionary logics of race-based citizenship and bordered sovereignty that European and American peoples developed in the nineteenth and twentieth centuries. Groups like the Tunica-Biloxis and the Pointe-au-Chien therefore represent the survival of these longer patterns of migration, international relations, and small, multiethnic community-building practices.

Of course, the stories of how exactly the diverse Indigenous peoples of the Lower Mississippi Valley employed these practices and chose to build their nations are complex and require attention to the many different paths these Native Southerners pursued. This narrative follows the stories of some of these resilient nations during the late seventeenth and eighteenth centuries. The Indigenous peoples at the heart of this history all lived in a region bounded by the Red River to the west and Mobile Bay to the east, the Yazoo River to the north and the Gulf of Mexico to the south. In these lands, peoples of more than forty distinct Indigenous polities made their homes. At the turn of the eighteenth century, larger political entities like the coalescent Choctaw and Creek confederacies and the Chickasaw nation controlled territory to the east of this region while Caddoan polities governed the land to the west, and Osages and Quapaws dominated the territories to the north. The space in between these groups was not ruled by any single Indigenous nation, but rather was a borderland and home to many small Native polities. For small nations, this borderland offered safety and a source of strength. I use the term *borderland* to describe the Lower Mississippi Valley not to suggest a European conception of a frontier or an unregulated space, but rather to mean a place with multiple and layered land rights. As the historian Brian DeLay has suggested, the "defining quality of borderlands regions is plural sovereignty—the presence of multiple polities claiming and exercising de-facto authority over place and people."[5]

This borderlands framework also helps translate Indigenous understandings of the control of space as a product of reciprocal relationships rather than the domination of a land and its inhabitants. As the Cree writer Emily Riddle explains when describing the historical practice of shared jurisdiction in Cree and Métis territories on the northern prairies, "European political traditions would have us believe that being sovereign means asserting exclusive control over a territory, whereas Prairie NDN [Indian] political traditions teach us that it is through our relationship with others that we are sovereign, that sharing is not a sign of weakness but of ultimate strength and diplomacy."[6] Essentially, the sharing of territory with different people empowers each group through their webs of interdependent relationships with others. This framing and the borderlands concept of overlapping and relational sovereignties also bring us closer to Indigenous conceptions of territoriality, belonging, and authority that scholars like Glen Coulthard and Leanne Simpson have described. These Native theorists describe governance as grounded in relations of reciprocal obligation not just to humans but also to land and to nonhumans such as rocks, fish, or forests. Indigenous conceptions of relational sovereignty therefore explain why small nations saw shared territory as a source of power rather than an indication of weakness.[7]

The small nations of these Indigenous borderlands were almost all polities that contained fewer than three thousand people. Many of these groups were communities of only a few hundred. While they were similar in size, these nations were incredibly diverse. The peoples of this region spoke at least six different languages, held distinct religious beliefs, followed diverse cultural practices, embodied different ideas of gender, and embraced a variety of political and governmental structures. Some of these polities were hierarchical theocracies with rigid class divisions, while others were loosely affiliated egalitarian villages governed by councils of men, women, and nonbinary leaders. French colonists collectively referred to the many small nations inhabiting this region as "*les petites nations*."[8]

I adopt the term *Petites Nations* with the intention of emphasizing Indigenous sovereignty and conveying this specific temporal and geographical context. I have capitalized the term to indicate that I am using it as a proper noun rather than simply to mean "small nations." Although Native American people in the modern era are frequently discussed as a minority group within the United States, or as people with a specific genetic or racial ancestry, ideas of Native nationhood that are bounded by race or framed in relation to the American settler states are relatively recent conceptions. Long before the creation of the United States, Native peoples of many ethnic backgrounds formed distinct political entities, established systems of governance, and developed relationships with, and obligations to, their lands and to each other. Early Native polities mostly did not look like modern, bordered, nation-states. They were nonetheless sovereign nations, and this long-standing, land-based sovereignty still grounds Native nations' claims to separate governance and autonomous territories today.

When they called these peoples "*petites nations*," French settlers understood few of the complexities of Indigenous politics and relationships. Nonetheless, Indigenous notions of nationhood in the seventeenth and eighteenth centuries have more in common with eighteenth-century European ideas of nationhood than with our modern conceptions of nation-states. In 1765 the French philosopher Denis Diderot defined "nation" as "a collective word that is used to express a considerable quantity of people, who live in the certain extent of country, enclosed within certain limits, and who obey the same government."[9] Applying his definition to Europe a century or two earlier, it would be difficult to draw firm boundaries around the groups of people inhabiting the Continent. The word *nation* had similarly flexible meanings in seventeenth and eighteenth-century England. As the historian Nancy Shoemaker has argued, "Even the word *nation* in early modern English was ambiguous, sometimes referring to a formal political entity and at other times to a vaguely defined body of people linked only by common language and culture."[10] Shoemaker further suggests that the vagueness of these early modern concepts of "nation" can be helpful, allowing us to talk about the many different ways that people formed collective political and cultural groups. Using the term *nation* to describe Indigenous polities therefore enables me to draw comparisons and emphasize parity among imperial and Indigenous settlements, political powers, territorial claims, and sovereign governments.

I recognize that *Petites Nations* is not a perfect term to describe this multitude of Native American peoples. Each of these groups had their own names for themselves. For example, Tunicas referred and refer to themselves as Tayoroni, and the people the French historically called Atakapa prefer to be identified as Ishak.[11] Still, Petites Nations allows me to employ a more flexible conception of nationhood to talk about the Indigenous past. Contemporary nation-states' ideologies, which treat citizenship as a status gifted by genetic descent and inherently exclude those beyond their borders, are at odds with most historical Indigenous notions of community, belonging, and expansive and incorporative kinship. Calling Indigenous polities nations, in this eighteenth-century sense of the word, therefore underscores the sovereignty and political authority of these groups while also emphasizing the capacity of these communities to naturalize outsiders.

The term *Petites Nations* also highlights the intentionally small size of these Indigenous polities. Throughout the eighteenth century, many of these peoples actively pursued strategies that allowed them to exist as autonomous communities of fewer people and avoid centralization or incorporation into such larger nations as the Choctaws or Creeks. Because of the lingering influence of anthropological theories of social evolution which posit that smaller polities or tribes are "primitive" and underdeveloped, we sometimes imagine that small political groups are only a step on the way to developing larger and more hierarchical systems of government. Many historians have portrayed small groups of Native people as "remnants" of formerly great nations, or "shattered fragments" of previous civilizations. Such wording suggests that small groups of Native people are in the process of decline. To counter this perception of smallness as brokenness or deficiency, I use *Petites Nations* meaningfully in my discussions of power and influence as a way of suggesting that smallness could also be a source of strength.[12]

Although each Petite Nation was independently small, they were collectively quite numerous during the 1700s. At the close of the seventeenth century, the total of the combined Petites Nations populations was roughly 17,000–20,000 people. For comparison, during the same era, there were about 7,000 Chickasaws and 21,000 Choctaws.[13] The total population of the Petites Nations remained larger than the total settler population throughout the French colonial era. When the French left Louisiana in 1763, there were roughly 4,000 French settlers and 5,000 enslaved Africans in the colony, while the Petites Nations population during that era was about 7,000 people, and the total population of Indigenous people in the Lower Mississippi Valley was roughly 25,000.[14] It was not until the late eighteenth century that European and American settlers and enslaved Africans began to outnumber the Indigenous inhabitants of the region.

In this era when Indigenous people were still the demographic majority, the Petites Nations' political networks and social policies shaped the trajectories of nations and empires in the Lower Mississippi Valley. This book opens in the late seventeenth century, with a chapter that focuses on the Yazoos, Ofogoulas, Tensas, and Tunicas and traces the origins of large as well as small Native nations in the region. As the Mississippian political world of the North American Middle Ages drew to a close in the Southeast, Indigenous communities created a new geopolitical order that built on this Mississippian past and was structured by practices of multinational settlement, migrant welcome, and extensive webs of international relationships. By the late seventeenth century, the Native nations of the Gulf South (both larger polities like the Creeks and Choctaws as well as the Petites Nations) had developed systems of multinational settlement and refugee sanctuary that helped migratory communities and groups in crisis leave their homelands and safely resettle alongside other nations. These practices of offering refuge and land to outsiders created communities that contained not just multiple independent nations but also people from a wide variety of ethnic, cultural, and political backgrounds. As the first disruptions from colonial incursions into the Southeast ricocheted along the Gulf Coast, and the rise of the Indian slave markets and growing Haudenosaunee (Iroquois) power transformed eastern North America, these Petites Nations' political practices became increasingly important tools to help them protect their nations in a dangerous world. The second chapter analyzes the ways that Biloxis, Bayagoulas, and Tunicas incorporated French settlers into these preexisting multinational settlements, and how these intimate relations shaped French settlement and colonial imperatives during the first decade of the eighteenth century. The first French towns at Mobile and Biloxi were both part of Petites Nations multinational settlements. At the same time, the Indian slave trades spread violence throughout the region and destabilized Petites Nations communities. These first two chapters lay out a framework for regional Indigenous political and social practices. In Chapter 3 the focus changes from Indigenous politics to the crises that colonial disruptions created within Tensa and Chitimacha communities between 1700 and 1720, as French settlers enslaved people of these nations. Louisiana colonists trafficked not only in foreign and enemy Indigenous peoples but they also traded women, children, and men who belonged to allied nations. During this era, the French even went so far as to manufacture a war against the Chitimachas to acquire enslaved laborers for the colony.

The middle third of this book centers on a series of conflicts between 1729 and 1750 that exacted high tolls on French, Indigenous, and African inhabitants of the Lower Mississippi Valley. Chapter 4 examines the 1720s and the growing resentment among Mobilian, Tohome, Chitimacha, and Natchez communities toward their French neighbors. During this era, several diplomatic shifts and a change in imperial administration enabled the rapid growth of the fledgling French colony. This period of colonial expansion emboldened settlers to begin to imagine a future of Louisiana without Petites Nations people. It also led colonists to attempt to break their obligations to the Petites Nations. Chapter 5 centers on the Natchez War of 1729 and the lasting consequences of this conflict for the peoples of the Yazoo River Valley. This chapter follows Tunica, Ofogoula, and Yazoo people as they were pressured by the Natchez, Choctaws, and French to fight in the conflict, and argues that the Natchez War took a high toll on Petites Nations communities in large part because the Louisiana colonists refused to respect the social and political norms that usually served to limit violence and conflict among both neighbors and combatants. The war among the Natchez, French, and Choctaws altered the geopolitical landscape of the whole Lower Mississippi Valley. It also solidified Choctaw dominance in the region, and the might of this nation would continue to shape both colonial and Petites Nations' political agendas throughout the remainder of the century. Chapter 6 discusses how French imperial anxiety generated a series of deadly regional conflicts with Louisiana's powerful Native neighbors. Following the Chakchiumas through the Chickasaw Wars and the Choctaw Civil War reveals how the Chakchiumas' relationships to Chickasaws and Choctaws shaped both of these conflicts and ultimately brought this regional violence to a close. At midcentury, the weakness of the French Empire, and Louisiana's concern over imperial competition, again created economic and political opportunities for the Petites Nations and revived interdependent diplomatic and economic relationships between these small polities and the colony.

The concluding third of the book examines the period between 1763 and 1800. The seventh chapter spotlights Tunica and Ofogoula people during the 1760s and 1770s as they navigated the imperial transition after the Seven Years' War, and traces the attempts by the new governments of British West Florida and Spanish Louisiana to control Indigenous territories. This chapter illustrates how Tunica and Ofogoula people wielded power and managed to use the new border to leverage opportunities for their peoples. Chapter 8 describes how Tunica and Petites Nations' fortunes shifted after the American Revolution as waves of settlers began to flood into the Lower Mississippi Valley. Tensions heightened among Tunicas and Choctaws during this era as the crush of settlement pushed Petites Nations people south and west and led to widespread dispossession. The ninth and final chapter examines the marginalization of Petites Nations communities in the years around the turn of the nineteenth century and the ways that Petites Nations people survived and remember this era. The book closes with a meditation on memory, American settlement, and the narratives of erasure that obscure the histories and contemporary vibrancy of the Indigenous nations of the Lower Mississippi Valley.

* * *

For American Indian people, how we tell these histories matters. The narratives of loss and erasure, or survival and power that historians weave in their writing fundamentally shape the ability of tribal nations to exercise rights and sovereignty in the present. In the case of early Louisiana Indigenous history, the stakes of this work are immense. In addition to suffering from discrimination and erasure in popular culture, several Native communities across the state are engaged in protracted legal battles with the federal government that center on how outsiders understand their histories. While four Native nations in Louisiana are federally recognized, the other eleven state-recognized Native nations are not, and this means that these nations' histories are current sites of political contest. Several of these non–federally recognized tribes, including the Pointe-au-Chien, United Houma Nation, the Grand Caillou/Dulac Band of Biloxi-Chitimacha-Choctaw, the Bayou LaFourche Band of Biloxi-Chitimacha Indians, and the Isle de Jean Charles Band of the Biloxi-Chitimacha-Choctaw Tribe, are descendants of the Petites Nations. In part, groups like the Pointe-au-Chien and United Houma Nation have been unable to secure federal recognition because of how historians and anthropologists have characterized Petites Nations' pasts as processes of decline and disappearance.[15] This scholarship gives readers the perception that Petites Nations peoples have vanished. Equally as significant, many of these nations have been unable to obtain recognition from the federal government because the Bureau of Indian Affairs' requirements for federal recognition are neither attentive to the historical processes that shaped Indigenous Gulf South societies, nor are they commensurate with Native understandings of community, nationhood, and belonging. Far from being removed from these contemporary political battles, early American Indigenous history is deeply imbricated in the ongoing contests over tribal sovereignty. Understanding the context of Louisiana nations' fights over federal acknowledgment is therefore an essential piece of these stories.

The federal acknowledgment process relies heavily on historical and anthropological scholarship. Indian nations that apply for federal acknowledgment are required to provide documentary evidence of their people's history and culture to the U.S. Department of the Interior. Archival research and historical narratives are therefore critical components of the application process.

Most Native nations have never had to apply for federal recognition. The U.S. government recognizes them as "authentic" Indian nations and sovereign polities because their ancestors signed treaties with the federal government in the eighteenth or nineteenth century and their nations have long-standing relationships with the United States. However, for groups that did not historically have relationships with the U.S. government—including those like the Pointe-au-Chien whose lack of formal relationships helped them avoid forced removal—the federal recognition process should theoretically provide a way for tribal nations to obtain official acknowledgment.[16]

Having recognition carries substantial advantages, but recognition does not *give* Native nations sovereignty. These nations were already autonomous political entities whose inherent rights to self-govern emerged through their relations to one another, to their lands, and to other Indigenous nations. Recognition, or the lack thereof, cannot create or extinguish the land- and kin-based relationships that form the basis of Indigenous people's authority to govern their homelands and people.[17] Even so, tribes with federal status have U.S. government support to legislate for their communities and manage their territories. They also have access to financial resources, federal healthcare, and business opportunities that unrecognized nations do not. If Pointe-au-Chien received federal recognition, they could gain access to clinical care through the Indian Health Service, and they might be able to shape the regulations on shrimping, trapping, and oil extraction in their homelands. These kinds of services, political powers, and economic resources can be crucial to ensuring the health and future of Native nations. Therefore, in the 1990s, the Pointe-au-Chien tribal leadership decided to pursue federal recognition in order to help sustain their community through the increasingly dire environmental crisis in their homelands.

My first ventures into early Louisiana history began in 2006 when I was working as part of a team collecting historical documentation for the Pointe-au-Chien Indian Tribe's federal recognition petition. From 2006 to 2010, I worked under the guidance of Laura Kelley, a history professor at Tulane University, who assisted the Pointe-au-Chien Indian Tribe in compiling archival evidence, and with Patty Ferguson Bohnee, a Pointe-au-Chien tribal member and law professor at Arizona State University, who serves as the tribe's general counsel and has helped direct the tribe's recognition efforts in recent years.[18] My job was to comb through archival documents to look for evidence of the histories of Native people who had inhabited the southern bayous before 1800. As I began this research, I was astounded by the quantity of colonial correspondence that dealt with Petites Nations, so, in the process of collecting evidence for Pointe-au-Chien, I became eager to understand a fuller picture of the early Native history of Louisiana.

By beginning my research for this book with a grounding in contemporary Southern Native communities, training in Native American and Indigenous Studies approaches and methodologies, and a deep, personal familiarity with insidious mythologies of disappearance that all Native people still confront in the United States, I was able to look critically at these colonial sources.[19] As early as the 1710s, some colonial observers began to claim that the Petites Nations were destroyed or dying out. However, in their next letters, or sometimes even further down on the same page, these French writers would proceed to lament the damage that these supposedly destroyed nations were causing to colonial farms, or comment on how the meat that these allegedly vanishing peoples sold in New Orleans kept the settlers fed. It would seem quite the challenge to both be dead and marketing venison in a bustling port city at the same time. In essence, by not assuming the inevitable demise of Native peoples, I was able to recognize that these French sources often conveyed more about imperial desires than Gulf Coast realities.

The more I researched and came to understand the political and social dynamics that shaped Petites Nations' communities and multinational settlements in the eighteenth century, the more I became troubled by the disjuncture between the historical evidence and the rigid definitions of community belonging and historical formation that the federal government uses to assess Native nations today. I have since come to conclude that the contemporary requirements for federal acknowledgment, and the Western ideologies of nationhood embodied in these regulations, have warped historians' expectations for early Native

American societies. This has led us to both overlook and misunderstand Petites Nations' stories.

Historians have long been drawn to large Native nations whose histories can be told as the development of centralized, coercive, political governments, or of powerful Indigenous empires with strong militaries. These stories sometimes mirror the ways that scholars talk about the creation of European empires or the coming together of the United States, making these histories accessible and the stories of Native nations legible for modern readers. This focus has produced important histories of large nations such as the Haudenosaunee (Iroquois), Comanches, and Osages. More recently, historians have also begun to pay attention to smaller and more fluid Native polities, and their scholarship on Shawnees, Anishinaabeg, and other Native nations with flexible systems of belonging and governance have upended our understandings of Indigenous politics and challenged the clean narratives we tell about the expansion of U.S. power and territory.[20] Nonetheless, historians' fixations on large and centralized polities still tend to obscure the stories of smaller nations. As this book illustrates, many Petites Nations rejected amalgamation into larger nations. Instead of seeking political centralization and hierarchy, Petites Nations like the Biloxis repeatedly split, migrated, adopted outsiders, and lived with foreign peoples in ways that would make no sense within the modern framework provided for federal acknowledgment.

Federal acknowledgment has therefore distorted the ways we think about what it meant to be part of a Native community in the past and has frozen Native peoples in time. The current federal recognition process requires tribal nations to provide histories that fit these expectations of centralized political power and ethnic homogeneity. Nations need to demonstrate the persistence of their Native American cultures, political organizations, and ancestries—the less change to any of these aspects of society, the better. Among other federal requirements are stipulations that Native people must prove that they were historically recognized as Indians by outsiders, that they provide evidence of governing documents and membership criteria, and that the tribe demonstrate authority or influence over tribal members. One of the criteria that has proven challenging for Pointe-au-Chien and other Louisiana nations is a requirement that nations "show that a predominant portion of the petitioning group comprises a distinct community and has existed as a community from historical times until the present." The tribe has struggled to provide archival evidence of the existence of their community in the period before 1830.[21] In essence, federal recognition rationale demands that the same group of people must have made up a distinct community and a mostly unchanging political entity for hundreds of years.

Current recognition mandates therefore explicitly exclude the capacity for political transformation or for the ability of Indigenous communities to integrate significant numbers of newcomers without diminishing the nation's sovereignty and national identity. This, of course, is at odds with the historical practices of multinational settlement, refugee sanctuary, and adoptions that were so important for eighteenth-century Petites Nations. Moreover, if we were to apply these same strict requirements in order to recognize U.S. authority over territories or grant U.S. citizenship today, many of the people and lands now encompassed by the more than fifty states and U.S. territories would fail to meet these same criteria for nationhood, citizenship, and valid sovereignty.[22]

Beyond the rigid historical misperceptions of Indian nationhood that underlie federal recognition requirements, a further difficulty the Pointe-au-Chien Indian Tribe faces is that their continuing presence in Louisiana defies the popular narratives of Southern Native history. In American high schools, students typically learn histories of Native Americans that conclude with the removal or the destruction of the Southern Indigenous communities. Even in recent years, as both early American historians and the U.S. public writ large have become aware of the importance of Native American peoples in American history, the stories that we tell about Native people generally follow predictable trajectories. They almost all end with dispossession, disappearance, or death.

My own nation's history somewhat mirrors these stories of removal. My people, the Peoria Tribe of Indians of Oklahoma, are descendants of the Illinois Confederacy. Like many other Native Americans, my ancestors were displaced from their homelands in Illinois and Indiana during the nineteenth century and ultimately removed to Oklahoma. But forced removal to Indian territory was only one way that Native people were dispossessed. Indeed, even as they lost land and battled settler encroachment, many Native communities across eastern North America found ways to remain in their homelands.[23]

Frankly, Petites Nations' histories are neither as unusual nor anomalous as they might initially seem. During the eighteenth century, most of the Indigenous polities of the Gulf Coast and the Lower Mississippi River Valley were similar in population to that of the present-day population of the Pointe-au-Chien Indian Tribe. This smallness and focus on local community attest to the endurance of a centuries-old system of political formation. Dozens of nations across the Southeast and Eastern Seaboard found ways to stay, avoid removal, and remain in their homelands as waves of American settlers flooded across their ancestral territories. Nations like the Pamunkeys in Virginia, Lumbees in North Carolina, Mashpee-Wampanoags in Massachusetts, Catawbas in South Carolina, and many others escaped forced relocation by moving to inaccessible areas and undesirable lands, or by living in small numbers on the peripheries of colonial settlements.[24]

So, while this study is rooted in the regional specificities of the Gulf Coast, the patterns and the experiences of these small Indigenous communities also provide frameworks that can help us understand how so many small and multiethnic Indigenous communities remained on their lands even as they were marginalized by different arms of the American state. Communities like the Pointe-au-Chien, United Houma Nation, and Lumbees challenge the political and racial logics that undergird contemporary American Indian policy and that leave little space for multinational or multiethnic Indigenous identities. Persistent stereotypes of American Indians as people who universally have tan skin, silky black hair, and who sing to raccoons, have made it difficult for Native people with black skin or blonde hair to be recognized as "real" Indians by many non-Indigenous people. And these stereotypes and phenotypical expectations have in turn influenced federal policy. The Pointe-au-Chien, Tunica-Biloxi, and United Houma Nation have all had state and federal officials, or even their neighbors, completely deny their Native ancestry and identities.[25] Essentially, the combination of popular perceptions of the South as defined by a Black and white racial binary, stereotypical imaginings of contemporary Native people, and historical erasure of peoples who avoided removal have all shaped how we have overlooked and misunderstood Petites Nations' histories.

Returning to the eighteenth century to examine how the smaller Indigenous polities of the Gulf South thought about practices of migration, refugee sanctuary, nation-building, and naturalization therefore sheds crucial light on both the past and present experiences of these Native American communities. Understanding these histories, and the betrayals, losses, dangerous diplomacy, compassionate caretaking, and high stakes conflicts that made the modern Gulf South requires avoiding projecting current U.S. beliefs about race, nationhood, and Indigenous decline into the past. Instead, this history demands heeding both archival trails and the knowledge of contemporary tribal communities. *The Great Power of Small Nations*, therefore, is attentive to the present with its potent ideologies, stereotypes, and ongoing contests over Petites Nations' histories even as it narrates events from three centuries before the present. This, then, is a story of Indigenous struggle, not one that ends with colonization or disappearance, but one that, like the people of this region, transforms and endures across generations and continues to shape the Gulf South.

CHAPTER 1

A World of Towns

In the last decades of the seventeenth century, Moncacht-Apé, a Yazoo man, undertook an epic journey. He left his nation's homelands just above the confluence of the Mississippi and Yazoo Rivers and set out in the direction of the rising sun. This Yazoo explorer and intellectual was on a voyage to uncover his people's history and to connect their distant past with their turbulent present. He wanted to know where his people came from, how they had come to live in this place, and what other Indigenous peoples knew of their own origins.

Moncacht-Apé's people were living through an era of momentous changes. During the 1600s, the steady growth of British, Spanish, and English settlements, along with the expansion of Haudenosaunee (Iroquois) power, transformed the geopolitical landscape of eastern North America. Then, in the second half of the seventeenth century, the development of the English colonies of Virginia and Carolina facilitated the growth of a wide-ranging traffic in enslaved Indigenous people across the Southeast. These trades in stolen Native women, men, and children carried violence and disease across the Gulf Coast and into Petites Nations territories. Meanwhile, Native nations who formed partnerships with English traders, like the Chickasaws, grew powerful and turned new European weapons against their southeastern neighbors. To protect their people from the violence unleashed by the slave trades and colonial incursions, the Yazoos relied on the time-honored practices of providing refuge for migrants and living in multinational settlements. Perhaps in order to make sense of the tumultuous present, Moncacht-Apé wanted to understand the past and his people's place among the many societies of Native North America. Interpreting Moncacht-Apé's world therefore requires attention to both the specific cultural and political contexts of the Lower Mississippi Valley as well as an examination of the wider transnational processes that transformed the Southeast in the late seventeenth century.

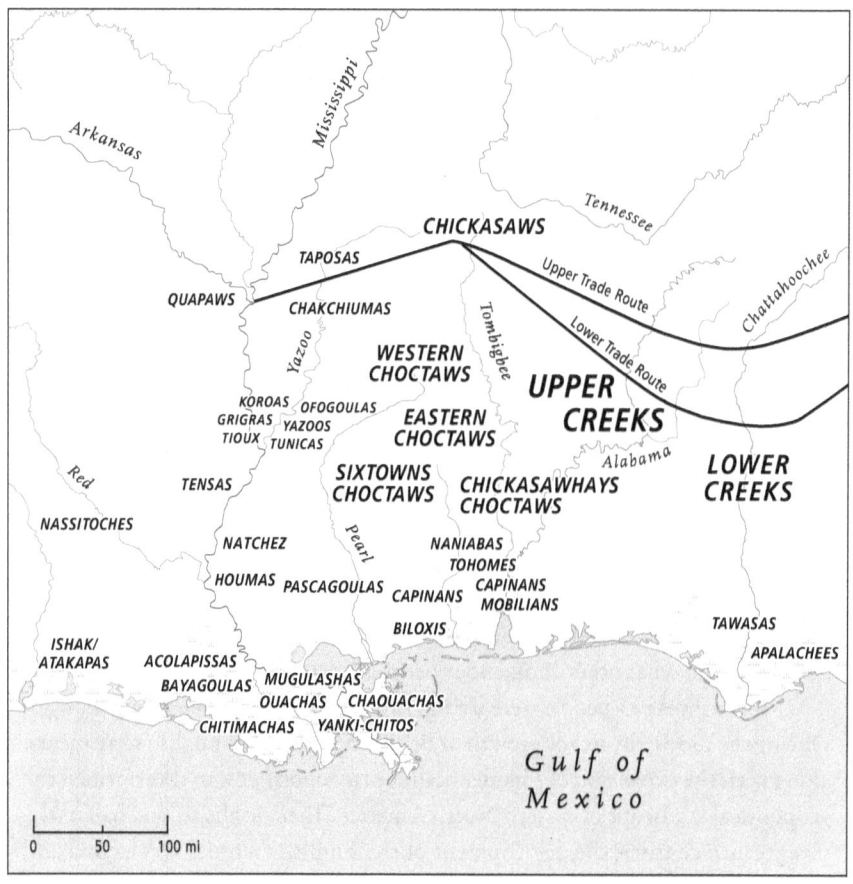

Figure 3. Select nations of the Lower Mississippi Valley circa 1699.

In the 1670s, the Yazoos lived alongside four other Petites Nations. Together, the Yazoos, Koroas, Tioux, Grigras, and Tunicas formed a cluster of settlements that contained about 3,500 people. As Moncacht-Apé walked through neighboring towns to buy salt or visit with friends, he would have heard women pounding corn and chatting in Tunica, his kinsmen calling greetings in his own Yazoo language, and foreign travelers selling hides or negotiating for bear grease in the Mobilian trade language that served as the lingua franca in the region. Growing up in this international hub, Moncacht-Apé frequently dealt with foreigners and heard stories of faraway lands. These moments must have sparked his urge to travel to see the wonders of the continent and its peoples for himself.[1]

As a young man, Moncacht-Apé left the multinational settlement where he was raised and set off across North America to uncover his people's history. He bid his wife and children farewell and journeyed east. Walking barefoot or in soft hide shoes, Moncacht-Apé relied on the well-trod pathways of the eastern woodlands to guide him to other Indigenous historians. This expedition would take him years and teach him much about the continent and its peoples.

Moncacht-Apé made the first stop of his grand tour at the nearby Chickasaw towns. He was likely impressed by the size, wealth, and grandeur of the Chickasaw nation. Perhaps he noticed that some men carried burnished muskets or that elite Chickasaw women wore brightly colored European manufactured cloth. The Chickasaws were allies of the Yazoos, so they welcomed Moncacht-Apé hospitably and entertained his requests for information. Moncacht-Apé explained that he wanted to know more of the region's history, and he asked the Chickasaws "if they knew where we all came from."[2] His Chickasaw hosts knew the stories of their own people's emergence and migration to this land, but they did not know the history of the Yazoos. Instead, they advised Moncacht-Apé to travel further north and east and to consult the peoples of that region. As he set out, they also cautioned him to travel carefully and to take paths that would "avoid passing by the big villages of the whites."[3] They were not sure that these "Blancs" (Frenchmen) would receive him kindly. Moncacht-Apé heeded the Chickasaws' counsel and kept to the routes that circumvented the French towns in Illinois and along the Great Lakes.

By relying on Native knowledge, hospitality, and networks of political connections, Moncacht-Apé was able to travel as far north as Niagara Falls and as far east as the Atlantic Ocean. As he wore out his shoes along the rocky paths of the eastern woodlands and sat with new friends beside small fires in the evenings, he shared stories of his people. In return, he gained a vast political and environmental knowledge of the continent and learned fragments of foreign languages and histories. Moncacht-Apé's journey east led him through more than nine different nations. He crossed through Shawnee lands in the Ohio River Valley, Haudenosaunee homelands in what is now Upstate New York, and along the peripheries of the growing English colonies in the Northeast. He then trekked through the frigid Northern Abenaki territories until he inhaled briny sea mist and gazed upon the roiling blue of the "great water."[4] Moncacht-Apé must have felt exhausted as he watched the waves crash onto the shore and stared out at the expanse. Despite all of his travel, he still could not find anyone who could tell him precisely where his own Yazoo people had originated.[5]

While Moncacht-Apé traveled east across the continent, new epidemics and shockwaves of colonial violence rippled west from the Eastern Seaboard, leaving death and destruction in their wake. As he journeyed, he took care to avoid villages where smallpox or influenza were raging. During Moncacht-Apé's time away, disease and raiders brutalized his own community. When he returned home, Moncacht-Apé was devastated to discover that his wife and children had died in this time of great suffering and illness. They may have been taken by one of the waves of disease or slave raids that scythed down the Mississippi Valley during this era. Like so many Native communities in the interior of North America, the Yazoos experienced European pathogens and epidemics long before they encountered flesh-and blood-colonists.[6] Both were deadly.

Moncacht-Apé fled his grief by throwing himself back into his mission. Again, he left his hometown in search of his people's origins, but this time he went west. He passed through the Quapaw, Missouri, and "Otter" nations in the windswept grasslands that are now Arkansas and Missouri and continued walking north through the territories of Northern and Western Plains nations. Finally, Moncacht-Apé stopped at a village a few days' journey away from the Pacific Ocean. His Native hosts warned Moncacht-Apé to be wary of the pale-skinned travelers who came on ships. These men had long, black beards and they covered almost their entire bodies in brightly colored fabrics. Even their feet were bundled in gold and red-hued cloth. Moncacht-Apé's Native hosts explained that these men came for a pungent yellow timber that could be used to make dye for their clothes. In addition to wood, however, the unwelcome invaders also came ashore to capture young people who they could traffic throughout the Pacific world. During one of these marauding seafarers' visits, Moncacht-Apé's hosts asked for his help defending their community. When they asked Moncacht-Apé to accompany them on a raid against these men who stole their children, he remarked that "my heart found that it was good for me to go with them," and Moncacht-Apé fought alongside his new friends. He may not have been able to protect his own children and his homeland, but he could fight for others. It is likely that he found comfort, on this distant Pacific coast, as he helped other Indigenous families defend their sons and daughters.[7]

It took Moncacht-Apé "thirty-six moons," or roughly three years, to make his journey to the West. Back in the Yazoo village, he sat up with his old friends and talked of his adventures. The knowledge he carried home earned him a reputation as a renowned linguist and scholar. The stories of his extraordinary voyages traveled beyond Native networks and reached French settlers. In later years, they sought him out for his expertise on the region and its history. During the

1720s, Moncacht-Apé sat down with the colonist Antoine-Simon Le Page du Pratz, who recorded some of these stories and published them in a memoir of his time in Louisiana.[8]

Moncacht-Apé's story provides a window into the wide world of the Petites Nations. He traveled through the lands of more than a dozen Native nations, and he collected intelligence about English, French, and possibly Japanese or Russian colonial schemes. As Moncacht-Apé's experiences illustrate, his people were part of far-reaching networks of Native economic, diplomatic, and intellectual exchanges. The Yazoos lived in the midst of an Indigenous borderland that brought them into regular contact with foreign diplomats, travelers, and traders. At home, they existed in a vibrant polyglot and multicultural settlement that was built on relationships of interdependency with their neighboring nations.

While Moncacht-Apé may never have uncovered exactly how or where his people had originated, he would have been familiar with the stories of his homeland from the past couple of centuries, and he would have understood the disruptions caused by the arrival of Europeans in the Southeast within the context of this longer history. For him, and for other Petites Nations people, it would be difficult to explain the fateful changes of the late seventeenth and early eighteenth centuries without speaking of the critical political events that were unfolding in the Haudenosaunee territories in the Northeast, in the new English settlements along the Atlantic Seaboard, and in the Creek, Chickasaw, and Choctaw communities of the Southeast. Decades before European settlers reached the Lower Mississippi Valley, Yazoo people were already experiencing the impact of these cross-continental developments in their homelands.[9]

The migrations of many new Indigenous people into the Lower Mississippi Valley and the expansion of the Indian slave trade in the Southeast were two of the most significant processes that reshaped Moncacht-Apé's homelands. In the last decades of the seventeenth century, large numbers of newcomers arrived in the Petites Nations' homelands. Several Indigenous groups made long and treacherous overland journeys to the Mississippi Delta from across the eastern woodlands, including a group of Siouan migrants, the Mosopeleas/Ofogoulas, who became the Yazoos' new neighbors. Some of these Native migrants came in search of economic opportunities. They were attracted by the environmental abundance of the region and the lack of a single dominant Native political power. Others came as refugees who fled from violence in their homelands. By the 1680s, Indigenous slave raiders and European colonists also began to arrive in the region. The expansion of the British settlements in Virginia and Carolina, coupled with French and Spanish imperial efforts to carve up the Gulf South, transformed the same pathways that Moncacht-Apé had used to seek knowledge and hospitality into vectors of European goods, pathogens, and violence. Perhaps most significantly, the escalation of the English trade in Indian slaves led to serious geopolitical upheavals and increased conflict across the Southeast in the last decades of the seventeenth century.

Native American immigration policies facilitated the mass migrations of Indigenous people across eastern North America and enabled the construction of the Petites Nations, Creeks, Choctaws, Natchez, and Chickasaws. In the mid-seventeenth century, the Indigenous peoples of the Lower Mississippi Valley were in the process of building new nations in the post-Mississippian South. During this era, Native peoples developed elastic political systems, extensive alliance networks, and innovative social policies adapted to the pressures wrought by the slave trade and the growing numbers of displaced migrants. Moncacht-Apé's Petites Nations contemporaries were the descendants of both large and small Mississippian polities, and these diverse peoples built many different kinds of societies. Crucially, all of these Native nations developed political systems that protected village-level autonomy and allowed for the integration of outsiders. During this era of crisis, Native Southerners developed regulations that protected migrants and helped manage the behavior of foreigners in their homelands. These political practices offered Lower Mississippi Valley nations essential protections and helped many nations survive colonial violence in the Southeast.

The Origins of the Petites Nations

Moncacht-Apé grew up in a landscape embedded with monuments of the region's grand past and in a society that was shaped by immigration. The dissolution of many Mississippian polities began a process of migration that continued and accelerated as European arrival and settlements in North America created conflicts and refugees across the eastern half of the continent. The Yazoos built on these Mississippian legacies and forged a new community alongside migrants from a wide variety of cultural backgrounds.

Between the eleventh and the sixteenth centuries, Mississippian iconography and material culture spread across eastern North America. In this era, both large and small Native societies produced the monumental architecture that is so emblematic of this cultural tradition. Mississippian societies came in many sizes and configurations. Some of the Mississippian polities had extensive corn agriculture, theocratic rulers, large and even urban populations, and societies that were marked by stark socioeconomic disparities. At Moundville, Spiro, and many other southern Mississippian epicenters, Native peoples hauled tons of earth and labored for decades to build enormous, flat-topped pyramids, expansive plazas for public ceremonies, and winding narrow ridge mounds that reminded visitors of the giant serpents that inhabit the underworld. Perhaps the largest and grandest of the Mississippian polities, Cahokia, at its height, may have been home to as many as forty thousand people. Located in present-day Illinois, residents of this metropolis constructed hundreds of earthen monuments, some of which were nearly a hundred feet tall. In the Lower Mississippi Valley, Native peoples had been building mounds for thousands of years before the Mississippian era. These Indigenous Southerners continued to maintain and expand some of these mounds long after the collapse of the Mississippian world. Such massive construction projects were not just the product of large and hierarchical Mississippian polities, but evidence of the architectural and organizational capabilities of smaller Native nations who collectively labored over long periods of time to build these important social, spiritual, and political spaces.[10]

During the thirteenth and the fourteenth centuries, the lands where Moncacht-Apé later lived were home to a great flourishing of Mississippian cultures. In the lower Yazoo Basin, northern, southern, and western styles from multiple Indigenous artistic, religious, and architectural traditions converged. This confluence created a distinct Mississippian culture that archaeologists call Plaquemine.

This region along the Yazoo Basin witnessed a proliferation of architectural and cultural production. In these lands, Plaquemine people built grandiose earthen platforms and durable stylized ceramics. During the thirteenth century, only a few miles from where the Yazoos later lived, Native Southerners constructed a massive political and ceremonial complex. Through long and painstaking labor, they built twelve impressive earthen mounds around a central plaza. Four hundred years later, as Moncacht-Apé traveled up the Mississippi River, he passed many of the mound and architectural complexes that remained throughout the Lower Mississippi Valley.[11]

The peoples who were the descendants of these Mississippian societies, like the Yazoos, embraced the cultural and social influences of their forefathers. In the late seventeenth century, the Yazoos and their immediate neighbors, the Koroas, were still building residences on top of mounds, and using these platform earthworks for political and religious ceremonies. Roughly 140 miles downriver from the Yazoos, the Natchez nation also maintained many of the same practices as their Plaquemine ancestors. When Moncacht-Apé stopped in the

Natchez villages on his travels, he almost certainly observed the splendor of the main plaza at the Natchez Grand Village with its six monumental flat-topped pyramids.

The Natchez built on these Mississippian legacies to become one of the most powerful groups in the region. Natchez people observed a strict social hierarchy that divided their community into commoners and elites. They were governed by theocratic rulers who traced their ancestry to the sun, and their leaders claimed divine political power via their connection to this life-giving, celestial body. Natchez people used these mounds for ceremonies that demonstrated their spiritual and earthly power. By incorporating refugee and migrant groups, the Natchez also developed a multilingual and multinational populace and extended their trade and diplomatic relationships. By the 1720s, Natchez had a population of between three and four thousand inhabitants and maintained close relationships with a variety of European and Indigenous nations.[12]

In the fifteenth and sixteenth centuries, many of the larger Mississippian polities collapsed or dispersed. While some of this political upheaval probably resulted from the combined political, biological, and ecological disruptions caused by the Spanish conquistador Hernando de Soto's expedition and other early European incursions in the Southeast, archaeologists emphasize that instability and the "cycling"—meaning the process of periodic collapse, fragmentation, and reinvention—of larger polities was a common occurrence in the Mississippian world. For example, Jeffrey Brain has suggested that both the Yazoos and the Tunicas possibly emerged from the demise of the sixteenth-century Mississippian polity of Quiz Quiz. Early European maps of the region substantiate this hypothesis and indicate that the Tunicas migrated south along the Lower Mississippi River after this collapse. By 1680 these two descendants of Quiz Quiz (the Yazoos and Tunicas) were again living as neighbors in a multinational settlement along the lower Yazoo River.[13]

The sixteenth and seventeenth centuries in the Southeast are sometimes referred to as "the forgotten centuries" because modern historians and archaeologists have only a vague grasp of the social, political, and demographic transformations that reshaped the region during this time. Moncacht-Apé was born into an era of geopolitical destabilization and reinvention, and he witnessed the rise and fall of numerous nations in the region over the course of his lifetime. If Moncacht-Apé's own people were a bit unclear on the deep origins of their people, European newcomers, who had begun to arrive in the last decades of the seventeenth century, were completely bewildered by the political formations of the region. These colonists struggled to comprehend the flexibility of these

Native polities, their structures of leadership, and the peoples' multitudes of relations.[14]

Moncacht-Apé's world was a place of towns, of small and malleable polities, in which separate, autonomous nations often lived in close proximity. Although many Mississippian people lived in large polities, most of the nations of the Lower Mississippi Valley had populations of fewer than two thousand people in the seventeenth century. These were smaller, less hierarchical, and less socioeconomically unequal polities that were composed of clusters of towns and villages. Whereas some of the larger Mississippian polities had relied on large, sparsely populated buffer zones to defend their nations, in the seventeenth century, smaller Petites Nations relied on proximity to and relationships with other nations, rather than isolation, to help bolster their defenses. There were some striking exceptions, like the Natchez, but in most cases, rulers of Petites Nations did not individually wield coercive or uncontested power. So, while Moncacht-Apé's people carried on many of the traditions of their Mississippian predecessors, the political and social environment they created was in significant ways distinct from that of their Quiz Quiz ancestors.[15]

Moncacht-Apé would not have seen his people as the broken or shattered remains of formerly great polities, and he would have understood his culture as a modern evolution of these Plaquemine pasts rather than a complete rupture from it. Undoubtedly the collapse and transformations of the Mississippian polities and the destruction wrought by European arrival exacted great tolls on the region's Native people. But groups like the Yazoos or Tunicas were not merely remnants of peoples who were formerly great. Despite scholars' overwhelming focus on the large and architecturally impressive chiefdoms of the Southeast, the archaeology of the region as a whole suggests that, during the Mississippian Era, most people actually lived in communities that had no more than a few hundred inhabitants. Petites Nations were therefore continuations of this pattern. These nations made intentional choices to build societies that were small and flexible instead of large and rigid, like the grand Mississippian chiefdoms of some of their ancestors. For example, the multinational settlements along the Yazoo River where Moncacht-Apé grew up were barely one-tenth the size of Cahokia at its height. At the end of the seventeenth century, there were roughly 1,200 Tunicas, 700 Tensas, and 400 Yazoos. Together with the Tioux, Grigras, and Koroas, these nations jointly numbered about 3,500 people.[16]

This fission of many of these larger Mississippian era polities also led to widespread population relocations that were ongoing long before the arrival of Europeans in the Gulf. During the seventeenth century, people moved both into, and out of, the Lower Mississippi Valley. Archaeological records indicate that, during the late Mississippian era, the Tensas River Basin was densely populated. However, by the seventeenth century, it was largely empty, and only the Tensa nation was living in the region. The low population density allowed new groups to move into the region and take advantage of the ecological abundance of the Mississippi floodplains.¹⁷

The Lower Mississippi Valley was already being transformed by migration and Indigenous nation-building when the shock waves generated by European trafficking in Indian slaves began to reach the region. The combination of the expansion of European and Haudenosaunee power in the mid-sixteenth century and then the rise of the Charleston-centered southeastern Indian slave trade in the late seventeenth century generated thousands of refugees. Many of those who fled escalating violence in their eastern homelands would find their way to the Lower Mississippi Valley.

As Moncacht-Apé traveled through the Haudenosaunee homelands on his trip to the Northeast, he might have come to understand how the expansion of this confederacy's power was part of what brought his new neighbors, the Ofogoulas, into Yazoo homelands. By the mid-seventeenth century, the powerful Haudenosaunee Confederacy established trading partnerships with English and Dutch merchants. The Haudenosaunee were a group of allied Iroquoian nations that resided (and still live) in the lands east of Lake Erie and Lake Ontario through the Mohawk River Valley. While many Mississippian polities were in the process of dissolution and reinvention, the Oneida, Onondaga, Cayuga, Mohawk, and Seneca nations forged a confederacy. Over the following centuries, this confederation grew in regional influence as the bonds among these nations increased its strength and minimized internecine conflicts. In the seventeenth century, European newcomers sought trade with this powerful polity. Haudenosaunee women cleaned, scraped, and prepared thick beaver pelts and supple deer hides to exchange with French and Dutch traders for woven cloth, guns, and metal tools. This trade enriched the already mighty confederacy, and they used their access to modern weapons to expand their influence and territory.

Moncacht-Apé would have been aware of the power of the Haudenosaunee nations as he traveled through their homelands. He may well have crossed paths with Haudenosaunee traders carrying bundles of hides and glinting muskets along the northeastern roads. As the confederacy asserted control of lands and resources further west, they fought with Great Lakes and Ohio River Valley nations. In addition to hides, during these conflicts Haudenosaunee men sought captives. When they returned to their villages, with their prisoners bound in cords trudging behind them, Haudenosaunee women decided who would be integrated into Haudenosaunee families to "cover the dead," and thereby fill the empty physical and spiritual space left by loved ones who died of disease or violence. If it were politically, economically, or spiritually necessary, women could also choose to have these captives ritually executed, or to trade or gift them to other allies.[18]

The Haudenosaunee Confederacy built an expanding sphere of political influence in the Northeast, and their nations became so powerful that their political pursuits shaped the lives of Native people across the Southeast. In fact, it is perhaps helpful to regard the Haudenosaunee as an expanding and incorporative Indigenous empire. The Native nations that lived on the peripheries of the powerful Haudenosaunee, French, Dutch, and English empires in the eastern woodlands and along the Atlantic Seaboard were faced with difficult choices as they were squeezed by their mighty neighbors. These smaller nations had to decide whether they would become a part of these empires, flee to other regions, or try to forge other economic and political networks that might counterbalance the power of these four large polities.[19]

One of the groups that was pushed out of the Ohio River Valley by these expanding empires, the Mosopeleas/Ofogoulas, ended up seeking shelter with Moncacht-Apé's own people. In the mid-seventeenth century, a group of Mosopelea men and women fled the Ohio River Valley to escape violent conflicts among Algonquian, Siouan, European, and Iroquoian people in their homelands. The Mosopelea families walked for months, carrying their young children and anxiously watching for raiders. We can imagine these Siouan-speaking migrants promising their weary sons and daughters that things would be better in a new land. As they traveled west to the Mississippi River, they were attacked by raiders, and some of their kin were captured by Quapaws in the Arkansas River Valley. During their dangerous journey, the Mosopelea families migrated in several different directions and found new communities in disparate lands.[20]

Sometime between 1673 and 1682, at least one group of the Mosopeleas crossed the Mississippi River and settled with the Tensas. The newly arrived Mosopeleas were probably impressed by the wealth of the Tensas. Their towns boasted grand cabins and temples that were covered in tightly woven and elaborately painted mats, while formidable defensive palisades surrounded their buildings. Elite Tensa men wore fine, white cloaks that Tensa women wove from tree bark, and their leaders claimed divine power directly from the sun. The Tensas had longstanding ties to the Quapaws, so, by forging an alliance and residing alongside the Tensas, the Mosopeleas were much less exposed to further Quapaw attacks. As the only nation in the Tensa River Basin, the Tensas had abundant land and resources to share with this refugee population.[21]

Petites Nations leaders, like the Tensa rulers, were adept diplomats who frequently dealt with foreign representatives and migrants. All Petites Nations peoples knew that outsiders could potentially be dangerous, so they relied on strict protocols to protect their communities. By the 1670s, the nations of the Lower Mississippi Valley had developed a highly structured series of meeting rituals that centered on the calumet ceremony. The calumet was a sacred pipe composed of a reed stem two to three feet in length with a polished stone bowl for tobacco. Native peoples (and later Europeans) who wished to negotiate with Native nations would approach a foreign village with the calumet held aloft, singing and dancing while processing toward the village. This performance was analogous to the European practice of raising a white flag to signal peaceful intentions. The archaeologist Ian Brown described the calumet as functioning like symbolic armor—a mechanism by which "groups that normally were mortal enemies could safely complete their transactions" for the purpose of either trade or diplomacy.[22] Petites Nations used the calumet ceremony to facilitate trade and diplomacy and to seek refuge in times of crisis.

This diplomatic ceremony helped the Petites Nations smooth the process of incorporating foreigners into their communities. The Tensas and Mosopeleas almost certainly engaged in a calumet ceremony upon meeting. After smoking with the leaders and honored men of their host village, foreigners partook in an evening feast, then listened to a series of speeches given by esteemed members of the local nation, and finally watched or participated in a night of dancing to celebrate the union of two peoples. After an initial gift exchange, the warriors and leading men and women of each nation recited their histories. They sang and danced with the calumet, performed renditions of daring military victories, and recalled the battles their nation had won and the captives they had taken. Native peoples sat patiently for hours, or even days, as they listened to these histories.[23] The performance and rituals associated with the calumet ceremony provided the opportunity for community members to tell both their personal and national narratives, and to inform outsiders of the relations and accomplishments that made their peoples powerful. Only with this proper personal and historical contextualization could Native people forge solid diplomatic and economic relationships with outsiders.

The calumet ceremony was an important part of the political culture that made it possible for Petites Nations to take in so many different refugees during the seventeenth and eighteenth centuries. Critically, the mutual expectations in-

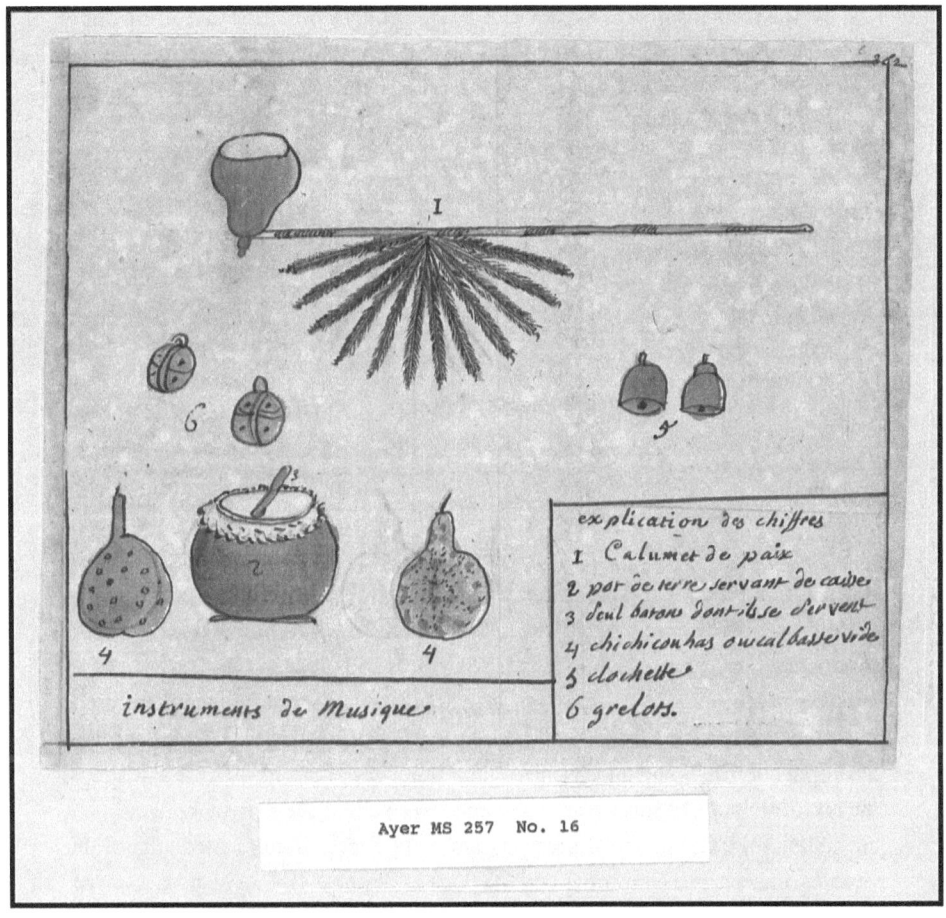

Figure 4. Calumet pipe and musical instruments. From Dumont de Montigny, Mémoire de Lxx Dxx officier ingénieur, contenant les evenements qui se sont passés à la Louisiane depuis 1715 jusqu'à present [manuscript]: ainsi que ses remarques sur les moeurs, usages, et forces des diverses nations de l'Amerique Septentrionale et de ses productions. VAULT oversize Ayer MS 257, figure no. 3. Image courtesy of the Newberry Library.

grained in this regional custom dictated that these nations must accept outsiders, feed them, and treat them as allies. Refusing to do so would be akin to a declaration of war.[24] This culturally institutionalized approach to negotiating refuge therefore represented a fundamental Petites Nations survival and caretaking mechanism.

While the Mosopeleas lived with the Tensas, they built useful relationships with neighboring nations. Their time with the Tensas allowed this nation to recuperate from its losses, and by the 1690s some of the Mosopeleas were on the move again. These Mosopeleas resettled with the Yazoos and Koroas. In this multinational settlement, this group of Mosopeleas became known by their neighbors as the Ofogoulas—the Choctaw term for "dog people." Moncacht-Apé likely witnessed the arrival of the Mosopeleas as a young man, and he would have remembered how they built a new village alongside his own. Refugees and migrants retained autonomy over their own community, but custom required that they respect their hosts' lands, waters, peoples, and leadership. The Ofogoulas would have followed these rules. Thanks in part to this culture of migrant hospitality, by 1690 the Yazoo River junction housed a densely populated multinational community. During this decade the Yazoos, Tunicas, and Ofogoulas, the Koroas, Grigras, Tioux, and possibly several other small nations lived as neighbors in the riverine settlements.[25]

In addition to welcoming foreigners and building strong international alliances, Petites Nations also fought to defend their lands and peoples. Many nations sparred with their neighbors. During the 1680s and 1690s, the Natchez fought with many of the Petites Nations, and the Tunicas and Quapaws engaged in a low-intensity conflict that simmered over these decades. Small-scale raids could be used to avenge the deaths of friends and family, and they also helped nations enforce territorial control. Some raids yielded small numbers of captives, and it was again the responsibility of Petites Nations women to decide if these prisoners would be integrated, sold, gifted, or executed. Occasionally, Petites Nations used large-scale violence, like when the Houmas and Okeloussas destroyed the Acolapissa town of Tangibao in the 1680s. However, conflicts among Petites Nations mostly did not lead to massive dispossession, extermination, or national collapse. Instead, low levels of violence could be productive, as captives played significant roles in most Native nations, and maintaining control of territories and reputations for military might helped the Petites Nations defend their communities.[26]

Calumet ceremonies, small-scale military operations, and practices of welcoming migrants protected and sustained the Petites Nations during the late seventeenth century. The multinational settlements that emerged from Indigenous immigration policies further strengthened the diverse peoples of the Lower Mississippi Valley and created a series of powerful networks for small autonomous communities.

In the last decade of the seventeenth century, however, these systems came under increasing strain as Moncacht-Apé's community, and many other Petites

Nations, encountered new dangers from Indian slave raiders. Between 1690 and 1715 Alabamas, Tallapoosas, Chickasaws, Abhikas, and other Native groups pummeled the Petites Nations, carrying off thousands of captives to sell to English merchants, who in turn sold them all over the English Atlantic world. The confrontation with these powerful networks of human trafficking brought the Petites Nations to a crisis point.

The Expansion of Indian Slave Trading in the Southeast

As Moncacht-Apé traveled east and west across the continent, he heard horrifying stories of men who raided villages and stole women and children. Like the Native nation that fought the cloth-wrapped sea voyagers, Indigenous communities across the Southeast faced new challenges in the last decades of the seventeenth century as growing European demand for Indian slaves fueled far-reaching captive raids. Through his conversations with men and women who had witnessed this violence or heard tales of the slavers from friends and family, Moncacht-Apé would have come to understand how the expansion of Haudenosaunee power, along with the growth of the English colonies of Virginia and Carolina, had increased captive raiding along the Eastern Seaboard and facilitated the expansion of these networks of Indian slaving into the Gulf Coast. This violence displaced thousands of Indigenous people and it also forced Native nations to make heart-wrenching decisions about whether they would participate in these networks of human trafficking or be forced to flee their homelands.[27]

The expansion of Charleston-based slave trade networks into the Lower Mississippi Valley during the 1690s unleashed incredible violence in the Petites Nations homelands, and these devastating raids threatened to destroy the small Gulf Coast polities. Faced with this new threat, the Yazoos chose to work with slave traders in order to defend their community. Their decision, as well as those of so many other Southeastern nations who felt compelled to participate in the captive trade, had devastating consequences for their Petites Nations neighbors.

When he passed through Haudenosaunee territory on his journey east, Moncacht-Apé would almost certainly have been warned to watch out for slave traders, and he likely would have heard the story of a people called the Westos who had once lived near these lands. In the early 1600s, the Westos, who were known by the English as the Eries, lived near present-day eastern Lake Erie at the northern and western edges of Haudenosaunee territory. In the 1650s, after the Haudenosaunee made peace with New France, they aggressively expanded their influence into the Ohio River Valley and waged a brutal war against this small nation. Like the Mosopeleas, who had been pushed out of the Ohio River Valley during this era by conflict, the Eries were also forced to flee. Instead of traveling south and west, like the Mosopeleas, the Eries moved south and east, and about 650 of these refugees resettled at the falls of the James River on the edge of the British colony of Virginia.[28]

In their new home, the Eries forged a political alliance with the English, using Indigenous captives to help secure this relationship. Early Virginia colonists were eager for workers to farm their tobacco plantations, and Native captives provided English settlers and merchants with a relatively inexpensive source of bound labor. In the South, the Eries became known as the Westos, and soon began raiding their smaller neighbors. In the late 1650s and early 1660s, the Westos and English settlers launched coordinated slave raids against Guale, Hitchiti, and Cusabo communities in the lands between the Spanish settlements in Florida and the English in the Chesapeake. By the 1670s, an Indian child was worth their weight in deerskins in the Carolina market, and a healthy adult might be valued at roughly the equivalent of two years of leathers generated by a Native trapper. As Moncacht-Apé traveled alone on these dangerous roads, he would have needed to be extremely cautious to avoid crossing paths with raiders. For the Westos and other early slave raiders, the economic and political power that resulted from trafficking Native children, women, and men made this brutal trade worth the risks.[29]

In 1670 the English founded Charleston. The city became a second nucleus of human trafficking in the South and the influence and captive trade networks of the Carolina colony soon expanded as far west as Moncacht-Apé's homelands along the Yazoo River. The nascent economy of Carolina developed concurrently with the expansion of the deerskin trade and created a buoyant demand for cheap labor in the 1680s and 1690s. Carolina merchants relied on the Indian captive trade to fulfill their labor needs in the era before enslaved Africans were readily available in the southern English colonies. Over the next decades, they formed close partnerships with Ocaneechis, Yamasees, Upper Creeks, Savannahs, and other local Native nations that supplied the colonists with Indian slaves. As more nations formed partnerships with Carolina merchants, their warriors pushed farther west in search of new sources of captives. This violent trade in Native men, women, and children supported the development of the Virginia and South Carolina colonies. Their growing prosperity only further fueled this vicious cycle of demands for even more unfree workers.[30]

In 1685 the Chickasaws forged an alliance with the English that expanded the Charleston-based captive trade as far west as the Mississippi River. Chickasaw women likely hoped that this relationship would protect them and their children from other slave raiders. This partnership supplied the Chickasaws with ample firearms, and they used this new weapons technology to lead devastating raids against other Native Southerners. The Chickasaws raided their old enemies and neighbors the Choctaws, then expanded their attacks across the Mississippi Delta. Although the Choctaws did not have access to European guns in the 1690s, they still vastly outnumbered the Chickasaws, and Choctaw revenge raids left many Chickasaw brothers, daughters, and wives in mourning. In 1700 the Chickasaws had a population of about 7,000 people while the Choctaws numbered 18,000. The Choctaws' retaliatory raids ultimately forced many Chickasaws to seek alternative targets.[31]

Unlike the large and powerful Choctaws, the Petites Nations of the Lower Mississippi Valley seemed to present less dangerous sources of captives. They lived in small communities, they lacked guns, and they were farther from the Chickasaws' homelands, which made it more difficult for their people to carry out retaliatory raids. The Yazoo River settlements—the place Moncacht-Apé called home—were particularly easy targets for these raiders because their villages were located along the western edge of the upper trade path that the Chickasaws and other Native raiders used to drag captives to the eastern markets.[32]

The escalation of slave raids by Chickasaws, Upper Creeks, and others in the Lower Mississippi Valley during the 1690s fractured the Yazoo River community that Moncacht-Apé had known as a boy and pulled the Yazoos into the violent networks of human trafficking. Although Yazoos, Koroas, Grigras, Tunicas, and Tioux had lived in close proximity in this multinational settlement for years, they pursued divergent strategies to safeguard their respective peoples and their nations ended up on opposing sides of the slave trade conflicts. The stark differences in their approaches to confronting the slave trade unraveled the ties that had bound together the Yazoos, Koroas, Grigras, Ofogoulas, Tunicas, and Tioux.

The expansion of the slave trade left Moncacht-Apé's people with a set of impossible options, and ultimately the Yazoos decided that they would participate in the violent exchange. Moncacht-Apé would have told his people of the horrors he had learned of during his travels. It is possible he even encouraged his people to maintain their alliance with the Chickasaws by supporting their new slaving enterprise, rather than become victims themselves. Perhaps, Yazoos concluded that trading captives to secure a partnership with the English would not only enable them to protect their families but also offer them access to valuable commodities. Yazoo women likely desired access to woolen cloth and metal hoes, which would make their work crafting clothing and farming their fields easier, and Yazoo men would have been eager for muskets. Even if Moncacht-Apé did not participate directly in these raids, he certainly would have witnessed the stolen women and children that were bound with cords and dragged through his village, and the frequent presence of Chickasaw raiders in his homelands would have been inescapable.[33]

Both the Yazoos and the Koroas were reasonably successful in their efforts to protect their nations by participating in the slave trade and strengthening their alliances with the Chickasaws and English. Throughout the 1690s and 1700s, it appears that neither of them suffered an attack by Chickasaw or English-allied raiders. Because of their collaboration with the Chickasaws, these nations were able to remain in their homelands, while almost all of Moncacht-Apé's other neighbors in the Yazoo River settlements fled.

In addition to protecting their people from eastern slave traders, the Koroas used their alliance with the Chickasaws to defend their people from local adversaries. During the 1680s, Tensa warriors raided Koroa villages and captured their children. Tensas sometimes sold these Koroa children to their allies or used them as diplomatic gifts. In 1682 the Tensas gifted a young, enslaved, Koroa boy to René-Robert Cavelier, Sieur de La Salle, the leader of one of the first French expeditionary forces to pass through the region. Unlike most captured Native children, this boy was ultimately returned to his people. While La Salle and his men were stopped at the Natchez villages, the Koroa boy's mother managed to rescue her child from the French convoy. One can only imagine the tears this mother must have wept as she held her son in her arms again. This, of course, was a very unusual outcome for a captured child, as most stolen boys and girls were never returned to their families' embraces. The Koroas used their relationships with the Chickasaws to try to protect their families from just this sort of danger. More than two decades later, in 1706, the Koroas' allies and neighbors, the Yazoos, attacked the Tensas with the support of Chickasaw warriors. It is possible that some Koroas joined this raid, but there is no documentary evidence to confirm this. Whether or not the Koroas participated directly, nations like theirs and the Yazoos' were able to work with the Chickasaws to target local polities that posed threats to their communities and had previously stolen their kin. Participation in the southeastern trades in Indigenous captives helped protect Yazoos and Koroas from both local and distant raiders.[34]

With the exception of the Yazoos, Koroas, and Ofogoulas, the Chickasaw and English-allied slave raiders forced all the nations of the Yazoo River settlements to flee from their homes. The Yazoos' and Koroas' partnerships with the Chickasaws and English opened up more of the Lower Mississippi Valley to eastern raiders and exposed their immediate neighbors to their violence. During the 1690s, the Tunicas, Grigras, and Tioux were either unable or unwilling to forge partnerships with the English and Chickasaws. Instead, the increasing presence of slave raiders in their homelands in the 1690s led the Tioux and Grigras to migrate downriver and seek refuge with the Natchez. This was a wise decision. There, the Tioux and Grigras were farther from the upper trade path. Moreover, some of the Natchez towns that allied with the Chickasaws now protected the Tioux and Grigras from Chickasaw attacks.[35] But Moncacht-Apé's peoples' partnership with the Chickasaws had devastating consequences for his Tunica neighbors.

In 1706 a group of Chickasaw warriors stormed into the region and attacked the Tunicas. This raid did not touch their Koroa or Yazoo neighbors, but it was so destructive and terrifying for the Tunicas that they fled downriver and sought refuge with the Houmas. While the multinational partnerships and physical proximity to the Yazoos, Tunicas, Koroas, Ofogoulas, Grigras, and Tioux functioned well in the 1680s, by the 1700s the escalation of slave raiding in the region made this settlement unsustainable. New political alliances forged through slave trafficking made conditions far too dangerous for the Grigras, Tunicas, and Tioux to stay near the Yazoos and Koroas.[36]

Although neither archaeological investigations nor written records have provided concrete numbers of captives taken from the Southeast, the historian Alan Gallay estimates that in the first two decades of the eighteenth century the Chickasaw, Natchez, Creek, and Yazoo raids in the Lower Mississippi Valley resulted in the enslavement of at least 3,000 Petites Nations individuals. By 1713 these groups raided as far south as the bayous below present-day New Orleans and carried off the children of the Chaouachas and other Petites Nations who lived in this region. Using John Swanton's very conservative population estimates for 1698, the Petites Nations collectively totaled 16,485 people. This means that as many as 18 percent of the Lower Mississippi Valley's Indigenous population was taken captive between 1700 and 1720 alone. All told, between 1685 and 1715 slave raiders stole between 24,000 and 51,000 Native people from across the Southeast to the slave markets in Carolina.[37] The expansion of the captive market along the Gulf Coast pulled the Petites Nations into a violent vortex that led to repeated social and political upheavals and severe population decline. Between

1680 and 1700, many Petites Nations people mourned the loss of nearly half of their communities.[38]

The small nations that survived this violence retained memories of the terror of slave raids for generations. Recollections of this horrific violence stayed with the Yazoos' Tunica neighbors for centuries. In 1933 the Tunica elder, Sesostrie Youchigant, recalled the tale of the fighting eagles to the linguist Mary Haas. His account provides a window into how Tunica people experienced and explained this horror. As he recounted, "At the place where the Tunica Chief lived, some other Indians were eating too many of his people. Now he got tired of it. He sent the other chief a challenge to fight. The other chief was willing to fight. Then they made hickory sticks. After they had made them just right they met in the woods. When they met, they fought. As they beat each other with the hickory sticks, they were whooping. They beat each other until each had killed the other."[39]

Memories of the trauma these raids wrought on the Tunicas illustrate the power of the violence, conflict, and dangers that threatened to destroy their nation. In his telling of the Tale of the Fighting Eagles, Youchigant also shared another critical piece of cultural context through his choice of terminology. Like Youchigant, when Tunica people tell this story today, they use the Tunica word for eat, *saku*, in the sentence "Tayoroniku kat'unahch, tonimahonsahuku uhk'oniseman namurikin'usakukatani" (Once upon a time where the Tunica Chief lived, some other Indians were eating too many people). Their use of *saku* to express the violence of this encounter conveys a specific Indigenous perspective on raiders.[40] In telling this story, Youchigant employed a centuries-old Southeastern Indigenous metaphor that used the analogy of cannibalism—or man eating—to talk about slavers. These men who came and stole women, children, mothers, sons, and aunts, who killed families, and who set homes and towns on fire, were effectively consuming—or devouring—the small nations of the Southeast. In the eighteenth century, Native peoples across eastern North America described this violent process using the metaphor of anthropophagy.

This verbal construction provides a window into how Indigenous Southerners conceptualized the destructive power of slave raiding. In Carolina, Sowee communities called the Westo slave traders who attacked their villages "man eaters." Likewise, Shawnees in the Ohio River Valley claimed that their nation was almost swallowed by Haudenosaunee raiders. This metaphor was even used by Southeastern Indigenous raiders themselves. In 1708 the Chickasaws threatened to attack the tiny French settlement at Mobile and "eat up a village of white men."[41] In this instance, the Chickasaws were not planning to literally consume the flesh of the settlers, but were instead looking for a way to express the complete destruction they would bring to bear on this colonial town. For all that documentary sources omit or obscure the experiences of Petites Nations peoples who endured this violence, their experiences live on in their oral histories. The stories that Native Southerners have passed down from generation to generation have enabled their own accounts of the slave trade to endure.

For the Tunicas, Yazoos, Koroas, and others, the expansion of the trades in Indigenous captives in the Southeast transformed their lives and communities in the decades around the turn of the eighteenth century. The escalation of raiding led many people to flee their homes, and even forced Native nations to relocate multiple times. Throughout this tumultuous era, many nations relied on the practice of refugee hospitality to provide them with safe harbors when they were forced to migrate. As Native people adapted to and fought to stymie the violence of the slave trade, they also aimed to build political and social structures that could withstand the challenges of this era. Drawing on long-standing relationships and cultural practices, both large and small nations worked to build societies that reflected their values and protected their families while also enabling their people to integrate the influx of migrants and refugees who moved across the Gulf South amid chaos.

Creating Petites Nations and Grandes Nations

Colonial violence and the slave trade broke apart Indigenous communities like the Yazoo River settlements where Moncacht-Apé lived, but it also forged strong ties between peoples and shaped the development of Native nations across the Southeast. The same practices that allowed Indigenous communities to protect and live alongside refugees and migrants also helped Native Southerners build powerful nations while preserving town-level autonomy. The layered and flexible political structures that enabled immigrants to govern their people also ensured that Native towns and villages would retain local control even as many of them chose to join or associate with larger nations and confederacies. In this way, the process of building larger nations, like the Choctaw, had much in common with how Petites Nations, like the Yazoos, integrated outsiders and organized their multinational settlements.

Moncacht-Apé's Southern neighbors pursued a wide range of political strategies and forged many different types of governments during the seventeenth and eighteenth centuries. Native Southerners constructed sprawling confederacies, built large and unified nations out of disparate polities, or relied on relationships with foreign nations to help them remain small and autonomous. Many nations included migrant populations and people of different ethnic and linguistic backgrounds, and they developed governance structures that could accommodate this diversity. The peoples of the Lower Mississippi Valley chose to build both large and small polities, and Indigenous people sometimes were part of both kinds of nations over the course of their lifetimes. In all cases, the political and social practices of multinational settlement and migrant acceptance facilitated both the construction and the resilience of these Southeastern nations.[42]

The pressures created by the slave trade and colonial incursions in the Southeast encouraged and further accelerated the processes of unification and confederation that had already begun to shape the Choctaw, Chickasaw, and Creek nations by the turn of the eighteenth century. The Chickasaws, Choctaws, and Creeks were all Muskogean-speaking nations that descended from Southern Mississippian polities. Their processes of ethnogenesis (coming together to form a shared cultural identity) and nation-building were part of centuries-long processes of migrations and social production that began long before the arrival of Europeans in the Southeast. However, for all three groups, the pressures of French, English, and Spanish colonization of the Atlantic and Gulf Coasts, coupled with the expanding southeastern Indian slave trades, encouraged Chickasaws, Choctaws, and Creeks to unify more rapidly and to intentionally incorporate outsiders to strengthen their nations.[43]

When Moncacht-Apé asked the Chickasaws "if they knew where we all came from," the Chickasaws would have been able to point to centuries of Chickasaw history in the Southeast. The Chikashsha, as Chickasaws call themselves, are the descendants of the Chicaza chiefdom and they carry a powerful military legacy that stretches back centuries. In the 1540s Chicaza people first encountered Europeans, and they defended their nation from the invading forces of Hernando de Soto. Shortly thereafter, the Chicaza polity collapsed. At least some of the people from Chicaza migrated away from the Tombigbee River into the uplands of the Black Prairie, resettling near present-day Tupelo, Mississippi. During this migration and political renewal, the descendants of Chicaza continually incorporated outsiders as they worked to rebuild and reinvent their nation. This practice helped their population grow such that by 1700 the Chickasaws had eighteen towns and roughly seven thousand people.[44]

The Choctaws—the Chickasaws' southern neighbors—similarly held longstanding connections in the Southeast, and in the late seventeenth and early eighteenth centuries they forged a large confederation of Muskogean-speaking people. Archaeologists describe Choctaws as the descendants of the Bottle Creek, Moundville, and Plaquemine peoples. These groups migrated into eastern central Mississippi between the late fifteenth and seventeenth centuries, and there they coalesced into a culturally cohesive group. Some Choctaw people also describe a similar process of migration, and Choctaw oral histories recount how both they and their brothers the Chickasaws, whom Choctaws recognize as kin, migrated from the West on a sacred journey to find new homelands. At some point in their odysseys, the two groups split, and the Chickasaws continued north. When the Choctaws came to the lands near present-day Bogue Chitto, Mississippi, their people were given spiritual signals that they had reached their new home. Here, they built an earthen mound, *Nanih Waiya*, to acknowledge their relationship to these sacred lands. Other oral histories suggest that the Choctaws physically emerged out of this Mississippian-style "mother mound." Through this earthen matriline, Choctaw people continue to trace their belonging to these lands where *Nanih Waiya* remains today.

In the late seventeenth and eighteenth centuries, the Choctaws, or Chahta as they call themselves, were not a single, centralized, political entity. Rather, as the archaeologist Patricia Galloway has described, the Choctaws were "a confederation of forty to fifty autonomous villages gathered in four groupings on the rivers that meet in what is now east-central Mississippi." Each of these four divisions, Chickasawhay, Sixtown, Eastern, and Western Choctaws, had separate appointed leaders and a council to help govern and negotiate on behalf of their people. This governance structure helped Choctaws resolve internecine conflict and made them a formidable regional power. These political divisions were likely shaped by diverse migrant populations, and through the eighteenth century, each division maintained cultural distinctiveness. Throughout the 1700s, the Sixtown Choctaws, who, Galloway hypothesizes, were the descendants of the Plaquemine culture, not only dressed and wore their hair in different styles than the Eastern or Western Choctaws, but they reportedly also spoke a western Muskogean version of the Choctaw language with "peculiar accents." It is easy to imagine that contemporary Mississippi Choctaws listening to their Choctaw Nation relatives speak with Oklahoma accents may well come to similar conclusions today. Their eighteenth-century predecessors' political structures made space for diversity and differences of political opinion even as they forged a growing sense of national identity. So, while Choctaw people collectively recognized each other as relations, and the four divisions did share a cultural identity and language, practical political power and critical markers of individual identity emanated from the town or division rather than national mandate.[45]

Creek people also prioritized local, town-level political power for most of the eighteenth century. The people who later became known as the Creek Nation, or the Mvskoke, as they call themselves, are from a wide variety of linguistic and ethnic backgrounds. During the seventeenth century, these groups migrated into the lands between the Ocmulgee, Chattahoochee, Flint, Alabama, and Coosa Rivers. These migrants, and the other ethnic groups that moved into Creek lands during the eighteenth century, were a tremendously linguistically and culturally diverse group. Creek communities spoke Muscogee, Hitchiti-Mikasuki, Alabama, Koasati, and Yuchi. By 1715, largely in response to pressures from the slave trades and British expansion, the people who became Creeks had organized themselves into loosely unified upper and lower divisions. The Upper Creeks—Alabama, Tallapoosa, and Abhika peoples—lived at the confluence of the Alabama and Coosa Rivers, while their Lower Creek relatives lived along the Chattahoochee River. Because the Upper Creeks were further west than the Lower Creeks, Upper Creek peoples had more frequent contact with the Petites Nations. By the turn of the eighteenth century, the Upper Creek population was more than ten thousand. As a result, they exerted considerable influence on their Gulf Coast neighbors and could pose serious threats to the people of Mobile Bay and the Lower Mississippi River.[46]

Creek leaders worked to protect local political power even as they developed national political affiliations. For both Upper and Lower Creeks, it was the town, not the national government, that was the most significant political unit. In Creek country, a town or *talwa*, referenced the larger group of people who shared square grounds and council fires (the sites of political and cultural activities), not simply their immediate village. As the historian Mike Green explains, a *talwa* was "an autonomous political and ceremonial center," and the source of local government. Some Creek towns were responsible for keeping peace, while others were led by powerful military leaders who took charge of matters of war. During the eighteenth century, there were between fifty-two and eighty towns that constituted the Creek nation. In addition to the town structure, Creek men and women relied on their clan leaders to regulate the behavior of those in their community and to resolve disputes. For many Creeks, the combination of clan and town identity remained much stronger than national identity throughout the eighteenth century. Town and clan leaders held the political power to make decisions for their people and guided their communities through the dangerous era of the slave trade.[47]

These flexible and locally controlled political and social systems allowed Creeks, Chickasaws, and Choctaws to incorporate outsiders into their nations.

Furthermore, they were also able to permit towns and families to leave their nations as needed. Historians and anthropologists have often examined Native nation-building by focusing on the process of incorporating larger and larger groups of people and developing more centralized systems of governance. But nation-building was a multidirectional process rather than one of continual growth and centralization. Native social structures generally left the door open for groups to leave these polities and reinvent themselves elsewhere, and they intentionally avoided centralizing governmental power. For example, in the 1730s, the leaders of the Chickasaw town of Ackia made plans to relocate their entire town and to join the Western Choctaw Division. Because Ackia shared close ties with the leaders and people of the Choctaw town of Coëchitto, the peoples of both Ackia and Coëchitto felt this would be an advantageous resettlement. Effectively, even among these larger confederated nations, and even as Choctaws, Chickasaws, and Creeks developed national identities that bound their people together, towns remained the critical political unit, and individual towns always had the option of fissioning, relocating, and reinventing themselves.[48]

Perhaps because in the nineteenth century Choctaws, Chickasaws, and Creeks made concerted efforts to transform their polities into hard-bordered nation-states, historians have been overly eager to see similar political rigidity and fixity in the eighteenth century. In the first decades of the nineteenth century, in order to be legible to the United States government and to hold on to their land in the face of American expansion, the Choctaws, Creeks, and Chickasaws endeavored to translate their traditional reciprocal relationships with lands and peoples into hard territorial borders and to codify their fluid and multipolar leadership and political power into centralized governments with coercive power. These efforts were pragmatic and set the parameters for much of modern Indian law and contemporary conversations about Native sovereignty. However, the political calculations of the nineteenth century were considerably different from the elastic and relationship-based geopolitical ideologies that Native people used to govern in the early eighteenth-century South.[49]

During the late seventeenth and for much of the eighteenth century, the Lower Mississippi Valley was a borderland that was free from the domination of any single polity. It was not a land of nation-states with hard borders. Petites Nations people at multinational settlements, like the Yazoos, who lived in places where multiple political authorities overlapped, had to continually negotiate these relationships with each other and with the land. Similarly, Native nations shared access to roads and to "other than human relations" (Native people mostly did not view what we might call "natural resources" as inanimate objects or inferior life-forms, but rather as relatives they had obligations to) like deer, fish, rivers, and salt. This ability to exist as autonomous polities while enmeshed in webs of relationships with other peoples is part of what made the region appealing for small Native nations. Petites Nations' fluid political systems, in which people primarily relied on persuasion and relationships of interdependency to exercise power, were similar in some aspects to the ways that people negotiated resources and political influence within the Creek and Choctaw nations. However, because Petites Nations did not often unify their governments, even within multinational settlements, Petites Nations people did not develop the same level of juridical or political superstructures to regulate interactions between nations as existed across Creek or Choctaw communities. So, unlike Creek or Choctaw councils that could manage violence, disputes, and national policy among larger bodies of people, Petites Nations chose to maintain full national autonomy and not to create confederated governance structures.[50]

The multinational settlements that supported Petites Nations' autonomy required continual cross-cultural and transnational negotiations. Nations within multinational settlements lived in neighboring hamlets that might be roughly the same distance from each other as between two towns within a larger confederated nation. Each Petite Nation might have several villages within the portion of territory their nation controlled, with their territories including residential and spiritual centers and farmlands. These settlements might directly abut or be within a few miles of their neighboring nations. While Moncacht-Apé lived alongside many foreigners, he clearly identified himself as Yazoo, and he described his nation as distinct from those of his neighbors. His people shared space and resources with the other groups, but they were not obligated to develop a shared foreign policy or to obey a unified political leadership. French observers often described these multinational settlements as the joining of nations. In 1699 a French missionary traveling down the lower Mississippi noted that, at the village of the Petite Nation of the Quinipissas, "there are about one hundred cabins, including the Bayagoulas and Mugulashas who have joined themselves to them (the Qunipissas)."[51] Nonetheless, the independent political identities of each group made clear that these nations had distinct identities and remained autonomous peoples.

Being a Petite Nation or living in a multinational settlement also did not foreclose the possibility that these smaller Native polities could become part of larger confederacies. Petites Nations and migrant towns sometimes remained within the territories of larger nations for years at a time. In some cases, Petites Nations were ultimately absorbed into these larger nations. This practice highlights both the flexibility of Southern nations and the overlap between the processes of political confederation and fission that generated both large and Petites Nations. When Yazoo relationships with Chickasaws brought too much violence to their homelands, the Tioux fled and sought refuge alongside the Natchez nation for roughly two decades before leaving in the mid-1720s. Similarly, in the 1690s, the Petite Nation of Napissas lived with the Chickasaws. However, instead of leaving, by the mid-eighteenth century it appears that the Napissas fused into the Chickasaws and were no longer a distinct polity.

Neither the systems of multinational settlements nor the practice of providing refuge or allowing outside groups to settle alongside other nations were unique to the Petites Nations. During the mid-eighteenth century, Upper Creeks allowed groups of Shawnees from the Ohio River Valley to settle with them for several months or even years at a time. Similarly, in the 1760s, a group of Alabamas left their homelands among the Upper Creeks, turned themselves into a Petite Nation, and journeyed west to join a multinational settlement with the Tunicas and Ofogoulas along the Mississippi River. The common phenomenon of hosting and providing refuge for outsiders and migrants therefore was an integral part of the process of nation-building in the eighteenth-century Southeast.[52]

The development of both large and small nations in the Gulf South was the product of these older Indigenous traditions of providing for migrants, living in multinational settlements, and international networking as well as the pressures wrought by European arrival and the growing southeastern slave trades. In the first decades of the eighteenth century, these same practices and pressures would come to shape how Native people treated the new set of European immigrants who arrived in their homelands. The frameworks Petites Nations people established for dealing with and taking care of foreigners would critically influence not just Indigenous nation-building projects but also European colonial development in the Lower Mississippi Valley.

Moncacht-Apé and his community first encountered Europeans in the 1680s, when French explorers paddled down the Mississippi, but until the first decade of the eighteenth century, most of the Petites Nations in this region did not have direct or sustained contact with Europeans. On his journeys, Moncacht-Apé had been warned about the dangers of these newcomers, and he had taken special care to avoid the French in his travels. Perhaps because of the intelligence that Moncacht-Apé and the Chickasaws provided to the Yazoos about the dangers of the French, Yazoo leaders remained wary of the Louisiana settlers through the first decades of their presence in the Lower Mississippi Valley. Little could Moncacht-Apé have known that within his lifetime French colonists would attempt to colonize his homeland and convert this space into a part of their global empire. However, for all the French government's dreams of colonial development, it would be Native communities, like Moncacht-Apé's, that determined the shape and limits of these imperial designs.[53]

CHAPTER 2

Establishing Relationships with the French

In late winter of 1699, the Biloxis and Capinans welcomed a group of strangely attired foreigners into their homelands. This group of men, and indeed they were all men, arrived on the Gulf Coast wearing layers of salt-encrusted woven cloth and leather over their arms, torsos, legs, and feet. Both their bodies and faces were missing the customary paint and markings that Native Southerners used to indicate their political affiliations and diplomatic purposes, so it was initially difficult for the Biloxis and Capinans to discern their reason for visiting the region. However, as they soon discovered, the unmarked French newcomers who stumbled ashore in their territories were seeking aid and resettlement. Biloxis and Capinans were familiar with these kinds of requests for help and refuge from strangers, and the leaders of these two Petites Nations seized the opportunity presented by their arrival to form trade and diplomatic alliances with these European immigrants. In doing so, they determined the first location of French colonial settlement in the Gulf South. Over the coming years, partnerships like those between the Biloxis and Louisianans would steer the course of imperial growth in the region and simultaneously alter the political and social worlds of the Petites Nations.

During the first two decades of the eighteenth century, many Petites Nations people developed close relationships with the French newcomers. As the frequency of slave raids into the Lower Mississippi Valley increased, the region's small Native nations clamored to find more effective ways to defend their peoples. Petites Nations leaders saw the French newcomers, with their high-tech weaponry, not just as potential military allies but also as immigrants who could be integrated into their multinational settlements. To incentivize the French to trade and to agree to live alongside their communities, many Petites Nations developed creative strategies to present themselves as valuable allies and appealing neighbors to the European settlers.

When French expeditionary forces arrived in Capinan and Biloxi territory in 1699, they entered into Indigenous homelands that had been thrown into chaos by far-reaching colonial networks. These nations were just recovering from a devastating smallpox epidemic that had spread through the land in the previous year. Everywhere the French envoy passed, they saw evidence of recent raids and fighting, and they observed the destruction wrought by the expanding Charleston-based Indian slave trade. As they traveled along the Mississippi River and Mobile Bay, they encountered abandoned villages, burned towns, and communities that were wracked with illness. Because raiders targeted women and children, many families were missing daughters, sons, sisters, and mothers.[1]

In the first decades of the eighteenth century, French immigrants in the Lower Mississippi Valley lived in precarity and privation. With only a small population of French settlers, and meager and infrequent material support from the French metropole, the first Louisiana settlers were left vulnerable and isolated. The harsh circumstances these early colonists encountered in Louisiana made them deeply dependent on their relationships with local Native nations. From the outset, the French Crown considered Louisiana to be a low imperial priority. As compared to the lucrative sugar-producing island of St. Domingue or the vibrant fur trade markets of New France, Lower Louisiana seemed to hold less economic potential than France's other North American possessions. The territory was of strategic defensive importance, but the land itself contained no gold or silver, and the swampy and sandy terrain of the Gulf shores seemed unlikely to nourish sugar or tobacco. Instead, during the 1700s and 1710s, settlers stationed in the new colony complained of floods, mosquitoes, and illness caused by the muggy climate. Colonists endured further deprivations as the outbreak of the War of the Spanish Succession consumed most of the empire's available resources. War raged in Europe between 1700 and 1713, and during this time Louisiana colonists received paltry and irregular assistance from the Crown. With little support from France, Louisiana settlers were forced to seek food, labor, and military aid from Indigenous nations. Isolation, supply shortages, and regional turmoil made the colonial government of Louisiana eager not just to pursue alliances with Native nations but to embrace opportunities to live in close proximity to Native peoples.[2]

Between 1699 and 1720, several Petites Nations welcomed French villages directly into their multinational settlements, and they integrated the European newcomers into their social and political networks in the same way they had brought in migrant Native nations for generations. The earliest Louisiana settlers all lived alongside Petites Nations, so the geography of colonial Louisiana was determined by these Indigenous people. The growth of early colonial Louisiana was therefore primarily characterized by incorporation of small French villages into Indigenous settlements rather than French imperial expansion and the incorporation of Native people into Atlantic networks and European political systems.

Before the French established the better-known posts of Natchez and New Orleans, Biloxi and Mobile were the primary nexuses of the French Empire in the Lower Mississippi Valley. In 1699 Biloxis and Capinans convinced the French to build their first settlement alongside their villages, and in 1702, the Mobilians invited all 140 French settlers to join them in their homelands along Mobile Bay where they lived with the Naniaba and Tohome nations. This French village within the Petites Nations' multinational settlements at Mobile functioned as the center of imperial Louisiana until the capital was moved to New Orleans in 1718. Although the French population of the Lower Mississippi Valley grew substantially from the few dozen soldiers and laborers who arrived on the Gulf Coast in 1699, the colony still had only 350–400 people dispersed among Indigenous villages and outposts throughout the Lower Mississippi Valley by 1718. During the first twenty years of colonization, the entire French settler population remained roughly the size of a single Petite Nation.[3]

In this era, many Petites Nations developed mutually beneficial and interdependent partnerships with the French settlers. Biloxis, Houmas, Mobilians, Bayagoulas, Acolapissas, and Tunicas all worked to build alliances with the European newcomers and to accommodate their strange new neighbors. The colonists' continual needs for labor, trade, and military assistance likewise forced them to adapt to Indigenous cultural and diplomatic practices. French settlers at Mobile had to respect Petites Nations women and nonbinary people, conduct political negotiations in accordance with regional customs, and provide their Native allies with military support. Petites Nations men and women also made efforts to adapt to the presence of the Louisiana settlers, and many of them incorporated Catholic beliefs, woolen cloth, or French language into their lives. These interdependent political and economic relationships shaped and sometimes curtailed the diplomatic and military pursuits of the Louisiana government. The presence and influence of these European settlers and their transatlantic networks in turn reconfigured the geopolitical networks and strategies of the Petites Nations.

Building Alliances Along the Gulf Coast

The Biloxis and Capinans were not initially eager to form relationships with the French newcomers. On February 14, 1699, groups of Capinan and Biloxi men and women watched with dread as European men disembarked from their ships onto the sandy shores of their Gulf Coast homelands. The men had pale, unpainted skin, strange hairstyles, and seemed to be a military force. In recent years, their communities had been terrorized by growing numbers of English and Indigenous raiders. So, upon seeing these men, the Biloxis and Capinans shouted warnings of the invading warriors, and their peoples ran to the woods. Among

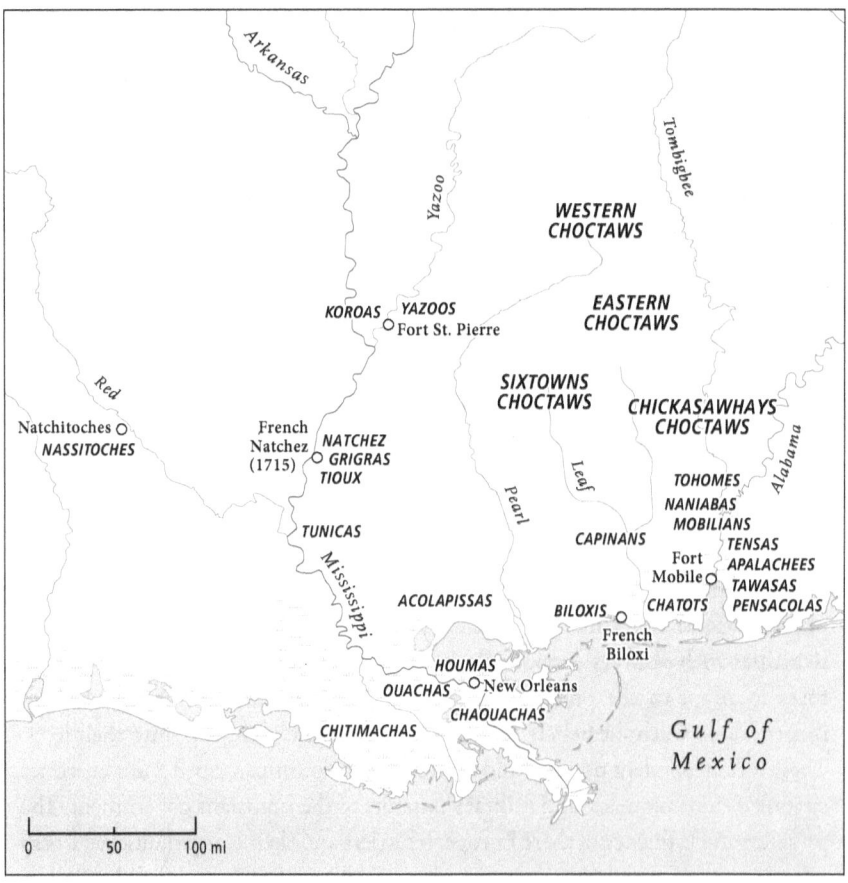

Figure 5. Map of selected nations circa 1720.

those who fled was an elderly Biloxi woman. Although she surely moved as fast as her aching hips and knees would carry her, she could not outpace the young men. These cloth-wrapped foreigners captured her and another elder from her community and held them prisoner at the Biloxi and Capinan campsite. The aged man had been unable to run at all as his leg was swollen with gangrene. Together they waited fearfully for their captors to decide their fates. However, to the woman's surprise, the men did not bind her or the other ailing elder. Instead, through gestures, they conveyed that they were from France, and that they sought only trade and friendship. To demonstrate their good intentions, they made these elders presents of tobacco and beads. Their gifts and gestures of peace allayed the woman's fears, and she promised that she would "grind corn to regale" the newcomers as soon as her people returned and could perform a proper calumet ceremony.[4]

Pierre Le Moyne d'Iberville, the Canadian leader of the French exploratory team that captured this Biloxi woman, was on a mission to determine if colonization of the Gulf South would be a worthwhile venture for the French Crown. Ideally, this Gulf Coast territory would form part of a chain of French controlled lands that would halt English imperial expansion. Through the hide and captive trades, the English had forged connections with Native peoples, like the Chickasaws, that expanded their economic and political networks from the Eastern Seaboard into the continental interior. French officials feared that this expansion of British influence put England in a position to claim a large swath of the North American continent, and this might ultimately block French territorial claims and trade networks in New France. If the French extended their dominion along the length of the Mississippi River and the Gulf Coast, they reasoned, they might be able to curb English expansion and even develop lucrative extractive economies of their own.

Nevertheless, during the first decades of French colonization of the Lower Mississippi Valley, their dreams of territorial domination and the reality of their quotidian lives were vastly divergent. Whatever the imperial designs Iberville and his men might have been ordered to carry out, these travelers urgently needed food, guides, and protection. Moreover, as they entered the region in 1699, walking into the turmoil created by English, Chickasaw, and Creek slave raids, they were pulled into a series of continental networks, conflicts, and intrigues which were easily as complex as the European competitions that shaped France's grand imperial aims.[5]

Iberville was well aware that his ability to claim the region for France would depend on alliances with Native nations like the Biloxis. The French Crown hoped to replicate the model of empire they had developed in New France, in which the colonial government claimed large chunks of territory and trade networks via their alliances with the Native nations that actually controlled this region. In practice, this meant that the Petites Nations initially had tremendous control over the French immigrants' diplomatic endeavors. Nations like the Biloxis introduced the French to their Indigenous allies and functioned as both their geographical and diplomatic guides in the region.[6]

Biloxis, Capinans, Bayagoulas, and Mugulashas were among the first groups to forge alliances with the French. The Biloxis and Capinans lived near present-day Biloxi, Mississippi, in a two-nation settlement of about 420 people. They were a fishing community, and they relied on the Gulf waters to supply their people with gar, oysters, and rivercane. The Bayagoulas and Mugulashas lived in another joint settlement also of roughly 450 people near present-day Bayou Goula along the Mississippi River.[7] The Biloxis and Capinans who had been captured by the French played an important role in facilitating relationships between their people and the newcomers. By returning the man, woman, and several of their kin, along with gifts, the French demonstrated their peaceable intentions. The Biloxi and Capinan leaders then conducted a calumet ceremony with the French to solidify the relationship. Iberville was familiar with the ritual from his experience with Indigenous peoples in New France, and he came well prepared. He impressed, and probably amused, the Biloxis and Capinans when he withdrew a rather odd calumet, one that was cast in iron and shaped like a ship, for the diplomatic occasion.

The Biloxis and Capinans invited the French into their villages on February 17, and they used this opportunity to convince the European immigrants to join their multinational settlement. Along with the French, the Biloxis and Capinans invited their allies—the Bayagoulas and Mugulashas—that evening. After welcoming Iberville's men into their village, the Biloxis and Capinans organized a large calumet ceremony for their guests. Hosting this kind of international summit required the Biloxis and Capinans to feed their guests, so the elderly woman Iberville's men had captured was likely able to make good on her promise to "regale" her guests with corn porridge. Together the Biloxis, Capinans, Bayagoulas, and Mugulashas ate, smoked, danced, and recounted their histories for the newcomers. In the firelight, men and women reenacted their valiant deeds as the flames flickered and cast shadows across their golden skin. Iberville was impressed by the fervor with which the warriors of these villages performed renditions of their military exploits and with the extent of their diplomatic connections. He recorded that the Biloxis, Capinans, Mugulashas, and Bayagoulas had alliances with the Ouachas, Chitimachas, Yakni-Chitos, Houmas, Pascagoulas, Natchez, Bayacchytos, and Amylcou.[8]

The Biloxis and Capinans were so successful in conveying their regional influence and military might that they managed to convince Iberville and his men to build the first French outpost alongside their villages. In the following weeks, Biloxi and Capinan men helped the French immigrants erect Fort Maurepas and set up a tiny French village. By persuading the colonists to base their operations out of their own settlements, Biloxis and Capinans acquired the support of armed French soldiers and access to valuable, novel goods like metal knives and sparkling beads, and strengthened their existing diplomatic networks. It was a brilliant tactical move.[9]

Native nations like the Biloxis and Capinans proved to be integral to the French establishment of Louisiana in large part because the French were deeply unfamiliar with the geopolitical terrain of the Lower Mississippi Valley. The French newcomers found the number and variety of autonomous nations and peoples in this region to be absolutely bewildering. They sometimes misunderstood how Petites Nations people identified themselves and what their relationships were to other nations. Moreover, the "infinité de Nations sauvages" that French settlers encountered challenged European notions about political order.[10] The many small and autonomous polities defied officials' hopes for centralized and coercive Native governments that they could use to mobilize the Indigenous population to the service of the French Empire. Still, the early Louisiana settlers clearly understood the importance of alliances with Petites Nations. Similarly, Petites Nations people may not have understood the specific Canadian and regional French identities of Iberville's crew, or the global extent of France's international networks, but they saw merit in relationships with the European settlers.

After meeting the French at the Biloxi and Capinan villages, the Bayagoulas and Mugulashas were eager to affirm their own alliances with the newcomers. Roughly one month after their initial meeting, the Bayagoulas received the French in their villages. They welcomed the foreigners and provided them with a tour of their homelands that showcased their agricultural bounty and spiritual power. Their guest, Iberville, seemed especially interested in one of their temples, so the Bayagoula leader paused during their tour of the village to let the Frenchman observe the evocatively carved and painted animal statues that adorned his people's house of faith.

In the midst of this beauty, the Bayagoula and Mugulasha communities were in crisis. Roughly a quarter of their kin had died in a recent smallpox epidemic. Many thatched-palmetto homes stood vacant, and most of their community were grieving the loss of family members and friends. On the outskirts of the villages, the Bayagoulas and Mugulashas wrapped their departed loved ones in woven-cane mats and placed them on elevated scaffolds. This allowed their flesh to decay and be picked clean by birds so that their bones could be reclaimed by their families. Shortly before Iberville's arrival, a group of Chickasaws and Napissas had attacked the Bayagoula and Mugulasha villages. Because slave raiders targeted women and children, the Bayagoulas had very few sisters, mothers, wives, and aunts still in their community. Surrounded by the mourning and the dead, a pervasive sense of loss was palpable in their villages.[11]

Bayagoulas and Mugulashas pursued innovative strategies to restore their communities, and they relied on social reproduction to sustain their populations in times of crisis. As such, some of the Bayagoulas and Mugulashas the French travelers met were not born into these nations, but rather were transformed into Bayagoulas and Mugulashas through rituals and relationships. As Iberville and his Native guides left the Biloxis and paddled up the Mississippi River on their way to the Bayagoulas, his party was met a couple of miles from the Bayagoula and Mugulasha villages by a diplomatic envoy. The representatives greeted Iberville on the water, and an elder presented Iberville with a grand, three-foot-long calumet. The man had painted his face and body in black and ocher for the ceremonial occasion. This elder had not always been part of the Bayagoula community. When he was younger, he had been taken captive by the Bayagoulas or Mugulashas, and the violence of his past was evident on his body. The deep-red and charcoal paint could not obscure the fact that he was missing a large part of his scalp. Still, the man had lived with the Bayagoulas and Mugulashas for long enough and built sufficient connections among his adopted nations that he had become an important and esteemed part of the community. He had even come to serve as their ambassador. Social reproduction—the ability to make kin out of captives, outsiders, and nonblood relations and thereby provide both the people and labor to sustain Indigenous communities—was critical for Petites Nations' survival. This was especially true because sustaining nations with strictly biological reproduction and obtaining sufficient feminine labor would have been extremely difficult with so many slave raids and epidemics. This encounter provided the colonists with a snapshot of two of the ways that Bayagoulas and Mugulashas were attempting to mitigate the damage of the slave trade by building alliances with foreign nations and integrating outsiders.[12]

While the French officials worked to strengthen their bonds to Native nations along the Gulf, their Atlantic networks remained feeble, and during their first years in Louisiana the settlers found themselves desperately isolated from the rest of the French Empire. In 1700 the king of Spain, Charles II, died without an heir and left his throne to the grandson of the French king Louis XV. If the English were already concerned about France's attempts to carve out territories in North America and growing French influence in Europe, the ascent of a French king to the Spanish throne seemed to confirm their fears that the Catholic monarchies were joining forces to dominate both Europe and the Americas. To prevent this consolidation of power, England declared war against Spain and France in 1702. The War of the Spanish Succession, as this conflict became known, sapped enormous resources from the Dutch, English, Spanish, and Austrian sovereigns. British, Spanish, and French troops fought across Florida, New England, and New France, until the Peace of Utrecht finally concluded the war in 1713.[13]

While France was embroiled in this conflict, the Crown had very few resources to devote to the colonies, so Louisiana, an imperial backwater of minimal value, was largely neglected. The few colonists at Mobile and Biloxi languished while they waited for the arrival of ships carrying critical provisions like grain, livestock, clothing, millstones, and gifts for Native leaders. Without regular supply lines to France, the colonists in Louisiana faced shortages of nearly everything. The situation was dire. Between 1708 and 1711, not a single supply ship arrived in Louisiana to aid the few hundred settlers, and the colonists suffered severe hunger and privation.

The isolation of the Louisiana colony left these settlers almost completely dependent on their Petites Nations allies. They relied on their Indigenous neighbors to guide them safely through the region, act as their emissaries with other nations, and provide enough food for their troops to survive the winters. French settlers had to ask Petites Nations men for military support and help building their outposts, and women for corn and bear oil. Even as these settlers turned out to be more impoverished allies than the Petites Nations had initially hoped, their presence in Petites Nations settlements, along with their military technology, provided additional protection from slave raiders, making their alliances worthwhile. In short, during the first decade of the eighteenth century, both the Petites Nations and the Louisiana colonists struggled to scrape by on the Gulf Coast, and they depended heavily on each other to protect their communities from the unfolding chaos in the region.[14]

Gender and Diplomacy

As French and Native diplomats forged alliances among their peoples, they relied upon gifts, performances, and cultural accommodation to make their relationships work. The Petites Nations and the French were relatively weak regional powers, at least compared to the Choctaws or Chickasaws, so these small nations (both Native and French) were willing to accept uncomfortable arrangements in order to sustain their partnerships. Building alliances across linguistic, cultural, and national boundaries required both Petites Nations and French settlers to adapt to uncomfortable social contexts. In addition to moving directly into Petites Nations territories and living alongside their Native allies, French officials were forced to deal with powerful women and nonbinary individuals who challenged their expectations about hierarchy and social belonging. Some Petites Nations embraced French material culture and spiritual practices, and most nations agreed to provide labor and services in exchange for military assistance and European trade goods. The desperate circumstances that plagued both Indigenous nations and Louisiana settlers at the turn of the eighteenth century encouraged Petites Nations and colonists to find ways to work with their strange new neighbors.[15]

These French immigrants did not come from a culture that believed women ought to serve as diplomats or as political representatives, but they arrived in a region where Indigenous people expected the presence and participation of women in politics and diplomacy. In fact, the lack of women among Iberville's forces caused Petites Nations concern, and their absence was a stumbling block for French diplomacy. One of the few activities that Petites Nations women did not normally participate in was warfare, so the appearance of an all-male French force traveling through the Gulf Coast likely led Petites Nations people to assume these foreigners were in the region to pursue combat rather than diplomacy. In fact, the exclusively masculine nature of Iberville's expedition presumably led the Biloxis and Capinans to initially flee from their approach. As the Frenchmen rowed upriver from the Biloxis' to the Bayagoulas' villages, Iberville noted that the groups of Ouachas and Bayagoulas they passed on the water traveled with at least one woman along with the men. Given the frequency of all-male parties of slave traffickers in the region, including women in hunting, diplomatic, and trade voyages may have been a critical way to signal peaceful intentions.[16]

Petites Nations women played central roles in international relations both inside and outside of their villages. This is especially evident in their involvement in calumet ceremonies. Like the elderly captive Biloxi who pronounced that she would "grind corn to regale" the foreigners, Native women understood the importance of their participation in these international summits. Being good hosts required feeding all of their guests, and preparing porridge for a large crew of hungry men necessitated a great deal of grinding, hauling water, and minding pots of boiling corn. If the visitors were lucky, the Biloxi women may have also thrown in bits of deer meat or bear fat to thicken the stew.[17]

Beyond preparing meals, Petites Nations women also participated directly in the portions of the ceremony that included performances of their nation's histories and military exploits. Biloxi warriors danced around the tall wooden pole that held the calumet in their village square, and they struck the pole with their "head breakers" (clubs) while they told of their valiant deeds in battle.[18] Iberville recorded that Biloxi women sang to him during his initial calumet ceremony and he had seen both Houma men and women dance and brag of their victories in war. They watched as Houmas recalled heroic battles and major accomplishments of their kin. One French explorer remarked with amusement that both men and women kept these boastful performances in check by teasing each other and accusing one another of "telling big lies" in the process.[19] We can imagine the women with their heads thrown back in laughter, waving their hands, as a young warrior made particularly outlandish claims about the incredible number of men he had singlehandedly defeated in combat. Likewise, at the Bayagoulas' village, Iberville remarked that both men and women, and even children, danced and joined in the ceremony. Women's participation in these diplomatic and military rituals, and their willingness to publicly tease and challenge men, suggests that Petites Nations peoples saw women as authorities within their villages. Their participation was clearly a crucial part of the diplomatic endeavors of their nations.[20]

Petites Nations women did not commonly participate in battle, but they nonetheless remained deeply involved in military affairs. Often women encouraged men to go to war in order to avenge losses, and they aided these efforts by preparing food and supplies for the men. Women were also responsible for making decisions about the fates of war captives. Sometimes they even partook in the torturing of prisoners of war to avenge the deaths of their loved ones. So even if women did not regularly go on raids, they were no less invested in these endeavors, and men clearly respected their guidance as they developed military strategies.[21]

To sustain relationships with Petites Nations people, French diplomats were forced to negotiate and interact with women who held political power. However, French diplomats floundered in mixed-gender settings and struggled to deal respectfully with Petites Nations women.

French mismanagement of interpersonal affairs with Indigenous women was so extreme that Bayagoula leaders were ultimately forced to provide explicit instructions to the colonists about how they must treat Indigenous women. While the French did not live alongside the Bayagoulas, Louisiana officials frequently turned to the Bayagoulas for guides and diplomatic aid. The Bayagoulas were sure to exact sufficient compensation for their labor, and they negotiated payments of beads, glass, coats, axes, blankets, and other manufactured items. French leaders chafed at Bayagoula demands not just for goods but for courtesy toward Bayagoula representatives. The Bayagoula leader, Antobiscania, and his wife found that they had to be very blunt with these foreigners about what they expected from their allies and trade partners. Not only did they have to make it plain that they should always be offered food and hospitality when they visited Louisiana villages but they also had to provide basic lessons in etiquette and proper conduct toward women.[22]

By spring of 1699, the governor of Louisiana, the Sieur de Sauvole, was thoroughly irritated by being forced to negotiate on Bayagoula men's and women's terms. In addition to continually asking for supplies for the fort, Sauvole had been attempting to convince the Bayagoulas to guide his men into the interior, and he was frustrated by the leverage that his peoples' dependency on the Bayagoulas gave Antobiscania. On May 17, 1699, Antobiscania and three of his men approached the French fort at Biloxi. Sauvole would have recognized them from a distance by their tattoos and their hairstyles. Although, like most of the Indigenous peoples of the Lower Mississippi Valley, these men were beardless, Bayagoula men also depilated most of their scalps, leaving only a small lock of hair on their crowns which they adorned with feathers. They left their chests bare to display their tattoos and wore cloths that were adorned with bells, feathers, and bits of copper around their waists, and their limbs bore bangles that created a soft tinkling as they walked.[23] Sauvole was wary of the Bayagoula leader's adept negotiating skills. As he recorded in his journal, Sauvole considered Antobiscania the "craftiest savage that I have yet seen, and the one that goes to the farthest ends" to achieve his goals.[24]

Antobiscania and his men arrived, and in compliance with Bayagoula decorum, Sauvole was required to offer them food before they began their discussion. After he finished his meal, the Bayagoula leader began to make demands. First, Antobiscania requested another thick red blanket. He claimed that the one the French had previously given him had burned in a fire during an attack on his town. Although Sauvole did not believe this tale, he felt compelled to provide the man with a replacement blanket. Bayagoula men and women typically wore clothes made of woven bark or capes made out of turkey feathers that were stitched together to form a warm, downy, covering. If Antobiscania could not acquire another blanket, he would have to hunt turkeys, and his wife would likely be responsible for the painstaking labor of plucking, cleaning, and sewing another cape or gathering bark and finger weaving a new coverlet. By requesting another blanket, Antobiscania was not only exercising his prerogative as a powerful ally but he was also reducing his wife's labor. Second, and perhaps more gratingly, Antobiscania wished to bring his wife on another visit to the French fort to meet with Sauvole and the other French officials. He stressed to Sauvole that it was extremely important that his wife be received with "the same homage as they give him."[25] By this point, Antobiscania would have known that he had to provide explicit instructions on acceptable manners in order to avoid awkwardness or offense should the French ignore or denigrate his wife during their exchanges.

While lavishing diplomatic ceremony and gifts on this Indigenous leader already frustrated Sauvole, he now found himself pressed to provide the same pomp and honors for a woman. This was utterly out of accordance with French understandings of gender and political decorum. As Sauvole admitted in his journal, he had not "considered that the savages were sensitive in that manner."[26] Presumably, the first visit of Antobiscania's wife had been difficult enough for the governor. The fact that Antobiscania felt compelled to provide such a frank breakdown of acceptable social conduct indicates that Sauvole had likely been quite rude to this elite woman during their previous exchange. Antobiscania's wife had probably arrived wearing a woven mulberry sash about her waist, leaving her chest exposed in order to display the tattoos that covered elite Bayagoula women's torsos to illustrate their social stature. As this was a special occasion, she may have also taken pains to freshly rebind her hair and blacken her teeth with a paste of ground roots. Regardless of her dress or her striking, inky grin, a woman at an international negotiation was sure to make an impression on Sauvole, and it was clear that both she and her husband expected him to respect her as a political representative.[27]

Because French officials often failed to recognize women as significant political actors, the documentation of women's political activities is thin. However, archival fragments hint at both the breadth and temporal expanse of women's roles, suggesting that women continued to participate in diplomatic endeavors and act as leaders throughout the century. For example, in the spring of 1771, Quitachoulabenaky, the ruler of the Ishak/Atakapas, received the French traveler Jean Bernard Bossu. Quitachoulabenaky welcomed Bossu to her village with food and drink and ordered her people to treat him hospitably. Bossu was engaged on a diplomatic mission for the Spanish to the Ishak/Atakapa nation. This community of about five hundred people lived near present-day Lafayette, Louisiana.

In his travel diary, Bossu described his stay with Quitachoulabenaky and the Ishak/Atakapas with awe. He reported that she was adored by her people and treated with their utmost esteem. As he described, "She rules with as much courage, wisdom and discretion as a man could. Consequently, the savages have nicknamed her woman of valor, that is heroine."[28] Bossu was so thoroughly impressed that he even compared Quitachoulabenaky to the English Queen Elizabeth and waxed poetic about the Ishak/Atakapa regent's moral rectitude.[29]

Selecting a young woman as their primary leader was an unusual practice for the Ishak/Atakapas, as they generally preferred to be governed by older men, yet Quitachoulabenaky's social and political abilities had garnered her such respect that she was promoted to this position at a young age.[30] While it was relatively uncommon for Lower Mississippi Valley nations to have women as their primary political leaders, Quitachoulabenaky's political position was not anomalous. In the early eighteenth century, the Natchez also recognized several elite women as leaders, and in 1722, a French official remarked that "there is among that nation a woman chief who has as much authority as the grand chief."[31]

Women's involvement in military and political matters meant that occasionally women and female nonbinary individuals could become esteemed warriors and leaders within their nations. Among the most extraordinary and powerful of these leaders was a masculine female Houma who rose to acclaim during the 1690s. In this era, the Houmas lived near present-day Pointe Coupée, Louisiana. Like the Tunicas, Grigras, and Tioux, the Houmas experienced grave loss and violence as colonial diseases and conflicts reached their homelands. During this decade of escalating slave raids and political upheaval, they turned to a formidable masculine leader to guide their people.[32]

In the summer of 1699, the French missionary François de Montigny recorded his surprise at encountering a female supreme leader when he visited the village of the Houmas. As he traveled down the Mississippi River and met with the leaders of the nations of the region, de Montigny negotiated primarily with men. Slave raiders targeted women and children, leaving behind societies with heavily skewed gender ratios. This also led many nations to keep women and children away from foreign visitors. When de Montigny visited the Natchez earlier that year, he reported that the women and children were all in hiding, as they were afraid that his entourage had come to attack their villages. So, when he reached the Houmas' village, he recorded with wonder that "they have a temple and some chiefs, but it is a woman [the masculine Houma leader] who appears to be the most esteemed."[33] More than the religious site, or the male leaders, de Montigny judged that this unnamed warrior was the most revered person in the

Houma nation. Unfortunately, welcoming de Montigny proved to be a fatal error for the Houmas. Some of de Montigny's crew were sick, and his visit brought a deadly illness to the community.[34]

Just months later, the French priest Jacques Gravier traveled through the Houma village and reported that the nation was mourning the death of this awe-inspiring Houma. The Houmas wept while they stored their beloved female leader's bones in the sacred temple. From the stories Houmas told of their life, Gravier gathered that this person had been a formidable warrior and a skilled tribal representative. Through their victories in combat, this person had proven to be a brave and skilled fighter, which earned them respect and a position as the head of the village. The leader ran calumet ceremonies, cut their hair like the men, and held the primary seat in the Houmas' councils. So, by embracing men's labor roles and sartorial trappings, this masculine female Houma was able to earn tremendous social prestige and assert considerable diplomatic power.[35]

Fragmentary evidence suggests that an elite and esteemed Tunica female may also have worn masculine clothing during their lifetime. Sometime between 1706 and 1731, the Tunicas buried an elite female dressed in fine men's clothing. As they interred the body, they placed a kettle containing a Natchez-made pot near their head and a lump of lead ore near their shoulder. Like the other Tunica women who were laid to rest at this site, they were buried with a ceramic pot and wore shell ear pins. During their life, someone had painstakingly woven hundreds of tiny glass beads into their hair. However, unlike the other Tunica women, this person appears to have been buried wearing a frock coat and possibly a pair of trousers, both of which were articles of French menswear. Only the most elite Tunica leaders wore European articles of clothing during the 1710s and 1720s. To be buried in these prized garments would have displayed tremendous status.[36] Furthermore, this person's dress in men's apparel may suggest that they held a traditionally masculine role, such as a high-ranking position of political or military leadership, but it may also suggest that this person lived as a man or as a nonbinary person during their lifetime.[37] Alternatively, the clothes may simply indicate the elite social status of this person.

Although French officials left fairly good records of their interactions with the Tunicas during the 1720s and 1730s, there is no mention of any female political or military leaders, so it is not possible to use the archives to uncover either the personal history or the gender of this elite individual. Tunica men already challenged the gender norms of the Native Southeast, as Tunica men (rather than women as was common nearly everywhere else) were the primary farmers, and it was their care for corn and sunflowers that nourished their people. It is not possible to identify a person's gender from their archaeological remains alone. All that archaeologists can definitively determine from human remains is a person's sex, so this Tunica individual may have identified as a man, as a woman, or as a two-spirit person. It is also possible that French observers could have perceived this female person to be a man, so they may not have noticed or recorded that there was anything special or unique about the gender and social role of this elite Tunica. Due to the archival silence, all that is clear is that whatever this individual's social roles, they were certainly an esteemed and elite member of their community to have received a burial with such material wealth.[38]

While *two-spirit* is a relatively recently popularized term within Indigenous communities, Indigenous people across North America have long conceived of gender as existing beyond a man/woman binary. To be two-spirit can signify a wide variety of identities and sexualities, and today it is frequently used as a catch-all term for queer Indigenous identities. The term also encapsulates people who identify as third, fourth, and fifth gender—all concepts of gender and sexuality that signify identities beyond man or women and that frequently embody both masculinity and femininity—so two-spirit can serve as a general categorization for Indigenous personhood and sexuality that defies the logic of settler heteronormativity. As the Anishinaabe scholar Niigaan Sinclair explains, the word *two-spirit* "is intended to gesture to Indigenous notions of gender outside of Western male and female binaries while at the same time suggesting that certain sexual, social, and relational identities exist in Indigenous communities beyond anthropocentric formations."[39] Essentially, while neither the Houma leader nor this elite Tunica would have used the term *two-spirit* to describe themselves, their gender identities do not fit neatly within a Western man/woman binary, so their bodies and lives presented challenges to colonial ideas about the natural orders of sex, gender, and society.

Some of the clearest evidence that at least some Lower Mississippi Valley nations may have embraced concepts of three and possibly four gender identities come from the accounts of early French travelers who visited the Natchez villages. In 1714 the French missionary François de La Maire recorded that he was deeply troubled by Natchez sexual and social customs. In addition to being convinced that the Natchez worshipped Lucifer and the sun, the holy father expressed his horror that some of the Natchez men profaned themselves by behaving in public as "prostitutes." He was especially concerned about males who "dress like women and are excluded from all the work of men."[40] As he noted, these Natchez who dressed as women also labored alongside other women. Seemingly then, these Natchez *were* women. Alternatively, they may have lived as neither men nor women but as Natchez people who embraced their femininity and womanly qualities, and we may no longer have language for or understanding of exactly how these Natchez femmes would have expressed their selves and sexualities in the early eighteenth century. Regardless, they were evidently accepted within Natchez society. Six years later, Vallette de Laudun, an officer in the French army, recorded similar observations about Native sexualities after he spoke with the French governor of Louisiana, Jean-Baptiste Le Moyne de Bienville, about the cultures of the Native people of this region. As he described, "A few days ago I talked to Monsieur de Bienville about the customs and religion of the savages. He told me that they gave in all vices ... that there were young men who seemed to have renounced their sex in order to serve uses so contrary to nature; that then they were no longer received in the society of men, and that they carried like a woman a band of skin which covered them in front, from the waist to the knees. He also warned that they were pushing youth so far, that at the age of fifty they did not return to their natural state, and that the savages still used them."[41]

Laudun's account offers no specific national or cultural context, so it is difficult to gauge the prevalence of two-spirit individuals across diverse Petites Nations societies. However, his phrasing suggests that this practice extended beyond just Natchez. In his 1753 memoir, the French lieutenant Jean-François-Benjamin Dumont de Montigny also described Natchez femmes who he referred to as "Chef de femmes" (chief of the women), suggesting that it is possible that other nations had similar practices. Like Le Maire and Laudun, de Montigny emphasized that these male Natchez did women's work and labored in the fields, that "they wear their hair long and in braids, and he wears [they wear] a skirt like the women" and Montigny expressed similar concern at what he believed to be their transgressive sexual engagements. During the 1720s, de Montigny lived alongside the Natchez for several years, so he would have observed these Indigenous femmes firsthand. His account, therefore, provides valuable testimony to the lives of these two-spirit Natchez.[42]

These passages perhaps tell us more about French morals and sexual restrictions than the experiences of Native people, but they are nonetheless rich and compelling sources. By 1720 Bienville had lived in Louisiana for nearly two decades and would have been in an excellent position to comment on the social practices of Native Americans. Likewise, Le Maire was a careful observer, working on preparing a natural history of Louisiana based on his travels in the country.[43] Both sources indicate that some Natchez who were biologically male wore women's clothing. These accounts also suggest that these Natchez who dressed as women also labored as women and performed women's roles in society. Their roles as women seem to have encompassed participation in all women's spaces and community gatherings as well as participating as femme partners in sexual relationships with Natchez men. Laudun was further disturbed that these Natchez did not seem to age out of their womanhood, and this suggests that the Natchez who dressed as women embraced their roles as women, men, third or fourth gender individuals, or two-spirit people for the duration of their lives.[44]

While Native leaders pressed French officials to respect people of all genders, they also worked hard to adapt to French customs and rituals. The people of the Petites Nations were used to living and interacting with foreigners whose practices differed from their own, and cultural adaptation and the ability to embrace new styles and ideas was a critical part of what made their multinational settlements work. Still, they struggled with many French customs. Native people found the brusqueness and chaotic order of European diplomatic meetings to be both brash and baffling. Among themselves, Native folks joked that the French talked over one another constantly, "like a flock of geese." It is easy to envision the raised eyebrows and pursed lips Native diplomats must have exchanged as they listened to colonists interjecting and tumbling over one another in conversation.[45]

In the same way that the French arrivals learned to engage in calumet ceremonies in order to forge alliances, some Native leaders also embraced aspects of French spirituality to help facilitate relationships. In 1699 the Tunicas were still living at the Yazoo River settlements. Like the Grigras and Tioux, the Tunicas were suffering from the smallpox epidemic and frequent slave raids. In fact, between 1680 and 1710 as many as half of their population may have perished due to this combination of biological and military assaults. Tunica families grieved almost continuously during this era. In hopes of halting this destruction, Tunica leaders reached out to the French to form an alliance that might protect their people.[46]

The Tunica leaders offered trade and military support, but they also promised a deeper spiritual alliance with the Louisiana settlers. Some Tunicas were open to receiving Catholic instruction, and their leader may have calculated that this cultural accommodation would help forge a lasting bond between their people and the French. Unlike most of the Petites Nations, the Tunicas requested the presence of missionaries in their villages, and their leaders also went out of their way to display Catholic devotion. The Tunicas correctly understood that these religious leaders influenced French colonial officials and that their presence would ensure stronger diplomatic ties with Louisiana officials. In 1699 the Tunica leader received Father Davion and eagerly submitted to a baptismal ritual in which he received the Christian name of Paul. While Paul may have been genuinely moved to convert and spread Catholicism among his nation, the rest of his community received the priest more tepidly. After months with the Tunicas, Davion wrote to his superiors to express his frustration that he had managed to baptize only three dying infants.[47]

The Tunicas' leaders continued to rely on French officials' perceptions of their nation as eager recipients of French culture to solidify their relationships with the Louisiana settlers through the 1720s. During the 1710s and 1720s, the next Tunica leader, Cahura-Joligo, delighted the French by permitting a missionary to baptize him along with his wife and son. In addition to welcoming missionaries in his village, Cahura-Joligo embraced the sartorial trappings of a friendly, Francophile diplomat. French travelers reported that Cahura-Joligo wore a European waistcoat and carried a gold-headed cane. On a ribbon around his neck he sported a French medal that was engraved with an image of the French king's wedding on one side and the city of Paris on the other. This dapper outfit, and his French medal, visually proclaimed his alliance with the French. By the 1720s, the leaders' appropriation of French culture, coupled with the Tunicas regular military assistance, convinced the Louisiana officials that the Tunicas were among France's most reliable Indigenous allies.[48]

Forging relationships among nations that had such vastly divergent ideas about gender, spirituality, and social order was undoubtedly challenging. However, the dire straits that both French and Petites Nations people found themselves in around the turn of the eighteenth century forced these nations to work past their differences and to accommodate their peculiar new allies. These relationships of necessity and interdependency would continue to define Petites Nations and French relationships for the first two decades of the eighteenth century.

Refugees at Mobile

Three years after the initial arrival of the Louisiana colonists, the political maneuvering of Petites Nations shifted the geography of France's Lower Mississippi Valley empire. At the dawn of the eighteenth century, the Naniabas, Tohomes, Capinans, and Mobilians—four Petites Nations that lived in a multinational settlement along Mobile Bay—were continually pummeled by Upper Creek raiders. As part of their efforts to defend their families from this onslaught of warriors, Mobilian and Tohome leaders persuaded French officials to establish a new village alongside their settlements. They hoped that the presence of these foreigners with their advanced weaponry would deter raiders. The new French colonial village, which the settlers called Mobile, would become the capital of Louisiana. While the Petites Nations' efforts to use the colonists to stop Upper Creek attacks had mixed success, the relocation of the Louisiana capital into the Mobile Bay multinational settlements both changed the seat of French power on the Gulf Coast and transformed the Mobilian, Naniaba, Tohome, and Capinan homelands into a hub for refugees who had been displaced by slave trade violence during the 1700s and 1710s.

The Mobilians, Capinans, and Tohomes had lived in the Mobile River region since at least the 1680s. These were small fishing communities whose people lived in villages that were proximate to those of their neighboring nations. The five towns of Mobilians housed some five hundred people, while the Tohome and Naniaba villages together were home to about three hundred. Their peoples had migrated west to the Mobile Bay region likely sometime during the 1600s. A small group of Capinans also lived alongside the bay. During this era, there were at least three autonomous Capinan communities in the region. In addition to the group along Mobile Bay, one group of Capinans lived alongside the Biloxis, and another lived west of the Biloxis near the Pascagoulas.

During the early eighteenth century, the Petites Nations along Mobile Bay faced some of the heaviest and most regular attacks from slave traders. Their lands were within a week's travel of not only the Chickasaws and Choctaws but also the Alabamas, Abhikas, Coosas, and Tallapoosas (Upper Creeks). Therefore, during the 1690s and 1710s, these Petites Nations confronted both Chickasaw and Creek raiders.[49]

By 1702 severe flooding at Biloxi led the French to accept the offer from the Mobilians to relocate their colonial post further inland to Mobile. Two years prior, in May 1700, several Mobilian and Tohome leaders had come to Biloxi to meet with Sauvole. They told him that their people had recently suffered a raid by the Conchas and Piniscas (Upper Creeks) and they desperately needed French help.[50] Over the previous year, the Mobilians, Naniabas, and Tohomes had brought supplies to the settlers who lived alongside the Biloxis and Capinans and strengthened their relationships with the Louisiana officials. Therefore, in their moment of need, they expected the French to provide military support. Sauvole recognized that "it is not a small obligation that we owe to those people there; they are the only ones for a hundred leagues around who could have aided us" in the event of an attack on the French fort. Moreover, he explained that "they fervently wish that we should go establish ourselves on their river."[51]

Sauvole ultimately decided to take the Mobilians up on their offer to have the French join their multinational settlement, and in 1702 some of the colonists migrated to this new site. The Mobilians provided food and supplies that the French desperately lacked, and their lands were superior to the swampy site that Iberville has selected for the first French fort near the Biloxi villages.[52] Still, the French battled starvation as the shortage of supplies and the soldiers' inability to farm created consistent provisioning crises. Sauvole even attempted to trade with the Spanish in Pensacola for flour, but he was unable to secure regular deliveries and keep the troops in bread. Instead, French settlers continued to depend on trade with local nations. The French governor sometimes even sent small groups of men directly into Petites Nations villages during periods of extreme hunger.[53] As they had done with countless refugees before, Petites Nations people received these desperate soldiers and offered them sustenance and shelter. This practice in turn helped reinforce the Petites Nations' connections to the French, and left these colonists indebted to their Native hosts.

During the first decade of the eighteenth century, the Mobile Bay Petites Nations developed service-based alliances with the French colonists who settled alongside their nations. These Louisianans purchased essential goods like poultry, corn, and wood from Naniaba and Mobilian women, and they counted on Tohome and Mobilian men to act as guides, porters, and craftsmen. The Mobile Bay Petites Nations also facilitated trade relationships among their Choctaw allies and the French newcomers, and they enmeshed their economic networks with those of their French neighbors. Like the Tunicas, some Mobilian people also embraced Christianity as they grew closer with their new neighbors.[54]

While some scholars have described Native communities that developed interwoven economic relationships as "dependent" nations, early French officials more often described themselves as the dependent party. Scholars may also need to reconsider the term *settlement Indians* as it applies to the Petites Nations of the Mobile Bay region, since it was in fact the French who gravitated to Native settlements rather than Native people flocking to the outskirts of a colonial city. As Sauvole made clear, it was the Biloxis and Mobilians who convinced the French to live near them rather than vice versa.[55]

Shortly after the arrival of the French, large groups of Apalachees, Pensacolas, Chatots, and Tawasas also came to seek refuge with the Petites Nations at Mobile. Between 1704 and 1706, a series of devastating raids by Alabama and Coushatta captive traders forced large numbers of Native peoples from northern Florida to flee their homes. In that year, groups of Apalachees, Pensacolas, and Tawasas arrived in Mobile and sought refuge at the Mobilian, Naniaba, Capinan,

French, and Tohome settlement. European observers and some subsequent historians have assumed that this move was the result of imperial designs. However, given the tiny population of French settlers, and the considerable influence of Choctaw-allied Mobilians, Tohomes, and Naniabas in the region, it seems almost impossible that these migrant nations from northern Florida would have been able to resettle in the Mobile Bay region without negotiating with the Petites Nations whose lands they were seeking refuge in.[56]

Furthermore, French officials' correspondence makes clear that the Louisiana government did not in fact orchestrate these migrations. Indeed, they had little control over the movements of these Indigenous refugees. The Spanish accused the French of luring away their Native allies in order to weaken the Spanish settlements in Florida and strengthen French power at Mobile. However, when the Spanish governor wrote to Bienville insisting that he "send back the four nations, Apalachees, Pensacolas, Choctaws, and Tawasas," Bienville explained that he was unable to do this, claiming "I had never been the first to propose to these nations to come and take lands in our region. . . . It was the Indians who had come to represent to me that the lands about Pensacola were not good for anything."[57] Therefore, while the presence of the French colonists made Mobile an appealing destination for refugee nations, it was multinational settlement and refugee acceptance practices, rather than imperial designs, that were the driving forces in facilitating Apalachee, Chatot, Pensacola, and Tawasa resettlement. Mobile Bay became a major hub for migrant populations and refugees in the first decade of the eighteenth century, and this in turn facilitated the expansion of French influence in the region.

Neither the Petites Nations nor the Choctaws initially perceived the Louisiana colonists as especially powerful or threatening neighbors, and French settlers struggled to rectify their aspirations for a grand empire in the Southeast with the privation and precarity of daily life in the colony. In fact, both the Petites Nations and the Choctaws sometimes considered the French to be akin to a nation of refugees. English travelers in the region repeatedly told Native Southerners that the Louisiana colonists were refugees from France, and this characterization seemed to fit with their desperate state. In 1708, nearly a decade after their arrival in the region, the French population numbered less than two hundred. The Mobilians alone had at least as many people as the entire French colonial population, and the Choctaw population was more than one hundred times that size.[58]

The French constituted only a small part of the Mobile Bay settlements, and their Petites Nations neighbors continued to prioritize their relationships with the Choctaws over their alliances with the Louisiana government even after the colonists moved into their homelands.[59] During the late seventeenth and early eighteenth centuries, the Mobilians and Tohomes specialized in the salt trade and carried saline crystals inland to sell to the Choctaws. In particular, they held very close relationships with the Chickasawhay Choctaws. After the arrival of the French at Mobile, their economic focus shifted away from the salt trade and toward labor services for the French. However, their alliances and trade with the colonists never supplanted their relationships with the Choctaws. Mobilians, Naniabas, and Tohomes regularly received Choctaws in their villages throughout the 1700s and 1710s, and they capitalized on these connections by serving as middlemen between the Choctaws and the French. The Mobilians', Naniabas', and Tohomes' close relationships with the Choctaws influenced their political agendas and made them valuable allies to the settlers at Mobile for generations.[60]

Still, neither French nor Choctaw alliances were enough to deter Creek and Chickasaw raiders from attacking the Mobile Bay nations. Instead, as the War of the Spanish Succession unfolded, the situation deteriorated further.[61] Certainly, by gaining even limited access to French guns and military support, the Petites Nations were better equipped to defend themselves, but their Louisiana partnerships also exacerbated their enmity with the Upper Creeks. By allying themselves with the French, the Mobilians, Naniabas, and Tohomes became antagonists of the English Crown and thereby prime targets of the English-allied Alabama raiders.[62]

The French and Mobilians responded to attacks from Alabama and Chickasaw raiders with very different tactics. In the Lower Mississippi Valley, Native nations had traditionally regulated violence and enforced their territorial control by conducting small-scale retaliatory raids against those who killed or harmed their kin. These attacks were usually directed at the family or village of the offending polity rather than at the precise individual who had done harm. This system served to dissuade future attacks and to build up individual nations' military and political clout. Thus, in 1704, when several Alabamas killed a French trader, the governor of Louisiana, Jean-Baptiste Le Moyne, Sieur de Bienville (the brother of Iberville), understood that their Native allies would expect the French to kill an Alabama in return. If they did not, the French would risk looking weak, and the other nations might assume that they could kill Frenchmen with impunity.[63]

Governor Bienville asked the Mobilians for assistance in exacting retribution against the Alabamas. His plan was to employ Mobilian, Tohome, and

Choctaw warriors to guide his sixty soldiers to attack the Alabama villages. The Mobilians, Tohomes, and Choctaws agreed and proceeded to purify themselves for battle. Once the men had cleansed and spiritually prepared themselves, the one hundred and twenty Mobilians, Tohomes, and Choctaws set out with Bienville and his troops in early June.[64] However, rather than helping the French assault the Alabama villages, the Mobilians and Tohomes led the French soldiers east on such a meandering path that the Choctaws abandoned the mission. Bienville also eventually realized that the Mobilians and Tohomes were taking his men on an exceedingly circuitous route. He became so concerned that the Mobilians and Tohomes were leading them into a trap, that he ordered his men to return to Mobile without attacking the Alabamas. When Bienville reported this mission to his superiors back in the metropole, he strove to cover up the botched military escapade. Instead of disclosing that he had been thwarted by Mobilian plotting, he suggested that the Alabamas were sufficiently frightened by the approach of the French forces that pursuing the matter further would hardly be worthwhile.[65]

Rather than sabotaging Bienville, it appears that the Mobilians were attempting to protect both themselves and their French allies from a disastrous military blunder. French records contain no explicit explanation of the Mobilians' and Tohomes' decisions to subvert French revenge against the Alabamas. However, it seems unlikely that the Mobilians approved of Bienville's plans for retaliation. The Mobilians understood the potential repercussions of an attack against the Alabamas. In 1700 the three nations that would later join to form the Upper Creeks—the Alabamas, Tallapoosas, and Abhikas—had upwards of 10,000 people. By contrast, the Mobilians, Naniabas, and Tohomes together numbered only about 1,225. Moreover, while the Alabamas were able to send raiding parties of 600–700 men to attack the Mobilians, French estimates suggest that the Mobilians, Naniabas, and Tohomes together could muster only about 350 warriors. The Alabamas were also well armed with English muskets.[66] So, had the Alabamas responded to French provocation with another raid, it could have spelled disaster for both the Louisiana colonists and their Petites Nations allies. Additionally, French troops transmitted a deadly "plague" to their Indigenous allies as they marched to the Alabamas, and the Mobilian and Tohome leaders watched as many of their men fell ill and were forced to return home.[67] Recognizing the slim odds for success, and the unfitness of their ill troops for combat, the Mobilians and Tohomes seem to have made a strategic choice to subvert the French plans and avoid the risks of an open conflict with the Creeks.

The location of the first Louisiana outposts within Petites Nations settlements at Biloxi and Mobile meant that French trade, diplomacy, infrastructure development, and even military capacity were dependent on Petites Nations' cooperation and directed by Petites Nations political priorities. As this failed raid in 1704 demonstrates, French imperial priorities were frequently thwarted or undermined by Petites Nations, and Petites Nations relationships to larger nations, like the Choctaws or Upper Creeks, often took precedence over their relationships with the Louisiana settlers. Instead, the Petites Nations seem to have treated the French much like other small nations that joined their multinational settlements, and they worked to find creative ways to accommodate their strange new allies.

Kinship, Captives, and Violence in Joint Settlements near Mobile

Despite the best efforts of Houma, Bayagoula, Tunica, Mobilian, Naniaba, and Tohome leaders to build alliances and develop strategies that would protect their peoples, the stories of the Petites Nations during the early eighteenth century are overwhelmingly characterized by the incredible levels of violence that their communities endured. Neither European partnerships nor living alongside foreign nations stopped either slave raiders from terrorizing communities and stealing women and children or European diseases from carrying off the young, old, and infirm. The mass mortality among Petites Nations communities also created another kind of danger. In moments of desperation, especially when communities had lost huge numbers of women and children, Petites Nations sometimes attacked their intimate neighbors and captured foreign women and children. They used these captives to rebuild their populations, and integrated outsiders by force. This brutal form of social reproduction could enable nations to recover from the gender-based violence of the slave trades, but it also came with tremendous risks. The stories of intimate violence at multinational settlements are horrific and painful, and they illustrate the specific way that the targeting of women and girls for human trafficking irreparably harmed Petites Nations communities. Both Acolapissas and Bayagoulas used surprise violence to forcibly integrate large numbers of captive women and children who had once been their neighbors as a means to rebuild their nations in moments of crisis. These episodes of betrayal and bloodshed illuminate the lengths that Petites Nations were willing to go in order to preserve their people, as well as underscore the limits of French alliances to protect Petites Nations.

Social reproduction in the era of the slave trade could be extremely violent, and the same ideology that allowed Petites Nations to convert outsiders into kin and to welcome people of all backgrounds also enabled them to kill in order to revive dwindling populations. Petites Nations had long forcibly integrated captives. For example, the Bayagoula man who served as an emissary, and greeted Iberville, was first ripped from his community, scalped, and taken as a prisoner. While he ultimately found belonging and respect within the Bayagoula community, he had nevertheless been made kin by force rather than by choice.

Shortly after they forged an alliance with the French, the Bayagoulas took more drastic measures to ensure the survival of their nation. Despite Bayagoula and Mugulasha efforts to leverage their alliances with the French to protect their people, slave raiders continued to assault their villages and the demographic crisis at the Bayagoula and Mugulasha settlement became dire. So many Bayagoula women and girls had been stolen that the nation seemed on the verge of collapse. Perhaps feeling that they had no other option, in 1700 the Bayagoulas fell on their Mugulasha neighbors. They killed nearly all the Mugulasha men and captured women and children. These captive Mugulasha women and children were made permanently part of the Bayagoula community. While the attack did help the Bayagoulas recover, it also destroyed the Mugulasha nation and sent the few Mugulasha survivors to seek refuge with neighboring nations.[68]

The Acolapissas employed a similar strategy to restore their community, and in a rare occurrence, French colonists were even witnesses to this intimate violence. In early 1706 the French soldiers at Fort Mobile were starving. Even with Mobilian, Naniaba, Capinan, and Tohome assistance, the Louisiana government was unable to feed their soldiers through the winter. In desperation, Governor Bienville ordered his men to seek refuge with various Petites Nations until the Louisiana administration was again able to support them. That winter, a small group of hungry Frenchmen traveled to the Acolapissas' village on the banks of Lake Ponchartrain, not far from present-day New Orleans. The soldiers and a carpenter, André Pénicaut, arrived in a miserable state. Like the other Petites Nations, the Acolapissas were used to taking in refugees and migrants in crisis, so they understood that it was their obligation to welcome and provide for these soldiers. In fact, the French were not the only foreigners who were seeking refuge with the Acolapissas at that time. The year before, a group of Nassitoches (another Petite Nation) had come to the Acolapissas seeking temporary resettlement. Heavy rains in 1705 had flooded their homelands on the Red River and destroyed their harvest, so many Nassitoches were forced to travel south to seek sanctuary.

When the French settlers came to plead for food and shelter, this group of Nassitoches was still living with the Acolapissas. The Acolapissa leader accepted the French men, and he and the Nassitoches leader determined that André Pénicaut would stay in their village as the Nassitoches leader's personal guest. As the hosting nation, and the original inhabitants of their homelands, the choice to provide refuge was ultimately up to the Acolapissas, and the Nassitoches leader explained to Pénicaut that he should consider the Acolapissa leader to be the voice of ultimate authority in the land. As migrants seeking hospitality, the Nassitoches would still govern themselves and engage with foreigners, but they expected to comply with their hosts' political and social expectations. Pénicaut, and the other Frenchmen, in turn would be expected to respect the customs and regulations of both the Nassitoches and the Acolapissas.[69]

Pénicaut loved his time with the Nassitoches and Acolapissas. In comparison to the time he spent starving with his fellow soldiers at Mobile, he relished the attention of the Nassitoches and Acolapissas and the consistent diet of boiled corn porridge and game. While the prudish carpenter was put off by the striking tattoos that adorned the bodies of the Acolapissa women, he was more comfortable around the un-inked Nassitoches women, and he enjoyed the company of the daughters and women relatives of the Nassitoches leader. During his stay, he practiced French with the Nassitoches leader's daughters Oulchogonime and Ouilchil. He also relished the raucous company of the Nassitoches and Acolapissa men who took him hunting and shared stories of their exploits. Pénicaut found that the men of both nations were great comedians, and he exclaimed that on numerous occasions their antics around the campfire had him and his French countrymen nearly dying of laughter. In his levity, Pénicaut even gave dancing lessons to the village inhabitants, and he endeavored to teach these Native men and women the strictly regimented European dancing techniques that would enable them to perform a proper minuet. When he left in 1707, he lamented that he would miss the affections of these peoples. At least, he hoped, he could look forward to a return to French wine.[70]

Five years later, Pénicaut was assigned to return to the Nassitoches and Acolapissa villages and travel with the Nassitoches to the Red River. The Nassitoches were ready to return home, and Pénicaut had been instructed to go with them and to establish a French post alongside their villages. From there, the Louisiana government could then establish trade and diplomatic relationships with the Caddoan nations to the west of the Nassitoches homelands. As they had at Mobile, the French again planned to rely on a mixed French and Indigenous multinational settlement to help them develop their imperial claims in the region.

This French outpost would later be known as Natchitoches. The Nassitoches agreed to return, and they were likely eager to reunite with their friends and extended kin in their own country.

For the Acolapissas, this plan presented an existential threat. In these French designs to relocate the resident Nassitoches, they saw a plot that would rip their community apart. As the Nassitoches were getting ready to leave, the Acolapissas suddenly attacked their departing guests. In the melee, they killed seventeen Nassitoches men and captured more than fifty women and children. It is possible that Oulchogonime and Ouilchil were among these prisoners. The Nassitoches who managed to escape ran to the surrounding woods and hid. Pénicaut watched in horror but could do nothing to stop the assault. Ultimately, he was able to reconnect with some of the Nassitoches who had escaped this attack, and he and the much-reduced group of grieving Nassitoches traveled north to their homelands.[71]

While we have no direct evidence to prove the Acolapissas' rationale, Pénicaut's account suggests that the Acolapissas assaulted the Nassitoches in order to maintain the Nassitoches women as part of their community. By 1712 the Nassitoches had lived alongside the Acolapissas for six years and many Acolapissas men shared intimate relations with the Nassitoches women and likely fathered children. Like other Petites Nations, the Acolapissas had been pummeled by Chickasaw raiders and had probably lost a disproportionate number of women and children to the captive trade.[72] Thus, when the Nassitoches threatened to leave and sever these kin ties, "the Colapissas were seized with jealousy or, rather, with rage. Seeing that the Nassitoches women, too, were leaving and were going away with their husbands, they fell upon the Nassitoches with blows of guns, arrows, and hatchets."[73] Pénicaut's focus on the significance of these Nassitoches women in motivating the attack suggests that the Acolapissas were unwilling to lose these migrants who had become critical parts of their lives and represented the reproductive future of their community.

Pénicaut recorded that the French were furious at the Acolapissas for this attack, swearing that the Louisiana government "intended to take revenge" for this slaughter. But this day of reckoning never came, and it seems that the French were unable to convince the Acolapissas to return these captured women and children. Perhaps the French calculated that they desperately needed an alliance with the Acolapissas to support their settlement at Mobile, or perhaps they thought that fighting the Acolapissas would be too costly. Whatever their reasons, the French were unwilling or unable to avenge this violence and were forced to adjust their plans for the Nassitoches settlement as a result.[74]

The purpose of examining these painful histories is not to suggest that Petites Nations were cruel or violent, but rather to draw attention to the extreme demographic crises that the slave trade created for these small Southern nations. The mass theft of Indigenous women and girls upended the ability of Petites Nations to grow, raise children, and provide for their communities. Therefore, in their desperation, they sometimes relied on massive adoptions of captives. Petites Nations used surprise attacks on their neighbors in joint settlements to address various issues—as the French would learn in later years to their peril—not just gender imbalances. However, the prevalence of attacks designed specifically to obtain women and children captives during the first decades of the eighteenth century underscores the multitude of ways that the expansion of the Charleston-based trade in Indian captives created crises within Petites Nations communities and refracted violence through the region.

* * *

The escalation of the southeastern Indian slave trade and the onslaught of epidemics at the turn of the eighteenth century created crises within almost every Petite Nation community. As Chickasaw and Upper Creek raids on Petites Nations increased in the years around the turn of the eighteenth century, the Petites Nations eagerly sought to use both violence and diplomacy to protect their people. As part of their strategic plans to build powerful political and economic networks, they enthusiastically incorporated French newcomers into their multinational settlements and built alliances and trade relations with the Louisiana settlers.

Although they were vulnerable to foreign raiders, Petites Nations exercised significant power within their homelands and their relationships shaped the lives of European and Indigenous people alike. During the first two decades of French settlement along the Gulf Coast, they forced the Louisiana colonists to adapt to their customs and politics and to pursue their military imperatives. Despite their stately rhetoric and claims to their superiors, Louisiana officials largely failed to counteract the prevailing image of French weakness among the Indigenous nations of the Lower Mississippi Valley, and they continued to depend on Petites Nations' support. Their endeavors were thwarted by Mobilian and Acolapissa priorities; their gender and cultural norms were challenged by Bayagoula, Tunica, and Houma people; and their physical locations were influenced by Tohome, Mobilian, Biloxi, and Nassitoches political strategies. The French struggled with the terms of their relationships even with steadfast allies like the Tunicas, and were forced to reckon with their position as one of the many international alliances that made up the Petites Nations' political and economic networks. Moreover, they could not stop or control Petites Nations' or large nations' use of violence against their Indigenous allies. Thus, within the first decade of their settlement, Louisiana's officials began to look for ways to improve their political and military reputation in the region so as to demonstrate to their Native neighbors that they could be dangerous enemies.

CHAPTER 3

Enslaved by Their Allies

Tensas and Chitimachas in French Louisiana

In 1718 an elderly Chitimacha diplomat recalled the previous decade with horror. As he recounted, "The sun was red, the roads filled with brambles and thorns, the clouds were black, the water was troubled and stained with blood, our women wept unceasingly, our children cried with fright, the game fled from us, our houses were abandoned, and our fields uncultivated, we all have empty bellies and our bones are visible."[1] Since 1706 his people had been at war with the French. He explained that his community was devastated, hungry, grieving, and desperate to put an end to the conflict. As he spoke, he recalled the hundreds of Chitimachas who had died in the conflict, the hundreds more who had fled to seek refuge with other nations, and his many kin whom French settlers held enslaved at New Orleans, Mobile, and Natchez. The Chitimachas had initially hoped that the French colonial government would help defend their people from slave raiders. In 1699 they conducted a calumet ceremony with Iberville and his men and negotiated a diplomatic and trade partnership. Within just a few years, their dreams for peace and safety were shattered. The Chitimachas' alliances with the Louisiana colonists failed to protect their people. Instead, the development of the settlements at Mobile and Biloxi heralded an expansion of slave raids into Chitimacha communities. Ultimately, many Chitimachas were enslaved by the very colonists they had hoped would protect their nation.

The establishment of French Louisiana created a new market for Indian slaves in the Southeast, and during the first decades of the eighteenth-century, settlers' demands for enslaved laborers led to war with the Chitimachas. Officially, the French administrators insisted that they did not traffic in allied Native peoples, and this claim was a core part of both the public image and diplomatic strategy of the Louisiana colony. In practice, French settlers bought, sold, captured, and enslaved a wide variety of Southeastern Indigenous people, including those from Native nations who held alliances with the Louisiana government. During this era, the Charleston-based Indian slave trade ripped thousands of people from their homes and flung Native captives across the Atlantic world, while a smaller-scale Indian slave trade in colonial Louisiana also tore Petites Nations peoples from their communities and forced them into slavery in French settlements at Mobile, New Orleans, Natchez, and Natchitoches. The combined British and French hunger for enslaved Indigenous laborers therefore subjected Petites Nations people to slave raiders from both near and far.

The Indigenous men and women who ended up laboring in colonial households and on plantations endured a wide spectrum of bondage and violence, and their gender profoundly shaped their experiences of enslavement. The documentary evidence of the lives of these enslaved men, women, and children is slim and often fragmentary. It is therefore difficult to discern how violence, negotiation, and coercion shaped labor and relationships among Indigenous people and colonists. Nonetheless, these terse archival records provide glimpses of the lived experiences of enslaved Native people. Native men and women found both large and small ways to resist the subjugation and abuse of their enslavement. In particular, Native people relied on kinship to mitigate the brutality of their daily lives and to build new family and communal ties.[2]

Both Chitimachas and Tensas were enslaved by French settlers at Mobile in significant numbers. Each of these nations also held alliances with Louisiana. The very different paths that led to the capture and enslavement of Chitimachas and Tensas by the Louisiana colonists offer evidence that the French claim that they did not enslave their allies was a fiction, and that enslaved Native people were a vital part of the early Louisiana economy. The experiences of free and enslaved Tensas and Chitimachas, and the relationships they built, illustrate the tremendous violence of the Louisiana Indian slave trade and provide glimpses of the ways Petites Nations men and women attempted to survive bondage within French settlements.

Labor Shortages and French Policy—Enslaving Native Americans

In 1702 Governor Bienville wrote to his superior in France with an urgent request for women. He begged for one hundred young women of good quality and strong moral character to help support the fledgling colony at Mobile. The first ships of explorers had not included any women, and colonial officials worried that the lack of women was hindering the growth of the colony. They were particularly concerned with the shortage of people who could do work that Europeans gendered as feminine, including washing and cooking. French women did not begin to arrive in Louisiana until 1704, and the first group of immigrant women was composed of only twenty-one settlers, rather than Bienville's requested one hundred. By 1706 the Louisiana colonists were also vociferously demanding that the French government send African slaves to the colony. They reasoned that enslaved laborers would remedy the shortage of workers and enable the development of plantations. Again, the French Crown processed the colonists' requests slowly and incompletely. The first Africans arrived in Louisiana in 1709, and until the 1720s, enslaved Africans constituted a very small portion of the colonial populace.[3]

French settlers relied on Petites Nations men and women for labor, but the services rendered by their Mobile, Tohome, Biloxi, and other Indigenous allies did not fulfill the settlers' domestic needs. The colonists also grew tired of having to negotiate on Native terms. French men were accustomed to working outside of their homes and to have women family members or hired servants take care of their households. Cooking, laundry, and cleaning required a tremendous investment of time and energy. Most of the first settlers in Louisiana were single French men who were unwilling or unable to do this labor. By 1708 there were 180 French men, 27 French families, and 60 French *coureurs de bois* (backwoodsmen) who lived within Indigenous towns. So, the vast majority of these early colonists did not live with women, or have access to women's labor.[4]

The low numbers of French women and enslaved Africans in the colony during the 1700s and 1710s led the Louisiana government to embrace Indian slavery. During this era, settlers both purchased Indigenous captives from Native peoples and conducted slave raids against local nations in order to secure slaves. Ultimately, the French need for workers, and their willingness to employ violence to secure servitude, led to the development of a range of coerced, slave, and wage-based Indigenous labor within Louisiana. By 1708 there were a total of 279 French settlers in Louisiana, not including the men living in Indigenous villages, and 80 enslaved Indians. This meant that nearly a third—roughly 29 percent—of the colonial populations at Mobile and Biloxi were enslaved Native peoples.[5]

During the first decade of the eighteenth century, Louisiana colonists enslaved Indigenous men and women, as well as babies, boys, and girls. Between 1702 and 1711, French settlers held 103 American Indian men and 80 American Indian women as slaves. By comparison, in 1711 there were only eleven enslaved

Africans at Mobile. So, during the first decade of Louisiana settlement, it was Indigenous people rather than Africans who made up the majority of the enslaved laborers in the colony.[6]

The era between 1700 and 1720 was the height of Indigenous enslavement in Louisiana. Between 1704 and 1738, more than 135 enslaved Native people appear in the baptismal records of Mobile, and this only indicates the percentage of Native people, most of whom were children, who were taken to be baptized during their bondage. Enslaved Indigenous men and women frequently served as diplomats and guides, and both enslaved Native men and women used their language skills and cultural fluencies to facilitate French relationships with other nations. If they were traveling with their owners, both Native men and women rowed pirogues, hauled firewood, trapped small animals, and fended off snakes and alligators. Within colonial settlements, Native women conducted domestic labor—washing, cleaning, mending clothes, and preparing food for French men—while enslaved Native men helped build the infrastructure of Mobile, Natchitoches, and New Orleans.[7]

In addition to forcing enslaved Native women to perform a multitude of household duties, many French men also expected to have access to these enslaved women's bodies. Enslaved Indigenous women at French settlements were raped or coerced into having sex with their French enslavers so often that early observers frequently labeled them as wives or concubines. While we cannot know what percentage of Native women endured a second phase of conquest and sexual violence, the archival records clearly indicate that French observers assumed that Native women who labored as domestics would also be sexually available to their owners. As the Indigenous feminist and scholar Sarah Deer has argued, the rape of Native women was part and parcel of the process of colonization: sexual violence is a critical component of colonial power. Stealing these Native women and continually assaulting their bodies on Indigenous homelands transformed the tiny pieces of French controlled territory within this Indigenous borderland into sites of colonial domination. While early settlements generally remained dependent on Native people and were spaces where colonists had to negotiate on Native terms, enslaved Native individuals within colonial households regularly experienced violence that was beyond the power of their people to control.[8]

The commonality of these violent coerced intimacies scandalized the French clergy who visited the region. In 1708 Father Henri Roulleaux de La Vente, who was stationed at Mobile, wrote back to his superior in France urging the administration to outlaw these types of relationships. La Vente lamented that Governor Bienville's familiarity with an Indian woman had scandalized the entire colony, and many priests found these relationships unhealthy and unholy. They were not so much concerned with protecting Native women from violence as they were with preventing what they viewed as immoral relationships. They believed that only a married man and woman should live under the same roof, and that these Native women had a harmful influence on Louisiana society.[9]

Some French officials also feared that these relationships could have dangerous consequences for the colony. They worried that the children of Native women and French settlers might not be loyal to the French king if they were too connected to their mothers. One official even prophesied with horror that if relationships between settlers and Indigenous women were permitted to continue, "the colony would become a colony of half-breeds who are naturally idlers, libertine, and even greater rascals, as those of Peru, Mexico, and the other Spanish colonies."[10] They dreaded that the physical and ideological contamination of these Native women would pollute their children and detract from the empire's mission.

Moralizing officials demanded that French women be sent to Louisiana as quickly as possible to offset these insidious intimacies. As one French official explained, without European women, they could not prevent this cross-cultural sex. The settlers would continue to engage in relationships with Native women because "the Indian women are easy, the climate is stimulating, and they are young men for the most part Canadians, that is to say very vigorous."[11]

The Catholic Church in Mobile also took steps to address the danger posed by the cultural influence of Native women in settler homes. Religious officials turned to French imperial slave codes for guidance on how to manage this growing enslaved population. The 1685 Code Noir had been developed to regulate enslaved African laborers in the French Caribbean. It specified that French colonists were responsible for providing baptism and Catholic education to their enslaved laborers. Church leaders in Louisiana hoped that religious conversion would help offset the threatening cultural influences of Indigenous mothers and Native blood in mixed-race babies. If these enslaved Native women could be made Catholic, perhaps they would not corrupt French households. During the first two decades of French settlement at Mobile, church officials baptized more than sixty enslaved Native American children and babies. Some of the enslaved who were dragged before the altar were children as young as two years of age. The presence of enslaved Native infants in these registers also suggests that their mothers were likely also held in bondage, even though these women often were not recorded as enslaved persons. Many wealthier Louisiana settlers—such as merchants, craftsmen, priests, and government officials including Governor Bienville—held Native children in bondage. In 1705 Bienville brought an enslaved boy to be christened Jean-Baptiste, and four years later he had a young Alabama girl who was ill and near death baptized as well.[12] Away from their communities and the care of their mothers, physically abused and surrounded by colonial diseases, many of these enslaved Native children and babies died.

Despite the objection of some priests and officials, French settlers continued to purchase, enslave, rape, and coerce sex from Indigenous women for decades. Many of the French soldiers had coerced sexual relationships with enslaved women and girls, and this violence produced a wealth of children. In 1716 the governor of Louisiana Antoine de la Mothe, Sieur de Cadillac complained to the superior council about the extent of these immoral relationships. As he reported, "All except for Sieur Blondel and the newcomers have Indian women as slaves who are always with child or nursing," suggesting that the sexual exploitation of enslaved Native women was ubiquitous in the colony. By September 1716, anxiety about the social impact of these unhealthy relationships forced the French council to recognize marriages between Catholic Indigenous women and French men.[13]

The creation of new legislation to regulate Indian slavery in Louisiana was designed both to satisfy the moral qualms of French priests and officials and to address French concerns about the very legality of enslaving Indigenous peoples within the colony. In 1709 Indian slavery was formally legalized in New France and Louisiana. This ordinance did not create the trade in Indian slaves through the French colonies, but rather sought to regulate an already widespread practice. In Lower Louisiana, Illinois, and New France, Native peoples often solidified diplomatic relationships with the French via gifts of Indigenous captives. The ability to give a life, either to remedy past violence or to seal a relationship with a living being, was one of the most powerful bonds of alliance for Native Americans across eastern North America. French officials worried that if the legal status of Native captives remained ambiguous, coureurs de bois would sell these captives to the English and thereby destabilize French claims into the continental interior.[14]

It was not just French colonial legislation for North America but also the global efforts of the French Crown to regulate slavery within its possessions that shaped the status of enslaved Native peoples along the Gulf Coast. As Article 9 of the 1685 Code Noir specified,

The free men who will have one or several children from their concubinage with their slaves, together with the masters who permitted this, will each be condemned to a fine of two thousand pounds of sugar; and if they are the masters of the slave by whom they have had the said children, we wish that beyond the fine, they be deprived of the slave and the children, and that she and they be confiscated for the profit of the [royal] hospital, without ever being manumitted. Nevertheless we do not intend for the present article to be enforced if the man who was not married to another person during his concubinage with his slave would marry in the church the said slave who by this means will be manumitted and the children rendered free and legitimate.[15]

According to these contemporary French legal codes, single French men who fathered children with enslaved women should be wed to their slaves. These marriages would legitimize the relationships in the eyes of the law and free their children from future bondage.[16] La Vente had lived in the Mascarene Islands where this law was in effect immediately preceding his arrival in Lower Louisiana. La Vente's efforts to push French colonists to wed the enslaved Native women they coerced sex from were therefore informed by legislation that was designed to regulate enslaved Africans on France's sugar plantations in the Caribbean Sea and Indian Ocean.[17]

Officially, French settlers were only supposed to possess slaves captured in just wars and preferably these captives should come from distant regions. Allowing the enslavement of Native people from local nations seemed to French officials to be bad policy since it might jeopardize Louisiana's alliances with its Native neighbors. French officials feared that enslaving Native peoples would also tarnish the image they wished to project of compassionate French diplomacy. Louisiana representatives repeatedly declared that they did not enslave their Indian allies—unlike the English—and Bienville believed this was a key tenet of official policy. The French colonists were poorer and militarily weaker than their English counterparts. To offset these deficiencies, Louisiana officials aimed to convince Native leaders that they were more just than their English competitors, highlighting the ways English merchants and officials had betrayed Native nations by enslaving their peoples. Bienville made a point of cultivating this image, and on several occasions he liberated captives taken from Native nations that were allied with the French. In 1711 Bienville claimed that refusing to traffic in Native peoples had incentivized the Chickasaws to stop attacking Mobile and consider peace with the French. As he explained, "I have disposed [them] in such a way that they prefer a small present from us to a much more considerable one from the English whom they like only because they give them a great deal and whom they despise because of the little scruple that they have against buying slaves of the nations with which they are not [at war], which we do not do at all."[18] The peace between the Chickasaws and France would not hold, but the French would continue to trade on their image of ethical conduct with Southeastern Native peoples in order to sustain alliances with other Indigenous nations.

As noble as this policy appears, it did not reflect the reality of enslavement in colonial Louisiana. The French continued to insist that they did not exploit and enslave people from allied Native nations. However, the baptisms, bills of sale, census records, and court cases from early Louisiana tell a very different story. Between 1700 and 1730, Native people who were allied with France—including substantial numbers of Chitimachas and Tensas as well as Nassitoches, Comanches, Paniouachas, Tawasas, Alabamas, Koroas, Apalachees, and Ouachitas—were enslaved by French colonists.[19]

The census records of slaves in Louisiana seriously undercount the number of enslaved Native people in the colony. The 1726 census of colonial Louisiana includes 159 Indian slaves, 1,385 African slaves, and 1,663 French inhabitants.[20] This record suggests that enslaved Indigenous peoples made up less than 5 percent of the total population. But this tally does not account for many of the Native women who were enslaved and living in coercive intimate relationships with French settlers. Moreover, while settlements in Natchez and New Orleans saw sharp increases in the number of enslaved Africans during the 1720s, enslaved Indian labor remained a crucial part of the economy throughout the decade in more remote settlements. At the tiny colonial settlement at Natchitoches, the 1722 census indicates that Indian slaves made up 30 percent of the enslaved labor force, and 13 percent of the total population.[21]

Both Chitimachas and Tensas were enslaved in substantial numbers by the French settlers, but the stories of how their peoples ended up in bondage are strikingly different. During the 1700s and 1710s, Tensa captives were bought, sold, and gifted to French settlers individually and in small groups by other Native peoples. By contrast, the French enslaved Chitimachas en masse during a genocidal war. Even once they became enslaved within French settlements, Chitimachas and Tensas had distinct experiences that varied depending on their ability to maintain kin connections and move beyond the confines of French homes and towns.[22] Comparing the stories of these two nations illustrates not only the variety of ways that Native peoples who were allied with France became enslaved, but also two vastly divergent Petites Nations' approaches to survive the multidirectional human trafficking networks that existed in the Lower Mississippi Valley.

The Tensas' World in Chaos

The second half of the seventeenth century ushered in an unceasing tide of violence in the Tensas' homelands on Lake St. Joseph. As refugees poured into the region between 1650 and 1710, and geopolitical metamorphoses transformed the Native Southeast, the Tensa nation struggled to defend their community. Their people endured violence from both English-allied slave raiders and neighboring nations. In the early eighteenth century, they were forced to flee their homelands and they attempted to rebuild their own community from the brink of dissolution. To save their community, the Tensas intermittently lived in multinational settlements and took in refugees, and they also employed violent tactics of forced adoption to restore their population.

Tensas had managed low levels of conflict with their neighbors for decades before the arrival of colonial slave traffickers upended their world. In the 1660s, the Tensas and their allies the Quapaws were at war with nearly all of their neighboring nations, and they endured attacks from Tunica, Yazoo, Koroa, and Natchez raiders. During this era, Tensa people relied on both military strength and spiritual power to sustain their community and protect their homelands.[23]

To mitigate the damage of these conflicts and upheavals, the Tensas sought help from the spirits. Tensa society was shaped by a strict social hierarchy and a powerful theocratic government. Similar to their Natchez neighbors to the south, the Tensas built earthen mounds to elevate their hallowed grounds, recognized the sun as a sacred power, and believed that their leaders held relationships to divine forces. Tensa families lived in homes that were made of thick clay walls with roofs of cane mats that were woven so expertly by their mothers, sisters, and aunts, that they even kept out the summer afternoon downpours. Their villages were organized around a sacred ceremonial center that held precious relics and housed their spiritual relations. At the center of this powerful space stood the grand temple, which was topped with three eagles, their carved wooden beaks beckoning in the direction of the rising sun. Inside this temple, spiritual leaders fed kindling to an ever-burning flame. This was the precious fire of the sun. It was given to the Tensas directly from the spirits via blazing lightning bolts. Should the fire ever go out, it was said, the Tensas' world would fall out of balance.[24]

The majesty and power of the Tensa village drew the interest of the earliest French explorers. In 1682 the leader of the Tensas received the French explorer Henri de Tonti at his village. The Tensa leader greeted La Salle in his magnificent home surrounded by his three wives and flanked by sixty headmen from the eight Tensa villages. Tonti was very impressed by this lavish reception and by the respect that the Tensas paid their leader. He recorded that the Tensas so esteemed this leader that when he died, one hundred young men were slain alongside him to accompany him to the afterlife. The bones of the leader and the young men were then stored in cane mats within the temple where they would be eternally cherished by the living. While this account was likely exaggerated, as the Tensas could ill have afforded to kill so many of their people in this dark era, Tonti's narrative nonetheless reflects the devotion these leaders inspired in their people.[25]

Despite the efforts of these elite leaders to protect their people, many Tensas fell victim to European diseases and slave raids. Because human traffickers targeted women and children, Tensas lost disproportionate numbers of aunts, mothers, daughters, and sisters.[26] By 1699 the nation was reduced to only seven hundred people. This was less than half of their population just twenty years earlier. To replenish their community, Tensas integrated small numbers of captives, but continued to lose women and children to raiders at still higher rates.[27]

The expansion of the British southeastern Indian slave trade led the Tensas to both establish multinational settlements and to use large-scale captive adoption to restore their declining population. During the 1680s, the Tensas welcomed Mosopelea refugees, but many of these migrants ultimately left Tensa settlements to form the new Ofogoula community along the Yazoo River. The Tensas again tried refugee integration between 1700 and 1706 as they welcomed fleeing groups of Ouachitas into their villages. This time, however, they attacked the migrants who were sheltering within their villages. Tensa warriors killed the men and forcibly incorporated the Ouachita women and children into their community to bolster their population.[28]

In addition to hosting Indigenous refugees and migrants and violently adopting foreign women and children, the Tensas forged an alliance with the French. In 1699 Tensa diplomats welcomed the French missionary François de Montigny into their villages. They received him generously and offered guides to escort him through the region. De Montigny had been instructed to survey the region and evaluate the viability of establishing missions among the Native populations. While de Montigny assessed the potential converts, the Tensas endeavored to have this priest use his role as a cultural go-between to end their war with the Natchez. In the summer of 1699, de Montigny mediated diplomatic discussions between the Tensa statesmen and their Natchez and Tunica adversaries.[29] Despite de Montigny's attempts to facilitate peace in the region, the nations of the Yazoo River region continued to suffer from raids and disease, so this partnership with the French missionary did little to aid the Tensas.[30]

By 1700 it seemed clear to the Tensas that they must have gravely erred and were experiencing divine punishment. In the spring of that year, a bolt of lightning pierced the sky and struck the Tensas' main temple. The cane mats and walls of the temple caught fire and blazed as the Tensa families cried out in horror. Tensas believed that lightning was the sacred fire of the sun, so they understood this lightning strike as the tangible embodiment of divine wrath. At the behest of the elderly guardian of the temple, the Tensas sang, blackened their tear-streaked faces with earth, and begged for the spirit to put out the flames. It was abundantly evident to them that the beings of the above world were furious with their people and that they needed to purify themselves and rectify their misconduct. As the flames continued to crackle, charring the sacred bones of their former leaders, several Tensa women came forward with their infants and made the ultimate sacrifice. They placed their children directly into the blaze to save their community. Iberville and Pénicaut watched in horror as Tensa mothers cast their children into the flames. Iberville recalled that he instructed his crew to restrain the bereft women and stop the sacrifice by force. In the aftermath of this incident, the Tensas' relationship with their French allies soured. They may have blamed the newcomers and their sacred, black-robed men for disturbing the spiritual balance of their world, and they were furious with Iberville for inhibiting their ability to use the lives of their children to restore spiritual order.[31]

The next decade brought no respite for the Tensas. Between 1700 and 1706, Chickasaw raids into Tensa territory continued to increase in frequency and severity. By 1703 these raids had ripped apart their communities, and half of the Tensa men had lost their sisters, wives, and children to the English-allied Indian slave traders.[32]

Further exacerbating this violence, and in response to the onslaught of slave raiders and the English presence around the Yazoo River region, some of the nations of the Lower Mississippi Valley also turned to slaving themselves in their efforts to forge alliances with the English and protect their people. In 1704, for example, the Tunicas captured twenty Tensas and sent them as a gift to Carolinian traders in an attempt to build a partnership.[33] The English in turn then gifted twelve of these Tensas to the Chickasaws in another gesture of friendship and alliance.[34] Given the tremendous volume of Indigenous captives the Chickasaws traded to the English, it is worth noting that, even as these captives were commoditized in Charleston slave markets, English traders continued to recognize the important roles captives played in Southeastern diplomacy.

In 1704 the barrage of Chickasaw raids drove the Tensas out of their homelands to seek refuge with the Bayagoulas. However, within just a couple of months of their resettlement, the Tensas killed many of the Bayagoulas in a predawn attack. We do not know what led the Tensas to assault their hosts, but it seems likely that the Tensas saw this as a prime opportunity to rebuild their population by forcibly incorporating captured Bayagoula women and children. Once they had killed many of the Bayagoulas and chased them from their village, they invited the neighboring Chitimachas and Yakni-Chitos to come share the calumet and feast on the Bayagoulas' provisions. The Chitimachas and Yakni-Chitos accepted this offer, and many of their people came to celebrate the Tensas' victory. However, the Tensas were not seeking peace. They took advantage of the safety offered by the calumet ceremony and attacked their visitors, again taking women and children. These violent adoptions increased the Tensa population. However, they also forced the Tensas to flee to escape retribution.[35]

While their partnerships with Europeans had failed to provide security for their people, the Tensas sought help from foreign nations. Instead of migrating south to the Bayagoulas, some Tensa families took refuge with the Natchez.[36] Other Tensas attempted to address the slaving problem directly. In the 1700s and 1710s, Tensa diplomats met with Chickasaw and English emissaries to discuss potential partnerships. In 1707 the Tensas received English traders in their villages in an effort to secure an alliance with South Carolina. The following year, Tensa leaders met with the South Carolina merchant Thomas Nairne. The English hoped that if they could gain the alliance of Petites Nations like the Tensas, then the French would be left isolated and unable to hold on to their territorial claims along the Gulf Coast. Nairne met with the Tensas, Tunicas, Koroas, Natchez, and Quapaws as he attempted to establish relationships between the English and the Mississippi River Valley polities.[37] However, the Tensas' efforts to secure an alliance with the South Carolina representatives came to naught, and they continued to endure raids and retribution from local Native nations.

In 1713 a group of Tensas fled east to the newly established French fort at Mobile and found refuge with these newcomers. At Mobile, the Tensas settled alongside the Mobilians, French, Naniabas, Tohomes, Apalachees, Tawasas, and

Chatots. In this multinational community, they were finally able to stop running and fighting and begin rebuilding their community.

Tensa Captives and Wives at Mobile

Of the many Tensas captured between 1680 and 1713, at least some of them were trafficked into the hands of French settlers. So, when the Tensas moved to Mobile, some of their kin were already living in bondage with their Louisiana allies. We can envision their grief as they moved through the French villages, recognizing stolen sisters and daughters. Over the prior three decades, the Tensas had maintained alliances with the French, yet their people were still trafficked into Louisiana settlers' homes. While the French did not themselves raid and capture Tensas, other Lower Mississippi Valley nations used Tensa captives to forge alliances with the colonists, and the French were willing to both receive and purchase Tensa captives.[38]

Almost all the Tensas whose age and sex appear on baptismal records from Mobile before 1712 were women and children. In these colonial registers, there are many entries listing enslaved Native babies who were less than a year old. For example, in 1708 Father Le Maire baptized a two-month-old Tensa infant who was owned by a merchant named Boutin. Although the priest recorded that this Tensa baby was named Vincent, he made no mention of the infant's mother or father.[39] It is hard to imagine that this child would have survived for very long without his mother, and it would be surprising if Boutin or other French colonists were willing to take a still breastfeeding child without a designated caretaker. Therefore, it seems likely that Boutin probably also owned Vincent's Tensa mother. This child and the many other infants were either carried to Mobile with their captive mothers or were the products of the rape their mothers experienced during their enslavement. It is possible that the French received these Tensas via diplomatic exchanges with other Native nations. However, it also seems that French settlers purchased these enslaved Native women and children from Native people and thereby created incentives for Native nations to raid Petites Nations for captives to sell to the Louisiana colonists.[40]

The parish priests who recorded the baptisms of these enslaved Native women and children sought to simultaneously whitewash and legitimize the coercive violence of the French settlers' exploitation of their slaves.[41] In 1709 a Native woman who was enslaved by the merchant Sieur Charli gave birth to a baby, and Charli had the child christened Nicolas Charli. It was very uncommon for French men to give enslaved children their last names. However, Nicolas's mother testified at the baptism that Charli was the boy's father, and it seems that Nicolas Charli the elder was willing to recognize this enslaved infant as his son. In March 1711, Charli went to church to have his infant daughter Jeanne christened as well. Unlike Nicolas, he did not give the baby girl his last name. Jeanne's mother was listed simply as "Tensa slave." The priest did not record the names of Nicolas and Jeanne's mother(s), so it is unclear whether this enslaved Tensa woman gave birth to both children or Charli held multiple enslaved Native women.[42]

Because French priests often recorded enslaved children's mothers as simply "Indian slave," without either personal or national identification, it is difficult to trace enslaved Tensa families within these archives. For example, in 1712 a Tensa woman who was enslaved by Sieur Rochon gave birth to a baby girl named Marie Rochon. If Marie's mother testified as to the paternity of this child, the priest did not record it. In 1722 Rochon had an enslaved Native baby named Henriette baptized. The priest recorded that Henriette was "an Indian" and that her mother was an enslaved woman who belonged to Rochon, but he did not record the baby girl's tribal affiliation, paternal relation, or last name. It is therefore not possible to tell whether Henriette and Marie were biological sisters, either via their mother or father.[43] If Marie lived through her early girlhood, we can speculate that she may have seen baby Henriette as her little sister, and felt a kinship with the similarly enslaved Native child.

These baptism records provide evidence of the sexual assaults that enslaved Native women experienced. Marie Rochon is listed on the register without any father, but by giving Marie his last name, Rochon seems to have tacitly acknowledged his filial relation to this child. Rochon was married to a French woman when he possibly raped this enslaved Tensa woman. His wife even served as godmother to the woman's child.[44] These baptisms sanctioned the violent, or at least coercive, relationships between enslaved Native women and their French owners, turning their children into French subjects. The frequency of these baptisms of infants with Native mothers suggests that the French men of Mobile did not share either Bienville's scruples about enslaving only enemies of French Louisiana or La Vente's concerns about unlawful intimacy.[45]

One of the clearest illustrations of the legal and semantic blurring of an Indigenous woman's status between slave and wife is illustrated by the marriage of Marguerite and Pierre-René LeBoeuf in 1712. In 1706 Pierre-René LeBoeuf left Mobile to build a new home on a small concession south of Mobile. He knew he would need help with domestic labor to maintain this new home, so he brought an enslaved Tensa woman with him. Five years later, she was baptized by a local priest. Marguerite, as she was christened at her baptism, first appeared in church records in 1711, where she was recorded only as "Indian," and as the wife of an enslaved Tensa man. The label "Indian" rendered her nationless, and racialized her in a way that was increasingly linked to slavery in the eighteenth century American South. It is not clear whether Marguerite and her Tensa spouse were enslaved together or they began a relationship during their bondage in Mobile. Evidently, the church refused to recognize the relationship of the two enslaved Tensas, or perhaps Marguerite's spouse died or was sold away because in the following year, 1712, Marguerite and LeBoeuf were wed by a Catholic priest and she was formally recognized as his wife. By 1713 she had given birth to a son, "Claude," whom LeBoeuf also had baptized. In the archival metamorphosis of Marguerite from slave to wife, we lose sight of the violence of her relationship with LeBoeuf and of the fact that her lived reality probably changed little after her wedding. Certainly, this marriage did not offer her freedom. Furthermore, while we cannot know Marguerite's individual religious preference, we should also consider that she may have experienced her inclusion within the Catholic Church as an additional site of cultural violence and coercion. Although some Tensas willingly converted to Christianity in the 1710s, given the centrality of spirituality to all aspects of Tensa life, both her own baptism, and the marking of her son as a member of the French church may have felt like assaults on the internal aspects of her Tensa identity in addition to her physical self.[46]

It is difficult to conclusively categorize the wide variety of relationships that existed between enslaved, unfree, and free Tensa women and French men at Mobile. In part, this is because Indigenous women and French settlers had different ideas about sex, bodies, and degraded labor. Tensa women's sexuality was notorious among the French, and officials feared that close contact with these women might result in moral lapses among the French men. Within Tensa society, women had considerable power over their bodies and their sexuality. Both Natchez and Tensa women were expected to marry, but they were not necessarily expected to have monogamous relationships. Especially in their youth, both Tensa and Natchez women were at liberty to pursue whatever relationships they saw fit, including relations with men for both personal pleasure and economic gain. When comparing what he perceived to be the moral behavior of Tunica women to those of their depraved neighbors, the Tensas and Natchez, the French missionary Jacques Gravier remarked with contempt that the Tunica women "are not as shameless or such libertines as the Tensas and Natchez women."[47]

Natchez and Tensa women may not have enjoyed full autonomy over their bodies, but their communities did not view sex as degrading, immoral, or detrimental to a woman's social standing. Natchez and Tensas had similar cultural, political, and spiritual practices, and they appear to have shared ideas about women's roles and sexuality as well. The Natchez were matrilineal, so it was the identity of one's mother, rather than one's father, that determined social standing and belonging. Natchez and Tensa women understood their children to be part of their matrilines, regardless of whether they had French or other Native parents. This also meant that at least some Natchez and Tensa women could choose to have multiple sexual partners, even after they wed. This was not the case for all Petites Nations women. Indeed, in many societies, women were expected to be monogamous after marriage.[48]

Natchez people understood sex to be an important part of diplomatic relationships, so Natchez leaders encouraged women to engage in sexual relations with French newcomers. As one stunned observer reported in 1735, "the sun [Natchez leader] and the other chiefs obligate the women to prostitute themselves to the whole world," but the woman "was not less esteemed for offering herself to strangers."[49] This observer believed the Natchez women were coerced into having sex with the French, and they may well have been, given how stratified Natchez society was and how much control Natchez elites held over the lives and bodies of lower-class Natchez. However, it is also possible that these women entered into these relations consensually and understood themselves to be diplomats who were charged with solidifying relations with the colonists. While it is impossible to read consent into these sources, it is clear that Natchez and Tensa women viewed sexual relationships and bodily autonomy differently than the French settlers did, and that they used sex along with other forms of labor to pursue their own or their community's gain.

Natchez and Tensa women were able to use their labor, including sex, to personal and familial advantage. In the 1720s the French traveler Dumont de Montigny recorded his disdain for Natchez women who worked outside of their homes and communities. At Natchez, he observed that "there were even some Indian women who came to offer themselves to the soldiers or habitants, to the officers and the sergeants, and this at a very cheap rate. But if you paid them a little more generously... then the Indian woman served as your wife and your slave all at once. She looked after the cooking, made the flour and the bread, both fluffed up the bed and helped to flatten it. Others hire themselves out for one or two days like field slaves to pound the corn and make flour."[50] De Montigny's observations provide us with crucial insight into both sex and labor relations among

Figure 6. Dumont de Montigny's illustration of Native American women. From Dumont de Montigny, no. 17, Mémoire de Lxx Dxx officier ingénieur, contenant les evenements qui se sont passés à la Louisiane depuis 1715 jusqu'à present [manuscript]: ainsi que ses remarques sur les moeurs, usages, et forces des diverses nations de l'Amerique Septentrionale et de ses productions." Ayer Collection, Newberry Library.

Natchez and French people in Natchez homelands. This description would seem to indicate that women who had to labor for settlers in order to support themselves considered sex work to be one more form of profitable exchange with the colonists and perhaps no more degrading or scandalous than washing linen or grinding corn. What de Montigny did not understand was that, unlike enslaved Native women, these Natchez and Tensas chose to labor for French men, and they reaped the financial rewards of their work. Additionally, de Montigny's remark that others hired themselves to work "like field slaves" would indicate that it was unusual for women to work in the fields, and that domestic labor was the more common job for Native women. His use of the terms "wife" and "slave" to describe the sexual and domestic work of these free women underscores how French colonists' choice of language—along with their conflation of sex with marriage, and agricultural labor with slavery—obscured the lived experiences of Native women.[51]

In Mobile, enslaved Tensas reconstructed their shattered lives by building new kin networks. In 1714 a Tensa woman who belonged to Sieur de Boisbriand and a Chitimacha man who belonged to Sieur de Châteauguay baptized their baby daughter Marie.[52] This relationship is remarkable given that only eight years prior the Tensas had slaughtered many Chitimachas on a raid to capture and forcibly adopted Chitimacha women and children into their dwindling nation. It is significant that both parents are named and claimed in the baptism, and thus were presumably in a sustained relationship, unlike the Tensa women whose children are listed without fathers. This unlikely union illustrates the close ties among enslaved people of various nations at Mobile, and the way that the common experience of captivity and servitude might bring together Native people of enemy nations.

Enslaved Native peoples formed close relationships that stretched across household, ethnic, and national boundaries, and Native families at Mobile straddled the boundary between slavery and freedom. Because of the small population, enslaved people likely came into contact with captured kin, their free brethren, and enslaved and free people from other nations on a regular basis. This close contact also meant that sometimes enslaved Native people formed relationships, married, and produced children with free Native people who lived in and around Mobile. In 1716, for example, a Native man who was enslaved by Sieur Duclos and a free Tawasa woman baptized their infant daughter Marguerite. In 1720 an enslaved Native woman and a free Chatot man named Capinan baptized their infant daughter Marie.[53]

Considering the wide scale of this enslavement and the relative proximity of the Chitimacha and Tensa nations, we are left to wonder how the French were able to sustain their alliances with these nations while they simultaneously held enslaved Chitimachas and Tensas in their villages. Although the Tensas surely resented that the French held enslaved Tensa women, given the immense number of captives among Lower Mississippi Valley nations, the Tensas were accustomed to negotiating with other nations that held their kin in bondage (sometimes in hopes of getting those captives back). For example, the Houmas agreed to negotiate with the Bayagoulas while the Houmas held Bayagoula prisoners in 1699. During the 1710s, the French continued to negotiate with the Natchez, Tunicas, and Acolapissas even as they held captives from other French-allied nations. As late as the 1740s, the French negotiated with Chickasaw leaders who took French prisoners as captives to use as leverage in diplomatic negotiations.[54]

Petites Nations peoples in the vicinity of Mobile also sometimes owned Indigenous slaves from other Petites Nations. This meant that free and enslaved people from the same Petites Nations might live in close proximity and attend the same mass. For example, Jean, a free Mobilian man, and his free Chitimacha wife, Marie Magdalene, jointly went to receive their baptisms from Alexander Huvé, one of the priests at Mobile in 1715. Within the same year, Huvé also performed two baptisms for two enslaved Chitimachas, one for a four-year-old girl named Marie who belonged to the leader of the Chatot nation, and one for Alexander, a fifteen-year-old Chitimacha boy who was enslaved by the missionaries of Fort Louis. The priest recorded that Salome, the wife of the leader of the Apalachees, attended Alexander's baptism and agreed to serve as his godmother.[55] Multinational settlements brought people of different nations and ethnicities into close contact, but they were also spaces in which free, captive, and enslaved Native peoples regularly interacted. While they might offer the opportunity to form relationships with others who shared their status—like Jean and Marie Magdalene or the Tensa and Chitimacha slaves of Sieur de Boisbriand and Sieur de Châteauguay—they were also places where people might interact with kin who had been captured or forcefully integrated into other societies. Although it was deeply painful for Chitimacha, Tensa, and other peoples to see their kin enslaved, it was not unusual for nations in this region to have to negotiate with those who held their people as captives.

Making "Just" Slaves of the Chitimachas

While most Tensas were individually gifted or sold to French men, Chitimachas were enslaved en masse as part of a genocidal war the Louisiana government waged against their peoples. Between 1706 and 1708, Louisiana settlers pursued a protracted conflict with the Chitimachas as a means to generate a cheap source of legal Indian slaves for the colony. The war was devastating for the Chitimachas, and hundreds of Chitimacha women, men, boys, girls, and babies were killed or enslaved during this era. Moreover, the French settlers' conduct—specifically their intent to exterminate the Chitimachas and their practice of enslaving all prisoners of war—set a dangerous precedent for future conflicts between Louisiana and its neighboring Native nations.

In 1699 the Chitimachas conducted a calumet ceremony with the French and welcomed them to their homelands. At the turn of the eighteenth century, the Chitimachas lived along the Gulf Coast to the west of the Mississippi River, between Bayou Lafourche and Bayou Teche.[56] They remained amicable with the French during the first five years of French colonization, but they did not develop close labor or trade-based relationships with the French in the way that many of the other Petites Nations did.[57] The Chitimachas' lands were far to the west of the Mobile and Biloxi settlements, so French officials did not regularly interact with the Chitimachas during this time.

In fact, French officials actively avoided Chitimacha territory because the Chitimachas' neighbors and close allies, the Ishak/Atakapas, had a well-known reputation for being fearsome man-eaters. Rumors of "wandering and man-eating Indians" made French colonists hesitant to venture into their territory.[58] Even the Choctaws respected the military capacity of these people, calling them "Atakapa," meaning "man-eater," in their language.[59] Additionally, both the Chitimacha and Ishak/Atakapa nations had sizable populations. In the years before the arrival of the French, the Chitimachas likely numbered more than 2,600 and the Ishak/Atakapas roughly 3,500.[60] Given the perception that there were large numbers of cannibals in the bayous west of the Lower Mississippi, French travelers generally avoided Chitimacha and Ishak/Atakapa territory. After their initial ceremony in 1699, the Chitimachas were not in close contact with the newcomers. So, although French officials claimed they held an alliance with the Chitimachas, they did not work to maintain diplomatic relations with the Chitimachas and the two nations had no close economic relationships to sustain their connection.

It did not take long for the Chitimachas to begin to suspect that the French had reneged on their promises of peace and friendship. After two years of minimal contact, the French commandant Juchereau de St. Denis led a contingent of French and Acolapissa soldiers into Chitimacha territory in 1702. They attacked a group of Chitimachas, who were out hunting, capturing twenty prisoners. St. Denis and his troops dragged these captives back to Mobile and sold them as slaves to the French settlers.[61] Governor Bienville reprimanded St. Denis and insisted that he return the Chitimacha captives. Bienville feared that St. Denis's raid would sever the alliance between the Chitimachas and the French, leading the

Chitimacha nation to retaliate. In his defense, St. Denis claimed that his men were suddenly attacked by the Chitimachas and were forced to defend themselves. His justification does not explain why his men chose to enslave these twenty Chitimachas. Bienville clearly believed St. Denis had entered Chitimacha territory looking to capture Indians. However it is plausible that there was some truth to St. Denis's story. It had been years since the Chitimachas last negotiated with the French, so the Chitimachas would likely have expected visiting Frenchmen to arrive bearing calumets or other signs of goodwill. The uninvited invasion of their lands by an armed contingent of French and Acolapissa men could have led the Chitimachas to mistake them for a war party and attack the group. In any event, Bienville's orders to St. Denis to return the captives were "poorly carried out," and the stolen Chitimachas were never returned.[62]

Four years later, the Chitimachas found an opportunity for vengeance. In November 1706, several Chitimachas killed the French priest Jean-François Buisson de St. Cosme as he traveled down the Mississippi River. In addition to the 1702 slave raid led by St. Denis, the Chitimachas had suffered a terrible assault by the Tensas, who were allied with the French, during the summer of 1706. This attack likely reinforced the Chitimachas' perception that the French and their allies posed threats to their nation. St. Cosme's incursion merely offered them the chance to communicate that French raiders would not be permitted to murder and enslave their people with impunity. The Chitimachas killed St. Cosme and his three French companions in their sleep, letting a young Natchez boy who was traveling with the party escape. The Chitimachas were allied with the Natchez, and presumably this boy would amplify their message by relaying what he had seen.[63]

The killing of St. Cosme frightened the colonial officials at Mobile and necessitated a forceful reply from the French.[64] Given their tiny population and weak military force, the French could not afford to look like easy prey. Much as the Chitimachas attacked St. Cosme to send the message that they would protect their peoples and territories, the French too feared what might happen if their colony appeared vulnerable to their Indigenous neighbors. In February 1707, Bienville expressed his concern that the Chickasaws and Choctaws, the two nations he saw as Louisiana's most essential allies, did not really believe that the French could defend themselves. He wrote that, after they heard about the murder of St. Cosme, the Choctaws and Chickasaws wanted to know "if there were really as many people in France as here" (Louisiana) and added that "if there were really as many people as I [Bienville] said, some of them would come here to avenge the deaths of the Frenchmen." If not, they told Bienville, the French "have no courage at all." The governor felt compelled to retaliate.[65]

Bienville understood the political need for revenge against the Chitimachas, but he also recognized an economic opportunity in this tragedy. Rather than orchestrating a single retaliatory raid, as would have been in accordance with Indigenous modes of justice, or demanding the heads of the murderers, as would have followed French norms of punishment, Bienville launched a war of extermination against the Chitimachas. He sent couriers to the villages of Louisiana's Native allies asking for support against the Chitimachas. By March 1707 he had recruited Bayagoulas, Biloxis, Chaouachas, and Nassitoches, to support the French troops. During their first assault on the Chitimachas, Bienville's coalition of Louisiana soldiers and Petites Nations warriors killed fifteen Chitimachas, wounded forty more, and captured an untold number of prisoners. Instead of ending this cycle of violence, this raid was merely the beginning of what would become a decade-long war.[66]

The killing of St. Cosme provided the French with the perfect excuse to declare war on the Chitimachas and thereby generate a ready supply of slaves. Bienville also hoped to use this conflict to demonstrate that those who killed French officials would be punished severely. In 1706 French colonists at Mobile were pleading for African slaves and lamenting the labor shortage in the colony, so French officials recognized that Chitimacha captives had the potential to solve both their diplomatic and labor problems.[67] Bienville even sent Juchereau St. Denis to lead an attack on the Chitimachas. With the support of Native allies, St. Denis and his forces stormed into a Chitimacha village near French settlements in Bayou Lafourche. His expedition burned the village to the ground and dragged eighty captives back to Mobile where they were sold to French colonists for 200 livres apiece.[68] Thus, the Chitimacha War, which was undoubtedly in part St. Denis's fault, ultimately provided St. Denis and many other Frenchmen with the opportunity to get into the lucrative business of human trafficking with officially sanctioned approval.

Bienville also had the Chitimacha man who killed St. Cosme publicly executed in Mobile. The man was tied to a wooden horse and the French executioner broke his head, scalped him, and then threw his body into the river. This execution should have ended the Chitimacha War, as justice had been served, but the economic appeal of Indian slaves was too great. The Chitimachas repeatedly asked for peace, but French forces continued to assault their villages and sell Chitimacha captives as slaves for nine more years. Meanwhile, the government offered bounties for the scalps of Chitimacha women, men, children, and elders.[69]

This war created an additional major vector of slave trafficking in the Southeast. In the following decades, and long after the decline of the Charleston-based Indian slave trade, the French would continue to enslave Indigenous prisoners of war. In effect, the Chitimacha War created a blueprint for future wars between Louisiana and Native nations. In subsequent conflicts, Louisiana officials would continue to treat women and children as enemy combatants, enslave prisoners, and offer no quarter to Indigenous refugees. The French Empire repeatedly waged wars to destroy Native nations, and both the Chickasaws and Natchez would endure French campaigns to similarly enslave and exterminate their nations during the 1730s and 1740s. So, in addition to the English merchants in Carolina and Virginia, the French settlers in Louisiana were also substantively responsible for escalating slaving violence in the Southeast.

In 1718 the French finally agreed to end the cruel war. Most accounts suggest that it was ultimately the frustration of the French planters who were subjected to Chitimacha raids that forced French officials to agree to peace. Pénicaut recorded that the concessionaires near Bayou Lafourche complained bitterly that their workers were constantly in danger of being killed and captured by Chitimacha warriors. Using these and other captive Frenchmen, the Chitimachas hoped to convince the French to grant them peace in exchange for returning the hostages.[70]

It is also likely that the French sense of the level of risk in trafficking local Indigenous men and women had increased. From 1715 to 1718, shockwaves from the Yamasee War reverberated across the Gulf Coast. After decades of growing frustration with the exploitive practices of British Indian traders, a coalition of Native peoples including Yamasees, Catawbas, Choctaws, and others attacked English merchants living within their villages and across the colonial settlements of South Carolina in 1715. These Native people were furious with English traders who beat Indigenous women, imprisoned their families, and stole property (allegedly to fulfill outstanding debts). Crucially, these Native nations also complained that some British traders failed to distinguish between captives from allied and enemy Indigenous peoples and thereby violated the terms of their relationships. This Native coalition fought with British officials for three years before finally losing the war. The carnage of the Yamasee War convinced British officials that it was too dangerous to deal in Native American slaves, so the conflict curtailed the Charleston-centered Indian slave trade. While the French had never orchestrated anywhere near the volume of Indian enslavement as their English counterparts in Virginia and Carolina, they would have recognized the potential for a comparable international attack on French settlements in response to slave raids against local and formerly allied nations.[71]

Moreover, in 1718 the French Crown transferred control of Louisiana to a joint stock company, and the company financed large transatlantic shipments of enslaved Africans to the colony. Within a year of the transition, shiploads of enslaved Africans began to arrive in Louisiana. As French settlers gained access to another source of enslaved labor, war with the Chitimachas no longer seemed like the most efficient method for acquiring slaves. After 1718 French settlers therefore transitioned their reliance on enslaved Indigenous laborers to enslaved African laborers.

In 1718, after nearly a decade of carnage and suffering, Governor Bienville invited a Chitimacha delegation to New Orleans to negotiate peace accords. The warriors, diplomats, and leading men and women of the Chitimachas processed into New Orleans singing the calumet. They sat silently for a long while, contemplating the gravity of the event and their relationship with the French. The French governor offered the Chitimachas peace and suggested that they relocate their villages closer to French settlements along the Mississippi. The Chitimachas replied to this offer with a response that was equal parts joy and anguish. A diplomat who spoke on behalf of the nation emphasized their grief and frustration that a murder committed by a single Chitimacha man caused so much bloodshed and loss for his entire nation. Yet he followed up this lament by expressing that, in comparison to the "red sun" and weeping women and children who had colored the last decade for the Chitimachas, "now the sun is warm and brilliant... the roads are clear... the game comes back, our women dance until they forget to eat, our children leap like young fawns, the heart of the entire nation laughs with joy to see that we will walk along the same road as you all, Frenchmen."[72]

Illusive Redemptions—Enslaved Chitimachas in French Louisiana

Peace came at a high cost for the Chitimachas. Governor Bienville's terms stipulated that the French would not return Chitimacha captives to their families. Instead, the settlers would keep these Chitimacha women, men, and children as slaves in perpetuity. Enslaved Chitimachas constituted the core of the enslaved population of colonial Louisiana through 1718, and these Chitimachas were forced to labor in the homes and fields of French settlers for decades afterward.[73]

Most enslaved Chitimachas remained within Lower Louisiana, but some were also trafficked out into the wider French Atlantic world. In 1717 the Pari-

Figure 7. Calumet ceremony. From Du Pratz, *Histoire de La Louisiane*, plate 1, vol. 1, 105. Image courtesy of the Huntington Library and Archives, San Marino, California.

sian newspaper *Le Nouveau Mercure* reported on the arrival of two young Chitimacha women in France. The article described the two women as of olive complexion with "bouquets of feathers on their heads," and glass adornments strung around their necks. The paper even presented the enslavement of these Chitimachas as an act of Christian charity. According to the *Mercure*, the Chitimachas were at war with their neighboring Native nations (not the French). As the writer explained, in Louisiana, when Indigenous people were taken captive by other Native nations, they were almost certain to be put to death. Therefore, "in order to save their lives and instruct them in the Christian religion, they [the Louisiana colonists] are forced to buy them [enslaved Chitimachas] although the King has not yet given permission to make slaves of them."[74] This transatlantic coverage of the war with the Chitimachas served to conceal the rationale of the conflict, and to preserve France's image as a benevolent and just ally of the Native peoples of the Americas.

Perhaps the most familiar account of the fate of one of these prisoners of war is that of the Chitimacha woman who was enslaved by the French planter Antoine-Simon Le Page du Pratz during the 1720s. Du Pratz arrived in Louisiana in 1718 and purchased a young Chitimacha woman from a French colonist outside of New Orleans. By the time Du Pratz bought this woman, she had already served several years in bondage. During these years she had not learned to speak French so when Du Pratz obtained her she initially communicated with him using hand signals. Within several months she managed to learn French and soon thereafter she began to serve as his translator and emissary in exchanges with the other Native inhabitants. While Du Pratz did not record her name, it is clear from his memoirs that she was instrumental in guiding him and helping him establish social networks in the colony. The few pages Du Pratz dedicated to this enslaved Chitimacha provide glimpses into her life and her efforts to mitigate and escape her bondage.[75]

Although she endured violence, alienation, and exploitation, this Chitimacha woman also survived bondage by embracing moments of joy and mirth. As Native people have for hundreds of years, enslaved Indigenous people in Louisiana sometimes confronted colonialism with stolen moments of humor that served to temporarily invert the power dynamics between enslaver and enslaved. One of the clearest incidents of this comes through in an exchange around a campfire shortly after Du Pratz had purchased this Chitimacha woman in 1718. One evening Du Pratz and this enslaved woman were sitting around the fire when she caught his attention. The young woman gestured to alert Du Pratz to a five-foot alligator that was approaching their fire. Upon seeing the alligator, Du Pratz leaped up and took off running. We can imagine him swearing some colorful oaths as he dashed back toward his house. Seeing this grown man shout and flee over a relatively small reptile, the Chitimacha woman broke out in a fit of laughter.[76]

Like all Chitimacha children, she had been taught to spot and kill alligators at a young age. Her community lived along the edges of lakes and depended on fish, shellfish, and rivercane. She had grown up spending time in the swampy homelands her people shared with the alligators. She would have known how to walk along the edges of the bayou by sweeping her legs in small arcs to catch the marsh grasses underfoot and prevent her ankles from sinking into the mud, and how to gather rivercane for her mothers and aunts to weave baskets. As a child, she had eaten alligator stew and learned to spot the ridges of these prehistoric reptiles' backs in the riverine shallows. During this era, alligators in Louisiana regularly grew to be twenty or thirty feet in length. In fact, Du Pratz later came across an enormous alligator that flourished a three-foot head, and he aptly described that reptile as "a very dreadful aquatic lizard and a frightful monster."[77] By contrast, this young alligator was hardly a cause for alarm, so the Chitimacha woman calmly selected a thick tree branch, as her parents had instructed her to do, and brought it down hard on the alligator's skull.[78]

When Du Pratz came frantically running back, musket in hand and ready to unleash his high-tech firepower against the already dead alligator, the woman could not restrain her giggles. She broke into an irrepressible smile as she considered her captor's ineptitude. In that moment, Du Pratz was forced to recognize both his dependence on this woman and the fact that he was the subject of her ridicule. While these moments are sparse, and their impact was fleeting within the larger structures of coercive violence that governed the lives of enslaved women, they are nonetheless powerful and perhaps help us better understand how Indigenous women emotionally endured slavery in French Louisiana.[79]

From Du Pratz's account, it is clear that this Chitimacha woman was raised in a preeminent Chitimacha family and had powerful kin. Her older sister was married to one of the Chitimacha leaders, and was probably respected as a ruler in her own right. The woman's father served as a diplomat and was partially responsible for helping finally end the Chitimacha War. During the conflict, her father helped the French execute the Chitimacha man who was responsible for killing St. Cosme. Executions like this were nearly unheard of in Southeastern Native societies, so this punishment would have carried a high risk for the executioner. Native people generally responded to killings by making reparations to the kin or nation of the deceased to "cover the dead," or by undertaking revenge killing. Therefore, a third party's intervention in a murder or assassination would throw off the spiritual and social rebalancing of the process of covering the dead, so it could necessitate further violence. By bringing another Chitimacha man to the French to be executed, the enslaved Chitimacha woman's father placed himself at risk of being killed by the executed man's family. This move would have alienated and endangered her father, but this was also an action of dramatic self-sacrifice that would fulfill the French leaders' demands for the murderer's head and thereby begin the process of bringing the war to a close.

This enslaved Chitimacha woman encountered her father, years after she was captured, during the diplomatic summit that concluded the Chitimacha War in 1718. Du Pratz had taken her along to New Orleans to help translate the proceedings for him. At the event, Du Pratz reported that she alternately smiled and cried as she listened to the Chitimacha leaders provide accounts of the war and saw her people negotiate peace. Her father, who believed that his daughter had died like her mother during the war, was overjoyed to discover her at the gathering. Du Pratz reported that the girl slipped away from him during the event and returned with her father. Du Pratz then invited the man to accompany them back to his home.

As two Chitimachas who were in isolated and vulnerable situations, this father and daughter tried to negotiate an arrangement that would help mitigate the woman's situation. At Du Pratz's home, the French settler gave the Chitimacha man "the best welcome he could hope for." Du Pratz was shocked that the man nonetheless "proposed to redeem his daughter for their nation." As we might expect, this father's priority was to secure his daughter's freedom from Du Pratz so that she could return with him. Du Pratz could not bear to lose this skillful diplomat and translator and bemoaned the fact that if he manumitted her, he would be without a domestic. In his account, he claimed that the woman refused her father's offer. According to Du Pratz, she said that she was very attached to Du Pratz and "she had lost the habit of living and going to that [Chitimacha] country." She also remarked that with her mother dead, she would expect no support at home. Furthermore, her father was very old and after his involvement in the war, he was "a dead man walking." Du Pratz countered by proposing that her father stay with them (presumably as a servant). Her father declined. Instead, the Chitimacha woman suggested that she, her elderly father, and Du Pratz should all instead go to Natchez where she could be with her other family.[80]

This brief account reveals a tremendous amount about Native and French kinship and labor expectations. Perhaps the simplest explanation of this exchange is that Du Pratz did not wish to manumit his slave, so he insisted that she actually wanted to stay with him. However, this account also provides a window into Indigenous expectations for captivity and enslavement in the Lower Mississippi Valley. By pointing out that her mother had died, she emphasized that the matrilineal kinship network that had conferred her status and belonging in her home village was severed, and she may not have expected either her sister or her shunned father would be in a position to take her in. Without kin, she might struggle to reintegrate into postwar Chitimacha society. Du Pratz's offer to her father also illustrates French labor expectations for Native people. It was not uncommon for free Native people to live on lands claimed by French settlers and to perform labor for French landowners. If he had accepted this offer, her father would not have been exactly "free," but as Christina Snyder has argued, freedom and independence were not concepts that made sense within Southeastern Indigenous worldviews where power and bodily autonomy were the products of relationships and bonds of mutual obligation to others. In effect, Snyder says, the opposite of slavery was not freedom, but kinship, because kin ties were what made someone a real person and allowed them to exercise influence over their lives.[81]

It seems that both the Chitimacha woman and her father were relying on making kinship with Du Pratz in order to improve the life of the Chitimacha woman. Her father even tried to forge a relationship with Du Pratz that could transform his daughter's status from that of an enslaved person into kin. After Du Pratz rejected her father's offer of redemption, her father endeavored to recognize his daughter's enslaver as family. This Chitimacha father attempted to use an adoption ceremony to generate bonds of mutual obligation among his daughter, himself, and her enslaver that would help protect his daughter. First, the Chitimacha father asked Du Pratz if he could give his daughter to him. Du Pratz responded by telling the woman that if she wished it, he would serve as her father, and she consented. The Chitimacha man then grasped Du Pratz's right hand and placed it on top of his daughter's head. He laid his own hand over Du Pratz's and spoke for a while in Chitimacha. Unfortunately, Du Pratz did not understand this speech, so he did not record the direct sentiments of the Chitimacha man. In summing up this extensive speech, the woman explained to Du Pratz that this oration signified that "he is giving me the girl as my daughter."[82]

It seems that both father and daughter thought that reformulating Du Pratz's relationship with this Chitimacha woman would be the best way to ensure that Du Pratz would take care of her. Now, instead of exploiting her as a slave, he was supposed to treat her as his relative. What Du Pratz seems to have missed, and what we can infer, is that this ceremony likely not only made this woman his daughter but also bound Du Pratz to both the woman and her father as kin through bonds of familial obligation. Moreover, in matrilineal Native societies, father figures had obligations to their children, but real authority was only held by their mothers, maternal uncles, maternal aunts, and maternal grandmothers.[83] Therefore, by calling him her "father" the woman and her Chitimacha father also gave terminology to the hope that, while they would be bound together, Du Pratz should have no coercive authority over this woman. The Chitimacha daughter might also have chosen to stay with Du Pratz because she believed that she was pursuing the same transformation.[84]

If we assume that Du Pratz's enslaved woman was pursuing the Indigenous path out of slavery by making new kin, it would help explain why she convinced Du Pratz to relocate to Natchez. Du Pratz was eager to set up a plantation, and this Chitimacha woman worked to persuade him to move to Natchez by regularly extolling the virtues of that beautiful land. As she explained, "I have parents who took refuge there during the war with the French, they will set us up with all of the things we need, they tell me the country is beautiful, and that the men live to be very old."[85] Again, she used her kin network and language skills to help Du Pratz navigate Natchez society. Her father's ceremony and her own efforts to position herself as kin to Du Pratz through services and familial ties did not release this women from bondage and subjugation. Nonetheless, it is critical to recognize these Chitimachas' efforts to use Indigenous systems and ideologies of relationality to redeem this woman from her enslavement.

At Natchez, this enslaved Chitimacha woman continued to translate, act as Du Pratz's go-between, and further his interests. As Patricia Galloway has suggested, Du Pratz was able to become highly influential at Natchez in part because of this woman's kin connections and her introductions into Natchez society. Although this enslaved woman's father died only a few days after his arrival at Natchez, the man and his daughter's connections facilitated Du Pratz's welcome into the community. At Natchez, Du Pratz regularly conversed with elite Natchez leaders, and both French and Natchez officials relied on him to conduct diplomacy and negotiate among parties.[86]

Regardless of this woman's motivations, it is evident that her and her father's efforts to force Du Pratz to see her as kin did not come to fruition. In fact, following the ceremony in which her father made his child Du Pratz's daughter, Du Pratz continued to refer to her as "my slave."[87] Not long after they arrived at Natchez, this woman disappears from Du Pratz's account, and it is unclear what became of her. Perhaps, having given up on making Du Pratz understand his paternal obligations, she fled, and was able to use her social networks to create a new life outside of the bondage and confines of colonial society. Whatever her ultimate fate, in the slim records left of her life we can see not only violence, exploitation, and family trauma but also the clash of Native and French perspectives on slavery, captivity, and kinship, as well as how the promise of redemption remained elusive for Native women who were enslaved in French households.

For many of the Chitimacha women who ended up enslaved at Mobile, their lives closely mirrored the experiences of the Tensa women who were enslaved by French settlers. Within the first year of the Chitimacha War, François Guyon des Prés Derbanne, the keeper of the king's storehouse at Mobile, purchased a Chitimacha woman named Jeanne de la Grande Terre. Earlier that year, Derbanne had moved to Dauphin Island to start a plantation of his own, and he evidently decided that he needed a woman's labor to manage his home. In addition to relying on her to help run his household, Derbanne began to rape or coerce sex from de la Grande Terre and she became pregnant. In 1710 Derbanne took his and de la Grand Terre's child to be baptized by the local priest Alexander Huvé. Perhaps under pressure from Huvé, who was a strong proponent of marriages between Indian women and French men, Derbanne eventually married de la Grande Terre and "they subsequently lived a long life together producing numerous children."[88]

Despite her marriage to Derbanne, Jeanne de la Grande Terre's status within colonial society remained ambiguous and malleable throughout her life. During 1710 English pirates attacked Dauphin Island and burned the farms of the French families there.[89] This assault drove Derbanne and his family inland, and by 1717 he and de la Grande Terre as well as their children had relocated to the new French outpost at Natchitoches, where Jeanne was regarded as a slave rather than as Derbanne's wife. Census records from their time at Natchitoches describe Derbanne as having two enslaved Native people working alongside enslaved Africans on his new plantation at Natchitoches. The 1722 census lists Derbanne as without a wife, the father of three children, and with three Indian slaves and four African slaves. Jeanne was almost certainly counted as one of the three Indian slaves. The absence of her as his wife on the census records likely indicates that Derbanne continued to view and treat her as a slave even after their marriage. In 1734 Derbanne died in New Orleans. Two years later, in 1736, de la Grande Terre also passed away, and when she was buried in Natchitoches she was formally recognized as Derbanne's wife. Unlike their mother, Derbanne and de la Grande Terre's children were fully accepted into colonial society. They even held enslaved Native people themselves. When Derbanne died, he passed François and Geneviève, two enslaved Native people who had labored for him at his home in Natchitoches, to his and de la Grande Terre's daughter Jeanne. Women like de la Grande Terre were forced to raise children who grew up socially, if not geographically, distant from their kin. Unlike Du Pratz's enslaved Chitimacha, it is much less likely that de la Grande Terre was able to travel throughout Louisiana to see her extended family and maintain relationships with her village. Although she may have been able to form relationships with the many other enslaved and free Native people at Natchitoches this alienation constituted another front of colonial violence.[90]

The Chitimacha war killed many, fractured Chitimacha villages, and turned hundreds of Chitimachas into captives and refugees. Like the relatives of Du Pratz's enslaved woman, some Chitimachas chose to leave their homes and seek refuge with other Indigenous nations to avoid the wrath of French soldiers, and the Natchez offered safe haven to many Chitimacha families. Those who remained in the southern bayous suffered hunger, fear, and grief. Their children grew so thin their ribs protruded through their chests. In 1699 French travelers estimated that the Chitimachas and their neighbors the Yakni-Chitos had roughly 700–800 warriors in their villages, or 2,450 to 2,800 people.[91] By 1720 French reports estimated that the Chitimachas had only 100 warriors remaining, meaning that their total population was only about 350. Over the prior twenty years, their nation may have decreased by 85–87 percent.[92]

The Chitimacha War not only caused a plummet in the Chitimacha population but it also at least temporarily forced the consolidation of the Yakni-Chitos and the Chitimachas into a joint polity. Before the war, Chitimachas, Yakni-Chitos, Ouachas, and Chaouachas all lived in close proximity to one another to the west of the Mississippi River in present-day Terrebonne and Lafourche Parishes.[93] All four of these nations were in close contact, but the relationship between the Chitimachas and Yakni-Chitos was especially strong, with the two nations frequently negotiating together during diplomatic summits.[94]

The Chitimachas and Yakni-Chitos were distinct polities, but their shared cultural contexts and close political and geographic ties led the French to attack Chitimacha and Yakni-Chito peoples indiscriminately during the war. Although many of the Indian slaves at Mobile do not appear in French records either by name or by tribal affiliation, some of the records of the forced marriages and baptisms of enslaved Chitimachas at Mobile help shed light on the identities of these captives. Several of the captives who became slaves at Mobile identified themselves as having the last name "Grande Terre" such as Jeanne de la Grande Terre and Marie Therese de la Grande Terre, the "wife" of the merchant Jacques Guyon.[95] While these women are labeled as Chitimacha slaves in the records, this epithet strongly suggests that they were Yakni-Chito.[96] In both Choctaw and

Mobilian *Yakni-Chitto* means "big country" and so these women were effectively identifying themselves as Marie Therèse and Jeanne of the Yakni-Chitos.[97]

By the close of the Chitimacha War, the Yakni-Chitos no longer appeared on French maps of the region and their nation had no more formal dealings with the Louisiana government. In the wake of the war against the Chitimachas, it seems that the Yakni-Chitos became enmeshed with the Chitimachas or migrated to seek refuge with the Houmas. While the descendants of the "big country" people mostly drop out of French records after the Chitimacha War, their people endured by forming even closer relationships with the Chitimachas and they may have sought refuge with the Chitimachas in the decades after the conflict. More than half a century later, in the 1770s, the surviving Yakni-Chitos were identified as Chitimachas of the Big Earth, suggesting a more permanent political affiliation between their nation and the Chitimachas.[98]

While the Tensa and Chitimacha nations had very different relationships with the French settlers during the first two decades of colonization, people from both of these nations ended up enslaved in colonial Mobile, New Orleans, Natchitoches, Natchez, and along the Mississippi River.[99] In the case of the Tensas, most of their enslaved were women and children who were taken by other Native nations then traded to the French. In contrast, the Chitimachas were taken as prisoners of war in a conflict that was specifically designed by the Louisiana government to generate an enslaved labor supply for the struggling colony, and both men and women were captured in large numbers. Both Chitimachas and Tensas held alliances with the French. The Chitimacha War also laid the framework for future conflicts between the Louisiana government and its Indigenous enemies. In the 1720s and 1730s, colonial officials would pursue similarly brutal campaigns to exterminate and enslave the Natchez and the Chickasaws.

Over the course of their first decades in the colony, French slave trading in Lower Louisiana created a major new vector of human trafficking in the Southeast. Consequently, as Chitimachas, Tensas, and their Native neighbors witnessed the expansion of the French colony during the 1710s and 1720s, as well as the growth of enslaved populations within the colony, many of the Petites Nations became increasingly troubled by the kind of society these settlers were building in their homelands. In the decade following the Chitimacha War many Petites Nations therefore began to seriously reconsider the merit of maintaining alliances with their French neighbors.

CHAPTER 4

Colonial Propaganda and Indigenous Defiance

In his 1725 memoir of his time in Louisiana, Jean-Paul Masclary penned a glowing and optimistic reflection on the future of the colony. As he explained, "Louisiana is one of the most beautiful and best countries in the world." With proper investment, the region had the potential to become a flourishing colony, perhaps even one comparable to Mexico, Virginia, or Carolina. Masclary's buoyant reflections were among the many exuberant tracts produced during the late 1710s and 1720s by colonial boosters who sought to generate immigration to and investment in Louisiana. Contemporary publications advertised the colony's numerous advantages, including the economic potential of the region, the fertility of the land, and the friendly relations that the government had with local Native peoples. After decades of struggle to establish a profitable imperial territory in the Lower Mississippi Valley, in the early 1720s it finally seemed that France's colonial dreams were on the cusp of becoming reality. Indeed, several significant political and economic shifts reduced some of the pressures that had stymied the development of Louisiana during the 1710s. By the 1720s, new leadership and policies appeared to herald a coming era of progress and prosperity.[1]

However, alongside the ebullient propaganda, another series of correspondence from Louisiana painted a much bleaker image of the colony. Instead of prosperity, reports from settlers told of a place of disorder, danger, and deprivation. When the French captain Vallette de Laudun sailed to Louisiana in 1720, he reported that the settlers were short on everything, and "the colony is in an extreme state of need."[2] In fact, they were so badly provisioned that Laudun even ordered his men to give some of his crew's own limited food stores to their starving French compatriots. The accounts from Louisiana's interior posts were similarly grim. Officials described the tribulations of settlers who endured famine and dwelt in fear of hostile Indigenous groups. Rumors of Chickasaw and Natchez attacks on French outposts and farms unnerved European families. In 1722 the commander of Natchitoches described the bleak conditions at this French outpost. After providing a count of the 34 settlers, 20 enslaved Africans, and 6 enslaved Indians at the settlement, he included chilling news of a recent Chickasaw attack. The commander described finding the remains of a French colonist in the woods near the fort. His scalped body had been left to be eaten by "birds and wild beasts," and the man's daughters had been kidnapped.[3] These dark tales portrayed completely different perspectives on Louisiana than the ones propagated by Masclary and his contemporaries.

The jarring dissonance between optimistic visions of a Louisiana that was on the cusp of developing into a lucrative imperial possession, and dire reports of privation, violence, and overwhelming Native power, reflect the strain that the colony underwent during the 1720s. In 1718 Louisiana was transferred to new management, and it began to receive more substantial funding. This investment generated a large influx of French and European settlers to the Gulf Coast, and it financed the trafficking of thousands of enslaved laborers from western Africa to the colony. Simultaneously, Indigenous nations across the Southeast made political decisions that benefited the Louisiana colony. During this era, Alabamas, Tallapoosas, and Abhikas (Upper Creeks) pursued new diplomatic strategies, the balance of power among the Natchez villages altered, and the conclusion of the Yamasee and Chitimacha Wars allowed French settlements to develop in slightly less dangerous conditions. Moreover, the conclusion of the War of the Spanish Succession relieved some of the British pressure on the French Empire in North America. Imperial administrators like Masclary sought to encourage this growth, and they saw the changing tides as portents of a bright future for France in the American South. However, even in this relative lull of conflict, and even with the arrival of the thousands of free and unfree immigrants and enslaved peoples into the region, the vast majority of the Lower Mississippi Valley remained Indigenous-dominated lands. Only in the areas that were most densely settled by Europeans—like Mobile, Biloxi, and the new settlements at New Orleans and Natchez—did the influx of settlers and enslaved people meaningfully shift power dynamics and relationships among Native people and their French neighbors.

This era of growth and success led to the emergence of transatlantic perceptions of the Petites Nations as vanishing and dying groups, and French settlers began to develop plans for Lower Louisiana's future without interdependent relationships and settlements with the Petites Nations. During the 1720s, many

French administrators even insisted that some nations—like the Bayagoulas, Biloxis, Chitimachas, and Mobilians—had already been mostly destroyed. While many Petites Nations did lose hundreds of their kin to disease and war in the years between 1700 and 1730, they were not cowed by the expanding French Empire. Instead, larger nations like the Choctaws and Natchez, alongside smaller nations, like the Chitimachas, Mobilians, and Tohomes pushed back against the expanding French Empire during the 1720s. Between 1718 and 1729, imperial policy and settler practice produced growing resentment among France's Indigenous allies and led Native communities to take steps to thwart colonial control. Therefore, rather than being an era that was primarily shaped by Petites Nations sliding into decline, dependency, and disappearance, this decade was defined by both profound and quotidian acts of Indigenous resistance that helped reinforce Native nations' autonomy over their lands and limit the extent of French power.

Geopolitical Shifts

Several diplomatic shifts substantially altered the political landscape of the Southeast during the 1710s. The combination of the conclusion of the War of the Spanish Succession and the outbreak of the Yamasee War weakened British relationships with Indigenous people in the region. This, in turn, diminished the threat of Chickasaw and Creek violence for the Petites Nations. The reduction of slave raids also opened up the way for new alliances among the Natchez and French and among the Upper Creeks and French. Collectively, these changes strengthened the Louisiana colony and bolstered the power of the Choctaws.

Between 1702 and 1713, the War of the Spanish Succession spilled the violence of English and French imperial conflict into the Native Southeast, and this war took heavy tolls on the Choctaws and Petites Nations alike. English officials and merchants at Charleston used the conflict as a justification to arm their Native trading partners and to send them on raids against Spanish and French allied Indigenous communities. Chickasaw warriors tore through the small riverine communities of the Lower Mississippi Valley and repeatedly attacked Choctaw villages. Likewise, Alabama, Abhika, and Tallapoosa (Upper Creek) raiders attacked the Petites Nations near Mobile. In the first years of the war, Lower Creek communities along the Ocmulgee River hammered the nations of northern Florida. These attacks destroyed entire communities and sent hundreds of Chatots, Tawasas, and Apalachees fleeing from their homelands to seek refuge in places like Mobile. Like the English, French administrators also armed their allies, and both Petites Nations and Choctaws led counterraids against Upper Creek towns. As the war dragged on and the slave trade shattered Native communities across the Southeast, Alabama, Tallapoosa, and Abhika communities grew weary of this violence and longed for peace in their communities. A decade of war had garnered the Upper Creeks a wealth of slaves, horses, trade opportunities, and expanded hunting territories for their people. However, it also left many Creek families grieving the loss of loved ones who were claimed by these conflicts. Therefore, in 1712 Upper Creek leaders reached out to the French at Mobile to ask for peace. The French used this opportunity to secure an alliance and trading partnership with the Upper Creeks. Their partnership with the Louisiana settlers enabled the Creeks to leverage French and British merchants and officials against one another to ensure good prices and policies for their people.[4]

The explosion of the Yamasee War in 1715 facilitated this Upper Creek and French partnership. The Yamasees were close allies of the Lower Creeks and had served as middlemen in the trade of Indigenous captives and deerskins among Creek people and merchants in Charleston. In the early eighteenth century, the Yamasees lived along the Eastern Seaboard about midway between present-day Charleston and Savannah (near present-day Beaufort County, South Carolina). This location provided them with easy access to English merchants. When Yamasees and other Native groups attacked their former allies, including the British traders within their villages in 1715, many Creek communities allied with the Yamasees and supported them in the war. In 1717 these Creeks were forced to admit defeat, and Lower Creek leaders journeyed to Charleston to negotiate a peace settlement. Although both the Upper and Lower Creeks restored their relationships with British traders in the years after this conflict, the Yamasee War had reduced their access to trade during these conflict years, encouraging them to seek additional alliances and trade avenues.[5]

In the midst of this conflict, in 1717 the French constructed Fort Toulouse, a tiny trading and administrative outpost, among the Alabama towns. Fort Toulouse provided Upper Creeks with more direct access to French goods and facilitated diplomacy and information sharing among Louisiana and Upper Creek towns. Critically, this new partnership also scaled back the Upper Creek attacks on the French and Indigenous towns along Mobile Bay and made it safer for French merchants and diplomats to travel through Creek country. This reduction in violence enabled the expansion of French settlements at Mobile and Biloxi.[6]

Despite the geopolitical significance of this alliance, as an economic enterprise the Creek and Louisiana partnership floundered. The failure of the French to provide a viable alternative to trade with the British meant that the Upper Creek and French alliance remained loose. Abhikas, Tallapoosas, and Alabamas continued to court British officials and build relationships with Carolina and Virginia traders. French merchants were never able to satisfy Creek desires for goods or to compete with British counterparts. Throughout its tenure, Fort Toulouse remained woefully underprovisioned. The French commanders regularly complained that they needed more goods, and they lamented that discerning Creek customers preferred higher quality British ribbons and cloth. It did not help that the British sold merchandise at roughly half the French price. Because French merchants could not satisfy Creek buyers, the Creek and Louisiana alliance primarily served political purposes rather than economic needs.[7]

The Yamasee War did not completely end the trafficking of Indigenous captives, but it did significantly reduce the scale of slaving in the Southeast, so the curtailing of this trade decreased the violence directed at the Petites Nations and their French allies. During the Yamasee War, the Chickasaws had resisted Creek and Yamasee appeals for support. Instead, they opted to back their British allies. However, despite the British victory, the Chickasaws lost economic and political power in the decade after the Yamasee War. For years, the Charleston-based captive trade provided the Chickasaws with a major source of revenue. After the war, this lucrative trade evaporated. Additionally, the Chickasaws' proximity to British traders had exposed their communities to epidemics. From roughly 4,000 people in 1715, the number of Chickasaws was further reduced to about 3,100 by 1730.[8]

With Chickasaw power on the wane, the Choctaws emerged into the post–Yamasee War world in a position of tremendous strength. Devastating epidemics and slave raids had killed many Choctaws. Some estimates suggest that, by 1730, the Choctaws may have numbered as few as twelve thousand. Still, the surviving Choctaw population was more than double the size of the entire enslaved and free populations of Louisiana. They were also empowered by their multiple imperial alliances. Following the War of the Spanish Succession and the Yamasee War, Choctaw towns continued to foster relationships with their French allies, and many also maintained relationships with British traders. This web of alliances provided them with steadier access to guns and multiple diplomatic channels. The Choctaws were then able to leverage their new security and imperial connections to exert pressure on both the Petites Nations and the French.[9]

The other key political development of this era was the establishment of French settlements among the Indigenous towns at Natchez. During the early eighteenth century, the Natchez people had welcomed Tioux and Grigras into their settlements, and these migrants established villages alongside the Natchez towns of White Apple, Jenzenaque, the Flour Village, and the Grand Village. During the 1700s and 1710s, several Natchez towns also maintained partnerships with the Chickasaws and English. Some Natchez even raided Petites Nations for captives to sell to their English and Chickasaw allies. Natchez political structures provided the ability for individual towns to pursue diverse diplomatic agendas and alliances, and this led to the creation of sharp political divides among different groups within the Natchez populace. By the 1710s, the towns of White Apple, Jenzenaque, and Grigra had all established relationships with the English. Meanwhile, the Tioux, Flour, and Grand Villages pursued alliances with the French. In 1714 these three Louisiana-allied towns facilitated the establishment of a French trading post at Natchez. This combination of the divergent political agendas among Natchez towns, coupled with the growing presence of French settlers in the region, created turmoil in Natchez homelands during the 1710s.[10]

Political competition among Natchez towns provided an opening for relationships with the Louisiana settlers. However, the contentious political climate at Natchez also laid the groundwork for the conflicts that would define the next two decades of French and Natchez interactions. In 1715, less than a year after the establishment of the French trading post at Natchez, several Natchez attacked and murdered a party of Frenchmen who were traveling down the Mississippi River from Illinois. The inhabitants of the Grigra, Jenzenaque, and White Apple Villages objected to French settlers' presence and influence at Natchez. They aimed to send a message that other colonists were not welcome in the region. However, rather than repulsing further French incursions into their homelands and waters, these murders only brought more French to Natchez.[11]

The Louisiana administration responded to the killings with a massive military mobilization, and Governor Bienville called on Louisiana's Petites Nations allies for help. In 1716 Louisiana and Petites Nations forces converged on Natchez. Bienville, who was leading the French troops, claimed he wanted to meet with Natchez leaders, and he used a calumet ceremony to gather the headmen of the Natchez towns of White Apple, Jenzenaque, and Grigra. However, when the leaders arrived, he entrapped them. Bienville held them hostage and used their captivity to force the Natchez villages to accept an unsavory peace agreement. The governor of Louisiana insisted that he would only grant peace to all the Natchez towns if they executed the leaders who Bienville believed were responsible for the murders; the Bearded of Jenzenaque and Alahofléchia of Grigra. He further demanded that the Natchez accept a French fort in their homelands. The people of the White Apple, Grigra, and Jenzenaque towns grieved the slaying of their beloved leaders, but Bienville's heavy-handed tactics did create certain advantages for the Grand and Flour Villages. Their French allies would now be within their homelands, and two of their most influential political opponents had been deposed. For the Grigra, Jenzenaque, and White Apple villagers this was not only a tragedy but also a dangerous development. Their leaders had been killed by outsiders in violation of Natchez systems of justice. Even worse, they were unable to seek immediate retribution because the Yamasee War strained their alliances with the British, choking off trade and leaving them without the support of these powerful allies. This moment had thereby enabled their rival towns to use the French to gain the upper hand in Natchez politics.[12]

The incidents of 1714–16 enabled Louisiana settlers to establish themselves alongside the Natchez and created closer (if not entirely welcome) relationships among all the Natchez villages and Louisiana. This partnership seemed to secure

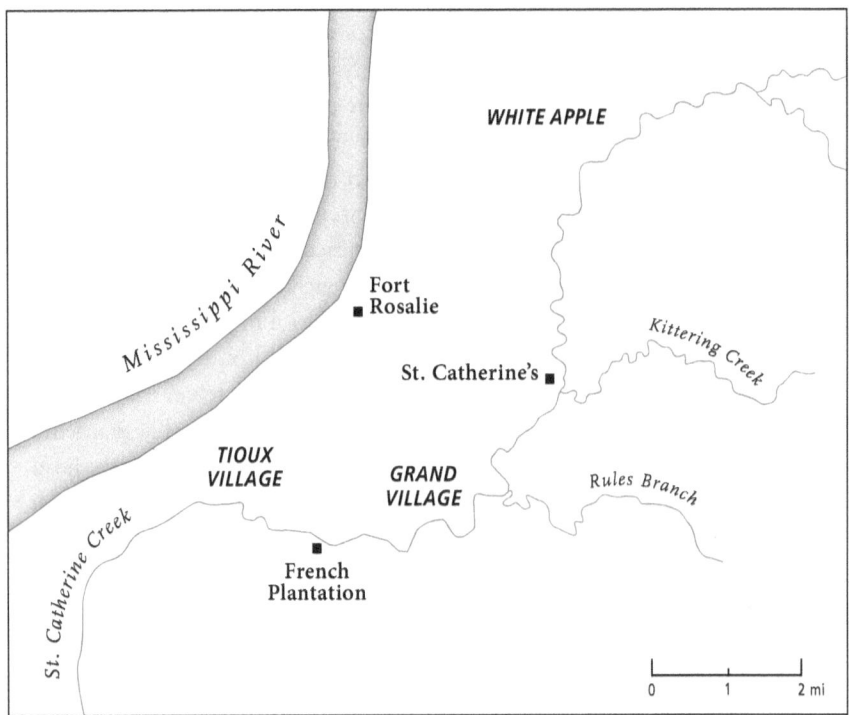

Figure 8. Interspersed Natchez, Tioux, and French settlements.

French control, or at least safe passage, over the lower Mississippi River. However, the violent and culturally unacceptable way the French had forged this alliance and their new settlements, with Natchez blood and diplomatic treachery, also sowed the seeds of destruction for the Natchez and Louisiana partnership and multinational settlement. But the culmination of this tension was still more than a decade away, and few could have predicted the scope of its impact. Nonetheless, in the closing years of the 1710s, with the British in turmoil in the East, and new partnerships with the Upper Creeks and Natchez, Louisiana seemed poised to expand its power in the Lower Mississippi Valley.

New Policy and Promise in Louisiana

During the 1710s, changes in the administration of Louisiana transformed the demographics of the fledgling colony. In 1712 King Louis XIV granted control of Louisiana to the wealthy Parisian financier Antoine Crozat. Crozat hoped that Louisiana would yield pearls, minerals, and other valuable exports. However, over the next five years, the Louisiana settlers neither discovered mines full of precious metals nor developed substantial agriculture. Crozat's administration also did not supply French officials with enough cloth, guns, and manufactured goods to support the deerskin trade with Indigenous Southerners. These failures to provide both diplomatic gifts and merchandise to Native nations strained the colony's relationships with its Indigenous allies. By 1717 Crozat had managed to convince the king to relieve him of this burden. The following year, the king transferred control of the colony to the Scottish financier John Law. Law proposed to manage and to fund the Louisiana colony via a joint stock company. Law's Company of the Indies, as the venture was known after 1719, had a bold new vision for Louisiana, and its investment would transform the colony seemingly overnight.[13]

During the 1720s, the Company of the Indies fostered large-scale immigration to Louisiana and financed the transatlantic trafficking of enslaved Africans. It planned to develop a mixed labor economy in Louisiana that would be composed of free and indentured Europeans as well as enslaved African laborers. During the 1700s and 1710s, few French subjects had been willing to emigrate to Louisiana. The country was widely, and correctly, perceived to be difficult and dangerous for settlers, and reports of the region's fearsome Indigenous inhabitants deterred potential migrants. In 1717, nearly twenty years after the French arrived, there were a scant four hundred French inhabitants in all of Lower

Louisiana. For the Company of the Indies to realize its plans, it would need to counter the prevailing dismal image of Louisiana and convince potential immigrants that this was a land of health and opportunity. To do this, the company launched a massive multicountry propaganda campaign and recruited French, Swiss, and German families, and indentured laborers. In addition to formal advertisements, the company ran a series of gushing accounts of the wealth and bounty of Louisiana in French newspapers. Like Masclary's account, these reports, which were often composed in the form of personal letters to loved ones back home in France, extolled the beauty and fertility of the Lower Mississippi Valley and potential avenues for fortune. One such account, published in the *Nouveau Mercure* in March 1719, framed as a husband's letter home to his wife, promised that "the colony is very vast and filled with gold, silver, copper and lead mines." Louisiana was indeed vast. Every other claim proved to be entirely false.[14]

The company's recruitment efforts paid off. Between 1717 and 1721, the advertisements helped recruit 2,462 indentured laborers and artisans, as well as 2,600 German, Alsatian, and Swiss immigrants to voluntarily migrate to Louisiana. French officials also relied on more coercive ways to generate immigrants for the colony. Famously, the company seized 1,200 convicts, deserters, vagabonds, and disorderly men and women from Parisian jails and loaded them onto ships bound for Louisiana. After riots broke out in the streets of Paris in 1720 in response to the forced transportations, the company was compelled to cease this practice.[15]

In addition to these free, forced, and indentured European migrants, the Company of the Indies also trafficked thousands of enslaved Africans to French Louisiana. By the end of 1718, the company had sent 1,284 enslaved Africans from the Bight of Benin, 323 from Senegal, and 294 from other parts of West Africa to Biloxi and Mobile. Between 1719 and 1723, they trafficked an additional 2,083 enslaved Africans, most of whom were from Senegambia. Enslaved Africans were an essential component of the company's plan for the colony, which envisioned these bound laborers as the key to developing productive plantation agriculture and the physical infrastructure of Louisiana's towns. This influx also led the French Crown to design a new Code Noir to regulate enslaved African laborers as well as relationships among enslaved and free persons of African descent and French settlers. In comparison to the 1685 slave code that was developed to regulate slavery in St. Domingue, the updated 1724 Code Noir placed tighter restrictions on the ability of slaveholders to manumit their slaves, drew firmer lines between Black and white populations, and attempted to regulate enslavers' use of corporal punishment. In effect, while the demographics of Lower Louisiana remained distinct from the overwhelmingly African and African-descended populations of the French Caribbean, the implementation of this code indicated the Crown's desire to transform this Indigenous borderland into a settler society fueled by enslaved labor that would mirror those of the Caribbean.[16]

The combination of the Company of the Indies' significant investment in enslaved Africans and forced laborers, along with its recruitment of settlers from across Europe transformed the colony. The population of Louisiana skyrocketed. In 1718 the colony had consisted of a mere four hundred people clustered among multiple Petites Nations towns. Over the next three years, more than seven thousand additional European settlers arrived in Louisiana. By the mid-1720s, the mass importation of Africans into Louisiana was also beginning to fuel the development of a marginally successful tobacco trade. French officials were hopeful that this enterprise might finally render the colony profitable. In less than a decade, the colonial population had more than quintupled, and the company's plans seemed to be working.[17]

Colonial Aspirations and Indigenous Power on the Ground

Although Louisiana grew dramatically during the 1720s, life in the Lower Mississippi Valley nevertheless remained harsh and precarious for most settlers. The colonists were still experiencing food scarcity, epidemics, and high rates of mortality. Moreover, outside of New Orleans, the Lower Mississippi Valley remained an Indigenous-controlled space, and French diplomacy continued to depend on Native alliances. Even as colonial boosters offered honeyed accounts of imperial success to their compatriots across the Atlantic, Louisiana's Native neighbors spoke far more critically of the colony. The behaviors of these immigrants were becoming increasingly unacceptable, so Native communities pushed back against the wave of imperial expansion, seeking to halt the misconduct of their French allies.

Of the thousands of French and European immigrants who had journeyed to the colony after 1718, less than half of these settlers remained alive and in the region merely a decade later. By 1726 there were only 2,228 European settlers, 1,540 enslaved Africans, and 229 enslaved Native Americans in Lower Louisiana. The company's drive to recruit immigrants had not been matched by a focus on logistics and provisioning, so the mass migration of the early 1720s resulted in some of the deadliest years for the colonists. While the Biloxis and Mobilians had been able to support a few hundred Frenchmen, and continued to take soldiers into their villages during the damp and chill winters, neither they nor the other Petites Nations were equipped to feed the thousands of immigrants who poured into their homelands. Left without food, medicine, and adequate clothing along the sandy, humid coast, these settlers experienced brutal deprivation during the winter of 1718–19. European families devoured the livestock that was intended to breed herds for the colony and they attempted to subsist on what they could forage close to the settlements. One account described the languishing migrants at Biloxi attempting to stave off hunger by foraging oysters. In their desperation, the starving settlers pried the sharp, gritty shells open and consumed their slippery flesh standing on the tidal flats. Many of these colonists "were reduced to eating herbs, and dying miserably on the sand."[18]

The shortages did not let up after 1719, and during the winter of 1720–21 this privation proved fatal. Between August 1720 and September 1723, 172 colonists died at Biloxi, with the winter months marked by spikes in mortality. This number is staggering considering that the total number of settlers who lived near Mobile and Biloxi was only 349 people in 1721. French officials were once again forced to send the soldiers stationed at Mobile to the villages of the Biloxis and Pascagoulas during the winter. Not surprisingly, many of the new arrivals returned to France at the first opportunity, and between 1719 and 1722, 1,000 colonists boarded ships to return across the Atlantic. They brought stories of suffering and rumors of bloodthirsty Indians that stemmed interest in voluntary migration. The enslaved Africans who had survived Atlantic crossings to reach Louisiana fared far worse. During this time of privation, their enslavers starved them to death. Thousands of African men and women died within only a few years of their arrival due to this abuse and malnourishment. By 1726 only 1,540 enslaved Africans remained alive in the colony.[19]

The scarcity of food and supplies continued to define life in colonial Louisiana throughout the decade. In 1728 the governor of Louisiana Étienne Périer wrote to the directors of the Company of the Indies begging for more supplies. The colony lacked essential provisions like rope and nails, and the government had no copper coin with which to pay the soldiers. Despite the influx of immigrants and enslaved Africans to farm the lands, the settlers were still largely unable to support themselves and the colonists had to depend on theft, illicit trade, and exchange with their Native neighbors to feed their families. Périer became frustrated and desperate. He grimly reported that "everybody is falling sick," and the colony "is without wine, brandy, flour, meat, and other dry merchandise," and it was also lacking in medicine.[20] Much of the wine and wheat that was shipped to Louisiana was sealed improperly and unsuited to the long voyage and damp, tropical weather. Barrel after barrel arrived soured or spoiled. Périer also complained of the quality of the dry provisions, as the company shipped him millstones so soft that they "fall to pieces like sand" and stockings and jackets for the troops that "are all so rotten there is no way to get anything out of them."[21] He also pleaded for the Limbourg cloth and light trade guns that Native people demanded. This brightly colored red and blue woolen fabric was used by many Native women to make blankets, wraps, and as a labor-saving substitute for fur or feather capes.[22]

These trade goods, and Louisiana's annual diplomatic gifts to Native leaders, were as essential as wheat and wine for the French colony. The settlers still relied heavily on exchanges with their Petites Nations neighbors for food and quotidian services. Likewise, Louisiana's military power, diplomatic influence, and territorial access were contingent on the colonial administration's relationships with both large and small Native nations. Without these gifts, Louisiana diplomats could not hold councils or ask for support from their Indigenous allies. Indigenous leaders required that the French provide access to reasonably priced European merchandise and distribute regular tribute gifts to their nations. These diplomatic presents demonstrated continuing French investment in the alliance. Although the French referred to these offerings as "gifts," they functioned more like tribute in that they were not reciprocated (Native people might offer captives or small gifts and services, but never outpourings of commodities), and that the Native people's support was contingent on the delivery of these goods. Each year, French diplomats would travel to the villages of the Choctaws, Natchez, Alabamas, Tunicas, and other Native polities, and Indigenous emissaries would come to Mobile and New Orleans to receive their gifts. Native people made it clear that they expected the French to be generous, and they should receive gifts of weapons, clothing, medals, and luxe novelty items like mirrors and cut-glass beads. In 1728 Governor Périer estimated the cost of these gifts at 19,000 livres. This was a lot of money for Louisiana, and indicates that rather than scaling back their spending on tributary offerings, the colony continued to increase its expenditures to maintain these valuable alliances. Twenty years prior, in 1706–7, the Louisiana administration had spent only 6,000 livres on gifts, so Périer's request indicated his desire for an increase in spending rather than a curtailing of this practice. Even as Louisiana grew, the endurance of tribute payments indicates the depth to which to the colony continued to rely on Native alliances.[23]

Louisiana's continual shortages of trade goods and gifts created friction with the colony's Native allies. In 1717 the governor of Louisiana Jean-Michiele de L'Epinay had offered the Petites Nations and Choctaws only meager gifts. Louisiana's commissary general nervously wrote back to the Council of the Navy to report on the damage done by the governor's parsimoniousness. The Choctaws were "very dissatisfied and they say among themselves that Mr. de L'Epinay was a mangy old dog whom the Great Chief on the other side of the great lake [the French king] had sent to this country, because he was dying of hunger in his village and he was an old woman."[24] From the perspective of his Indigenous allies, L'Epinay's inability to fulfill his diplomatic requirements rendered him unfit to lead and unworthy of their respect. Moreover, by describing him as an "old woman" the Choctaws highlighted the governor's lack of military capability, and they drew on a widespread Indigenous lexicon that associated femininity with an inability to participate in combat. In no uncertain terms, the Native leaders emphasized the French official's weakness, his unmanly conduct, and his dependency on others to care for him.[25]

The Choctaws were essential allies of the Louisiana colony, and French officials were also aware of the potential threats posed by their powerful neighbors. Even during the 1720s, when the Choctaws were weathering waves of epidemics on the heels of decades of slave raids, they still numbered roughly fifteen thousand people. This reduced Choctaw population was more than six times the size of the European population, and their military forces could have easily overpowered the small French garrisons spread along the coast and Mississippi River. As Bienville explained in 1711, the Choctaws "are the key to this country," and their alliance was critical if the French were to keep the British at bay.[26] France relied on their alliance with the Choctaws to secure French claims to the interior Southeast and to keep British representatives from the territory. But the French were never able to make good on their promises of generous tribute and consistent trade. So, Choctaw towns continued to receive British merchants and emissaries, and some also sustained relationships with the Chickasaws. Both British and Chickasaw representatives continually stoked Choctaw anger with their French allies to persuade Choctaw leaders to trade with merchants from Charleston and Williamsburg instead of Mobile and New Orleans. Choctaw leaders in turn leveraged their courtship by rival British and French emissaries to pressure Louisiana officials to provide adequate tribute and trade.

Even during the halcyon days of the 1720s, the French colonists feared the Choctaws. Rumors of these British representatives in Choctaw villages unnerved the settler families who lived closest to Choctaw territories. In 1729 Bernard

Diron d'Artaguiette, the commander of the fort at Mobile, reported that "the English have already made the Choctaws threaten us, [saying] that they cut the throats of the French of this colony."[27] It is unlikely that the Choctaws were seriously planning a large military assault against the French in 1729, as it was broadly in their interest to hold alliances with two imperial powers and maintain access to multiple vectors of European trade. Nonetheless, it is clear that Louisiana administrators' failures to adequately supply the Choctaws, and thus to maintain the obligations of their alliance, created real danger for the colonists.[28]

While the Choctaws continued to intimidate Louisiana officials, the French administration's grandiose visions obscured their ability to recognize the enormous continued value of their Petites Nations allies and neighbors. Choctaw, Upper Creek, and other large nations remained integral to French plans for the region, but by the 1720s the Petites Nations no longer formed part of this "future wish" for the colony—except in their absence.[29] The company's vision for a Louisiana society, one that used the labor of imported enslaved Africans and voluntary European migrants to develop and extract resources from Indigenous lands, represented a shift to a different kind of colonial project. Instead of constructing an empire based on interdependent relationships with the Petites Nations, these settlers sought to build a colony on Petites Nations land and to develop a society that had no place for Petites Nations people. Historians and Native American studies scholars describe this kind of imperial process as settler colonialism. Critically, the framework of settler colonialism emphasizes not just the presence of many settlers in a region, and settler control of land, but also the intellectual and ideological work of visualizing the disappearance and eventual eradication of Indigenous people, followed by the replacement of Native societies with new, imported ones. We can see evidence of these dreams of Native land without Native people in many of the propaganda pieces circulated during the 1720s. For example, in his same 1725 reflections on Louisiana, Masclary followed his account of the fertility of the country and the potential wealth that could be extracted from it with an insistence that "the number of savages in Louisiana is diminishing daily" due to sickness and the wars among the nations. Referring specifically to the Petites Nations, he explained that all that remained of many of these nations are "two or three families."[30]

Other French writers echoed the narrative of the Petites Nations' destruction and emphasized that their land would shortly be available for colonists. This logic is especially clear in the correspondence of the traveling Jesuit priest Pierre Charlevoix who passed through the region between 1721 and 1722. In a letter from New Orleans in 1721, he described the alleged destruction of the Bayagoulas. On his trip down the Mississippi, he saw the "ruins of the ancient village" of the Bayagoulas and recounted the grim fate of their people. "It [the Bayagoula village] was very populous about twenty years since. The smallpox has destroyed a part of its inhabitants, the rest are gone away and dispersed: They have not so much as even heard any news of them for several years, and 'tis a doubt whether is a single family remaining." In the very next sentence Charlevoix continues, "The land they possessed is very rich. Messieurs Paris have a grant here, where they have planted in rows a great number of white-Mulberry trees. . . . They also begin to cultivate here, with much success, indigo and tobacco."[31] Charlevoix narrates an end of the Bayagoulas that conveniently opened up their fertile lands for French settlers. He similarly notes that "the nation of the Chitimachas is almost entirely destroyed; the few that remain are slaves in the colony." Likewise, the Mobilians were formerly "very powerful" although "at present there are hardly any traces of them." To read these letters is to be led into a story of Louisiana that places Petites Nations as remnants of a dying past and French settlers as the future of the land.[32]

In reality, both the Bayagoulas and the Chitimachas remained very close to their allegedly emptied homelands for decades after the arrival of Charlevoix and the Parises, and this makes the priest's assertions all the more insidious in their ideological violence. Paris may even have lived alongside the Bayagoulas during 1718 and 1719. The Bayagoula people did not die or vanish during this era. Instead, in the mid-1720s, the Bayagoulas relocated further downriver, closer to the new town of New Orleans. They may have felt pressure from the invasion of the Paris family on their lands, or they may have been seeking new trade opportunities with the growing colonial populace. During the Chitimacha War, or perhaps at the very end of the conflict, a community of Chitimacha people also sought refuge with the Bayagoulas, and the two groups lived together on this land. Even after the Bayagoulas relocated downriver, the Chitimachas remained in these lands near the Parises' plot.[33] Charlevoix's insistence that this was vacant land, even as Bayagoula and Chitimacha people continued to live as neighbors to French settlers, helped create the ideological scaffolding for the later processes of dispossession and alienation of Indigenous territories. The erasure of Native people went hand in hand with the expansion of French settlement and land claims during this era. Fictitious stories of dying nations and empty homelands were integral parts of broader imperial efforts to increase French settlement and develop a plantation economy in Petites Nations' homelands.

Colonial Propaganda and Indigenous Defiance   123

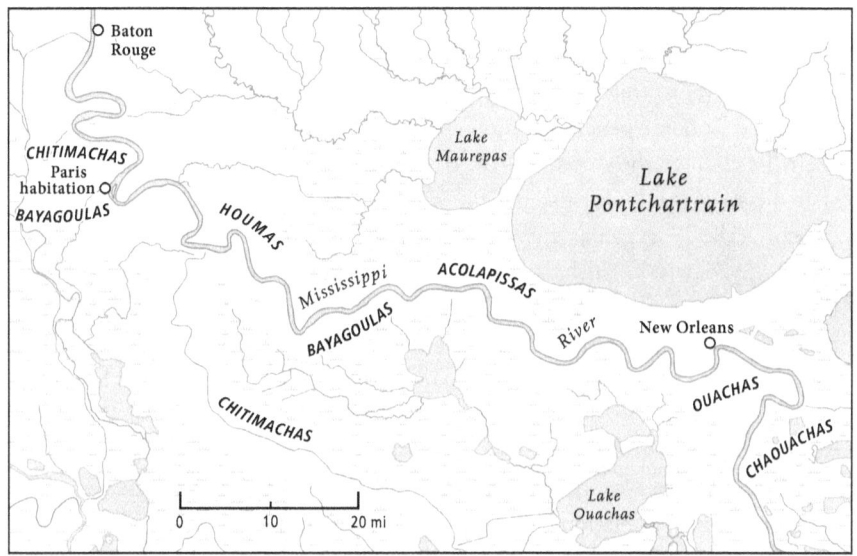

Figure 9. Selected Petites Nations locations along the Lower Mississippi River circa 1720.

Stories of Petites Nations destruction and erasure were so common during this era that they even appeared in metropolitan French newspapers. One 1717 report in the *Nouveau Mercure* declared that "there remain no more than five or six families" of Biloxis left in Louisiana. This author also used the same term *remains* or *reste* in French, to talk about the condition of the Petite Nation of Chakchiumas. As he commented, "There is between the Choctaws and Chickasaws the remains of the Nation of the Chakchiumas, who serve us usefully by discovering all that our enemies plot against us."[34]

The dichotomy between colonial desires for the disappearance of these small nations, and the reality that French settlers heavily relied on the vital services of the Petites Nations, reflects the tension that was generated by the continued interdependence of French and Petites Nations peoples as the colony rapidly expanded. Even Bienville, who was routinely engaged in missions alongside Petites Nations warriors during the 1720s, proclaimed in 1725 that the Lower Mississippi Valley was "formerly the most densely populated with Indians but at present of these prodigious quantities of different nations one sees only pitiful remnants that have escaped the fury of the continual wars that they had among themselves and which were still lasting in the year 1699.... Several have been entirely destroyed."³⁵ This rhetoric stands in stark contrast to the continued presence of Biloxi men and women who came to Mobile from their villages on the Pearl River to trade fish and game, and the regular French requests to Mobilian and Tohome people for guides and porters during this same era. Even as Bienville claimed the destruction of the Petites Nations in 1725, he recognized that the Acolapissas "furnish us almost all the meat that is consumed at New Orleans," the Pascagoulas and Capinans were "very good hunters and fishermen," the Biloxis "furnish an abundance of meat to all the French," and even the Chaouachas, whom he considered "by nature slothful and indolent," also produced and sold substantial quantities of corn to the French.³⁶ Thus, the inhabitants of Mobile and New Orleans were able to eat in large part because these supposedly vanishing Native people continued to supply the colonists with food and services.

Colonial observers became convinced of the inevitable and imminent demise of the Petites Nations. This perception has been echoed in more recent historical literature. Emphasizing the damage that colonization, slavery, and biological invasion wrought on these small nations, many scholars have characterized the era between 1700 and 1730 as a period of Petites Nations decline in which these polities "dwindled into small dependent communities" and "accepted French domination." Articulated most succinctly, one scholar argues that, "as their usefulness to colonists diminished, so did their overall numbers, and settlement Indians and *les petites nations* slowly faded out of the historic record and into extinction."³⁷ These assessments emphasize the destructive power of colonization and the violence that French settlement wrought on Indigenous peoples. They correctly highlight the immense pressure that the growing Louisiana colony placed on Petites Nations communities. They also underscore the damage wrought by the massive population declines that Petites Nations people experienced. However, these narratives leave very little space for seeing the Indigenous resistance and resilience, and do not help us understand how so many of these communities managed to survive.

European colonization did take an immense toll on Petites Nations people. During the first three decades of the eighteenth century, the combination of the multidirectional slave trades and the onslaught of European diseases drastically reduced the number of Petites Nations people. Disease spread like wildfire among the coastal communities who lived in multinational settlements with French newcomers. The sick and starving settlers who arrived between 1717 and 1723 transmitted a multitude of illnesses to Mobile and Biloxi Native communities. This combination of migration and disease reversed the demographic ratios at places like Biloxi and Mobile. Rather than being Petites Nations' multinational settlements with just a few small villages of French colonists, by the mid-1720s colonists outnumbered Mobilians, Apalachees, Tohomes, Chatots, and Biloxis in their homelands. In 1699 there were between 2,100 and 2,450 Mobilians and Tohomes living in the vicinity of Mobile. However, epidemics of disease and violence caused by the colonial slave trade killed more than 90 percent of their population during the first two decades of the eighteenth century. By 1725 there were only 210 surviving Mobilians and Tohomes and many of their villages lay deserted. In 1726 there were 528 settlers and enslaved persons living in Mobile. There were now twice as many colonists as Mobilians and Tohomes.[38]

It is more difficult to estimate the total population of the Biloxis during this era. In contrast to the *Nouveau Mercure* article that described the Biloxis as constituting merely two or three families, Bienville estimated that the Biloxis had about 40 men, or 140 people in total in 1725. In 1731 a traveling priest estimated that the Biloxis had 160 warriors, or about 560 people. Seventeen years later, another French colonist estimated the population of the Petites Nations near Mobile—which included Apalachees, Tensas, Biloxis, and Mobilians—to be only about 250 warriors. This would suggest that by midcentury these nations might have numbered fewer than 1,000 people combined.[39] While it is clear that new pathogens and the disruptions of the slave trade killed thousands of Mobile and Biloxi River peoples, the Mobile Bay nations were not eradicated. Although they endured much grief and changes, these communities continued to persist and form critical economic partnerships with their French neighbors.

Compounding the misinformation in colonial propaganda, French administrators' misunderstandings of the identities and political evolutions of Petites Nations also led to perceptions of Indigenous decline and disappearance. In the 1720s, many Petites Nations migrated away from the crush of settler populations and resettled in the ways they had always done. When they left, settlers concluded that these groups had vanished. For example, during this era, the Biloxis moved away from the expanding colonial settlements near their homes on the coast by the Pearl River to a location further west (near where the Acolapissas had formerly lived), rebuilding their villages there. Many Native towns moved independently, or recombined their towns with other groups, as they migrated to avoid the pressures of the slave trade and colonial settlements. For example, after the 1710s, the Capinans of Mobile Bay mostly cease to appear in French records. This would seem to indicate that they were destroyed by the arrival of the French. As they lived near the French at Mobile, the settlers would presumably have been in regular contact with Capinan men and women, so it is hard to imagine that they could overlook an entire group of their Indigenous neighbors. Nonetheless, archival records indicate that the Louisiana settlers did just that. Rather than being eradicated, the Capinans blended in with their neighboring communities and French observers counted them as part of the Mobilians or Tohomes. If they remained in the Mobile region during the 1710s, they did not push for strong nation-to-nation relationships with the French like their Tohome and Mobilian neighbors. During the 1720s, some Capinans lived with the Pascagoulas along the Pascagoula River. Then, in 1731 a group of Capinans appear on a traveling priest's tally of local populations near Mobile, and in 1738 they moved to an island off Mobile Bay. In 1764 they again appear on a map of the Mobile Bay region west of Mobile along the Pascagoula River, living in an autonomous settlement. Therefore, rather than a straightforward story of physical extermination, the Capinans' disappearance is a story of intentional distancing from European settlers. During the early 1700s, they settled so closely alongside the Naniabas, Tohomes, and Mobilians that they were overlooked and confused with their neighbors. Then, as Mobile expanded, they moved further from the crush of European colonists and formed new settlements, sometimes with other Petites Nations or on their own. Their absence from diplomatic records and the sparse documentary trail they left therefore indicate more about their efforts to avoid close interactions with Europeans than about community demise.[40]

In 1718 the French priest Father Le Maire specifically commented on the phenomenon of mobility and geopolitical fluidity that sometimes rendered Petites Nations people invisible to settlers. Le Maire noted the discrepancies between late seventeenth-century French maps that charted dozens of Lower Mississippi Valley nations, and the absence of many of these groups from maps and accounts from the 1720s. But the disappearance of these nations was not simply the product of the slave trades and disease. Instead, some of the disappearances were also the product of French ignorance. On older maps, he explained, towns were often listed by their individual names, rather than by the names of the larger polities to which they belonged. As he related, "These [people] are less parts of different nations, than [at a] distance between the same nation, which in order to find their own land, have separated from the principal village." Essentially, French observers often struggled to understand the political compositions of these multinational settlements and they confused separate towns for separate nations, as well as separate peoples as the same polity. Le Maire's observations explain why groups like the Capinans and Naniabas might vanish during this era, only to again reappear years later. Simply put, some of this perceived destruction of the Petites Nations was purely the result of French misunderstandings of Indigenous political systems.[41]

Despite the power of these colonial narratives, the boom in French settlement during the 1720s did not lead to an end of Louisiana's dependence on their Native allies or to an end of the Petites Nations. Throughout the decade, colonists continued to suffer from regular shortages of food, medicine, and essential supplies, and they relied heavily on trade with local Native people to sustain their communities. These continual shortages, coupled with growing numbers of settlers, led the Choctaws to take action to force the Louisiana settlers to change their behavior. Some Choctaw leaders threatened and derided the French or strengthened their relationships with the British. While this influx of immigrants, and the pathogens they carried, led to the deaths of thousands of Petites Nations people, especially those nearest to Mobile and Biloxi, it did not lead to an end of the interdependent relationships among settlers and Petites Nations communities. Instead, these same connections among Petites Nations, large nations, and the French newcomers that had sustained the Louisiana community throughout the first decades of colonization continued during this era. Still, this influx of settlers did meaningfully shift more power and land to Louisiana colony. Petites Nations were therefore increasingly forced to negotiate with immigrants who outnumbered their communities and who began to transform their homelands into colonial settlements. As the settlers grew bold and began to ignore their obligations to the Petites Nations who hosted them in their homelands, many Petites Nations communities developed strategies to push back against the expansion of colonial power.

Countering Colonial Incursions

In the wake of burgeoning French settlements, declining Indigenous populations, the violent executions of Natchez leaders in 1715, and the brutal Chitimacha War, one might expect that Petites Nations would become more malleable to French desires and more desperate to preserve their relationships with the Louisiana government. However, the actions of the Natchez, Chitimachas, and Mobilians during the 1720s indicate that they did not perceive themselves to be conquered, dependent, or on the verge of destruction. These three nations had all experienced tragedy as the result of French colonization, and we might therefore expect them to be hesitant to push back against the growing might of the Louisiana colony.

Instead, during this era Natchez, Mobilian, and Chitimacha leaders defied French attempts to demand labor, land access, and political subservience from their people. Their people's profound and quotidian acts of resistance indicate Petites Nations' determination to defend their sovereignty and prevent the Louisiana government from asserting authority over their lands and people.

Following the Natchez conflicts of 1714–16, French settlers flocked to Natchez. Grand Village–allied Natchez welcomed French settlers and provided them with parcels of land to set up their own settlements interspersed among Native towns. These adjoining French, Natchez, and Indigenous migrant communities and towns in Natchez homelands created similar patterns of multinational settlement as those that had shaped Petites Nations communities at Mobile, Biloxi, Natchitoches, and Yazoo. But the new land-use arrangements angered many Natchez and left them frustrated with Grand Village's growing political authority. Antoine-Simon Le Page du Pratz, who had been encouraged to move to Natchez by his enslaved Chitimacha woman, arrived at Natchez in 1720. He purchased two parcels of land and was disturbed to find that these titles did not ensure that the land was fully vacant. One Natchez man refused to leave or sell his home and land, and he cared little for Du Pratz's claims of ownership. Like many Natchez, he rejected the authority of the Grand Village to sell his land out from under him and resisted this settler invasion. This remarkable man refused so steadfastly that he actually managed to convince Du Pratz to recognize his right to remain. Since Du Pratz could not remove the man from his home, he extracted a promise from the Natchez resident that he would hunt, fish, and provide light labor for Du Pratz as needed.[42]

The flood of settlers into Natchez homelands increased the tension both among Natchez political parties and between settlers and Indigenous residents. Between 1715 and 1723, 183 French colonists moved into Natchez territory where they joined the Tioux, Grigra, and Natchez populace. The company's financing of transatlantic slave ships enabled elite landowners to buy enslaved Africans to work on their plantations, further transforming the demographics of the region. By 1723 there were 100 enslaved Africans in the Natchez homelands. These enslaved laborers' toil and agricultural expertise made the cultivation of tobacco possible and led to the development of a nascent plantation economy in Natchez homelands.[43]

The Louisiana settlers were bad guests and neighbors. They exploited enslaved Africans and carved up Natchez land to grow tobacco. They brought large grazing animals that trampled Natchez cornstalks and fouled the earth. Settlers' horses, cattle, and hogs repeatedly wandered out of the French villages and into Indigenous gardens and food stores. Natchez villagers grew frustrated with these immigrants' mistreatment of their lands and the destruction wrought by their invasive animals. By 1722 some Tioux and Natchez had turned to stealing, killing, or maiming these livestock in order to force the French to control their nonhuman relations.[44]

During 1722 and 1723, the tension over land use and French conduct at Natchez repeatedly flared into open conflict. In late October 1722, a French sergeant demanded an outstanding payment for merchandise from a Natchez man from White Apple. The Natchez man was unable or unwilling to pay at that moment, and he allegedly threatened the sergeant in response to his rude demand. While the men argued, a group of French soldiers arrived. As tempers flared, the soldiers shot and bayoneted the Natchez man and one of his companions. The wanton bloodshed shocked the Natchez populace and catalyzed a series of skirmishes between Natchez inhabitants of White Apple and the French. Meanwhile, the Grand and Flour Village Natchez feared the damage this would cause to their partnerships with the French, and they took steps to speedily resolve the conflict. Natchez from the Grand and Flour Villages, as well as some of the Tioux, assisted the French with logistics and acted as mediators between their warring neighbors. Tattooed Serpent (a military leader) of the Grand Village along with his wife (a political leader in her own right), "the Woman Chief" (another elite political leader), and the head of Flour Village all worked together to negotiate a peace. The Tattooed Serpent blamed the inhabitants of White Apple as well as Grigra migrants for fomenting this conflict, and used his authority to pressure the villages to cease fighting.[45]

Less than a year later, in the fall of 1723, the White Apple villagers again came to blows with the French over the same issues of land use and mistreatment of Natchez people. Frustrated Natchez lashed out at the livestock that had destroyed their crops. They cut off cows' and horses' tails and left warning marks on the beasts. Instead of understanding the mutilation of horses and cattle as messages to better control their animals, the French responded to these assaults by directing violence at Natchez men and women. The Grand Village leaders again blamed the White Apple Village as well as the Tioux for harming the animals and inciting conflict, and again the Tattooed Serpent mediated peace between White Apple and the French. This time, Governor Bienville demanded not only the heads of the ten Natchez he believed had incited this violence but also that the Tattooed Serpent deliver the men's families to the French. These women and children were to be enslaved as punishment. Bienville also used this opportunity to insist that the Natchez leaders execute a free Black man, who had nothing to

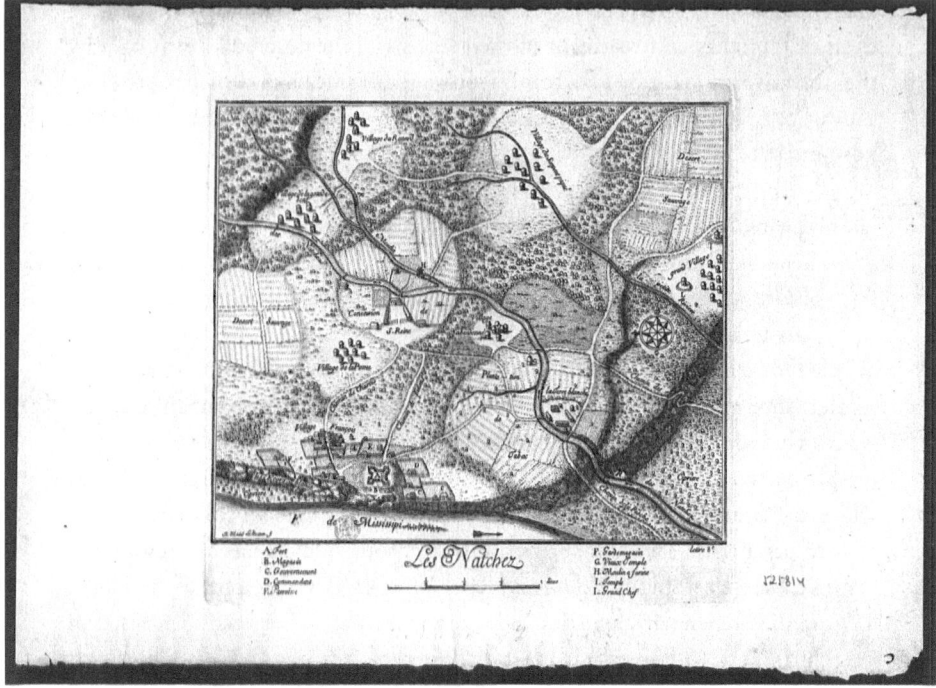

Figure 10. Map of Natchez showing interspersed French and Natchez settlements, by Jean Baptiste Michel Le Bouteux. Bouteux's map displays the White Apple, Grand, Flour (here listed as Renard), and abandoned Natchez villages alongside French plantations, Native and French cultivated crop and tobacco fields, and the roads that linked these multinational settlements. Jean Baptiste Michel Le Bouteux, Les Natchez, ca. 1750, Biblioteca Nacional de Portugal, Registo Nacional de Objetos Digitais, C.C. 55 P2.

do with the conflict, but was living at Flour Village. Bienville feared the social implications of allowing free African people to find permanent refuge with Native nations and used this peace agreement to end this man's life and liberty. The French also demanded three Grigra scalps and annual payments of meat, bear oil, and other food supplies from White Apple Village as recompense for the deaths of so many livestock and the damage of the war. The Tattooed Serpent only partially complied. He brought Bienville the heads of two of the alleged leaders of the insurrection, as well as the head of the free Black man, but he refused to enslave the families of the executed Natchez men.[46]

The village of White Apple as well as some of the Tioux and Grigra migrants grew more and more enraged by the presence of French settlers and fearful of the violence and the environmental destruction these colonists brought into Natchez homelands. Still, the leaders of Grand and Flour Villages continued to see benefits to having the French as neighbors and political allies. With each conflict, Grand Village was also able to expand its political power. Nonetheless, White Apple would not be cowed by French brutality. The White Apple people continued to enforce their governance on their own lands and to find ways to limit the abuses of French settlers. Their experiences of trespass and resentment would grow to explosive proportions by the end of the decade, but during the mid-1720s the Flour and Grand Villages leaders were still able to mediate among their Natchez compatriots and their French neighbors.

Petites Nations' military assistance was key to the ultimate French, Grand Village, and Flour Village victory in 1723. In late September that year, Bienville stopped in Petites Nations villages along the Mississippi River to request aid, supplies, and men to join his small French army. He had only 211 French soldiers and volunteers while the Natchez had roughly 500 warriors.[47] Nearly 200 men from the Petites Nations of the Ouachas, Chaouachas, Acolapissas, Houmas, and Tunicas joined the expedition. These Petites Nations warriors understood that through their military assistance they were strengthening their ties to the French and generating relationships of obligation among their people and the colonists. As compensation, Petites Nations men would expect to receive military supplies, and they would be allowed to keep any Natchez people they captured in battle. These Petites Nations men provided critical military assistance to the French, and the Tunica leaders in particular were recognized by the French for their outstanding military assistance and bravery. Remarkably, thirty Chitimacha men also served with the French forces. However, unlike the men of other Petites Nations, it appears that they resented being asked to participate in this conflict with the Natchez.[48]

One of the Chitimacha men who joined Bienville's 1723 expedition against the Natchez was a military leader who was both a veteran and victim of the Chitimacha War. This man was captured during the war and enslaved by Bienville during the 1710s. Somehow, the man managed to convince Bienville to emancipate him. Ultimately, the man was able to return to his nation, and by 1723 he was regarded as an esteemed military leader among his community. French records refer to this man as "Framboise" (Raspberry), a diminutive name that Bienville likely gave him in order to humiliate and belittle him during the time he was enslaved. That Bienville and other French leaders continued to call this man

"Framboise" even after he had been emancipated and was acting as the military leader of the Chitimacha detachment assisting the French, rather than recognizing him by his title or Chitimacha name, illustrates the profound and enduring violence of this man's enslavement even years after his formal liberation and return to the community. This history of violence, and the latent threat of enslavement, also helps explain why this Chitimacha leader and his compatriots felt they were not in a position to refuse assistance to Bienville outright in 1723.

Even if the Chitimacha military leader was compelled to participate in the war, from within the joint Petites Nations and Louisiana forces, he managed to subvert French military aims and limit the considerable violence that the French leveled against the Natchez village of White Apple. This man was forced to watch and assist French troops as they burned White Apple cabins; killed Natchez of all ages, including elderly women and babies; and as French settlers enslaved dozens of Natchez women and girls. In November, after more than a month of battle, and after Tattooed Serpent had already come with a calumet to sue for peace and delivered the heads of two of the leaders of the White Apple–allied villages, the Chitimacha military leader was dispatched on a mission to chase down a group of fleeing White Apple villagers. With twenty of his own men and twelve French soldiers, this leader was ordered to attack the White Apple refugees. The Chitimacha military leader did as he was told and left with his men, but after reconnoitering the area, he returned to the fort empty-handed. The French commanders were furious with the man they called Raspberry, and one of them asked this leader "if his men had the intention of giving [the Apple Villagers] the upper [hand] to which he responded that there was not enough time because if the savages [Apple Villagers] saw that they were returning to them, they would flee."[49]

By following the broad mandates of the French military commanders, but failing to capture the refugees, and perhaps even being intentionally loud and indiscrete as he traipsed through the woods, this military leader had evaded having to attack and enslave the Natchez while maintaining plausible deniability. Many Chitimachas had taken refuge with the Natchez during the Chitimacha War, and some families remained with the Natchez even after the conclusion of the conflict. So this military leader may also have feared attacking Chitimacha kin or betraying the sanctuary that the Natchez had offered his own people if he followed French orders to hunt down these refugees. Initially, the French intended to use the war of 1723 to "destroy" the White Apple and Jenzenaque towns and enslave their people. However, after months of fighting they finally had to admit that destroying these towns was an "impossibility" because of the "inaccessible country."⁵⁰ The Chitimacha leader's failed mission helped reinforce the perception of the difficulty of pursuing Natchez in their own lands, forcing the French to call off their hunt for the refugees. Shortly thereafter, the Chitimachas, Houmas, Acolapissas, Ouachas, and Chaouachas ran out of food. Since the French could not supply them, their warriors returned home. By drawing out the timeline of the war, and the expenses the French were forced to incur to support their allies, this Petite Nation leader also helped thwart a crushing French victory.⁵¹

The Chitimachas who were pressured to participate in this campaign would have empathized with Natchez villagers who tried to regulate the environmental destruction of French colonization, and some of their own people even engaged in similar tactics in their own homelands. In November 1723, after he secured peace with the Natchez, Bienville returned to New Orleans. As his troops canoed downriver, he was stopped by Monsieur Buisson, the French planter who had moved in next to Paris near the old village of the Bayagoulas and alongside the Chitimacha village. This planter complained to Bienville that a Chitimacha man had recently attempted to destroy his farm. Buisson reported that he caught the Chitimacha burning down the palisade that enclosed his animals, and that "the beasts had ravaged his lands and his garden."⁵² When the planter tried to stop the Chitimacha man, he fled. Bienville and his troops tracked down the arsonist, and captured him with the intent of imprisoning him when they reached New Orleans. In unleashing the animals on the planter's garden and lands, the Chitimacha man exposed the colonist to the same destruction that these animals and French farming methods had wrought on Chitimacha lands. He also made it clear that this planter was not welcome and should not feel safe in Chitimacha territory. Buisson and the other encroaching French settlers were likely putting pressure on their Chitimacha neighbors, and surely their roving horses and hogs were a menace to Chitimacha crops and medicinal plants. The Chitimachas therefore challenged French claims to the riverine plot by attacking the physical markers of their property and the animals that destroyed and transformed these lands.

The efforts of Chitimachas to place limits on French colonization and to inconvenience, or even imperil, French missions did not stop in 1723, but rather continued throughout the decade. One of the most spectacular and best recorded of these incidents again included the Chitimacha leader that the French continued to call Raspberry. In the spring of 1727, the Jesuit missionary Father du Poisson began an arduous journey up the Mississippi River. Du Poisson had been

Figure 11. Map of New Orleans and environs including Chitimacha settlements to the west of the city along la fourche de Chetimachas. Jean Baptiste Michel Le Bouteux, Carte des environs de la Nouveile Orleans, 1750, Biblioteca Nacional de Portugal, C.C. 362, P2.

assigned to establish a mission in Quapaw territory, instruct the nation in the Christian religion, and affirm the Quapaws' alliance with the French. The spring flooding had swollen the muddy river and made the current nearly impassable, so du Poisson and his men advanced upstream very slowly. The exhausted travelers had to stop frequently and stay overnight at Indigenous villages along the river. Du Poisson and his men expected to be received, fed, and welcomed into these villages as allies. While they were staying at the villages of the Bayagoulas, the party chanced to run into the formerly enslaved leader of the Chitimachas, who was also visiting with the Bayagoulas. Seeing that the travelers were weary, hungry, and unable to cook dinner on account of the soggy ground, the Chitimacha leader invited them to dine that evening at his people's village further upriver. This leader left a young Chitimacha with instructions to guide the priest and his men to their village. Du Poisson and his men eagerly accepted this invitation and packed their things back into the pirogues to travel to the Chitimachas.

Du Poisson's party set off behind the Chitimacha youth along the swollen river in pursuit of the promised meal. The Chitimachas had withdrawn further from the river to escape the flooding, so they were lodged in a particularly inaccessible portion of the swamp. These travelers shortly had to get out of their canoes and slog over tree branches and through the mud in their long robes. Father du Poisson found fighting the mud and the tangled bayou vegetation exhausting. He explained that they continued only because the guide "assured us that it was only a step farther, [so they] pushed the pirogue by main strength, for the hope of feasting with Framboise encouraged them; but, at length, we found only overthrown trees, mud, and some low ground where the water was stagnant." Then, when the explorers had pressed themselves thoroughly into the wilderness, "the little Savage left us there, and disappeared in a moment. What were we to do in these woods without a guide? Father Souel jumped into the water, and we did the same; it was somewhat amusing to see us splashing among the thorns and briers knee-deep in water; our greatest trouble was to draw our shoes out of the mud."[53] The guide had abandoned them deep in the woods and far from the river. This was a serious predicament as French soldiers and travelers frequently starved to death or ran into trouble and died when they became lost in the Louisiana country. Yet du Poisson and his men failed to get the message and pressed on in what they hoped was the direction of the village.

Miraculously, du Poisson and his sodden companions did manage to toil their way through the marsh and locate the Chitimacha village, yet they found no respite upon their arrival. Rather than greeting them hospitably, the Chitimacha leader made clear that the Frenchmen were not welcome in Chitimacha territory. Addressing the weary travelers in their mud-caked robes, he coolly told the missionaries that he "had nothing" for them. After this jarring reception, du Poisson correctly assessed that his men must immediately flee from the village and return to the canoes, in spite of his party's exhaustion. Southeastern diplomatic etiquette required that travelers were always received and fed at the villages of their allies no matter the inconvenience to their hosts. To turn away the French party and refuse to feed them was therefore an overtly hostile act. Perhaps the Chitimacha leader had expected that these travelers would meet their end mired in the bayou before they ever reached the village, or perhaps this encounter would have turned violent had the French attempted to stay the evening. In either case, the formerly enslaved Chitimacha leader clearly conveyed that the Chitimachas did not wish to help the missionaries or welcome French travelers in their territory.[54]

The Louisiana administration's insistence that nations like the Chitimachas be conquered was part of imperial efforts to assert control over the Petites Nations and claim the lands of the Lower Mississippi Valley. The Chitimacha leader and his peoples' efforts to thwart the French missionary and destroy French property were direct challenges to imperial power, and served to hinder and limit French trespasses on their lands and against their people. Throughout the 1730s, the French continued to couple descriptions of the Chitimachas as "destroyed" and "wandering" with complaints about their attacks on colonists and property. For a nation that was allegedly conquered and subdued, the Chitimachas remained a considerable preoccupation for French officials. In Bienville's 1732 memoir to the king, he again insisted that the Chitimachas were greatly reduced from their former glory, having at present only 40 warriors, or roughly 140 people. However, even as he emphasized their weakness, he lamented their continual harassment of French settlers, saying that they had recently killed two Frenchmen in their territory and burned a plantation.[55] In effect, then, rather than continuing to openly fight the French after 1718, the Chitimachas shifted to subversive resistance tactics. Even after the formal conclusion of their war with the settlers, they continued to stymie the growth of colonial Louisiana and fight to protect their remaining homelands and people.

By the end of the decade, even France's most steadfast Petites Nations allies were growing frustrated with the Louisiana settlers' treatment of Petites Nations peoples and lands. While the Chitimachas and Natchez people both fought wars with the French, Mobilians had maintained strong alliances with French settlers at Mobile and continued to live alongside the colonists in the Indigenous and French multinational settlements in their homelands. However, as the French settlements at Mobile grew, and the Louisiana government became increasingly fixated on their larger allies like the Natchez and Choctaws, they began to also violate the terms of their relationships with their most intimate Petites Nations neighbors. By 1729 the leader of the Mobilians was pushing back against French misconduct, stymying governmental operations as a way to force a restitution of the proper forms of relationships between his people and the Louisiana settlers.

That year, the French lieutenant Regis du Roullet found his diplomatic mission to the Choctaws hamstrung by the Tohomes and Mobilians. Du Roullet was on an assignment to travel from Mobile to meet with the leaders of several Choctaw villages. The shortage of French trade goods and the failure of the French during the previous year to distribute annual tribute gifts to the nation convinced many Choctaw leaders to rely on British merchants instead. Du Roullet's crucial assignment was to meet with these Choctaw leaders, listen to their complaints, and assure them that they had the firm support of the French king. He was also to talk them out of pursuing further diplomatic and economic relationships with the British. To convince them that the French really could supply their people, he was bringing hundreds of pounds of coats, leggings, Limbourg cloth, shirts, blankets, knives, beads, scissors, gunflints, gunpowder, vermillion, brass bells, and other gifts for the Choctaw village leaders. Du Roullet required porters to transport these goods, so he asked the commandant of Mobile to supply him with seventeen Petites Nations men to carry the load. The commandant promised to order the Tohomes and Mobilians to supply nine men from their villages. He would also request assistance from the Chickasawhay Choctaws. The commandant was promptly forced to write back to du Roullet to say that, although he was "greatly mortified by this mistake," he simply could not convince the Tohomes and Mobilians to carry the bales of goods.[56]

As the Tohomes and Mobilians would receive no part of this wealth of merchandise, they refused to carry the burdens. Like their Choctaw allies, they were in serious need of cloth, gunflints, bullets, and the other valuable manufactured goods that du Roullet was carrying. The French had not given the Mobilians and Tohomes proper tribute gifts or merchandise access in years. Since the Louisiana government had failed to maintain their diplomatic agreements to adequately supply the Mobilians and Tohomes, these nations were under no obligation to continue to fulfill French requests for assistance. Refusing to accept defeat, du Roullet decided to try his luck negotiating with the nations directly. He first visited the Tohomes and asked for porters. The Tohomes had long supplied the French with labor, so du Roullet hoped he could convince the men to do so again. All except two Tohomes refused this request. The leader of the Tohomes did not reject du Roullet outright, but demurred, claiming that he lacked the authority to make his men carry burdens for the French.

Du Roullet next stopped at the village of the Mobilians and made the same request. Their leader, Tonty, bluntly and emphatically refused. He recalled the long service of the Tohomes and Mobilians to the French, and he emphasized his people's connections to the settlers. As he explained, "Whenever the French needed porters or any other commission it was to those of the river [the Mobilians and Tohomes] that they applied" and the Mobilians had fulfilled their requests for help. But Tonty was stung by the French failure to bring his people trade goods. Their alliance was no longer as it had been, so the Mobilians refused to provide for the settlers until they made good on their promises. Instead, he sharply suggested that "the Choctaws who were flush with provisions could carry the bullets powder and other goods that [du Roullet] had, since they were for them."[57]

The Mobilians and Tohomes were in great need of manufactured goods, but they clearly were neither so desperate nor so dependent on the French that they felt they could not reject or chasten their Louisiana allies when appropriate. By the end of the 1720s, both groups were angered by the repeated failures of the French administration. Tonty complained that the French lacked sufficient ammunition to keep his people from "being defeated like women." For the Mobilians, the primary goal of living with these colonists was to help them better defend their people. If the French could not provide guns and gunpowder, their relationship was not achieving its diplomatic purpose. Asking the Mobilians and Tohomes to carry desperately needed trade goods to the Choctaws was beyond obtuse; it was deeply insulting. So, while this incident did not cause a major rupture between the Mobilians and Tohomes and the French, it does indicate that, by the end of the 1720s, the relationships even among even closely allied neighbors had become strained as a result of the growth of Louisiana and the changing political priorities of the French administration.

Du Roullet did eventually manage to get most of his goods to the Choctaw villages with the help of the Chickasawhays, but the refusal of the Mobilians and Tohomes delayed him and imperiled his diplomatic mission. For nations that were allegedly destroyed and dependent, the decisions of the Mobilians and Tohomes to reject French requests for assistance indicated both their continued autonomy and their efforts to pressure their Louisiana neighbors into upholding the obligations of their alliance. After all, the Mobilians and Tohomes still had very close ties to the Chickasawhays, and since the Choctaws were far more powerful than their French neighbors, these relationships continued to give the Mobilians and Tohomes both political leverage and economic alternatives to the Louisiana colony.

Taken together, the resistance of the Chitimachas, Natchez, and Mobilians to French colonization during the 1720s suggests that instead of moving toward a flourishing Southeastern empire, Louisiana settlers' conduct in the Lower Mississippi Valley was fraying the critical ties to Indigenous communities that kept the colony afloat. Moreover, although the Petites Nations endured calamitous epidemics during this decade, it is clear that they still saw themselves as dependent on the French. But many nations entertained the possibility of concluding or at least scaling back their relationships with the Louisiana settlers when they failed to benefit their communities. Persuasive as the Company of the Indies' propaganda might have been, the Petites Nations were not in fact disappearing and destroyed, but instead were engaged in subversive and overt resistance in ways that continued to limit and imperil French imperial authority in the Lower Mississippi Valley.

During the late 1710s and the 1720s, colonial Louisiana grew rapidly, and the colonial administration secured important alliances with Upper Creek and Natchez polities. However, both the rate and manner of this growth put increasing pressure on their alliances with Choctaws and Petites Nations. The Louisiana government's failure to uphold the obligations of their alliances and French settlers' abuse of Indigenous lands led to conflicts with the Natchez and Chitimachas and strained the administration's relationships with the Choctaws, Mobilians, and Tohomes. Thus, despite all the French bluster about the success of the colony, the actions of the Louisiana settlers set the colony on a collision course with its Indigenous neighbors that would lead to catastrophe before the close of the decade.

CHAPTER 5

French Transgressions and Natchez Resistance

The leader of the Natchez village of White Apple raised the calumet before him so that the red and white feathers that dangled from the pipe stem fluttered and twirled in the crisp fall air. He signaled that his men should begin the diplomatic ritual, and they gathered in formal procession. As his retinue approached French Fort Rosalie at Natchez on a November morning in 1729, the men sang, danced, and rhythmically lifted the pipe in greeting. They fervently hoped that the French would not suspect that anything was amiss. The commander of the Natchez fort, Sieur de Chepart, heard their singing, and saw with delight that the Natchez had come with gifts of corn, chickens, and bear grease. Chepart eagerly welcomed them through the fort's gates. To the White Apple men's immense relief, their plan was unfolding perfectly.[1]

Chepart had been waiting for this moment for months. In spring of that year, the commander had demanded that the inhabitants of White Apple relocate their entire village to make way for the tobacco plantation he planned to build on their homelands. The White Apple women and men repeatedly refused his appalling request. But Chepart remained obstinate and responded to their rejections with anger. He threatened the men and women with violence and enslavement and continued to insist on his right to take their lands. Ultimately, these Natchez were forced to accede to Chepart's demands—or so the commander believed. They only pleaded that Chepart allow them to remain until the end of the fall harvest, so they would not lose the corn that would feed their people through the winter. That morning, on November 28, the French commander believed his bold tactics had paid off, and that the grateful headmen of White Apple had come to repay his kindness in extending their tenure with offerings of food and words of friendship. He greeted the men and approached the group to receive his tribute.

Chepart had grievously underestimated the people of White Apple. Instead of affection, the commander and his troops were met with a hail of musket fire and blows from axes and clubs. After the warriors from White Apple dispensed with the Louisiana garrison, they collected ammunition from the fort and turned their attention to the French plantations that surrounded the Natchez villages. Within hours, these Natchez killed at least 229 colonists. They also took 50 French women and children and 300 enslaved Africans captive.[2]

This bloodletting was the culmination of more than a decade of tension and unresolved political battles between White Apple and the French colonists who had joined the Natchez settlements. Rather than deferring to their Native hosts, French newcomers repeatedly broke with the Natchez community's expectations. They did not understand, or refused to recognize, that their right to remain on the land was dependent on their ability to maintain good relationships with the Natchez people. What were the Natchez to do with a growing group of neighbors who violated all the political and social norms of their nation?

Once it became clear that the Louisiana settlers no longer had any intention of abiding by Natchez regulations of shared land use and respectful conduct within a multinational settlement, the Natchez were forced to take drastic measures. In the decade before the war, French colonists had seized prime Natchez land to grow tobacco, imported hundreds of enslaved Africans to work their fields, permitted their cattle to run into Natchez cornfields, and mistreated Natchez women and elders. They had also killed White Apple political leaders and enslaved women and children from their village. For years, Grand Village and Flour Village had worked to tamp down White Apple's political resistance and restore peace among their Indigenous and European neighbors. However, Chepart's latest brutal demand to displace the entire village, and his threats of slavery, as well as White Apple's violent response, were too severe transgressions to be restored by peaceful mediations. Instead, the 1729 conflict unified the Natchez nation, and all the villages fought a joint war against the French. Turning to a military strategy of mass violence in their desperation, the Natchez killed their French neighbors in order to eject the Louisiana colonists from the multinational Natchez settlements by force.[3]

The shockwaves from the killings at Natchez rippled across the entire Gulf Coast. Over the next year, both the French and Natchez frantically attempted to recruit the aid of their Indigenous allies. Louisiana had insufficient troops to independently wage a war against the powerful Natchez. In the mid-1720s, the

Natchez were roughly 1,750 people and could field about 500 warriors. The French had merely 325 soldiers in the entire colony.[4] Nonetheless, the Louisiana government absolutely could not let an attack of this magnitude go unavenged—to do so would be political suicide—so they begged the Choctaws, Quapaws, and Petites Nations for assistance. The Natchez may have been larger and more powerful than the French, but both nations recognized that the conflict would ultimately be determined by the decisions of their Indigenous allies. If their Native neighbors chose to support the French, the Natchez could expect to suffer tremendous losses. If they chose to back the Natchez, it could spell the end of the Louisiana colony.

The Petites Nations found themselves caught in the middle of this conflict and simultaneously pressured by their French, Natchez, and Choctaw allies to join the war. By 1729 many of the Petites Nations had constructed extensive webs of alliances that linked them diplomatically and economically to either the White Apple or Grand Village–allied political parties of the Natchez villages. Most Petites Nations also had relationships with at least one of the larger Native nations and imperial powers in the region, including the French, Choctaws, Chickasaws, and British. The involvement of these larger nations would entangle many Petites Nations in the fighting. Therefore, when White Apple violently severed their relationship with the French and expelled these foreigners from their homelands, many Petites Nations people found themselves caught between opposing sets of diplomatic obligations. Their situations were made more difficult by the fact that the French administrators chose to seek the destruction of the entire Natchez nation rather than opting to only punish individual towns as they had done during previous conflicts.

As it became evident that the French would also not follow Indigenous norms of warfare, and that they were willing to use extreme violence against their enemies and allies, combatants and women and children, the Petites Nations found themselves dragged into a conflict that seemed almost limitless in its scope and brutality. Multinational settlement at Natchez and the interdependent relationships and networks of exchange that the Petites Nations and Louisiana settlers had developed in the Yazoo River and Natchez region made it difficult for nearby Indigenous communities to escape the conflict between the Natchez and the colonists. Instead, the outbreak of the war between the French and the Natchez forced the Yazoos, Koroas, Tunicas, Tioux, and Ofogoulas to make impossible choices that embroiled their people and homelands in tremendous violence. Outside of the Natchez and the French, these Petites Nations bore the highest tolls of the conflict. The radiation of this conflict across the Lower Mississippi

Valley through Natchez and French networks permanently altered the political landscape of the region and brought the expansion of colonial Louisiana to a grinding halt.

Unsustainable Futures at Natchez

Although the causes of the Natchez War are complex, several long-standing disputes between Natchez towns and the Louisiana settlers help explain the Natchez's decision to execute their Louisiana neighbors en masse. First, this conflict was clearly an outgrowth of the contests over land use, social behaviors, and political relationships that characterized French settlers' relationships with White Apple through the 1710s and 1720s. Second, the physical abuse of Natchez men and women unnerved the people of White Apple and made them fear for the safety of their families. Third, this ongoing abuse, coupled with growing Natchez anxiety about French practices of slavery in the Lower Mississippi Valley, led White Apple townspeople to conclude that they could not be safe in their own homelands while the colonists remained there. As the influx of both Louisiana settlers and enslaved Africans continued, the issues of land use, fair modes of exchange, and roaming livestock became more severe. By the late 1720s, the French conduct had become so offensive that the Natchez political factions were able to unify their polity in opposition to their voracious French neighbors.[5] Essentially, the French refusal to respect the social and political regulations set forth by their hosts ultimately catalyzed the violence of 1729.

The French conduct at Natchez is perhaps the most extreme example of the Louisiana administration's efforts to dispossess Native people, and it also represents the fundamental clash of Indigenous and European social ideologies. The Natchez people, or at least those allied with Grand Village, believed they were inviting these immigrants to share their homelands and act as their trade partners and political allies. They also expected that the colonists would still be accountable to the leadership of Grand Village. Effectively, they anticipated that the French would be good relatives and would comply with their social and political norms, as Tioux and Grigra people had, since they would have understood the Louisiana settlers' rights to use the land to be contingent on their relations with the Natchez people. If pigs, horses, and other livestock had been violating their expectations of respectful relations to the land and people for more than a decade, Sieur de Chepart's 1729 demand that an entire town of Natchez relocate to make way for his plantation surely felt like an extension of these transgressions.

Given White Apple's experience with the French settlers over the previous decade, they would have had no reason to believe that this behavior was likely to stop or change.

From the perspective of the White Apple townspeople, the very foundations of the Louisiana and Natchez alliance were rotten to the core. When the French executed prominent Natchez leaders in 1716, Sieur Duclos, the commissary general of Louisiana, concluded that this overreach of French colonial justice had poisoned White Apple and French relations and would have deadly long-term consequences. As he explained, "judging us by their principles" the people of White Apple "would always fear that sooner or later we should have them tomahawked" and that "in order to prevent it they would not fail immediately or later as soon as they found a fine opportunity to play some bad trick on the French." As he understood, the diplomatically transgressive killing of these leaders meant that French settlers "would not be safe at all and would even run the risk of being massacred there some day."[6] In essence, because the French had rejected Indigenous norms of justice and warfare, and instead used execution to force the people of White Apple into compliance, these Natchez would eternally live in fear that the French would again use violence against their people to quash disputes. Thirteen years later, Duclos's bloody premonitions came to fruition.[7]

Although the alliances of the Flour and Grand Villages had long held together the Natchez and Louisiana partnership, by the mid-1720s even these towns became resentful of their Louisiana neighbors. An elite Grand Village man explained the causes of his people's changing feelings toward the settlers to Le Page du Pratz in the 1720s. The man was the brother of the leader of Grand Village and he had become a friend of Du Pratz's when the planter had settled at Natchez. Du Pratz called this man by his formal political title, Serpent Piqué (Tattooed Serpent), a reference to the inked snake on his body that indicated his status as a military leader, rather than by his personal name. Following the 1723 war, Tattooed Serpent's relationship with Du Pratz soured. Shortly after the conclusion of the conflict, Du Pratz caught up with Tattooed Serpent and tried to ascertain what had destroyed their formerly companionable relationship. He asked the man why he had not come to call recently, and whether this meant that they were no longer friends. "I do not know," responded Tattooed Serpent. The man explained that, in the preceding years, it seemed that the French had turned against his people. Why had the French become such bad relatives? "Do the French have two hearts, a good one today and a bad one tomorrow?" he asked. Even in times of peace, they used force against the people who were so generously hosting the colonists in their homelands. He blamed the French for starting the 1723 conflict and explained that "we do not know what to think of the French, who having started the war, offered peace themselves; then during the times that we are tranquil and we believe at peace, they [the French] come to kill us without saying anything." Something had broken between the Natchez and French during the 1722–24 conflicts, and the sentiments among Grand Village and Flour Village Natchez began to shift. Even Tattooed Serpent, who had long supported the pro-French political party, was deeply concerned about the growing list of social and political violations the French committed daily against his lands and people.[8]

In the years after the 1723 war, the Tioux made the wise decision to leave the deteriorating situation at the Natchez settlements. The colonists were not responsive to Tioux and Natchez demands that they better control their animals and respect their Indigenous neighbors. Seeing the way the Louisiana government had killed and enslaved the Natchez who defied them, and having lost the support of Grand Village—the Grand Village leadership blamed the Tioux for the 1724 war—the Tioux may have understood that the time when they were welcome to live alongside the Natchez was drawing to a close. So, unlike their French neighbors, who stubbornly insisted on remaining when it was clear that they were no longer welcome, the Tioux moved out of Natchez and resettled independently.[9]

In conjunction with the mounting friction over land use and rampaging livestock, the Natchez people objected to the French settlers' abuses of Native people and particularly of Natchez women. Natchez women were respected as authorities within their families; they could serve as political leaders and held significant bodily autonomy. Natchez men and women therefore were enraged when French settlers and soldiers assumed that, like the land, these women were available for their use. In 1733 a Choctaw leader who recounted the causes of the 1729 war explained that the Natchez attacked their French neighbors in part because "French warriors carried away their women by force."[10] As the people of White Apple understood, the exploitation of women and land were deeply connected processes. They could not permit the French to remain and extract more profit from the land without opening up themselves, their wives and daughters, their mothers and sisters, and their leaders to greater violence.[11]

Part of the Natchez's objections to French use of their territories was also connected to their abuse of Africans and practice of slavery. Between 1719 and 1731, more than 5,951 enslaved Africans were sent to colonial Louisiana. These influxes of enslaved laborers transformed the Natchez settlement during the

1720s. In 1726 there were 150 French settlers and 74 enslaved Africans living alongside a Natchez population of roughly 1,750. Over the next three years, the colonial population more than tripled. By 1729 there were 400 colonists and 180 enslaved Africans. Seemingly overnight, these Louisiana settlers and slaves had become nearly one-third of the entire population at Natchez and huge chunks of Natchez land were being used as tobacco plantations. French settlers physically abused enslaved Africans, forced them to labor in their fields and their homes, and excluded them from political leadership and familial belonging. While the Natchez had long practiced Indigenous forms of slavery and captivity, and certainly committed severe violence against captives, the racial structure and intergenerational nature of French slavery was fundamentally distinct from these Indigenous practices.[12]

Likewise, the Natchez were abundantly aware that the French enslaved Native Southerners, and they treated these captives in ways that were contrary to the accepted Indigenous practices of slavery, which often left pathways open for social acceptance and eventual inclusion in society. By the second decade of French settlement, many Louisiana settlers held Native people in bondage, and the colonists showed no sign of ceasing their trafficking of Indigenous women, men, and children. Moreover, it was clear that the colonists were willing to enslave Natchez people as well as those from other Lower Mississippi Valley nations. During the 1723 war between the Natchez and the French, the Louisiana troops enslaved more than a dozen Natchez women. Some of the Natchez's French neighbors, like the planter Monsieur LeBlanc, personally captured and then sold Natchez women while simultaneously owning property near White Apple. By 1726 there were nine enslaved Native people laboring for French colonists at Natchez. It was clear to the people of White Apple that the presence of Louisiana settlers in their homelands constituted a serious threat to the safety and liberty of their families.[13]

The Natchez people observed the French abuse of both enslaved Africans and Natchez people and were unnerved by instances in which French individuals treated free Natchez men and women as they did their enslaved African and Indigenous laborers. As one colonist explained, French soldiers and the commander "threatened to send them [the Natchez] to the Islands [enslave them]" if they did not comply with orders. Moreover, if a Natchez father or husband stepped in to stop a French man from abusing his wife or daughter, "they [the French] knocked them out with sticks," and beat Natchez who protected their families.[14] The way Chepart and some of the other colonists treated the Natchez indicated that they believed they had the right to corporally punish and enact physical and sexual violence against free Natchez men and women, and to enslave Indigenous resisters as they saw fit. Reflecting on the settlers' conduct, this colonist could only conclude that the Natchez people became "obligated to destroy those who caused them so much harm."[15]

Chepart's threats to enslave Indigenous resisters and his physical abuses of free Natchez people seemed to confirm the Natchez peoples' worst fears about their French neighbors. Both Le Page du Pratz and a French officer named de Laye reported witnessing the cruelties of Commandant Chepart. Du Pratz recounted that the commander spoke to the head of Grand Village as though the leader was "a slave whom he could command absolutely." Chepart threatened that if the leader did not deliver the payments of corn and goods on time, he would have him "bound hand and foot [enslaved] and sent down the river to New Orleans."[16] De Laye likewise explained that Chepart "had mistreated them [the Natchez] and made them work like slaves without paying them."[17] For both de Laye and Du Pratz, it was clear that by fall of 1729 the commander's conduct had convinced many Natchez that their French neighbors were plotting to enslave their people.

Throughout the summer and fall of 1729, the Natchez community met to discuss the horrific behavior of their French neighbors and to strategize ways to respond to Chepart's obscene demands. By autumn of that year, it had become clear that the situation was urgent, and that French and Natchez cohabitation was rapidly becoming untenable. Du Pratz reported that, at one of these meetings, a Natchez elder from White Apple made a rousing speech that articulated Natchez concerns about violence, dispossession, and enslavement. As the elder proclaimed,

> It has been a long time that we have perceived that the neighborhood of the French has made more bad than good.... Before the arrival of the French within this country, we were men who were content with what we had, and it was sufficient for us, we boldly walked every road, as then we were our own masters; but today, we go groping, with the fear of finding thorns [in our path], we walk as slaves, and it will not be long until we are [slaves] of the French, since they already treat us as if we were. When they are strong enough, they won't use politics anymore; [for] the least thing that our young men will do, the French will tie them to a post, and they whip them as they whip their black slaves, have they not already done so to one of our young men, and is death not preferable to slavery?[18]

Chepart's abhorrent conduct and the growing Natchez fear about French practices of slavery helped unify the divided political parties and villages of the Natchez nation. In this moment of collective threat, the White Apple villagers were able to generate support for a plan that would finally evict the French from the Natchez homelands once and for all.[19]

Ultimately, the Natchez people feared for their liberty and the safety of Natchez women and girls, which along with their fear of dispossession of their land led them to seek violent recourse. The French would not leave of their own accord, and increasingly appeared determined to force the Natchez out of their own territory. War, it seemed, had become their only option.

When the Natchez did strike, they relied on the same military tactics that many other Petites Nations had used to expel unwanted neighbors when relationships broke down at multinational settlements. Like the Tunica eviction of the Houmas in 1706, or the Bayagoula attack on the Mugulashas in 1699, the village of White Apple remedied an untenable political situation using violence and subterfuge. Although some contemporary reports suggested that the Natchez attack was part of a general Indian conspiracy—which allegedly involved the Choctaws and Petites Nations and was designed to wipe out all the French in Louisiana—it seems clear that this attack was in fact limited to evicting the colonists from Natchez and the Yazoo River region rather than a coordinated assault with Choctaws and other distant nations.[20]

It is unclear what future Natchez people envisioned for the Africans who had been enslaved by French settlers at Natchez. Natchez people did not share the same racial ideologies as Europeans, and indeed, neither race nor religion played a central role in justifying slavery or captivity within Native nations. But Natchez people did perceive African people as outsiders and as distinct from other Indigenous captives. French sources that describe Natchez relationships with enslaved Africans are ambiguous. The French officer de Laye recalled that, days before the November attack, several Natchez women had gone to the Kolly and Longraye plantations to warn some of the enslaved women there to be on their guard.[21] Other Natchez reportedly promised enslaved Africans that "they would be free with the Indians" after the war.[22] As both Jessica Marie Johnson and George Milne have argued, enslaved Africans may have seen the war as an opportunity to fight for their own freedom, and some of them even took up arms to assist the Natchez. While the Natchez killed many French men during their November attack, they did not aim to kill African men, and instead kept African men, women, and children as captives. Still, it quickly became clear to these African men and women that the Natchez did not intend to either liberate them or fully integrate them into Natchez society. Instead, it seems that the Natchez used their labor to support their war efforts, and that they intended to sell at least some of these captive Africans to their Chickasaw and British allies. So, while some Africans may have hoped for and found a modicum of self-determination or freedom from bodily violence alongside the Natchez, the war did not offer true emancipation or social inclusion to the many enslaved Africans who were caught within the conflict.[23]

The Natchez assault in November 1729 embroiled African, European, and Indigenous peoples in the conflict, and the upheaval caused by this event quickly spread violence beyond the confines of the Natchez villages. This brutal rupture among allies and neighbors transformed the expulsion of transgressive immigrants from Natchez into a massive regionwide war. In the days and months after the attack, both Natchez and French leaders sought aid from their networks of diplomatic allies. In the coming years, the French and Natchez conflict expanded, ensnaring nearly all the Petites Nations as well as the Chickasaws, Quapaws, and Choctaws.

Choosing Sides

In the aftermath of the November attack, both the French and the Natchez urgently sought aid from their Indigenous allies. For Petites Nations like the Tioux, Tunicas, Koroas, Yazoos, and Ofogoulas, all of whom had relationships with both the Natchez and Louisiana, this put their nations in dangerous positions. To support either side would mean betraying their other allies. But by not choosing sides, they also risked becoming targets of either Natchez or French attacks. Tioux, Tunicas, Koroas, Yazoos, and Ofogoulas all wrestled with their decision about which side to support. Ultimately, these former allies split into three distinct camps, and they ended up on opposing sides of the conflict. Tioux, Yazoos, and Koroas supported the Natchez; Tunicas supported the French; and Ofogoulas struggled to maintain neutrality amid the unfolding chaos in their homelands.

Of all the nations that ultimately became embroiled in this conflict, none would have as significant an impact on the outcomes of the Natchez and French War as the Choctaws. Both Eastern and Western Choctaws had long-standing adversarial relationships with the Natchez, and after careful deliberation, many Choctaw leaders decided to collaborate with the French to neutralize the threat posed by their old Natchez enemies. Their entry into the war in late winter of

1730 would reverse the tide of the battle and draw many Petites Nations into the fight on the side of the French.

In a war in which Louisiana settlers repeatedly violated Indigenous ethics and codes of conduct, the Choctaws also fought to mitigate the scope of violence and to maintain norms of warfare and diplomacy. Over the course of the conflict, their participation protected Petites Nations from assaults by French troops, limited the genocidal campaigns of the Louisiana government, and forced the French to abide by Choctaw expectations for alliance and compensation during war. The critical decisions that Choctaw and Petites Nations men and women made would ultimately determine the fates of the Natchez and the Louisiana.

The Petites Nations closest to Natchez were the first to be pulled into the conflict. Several days after the November 29 attack, the Tioux received four bedraggled French refugees. In keeping with Indigenous diplomatic protocol, they welcomed their former neighbors kindly and provided them with food and shelter. Tioux men and women listened with concern to the survivors' stories of Natchez brutality, and comforted them saying that "they would like to avenge the deaths of the French."[24] The colonists' accounts raised grave concerns among the Tioux, so they promptly dispatched emissaries to Natchez to gather more information.

For several years, the Tioux had aimed to distance themselves from the powder keg of Natchez politics, but the arrival of these French refugees in early December 1729 thrust them back into the very conflict they had tried so hard to avoid. When the Tioux had left Natchez in 1727, they had chosen to remain in the region, but did not continue to have intimate and regular dealings with the colonists. Their judicious migration allowed them to avoid fully severing their relationships with either the French or the Natchez and becoming caught up in further disputes. The arrival of French refugees ended their peace and neutrality.

The Tioux diplomats who were sent to Natchez to investigate the survivors' claims listened with empathy as the Natchez recounted their grievances and asked for aid. Natchez men and women passionately explained that the French posed a grave danger to their people, and they likely reminded the Tioux of how, for many years, they had sought to force the French to be good relations and neighbors to no avail. They may also have appealed to the Tioux by reminding them of the abhorrent conduct of the settlers toward both of their peoples. Moreover, as George Milne has shown, by the late 1720s the Natchez were drawing on the language of race to articulate a sense of Indigenous solidarity using the language of "red men" and the Tioux may have found this rhetoric persuasive. Perhaps the Natchez recalled the long history of relations between their peoples and reminded the Tioux that their people had once come to the Natchez asking for lands and refuge for their people. Natchez men and women also promised the Tioux gifts and the spoils of the war if they would assist in driving the French from their homelands. The Tioux diplomats returned to their people carrying the Natchez's message and convinced of the justness of their cause. Shortly thereafter, the Tioux executed the four French refugees.[25]

Over the next weeks, Natchez representatives solicited aid from the Petites Nations, and the Tioux reached out to the Tunicas on their behalf. The Tunicas received the Tioux diplomats and listened to their requests, but did not make a firm commitment to the Natchez. During previous conflicts, the Tunicas had supported Grand Village, Flour Village, the Tioux, and the French in their fights with White Apple, Grigra, and Jenzenaque, and had lost warriors and leaders in the bloodshed. Now, with the Natchez polity unified, Grand and Flour Villages again called for their aid, but this time it was for help against Louisiana rather than against White Apple.

The Tunicas were divided over their response to the killings in 1729. Many of their nation had close ties to French officials, including the few Frenchmen who lived within their villages, and they saw the advantage of sustaining these trade relationships. Other Tunicas, who may have empathized with the Natchez's fears and resented the conduct of the Louisiana settlers, argued in favor of supporting the Natchez. The Tioux had been their allies for many years, and surely the Tunica elders recalled their time living alongside the Tioux community on the Yazoo River. There seemed to be no way they could protect all their friends and trade partners. So, despite their reputation among the French as "the only Savage Nation [that is] truly friends of the French," the Tunicas also did not jump to the aid of their Louisiana allies.[26] Given their entangled webs of relations, as well as their concerns about whether the powerful Choctaws would join this conflict, they decided that the most prudent course of action would be to try to avoid this bloody conflict among their allies.[27]

Most Tunicas initially aimed to stay out of the fighting, but some rallied to aid their Native neighbors. A young Tunica man who supported the French described the friction the Tioux diplomats' entreaties had created within his nation. As he reported, among his people there were "some who have a badly made heart.... Some of them were doing what they could to engage us, they do not regard these people as Tunicas, even though they are of the same nation, that the Tunicas have French hearts, that they would die alongside them [the French] rather than betray them, that they did not value at all those who went with the Tioux [to fight with the Natchez] and that they would perish [Tunicas who supported the Natchez] by their own hands if they could catch them."²⁸ This young man aimed to assure the French officer that the Tunicas were indeed their trusted allies, and the majority of the Tunicas would later join the fight on the side of the French. Nonetheless, the man's anger with his Tunica kin who had "badly made" hearts illustrates the strain this conflict created within the communities who lived in the Natchez and Yazoo River region.

The Yazoos and Koroas were more receptive to the Natchez entreaties for support. These nations had long-standing relationships with the Natchez, and they had only reluctantly established alliances with Louisiana. Although the Yazoos and Koroas had received French travelers in the 1680s, they did not pursue diplomatic ties or joint settlements with the French during the 1700s. Instead, during this era, the Yazoos and Koroas sought alliances and trade relationships with the Chickasaws and English. When the Yamasee War choked off British trade networks throughout the Southeast, the Yazoos and Koroas were forced to find other economic avenues. Like their Natchez neighbors, in 1716 they agreed to host a few French settlers. Three years later, a little contingent of French troops arrived in their homelands and erected a small fort. These few colonists joined more than seven hundred Koroas and Yazoos on lands that had previously housed other Native nations. During the 1720s, the Louisiana settlers became the most recent immigrants to join the long-standing multinational settlements on the Yazoo River.²⁹

Although the French called the outpost at St. Pierre a *fort*, this term implies a greater level of French establishment and military control than actually existed in the Yazoo and Koroa homelands. In 1727 a French priest who visited the outpost remarked that the fort is actually a "hut ... surrounded by palisades, its sole defense consisting in the position it occupied at the top of the bluff." This tiny shelter had only twelve soldiers and four other inhabitants. Although by 1729 the post had increased to about eighty people, including the garrison, this settlement remained small and heavily dependent on the Yazoos' and Koroas' services and generosity. Louisiana settlers reported that the Yazoos and Koroas talked derisively of their French neighbors, calling them "beggars," and grew frustrated with their failure to provide the trade goods they had promised to the Koroas and Yazoos. The Louisiana administration's inability to uphold their promises and properly supply the Yazoos and Koroas likely factored into the Koroas' and Yazoos' decision to participate in the Natchez War.³⁰

By mid-December, the Koroas and Yazoos had decided to back the Natchez, and their entrance into the war opened a second front of military conflict against the French. In a move that almost directly mirrored the tactics the Natchez had used at Fort Rosalie, Yazoo and Koroa warriors entered Fort St. Pierre under the guise of a calumet ceremony and attacked the small garrison and inhabitants on December 12, 1729. They killed many of the men, sparing only a tailor and a porter, leaving seventeen colonists dead. The Koroa women felt that it would be cruel and imprudent to kill the women and children, so they held many of these surviving colonists as captives. This was a major victory, and the Koroas and Yazoos were perhaps optimistic about what a future without French settlers in their homelands would look like for their children. They sent representatives to spread the good news and to recruit further support.[31]

The Ofogoula women were making pots when the Yazoo diplomats arrived with arresting news. They told their allies and neighbors of how they had valiantly defeated the French, of the clothes and muskets they had captured, and they spoke of the potential of a colonist-free Yazoo River. Several Ofogoula men congratulated the Yazoos, lamenting that they had not been part of the fight. Some of the younger Ofogoula warriors were so energized by the Yazoos' reports that they took off toward the Mississippi River in hopes of catching unsuspecting French travelers. As the women rubbed at the dried clay that clung to their cuticles, they may have been wary of this enthusiasm for war, and after the Yazoos left, some of them would have offered more cautious counsel.[32]

Perhaps these women were persuasive because despite the initial enthusiasm of some of the men, the Ofogoulas were hesitant to join the Natchez. They too were frustrated by the failures and transgressions of their Louisiana allies, but the Ofogoulas knew all too well the dangers of war. Many remembered the losses and horrors their great grandparents spoke of as they recounted fleeing conflict in the Ohio River Valley. As these tradeswomen likely reminded them, there were significant economic advantages to their relationship with the French. Once their earthen pots were polished, dried, and fired, Ofogoula women would fill the containers with rendered bear fat and sell them to local French soldiers and inhabitants. The colonists had relied on the Ofogoulas, Yazoos, and Koroas to supply them with essential food items like meat and bear grease, and this exchange provided the three nations with ready access to tailors, gunsmiths, and European trade goods.[33] Now that the fort was gone, the Ofogoula women must have wondered what would happen to their community's economy, and where they might sell the next batch of bear grease.

The Ofogoulas managed to avoid making any military commitments until they were sure of the Choctaws' course of action. In early December of 1729, both the French and the Petites Nations were unsure whether the Choctaws would decide to fight. Knowing if the powerful Choctaws would offer their support to either side would allow Petites Nations like the Ofogoulas to better assess the risks of committing to defend their Natchez or French allies. The Ofogoulas received Natchez envoys and tried to maintain their delicate neutrality while the French urgently pleaded with the Choctaws to send their warriors against the Natchez.[34]

The Choctaws' slow deliberations frustrated Louisiana officials so, seeking some kind of immediate retribution, the French governor channeled his wrath into a genocidal plot to destroy the small Chaouacha nation. Feeling impotent to pursue retribution against the Natchez, Governor Étienne Périer sought other, less dangerous, Indigenous communities that he could use as fodder for French vengeance. He was desperate to take some action that would counter the prevailing image of French military weakness and thereby stave off further attacks on French settlements. Périer found the small, Louisiana-allied Chaouacha nation to be ideal prey. In targeting the Chaouachas, the Louisiana government would once again violate Indigenous ethics by launching an unprovoked raid against one of their most vulnerable allies.

On December 5, 1729, the governor ordered a company of free Black militiamen to march south into the swampy homelands of the Chaouachas and kill every man, woman, and child.[35] This Petite Nation provided meat and produce to the inhabitants of New Orleans, and they had long-standing relationships with the colonial government. Their tiny community only had about 105 people before this attack, and the assault killed more than 10 percent of their nation. Périer eagerly proclaimed this mass killing a success, and boasted to his superior that "this example carried out by our blacks has kept the other petites nations up the river in a respectful attitude."[36] He further wished that he had "destroyed all of those petites nations that have no use to us, and which on the contrary, might push our blacks to revolt" and follow the example of the Natchez.[37] In essence, Périer thought he had executed a brilliant political move. By relying on Black soldiers to attack the Chaouachas, he hoped to foster animosity among Indigenous and African peoples and thereby prevent the Natchez War from turning into a joint African and Native American uprising. Critically, he also expected that by killing Chaouacha men, women, and children, he could terrorize the other Petites Nations into submission.[38]

Périer targeted the Chaouachas because of their vulnerability, not because they posed any threat to New Orleans or supported the Natchez. The Chaouachas had been staunch allies of the French for decades before this attack. They were also longtime enemies of the Natchez.[39] In 1713, the Natchez, along with their Yazoo and Chickasaw allies, conducted a slave raid against the Chaouachas.

Under the guise of a calumet ceremony, these raiders entered the Chaouacha villages and killed several Chaouachas, including their primary leader and several of his family members. They then dragged eleven Chaouacha prisoners, including one of the leaders' wives, back to Natchez where they sold these women and children as slaves to the British.[40] Moreover, the Chaouachas had also volunteered soldiers and support during the Louisiana settlers' wars with the Chitimachas and with White Apple and Jenzenaque in 1723. So the Chaouachas were definitely not allies of the Natchez.[41] This was a massacre of convenience.

When they learned of the French killings of the Chaouachas, the Choctaws intervened to prevent more bloodshed. The unjustified slaughter of their Petites Nations allies by the French was intolerable, and they would not permit Périer to fulfill his lust for further atrocities against downriver Petites Nations. Instead, the Choctaws encouraged the Petites Nations closest to New Orleans—the Bayagoulas, Houmas, and Acolapissas—to temporarily relocate upriver to the safety of their territory where they would be protected. Périer celebrated their migrations and saw the nations' temporary relocations as evidence that his policy was working. In April 1730 he icily reported that if the Petites Nations had not relocated away from the city "we would be obligated to destroy them, above all the Houmas, the Bayagoulas, and the Acolapissas, who were in the general conspiracy, they are under obligations to us, and they are very near us."[42] Choctaw interventions protected these nations at a critical moment, and their hospitality and welcome of their migrant allies further strengthened the relationships among the Houmas, Acolapissas, Bayagoulas, and Choctaws.

Despite their objections to Périer's cruelty, the Choctaws did ultimately choose to support the French. They recognized a valuable opportunity in the crisis between the Natchez and the Louisiana settlers, and used it to pursue their own political goals. Over the previous three decades, the Choctaws and Natchez had often been in conflict. During the 1700s and 1710s, the Natchez allied with Chickasaw and British slave raiders who repeatedly attacked the Choctaws and stole their mothers, sisters, wives, and children, making them enemies of the Eastern, Western, and Chickasawhay Choctaws. The Charleston-based Indian slave trade had significantly abated by the 1720s, but the dull ache of the grief from the losses of beloved kin remained omnipresent in many Choctaw homes.[43] Just three years before the 1729 outbreak of violence, the Choctaws and Natchez had fought their own "small war" and the memories of this conflict were fresh within Choctaw communities. French administrators were not privy to information about either the cause of this 1726 conflict or its resolution. Still, they were comforted to learn that by 1727 the two nations had made peace. The Louisiana officials feared that this détente would not last, and they worried about the implications for their settlements at Natchez if the conflict resumed.[44] In the mid-1720s, the French were more concerned by the danger the Choctaws posed to the colony than about threats from their Natchez neighbors, so Louisiana officials repeatedly advocated for peace.

Choctaw conflicts with the Natchez presented serious threats to French colonial development in Natchez homelands. In October 1729, merely one month before the Natchez attack on the colonists, a French commander learned that the Choctaws were rumored to be seeking to destroy the Natchez. In his report to the French minister of the marine, Diron noted that he had intervened in these Indigenous affairs and sought to calm the Choctaws. He explained that "the Choctaws want to ruin the Natchez and abolish that nation," which would "bring completely prejudicial [impacts] to our establishments." He insisted that, by talking to a group of Choctaws who were traveling through the area, he had prevented an assault and "made peace [between] the Choctaws and Natchez." The events of the next few months suggest Diron had been overly optimistic.[45]

The Natchez also voiced concerns over the danger posed by their Choctaw enemies in the fall of 1729, and they even used this pretext to facilitate their attack against the French settlers. When the Natchez men who had orchestrated the Fort Rosalie assault asked to borrow the French settlers' guns—weapons they would soon turn against the French—they claimed that they needed them to hunt and fend off potential Choctaw raids. It is plausible that this was an ingenuous explanation that the Natchez gave the French because it would make their request to borrow weapons seem credible, but it is also possible that the Natchez were leveraging their fears of a Choctaw attack, fears the French shared, to gain access to French weapons.[46]

After months of deliberation, Eastern and Western Choctaw leaders decided to use the French conflict to deal a crushing blow to their Natchez enemies. In early 1730, Choctaw warriors began their spiritual preparations to go to war. During the first major retaliatory push by the French in late January of that year, eight hundred Choctaws helped the colonial militia secure a decisive victory.[47]

The Choctaws' entry into the war dragged additional Petites Nations into the conflict. Houmas and Acolapissas, both of whom were seeking refuge in Choctaw homelands, were among the first lower river Petites Nations to be pushed into the war. Choctaw pressure also convinced the Tunicas to back Louisiana, and their homelands became a central organizational hub for the joint Indigenous and French forces. As they had in the previous wars, the Tunicas allowed the Louisiana troops to use their lands as a staging ground for their missions, and Tunica women and men arranged logistics and provisioning for the soldiers. Relatively small numbers of Petites Nations warriors supported the French during this early phase of the war. Merely 300 men from all the Petites Nations south of the Tunicas arrived to support this first wave of attacks.[48] Given that France's Petites Nations allies could collectively field nearly 1,800 warriors, this means that fewer than 17 percent of Petites Nations men answered Louisiana's urgent pleas for military assistance.[49]

Unlike most Petites Nations, the small northern nation of Quapaws was eager to respond to its French allies' requests for support. Like the Choctaws, the Quapaws had long-standing conflicts with the Natchez, and they were also old enemies of the Yazoos. The Quapaws found that the war presented them with a convenient opportunity to renew their fight with the Natchez and strengthen their alliance with the French. So the Quapaws promptly and enthusiastically joined the war, and some even swore that as long as a single Quapaw remained standing they would continue to fight the Natchez and Yazoos.[50]

Choctaw support definitively turned the tide of the conflict. In early 1730, they led a series of attacks that left the Natchez and their allies on the defensive and reversed the momentum of the war. First, on January 27, 1730, 500 Choctaw warriors assaulted the Natchez villages. They caught the nation off guard and managed to kill 60 Natchez, liberate 54 French women and children, capture 100 enslaved Africans, and collect at least 15 Natchez prisoners. Many of the fleeing Natchez sought refuge in two palisaded forts within their villages or hid with their loved ones in the woods. Over the next several weeks, as the battle stagnated, the Choctaws and French laid siege to these ensconced Natchez. By late February 1730, the French, Choctaws, and Quapaws seemed to be winning the war.[51]

As the conflict dragged on, Choctaw emissaries continued to pressure Petites Nations to support their fight against the Natchez. In late 1730, French officials recorded that the Choctaws "have been intimidating the small nations along the Mississippi River and on the Mobile River," and their heavy-handed persuasion succeeded in generating more support from the downriver Petites Nations, like the Houmas and Acolapissas, as well as upriver nations like the Ofogoulas.[52] Were it not for the Choctaws, many of the Petites Nations would likely have abstained from the conflict, and more of them may even have backed the Natchez. As the French officer Ignace-François Broutin bleakly concluded in 1730, even "the Tunica would take the stronger side as all the Indians would infallibly have done if the Choctaws had taken arms against us."[53] In effect, then, the Petites Nations were not so much joining the French as they were agreeing to support their Choctaw allies.

The conflict reinforced Louisiana's dependence on their Indigenous allies and neighbors, and French officials resented having to supplicate the Choctaws. The increased confidence of the Choctaws and the desperation of the French was a miserable pairing for Louisiana officials. French officials purchased Natchez scalps from the Choctaws "at very dear prices," and they were resentful that the Choctaws did not seek to destroy the Natchez with sufficient vigor.[54] Governor Périer begged the comptroller of finances to send him more money and remarked that the lack of funds and men made the Choctaws "think we use them only because we are not capable of making war. [This is] the idea we have given them of us by using them in our defense. The least little nation thinks itself our protector in the situation in which we are."[55] The Choctaws' perceptions were wholly accurate. As Governor Périer could only contribute two hundred French soldiers to fight the Natchez, the war relied almost entirely on Choctaw, Quapaw, and Petites Nations support.[56]

In return for their military services, and for securing the support of the Petites Nations, Choctaw leaders pressed the French to provide their warriors with generous compensation. Choctaw combatants fought on their own terms, and they sometimes thwarted or undermined French military strategies. They developed independent battle strategies and held on to war spoils, including French and African captives, in order to force the Louisiana officials to compensate them for their service. Choctaw leaders had extensive experience with French representatives breaking their promises for gifts and payment, so they knew it would be unwise for them to promptly return these captives if they expected to get paid. By late February, many Choctaws had tired of the war and Louisiana officials' parsimonious remuneration. They began to talk of retiring from the conflict.

In March 1730, the officer Joseph-Christophe de Lusser was sent to the Choctaws to hear their grievances and negotiate the return of several of the French prisoners. Rather than returning these terrified colonists outright, the Choctaws brought them back to their own towns and waited for the French to come "repurchase" their kin. The Choctaws claimed that they were holding these French men, women, and children because the French had not justly rewarded them for their assistance in the war, and their leaders had no right to strip their warriors of their hard-won captives without proper recompense. Choctaw leaders took this opportunity to remind French officials of their obligations and indebtedness to their people and to force them to comply with Choctaw expectations for diplomatic partnerships. As the Choctaw leader of Yellow Canes recalled in 1731, without the Choctaws and other Native nations, the French military was useless. Their soldiers did very little damage in battle, and although "the cannon of the

French made much noise [it] had had little effect.... It was as if one was spitting on the ground." Furthermore, he stressed that "the Tunicas and other little nations had not wished to fight for the French because the French had put some of them in chains and treated the red men like slaves" and that "they stole the skins of the Indians by not giving them fair compensation for their goods."[57] With this withering commentary, the Yellow Canes leader reminded the French settlers that they direly needed the Choctaws, and they should be extremely grateful for their continued support. With no other options, the French were repeatedly forced to pay the ransoms to secure the release of the Louisiana colonists from the Choctaws and to accept that the Choctaws would fight on their own terms.

By late spring of 1730, the Choctaws had achieved their war aims, so they largely withdrew from the fighting. Their support had driven many of the Natchez from their homelands and shattered the polity into various bodies of refugees. Critically though, unlike the French or Quapaws, they were not seeking the complete annihilation of the polity, so they did not feel the need to continue the war. While some Choctaws continued to provide aid, most of their warriors returned home by that summer. Choctaw support had helped the French crush the Natchez military, but their withdrawal also prevented the French from fully exterminating the Natchez. Their conduct, and specifically their refusal to hunt down fleeing refugees, upheld Indigenous norms of warfare and stymied French efforts to kill or enslave surviving Natchez families.

The Choctaws' withdrawal from the war did not free Petites Nations people from their entanglement in the conflict, and it did not halt the expanding waves of violence that spread across the region. Once this large and powerful nation pulled out, French officials were again left to depend on their Petites Nations and Quapaw allies to carry out the combat, intelligence gathering, and supply line support to sustain their war. Moreover, since Petites Nations people had now also fought against Yazoos, Koroas, Tioux, and Natchez, these nations sought their own retribution for lost kin. Without the backing of the Choctaws, this war turned even more deadly for many of the small polities who were then forced to bear the brunt of this conflict.

Deadly Tolls

The years 1730 to 1731 were perhaps the most violent two-year period of the entire eighteenth century for the nations of the Yazoo River and Natchez region.

As French and Choctaw leaders drew in Petites Nations combatants, the Natchez War turned into a multidirectional conflict that pitted former neighbors and allies against each other and led to the death or displacement of roughly half of the regional population. Both the Louisiana and Natchez polities waged a total war, and during the ensuing years, not just Petites Nations warriors but also women, children, and elders became targets and victims of this violence. By 1731 when Governor Périer declared French victory over the Natchez, not a single polity between Pointe Coupée and the Yazoo River had emerged unscathed, and by the end of that year all but two of the nations in this region had suffered losses of at least 50 percent of their populations. For the Natchez and their Petites Nations neighbors, the scope of this violence was devastating.

Choctaw participation in the war proved disastrous for Yazoos. In addition to attacking Natchez villages, in early 1730 Choctaw raiding parties turned their attention to the Yazoos and Koroas. In February, shortly after they had attacked the main Natchez villages, a group of Choctaws entered the Yazoo village under the pretext of wanting to trade bear oil. Once inside, they killed several Yazoos and retrieved some of the French captives. A second group of Choctaws also attacked a Yazoo trading party as they attempted to take several other French captives to sell to their allies the Chakchiumas. The Choctaws routed the Yazoos and captured these French prisoners.[58]

The Chakchiumas were a Petite Nation that was situated in the borderland between the Chickasaw and Choctaw nations, and like the Tunicas and Ofogoulas, they were hoping to avoid being drawn into this war. In fact, perhaps more than any other nation in the region, the Chakchiumas had long succeeded in avoiding entanglement with any European empires. This nation had close political alliances and kin ties with both the Choctaws and Chickasaws, which allowed them to pursue only very loose connections to British and French traders and officials. The Chakchiumas had maintained a distant alliance with the French throughout the 1710s and 1720s by periodically providing intelligence about Choctaw and Chickasaw politics to French administrators. They likewise traded with the British through the Chickasaws. However, they did not host any French settlers or military posts and instead lived in an all-Indigenous multinational settlement. In 1725 they were living alongside the Taposas and Ibitoupas. Together, these three Petites Nations numbered roughly seven hundred people. All three groups dealt only infrequently with European officials. The Ibitoupas, and possibly also the Taposas, had been part of the pre-eighteenth-century Yazoo River settlement that included the Koroas, Ofogoulas, Yazoos, and Tunicas. So the Yazoos and Koroas were likely counting on these long-standing connections, and the nation's scorn for the French, to ensure that the Chakchiumas would be sympathetic to their cause.⁵⁹

This was a grave miscalculation. The Choctaws' entry into the war likely left the Chakchiumas with no choice but to support their Choctaw allies in their fight against the Natchez. The Chakchiumas rejected the Yazoo attempt to sell them French captives, and in late February, along with Choctaws and Taposas, attacked the Yazoo and Koroa villages. The Choctaws presumably pressured their Chakchiuma allies for support and pulled them and their Taposa neighbors into the fray.⁶⁰

In the ensuing months, the Choctaws, Quapaws, and the French and their Petites Nations allies made it clear that they intended to fully extirpate the Koroas, Yazoos, and Tioux from their homelands. If Moncacht-Apé lived to 1731, he would have been devastated to witness the tragic destruction of his community. Following the Choctaw and Chakchiuma assaults in February, the French gave the Tunicas instructions to attack the Yazoos and Koroas in March. It is impossible to know what conversations took place among the Tunicas as they prepared to undertake this mission. Did their elders recall their time living alongside the Yazoos and Koroas and entreat the younger men to avoid this assault? Was it the Tunicas' fear of Choctaw or French retribution that drove them to carry out this task? Or did they see an opportunity to strengthen their relationships with both the Choctaws and the French and neutralize the threat of the Natchez and their Chickasaw and British allies? After what was surely a long and painful deliberation, they ultimately decided to carry out the orders.

These final assaults drove the Koroas and Yazoos from their settlements and dispersed their people in multiple directions. The attacks also frightened the Ofogoulas and sent them fleeing from their settlement with the Koroas and Yazoos. They traveled south and asked for refuge with the Tunicas, who allowed them to settle alongside their town. The Ofogoulas likely feared that if the Choctaws attacked the Yazoos and Koroas again, they might also target the Ofogoulas. These attacks not only persuaded the Ofogoulas to geographically relocate their people but also forced them into alliance with the Tunicas and French. One group of Yazoos fled west to the homelands of Moncacht-Apé's forefathers along the Red River. Other families sought refuge with the Natchez and Chickasaws. Over the summer and fall, Tunicas continued to pursue these bands of Yazoos and Koroas, and Chakchiuma warriors carried Yazoo and Koroa scalps down to New Orleans where Governor Périer received these bloody gifts with pleasure and payment. By April 1730, Périer declared that the Yazoos and Koroas had been thoroughly destroyed. The following year he rejoiced that "there are not more than forty men [Tioux, Yazoo, and Koroa] remaining dispersed and pursued by the other nations."[61]

The Tunicas likewise experienced tremendous losses as a consequence of their involvement in the war. One of the most devastating episodes of this conflict began when the Tunicas were forced to directly confront their old allies, the Flour Village Natchez. In previous conflicts, the Tunicas had supported the Grand and Flour villagers in their clashes with Jenzenaque and White Apple. However, in 1730 they sided with the Choctaws and French against all the Natchez, and Tunica warriors killed and captured Flour and Grand Village men and women. On one of these spring raids, the Tunicas captured the wife of the leader of Flour Village. This woman was a political leader in her own right and a respected member of the Natchez community. As a way of demonstrating their commitment to the French and to reaffirm their relationship with the Louisiana government, they gifted this woman to Governor Périer. On April 10, they arrived in New Orleans to formally present this woman and several other Natchez captives to the Louisiana leader. Governor Périer received the Tunicas graciously, but returned the captives they offered. The historian Sophie White has suggested that Périer declined to accept these prisoners so that he would not have to try them in a French court and execute them according to French laws. By leaving the captives with the Tunicas, he expected that the revenge would be swift and their deaths would be cathartic to the terrified French citizens. Indeed, in the public square, Tunica warriors and French colonists jointly tortured and executed these captives. French observers who witnessed this horrific spectacle were deeply impressed by this prominent Natchez woman's resolve. As she endured the torments, she hurled insults at her attackers and cursed the Tunicas. She promised that the Natchez would make the Tunica men pay dearly for what they were doing to her, maintaining her spirited verbal resistance until her body gave out.[62]

The people of Flour Village sought vengeance for the death of their beloved leader and for those of their kin, even as their situation grew more desperate. In April 1731, as they battled hunger, sickness, and the onslaught of French and Petites Nations attacks, the leader of Flour Village approached the Tunicas to ask for refuge for his people. He entreated the Tunica leaders Cahura-Joligo, Lattanash, Dominique, and Bride-les-Boeufs to allow Flour Village families to settle alongside their villages and cease the war among their peoples. The Tunicas received their request and sent a representative to ask the French governor whether he would approve of this plan. The French were also exhausted by this war and running out of resources. Périer was therefore willing to accept their offer and instructed the Tunicas to proceed with the plan to resettle these Natchez alongside the Tunica and Ofogoula villages. Over the next months, the Tunicas, Natchez, and French coordinated the Flour Village relocation. On June 13 the Natchez families arrived at the Tunicas' village and the nations' leaders began the diplomatic protocols and welcoming ceremonies that would bring together their peoples. Men and women of these war-torn nations feasted together and danced through the evening, rejoicing in the newfound peace. By some accounts, this group of Flour villagers even included refugee Koroas and Chickasaws. The Tunicas generously received them all.

But the Natchez were seeking vengeance, not peace, and in the pale, predawn hours, the Natchez betrayed their refuge and the Flour villagers and their allies attacked the sleeping Tunicas. Cahura-Joligo was among the first slain. The Flour Village warriors managed to slaughter nearly half of the Tunica people, including elders, women, and children, and they took Tunica prisoners as well. For five days, the Tunica men fought valiantly, battling exhaustion and desperation, to retake the village. Meanwhile, the women, children, and elders who had managed to flee collected their surviving kin and mourned the devastating losses of their loved ones.[63]

In the aftermath of this betrayal, the Tunicas were grieving and furious, and blamed not just the Natchez but also French mismanagement of the war for this massacre. They sharply criticized the Louisiana troops' obsession with capturing and enslaving Natchez people (instead of killing them) and their continued willingness to negotiate with the Natchez. The Louisiana military's approach to combat had undermined French success and proved deadly for the Tunicas. In late June, Tunica and Petites Nations leaders met with the commander of the Louisiana troops, the Baron de Crenay, to discuss their joint military strategy and the next steps in the war. The French had recently botched an attack on a group of Natchez allowing many Natchez to escape and wreak havoc on several French forts. The Tunicas and Petites Nations representatives who met with the commander were livid, and they scathingly criticized the French for their failure to be good wartime allies. Tunica and Petites Nations leaders demanded that the Natchez "dogs and traitors" be burned alive. Without their deaths, the Tunica people could expect no closure, and they could not rebalance the spiritual forces that had been disrupted by the Natchez's slaughter of their people. Baron de Crenay attempted to calm the furious and grieving Tunica and Petites Nations leaders with gestures of peace and alliance. Instead of executing the Natchez, he handed the Tunica military leader a calumet and again promised the loyalty and support of Louisiana. In his rage and frustration, the Tunica leader made clear what he thought of the state of the alliance between his people and the French. He threw the sacred pipe to the ground and trampled it under his feet. Hollow gestures and empty promises could not restore the badly damaged relationship between the Tunicas and the Louisiana government. The Tunicas demanded action.[64]

After escaping from the Tunicas, the Flour Village leader and his band of refugees assaulted the small French post at Natchitoches. In October of that year, Natchez warriors besieged the Petite Nation of Nassitoches and the French outpost alongside their village. St. Denis (who was still commanding the Natchitoches post) had to ask for emergency support from not just the Nassitoches but also the Ishak/Atakapas, Caddoan peoples, and even several Spanish soldiers who were posted nearby. After depleting nearly all the Natchitoches fort's resources and withstanding heavy losses, the combined forces managed to defeat the Natchez. The Flour Village leader was among those killed in battle. Most of the surviving Natchez were either captured by the Nassitoches, Caddos, and Ishak/Atakapas or enslaved by the French. Since the Flour Village group was largely composed of families, many of these enslaved were women and children. Thus, St. Denis (the same man who arguably began the Chitimacha War to acquire Indigenous captives) was once again profiting by trafficking in Indigenous people during a genocidal French war.[65]

The attack at Natchitoches was the last major campaign of the Natchez against Louisiana, and by the winter of 1731, most of the Natchez who had not died or been captured were living as refugees. Some bands did remain in the woods and bayous north of their old villages, but most Natchez relied on the Southeastern custom of refugee sanctuary to help them find asylum with other nations. Many sought and found safety with the Chickasaws during 1730 and 1731. Other groups of Natchez chose to move even further beyond the reaches of French imperial networks, resettling permanently alongside Cherokee and Creek towns. One small group of Natchez even migrated all the way east to Catawba territory, and subsequently found more long-term sanctuary alongside the small nation of Peedees by securing land through the British government of Carolina.[66]

Natchez people who remained free and found refuge either in the lands north of their former homes or with other Southeastern nations continued to harass Ofogoulas, Chakchiumas, and Tunicas for years after the formal conclusion of the Natchez War. In 1732 a combined force of Chickasaws, Yazoos, and Natchez attacked the Chakchiuma villages in the dead of night. These raiders killed four men and four children and took eleven women as prisoners. Natchez

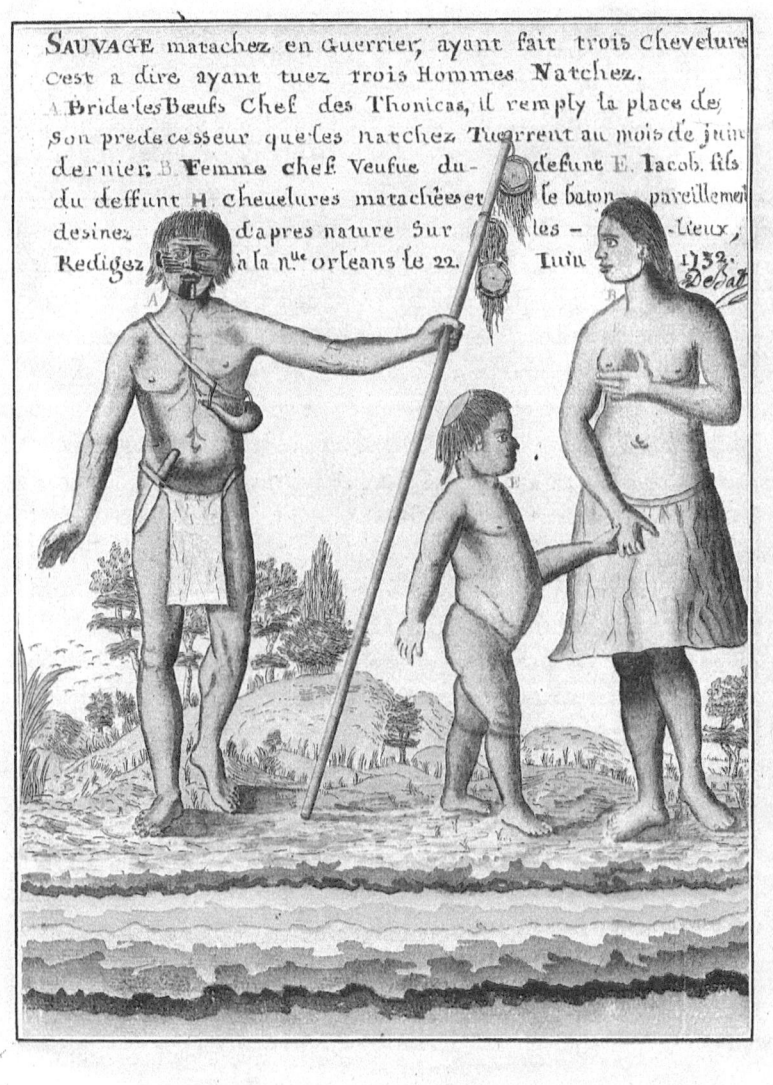

Figure 12. Depiction of the Tunica leader Bride-les-Boeufs with the widow and child of the former Tunica leader Cahura-Joligo. Alexander de Batz, *Sauvage Matachez en Guerrier, Nouvelle Orleans*, 1732, Peabody Museum, object, 41/72/10/18. Reproduced with permission of the Peabody Museum of Archaeology and Ethnography, Harvard University, Cambridge.

refugees also targeted the Ofogoula and French settlements at Pointe Coupée alongside the Tunica villages. During 1732 repeated attacks by combined groups of Chickasaws and Natchez wreaked havoc on the post. In March of that year, Natchez people attacked a French plantation, killed and captured enslaved Africans, slaughtered cattle, burned buildings, and terrified the French inhabitants. In June Chickasaw and Natchez parties again attacked French farms, where they stole cattle and burned fields, and raided the Tunicas' and Ofogoulas' villages.[67]

While the Tunicas seemed to have been strong enough to repulse Natchez raids without substantial damage, the Ofogoulas were again forced to relocate to protect their people. In 1733 they left the Tunica villages and moved north to the restored French fort at Natchez. There, they established a village that was within the cannon range of the French garrison and so would be better protected from Indigenous attackers. They also seem to have resumed negotiations with the Natchez in an effort to stave off future assaults.

In spite of their long efforts to live in peace and neutrality, the Ofogoulas were still caught in the conflict between the French and the Natchez. French military leaders at Natchez and Pointe Coupée insisted that both Tunicas and Ofogoulas track down the Natchez who had been attacking French villages and travelers along the Mississippi River. Given their interdependent relationships with the French at their new home alongside the Natchez post, the Ofogoulas felt obligated to provide this service. As so many other Petites Nations did when their French allies pressed their nations to take objectionable actions, the Ofogoulas largely led ineffective raids. Sometimes Ofogoula people destroyed Natchez fields, but they seem to have rarely killed or caught any Natchez people in these raids. In fact, while they continued to furnish the garrison and provide intelligence on Natchez movements, the French became so distrustful of the Ofogoulas that they began asking small groups of Choctaws to accompany and supervise the Ofogoulas on these missions to ensure that they were not deliberately fumbled.[68]

Throughout the 1730s, Natchez people raided French settlements along the Mississippi River near Pointe Coupée and Natchez, and Ofogoula and Tunica people continued to lead small and largely unsuccessful retaliatory raids. The steady violence against French homes, enslaved Africans, fields, livestock, and the Ofogoula and Tunica nations indicates that Natchez resistance did not end in 1731, but endured throughout the 1730s.

Hundreds of the Natchez men, women, and children the French combatants had captured during the war were enslaved and destined for brutal lives of bondage and death. French officials believed that these Natchez were too dangerous to keep within the Louisiana colony, so most of the captives were sent to be worked to death on sugar plantations in the French Caribbean. The Company of the Indies also hoped that the sale of these captives would help cover a portion of the costs of the war. Of the 450 Natchez that French soldiers captured during the fighting, 300 were crammed into slave ships and sent to St. Domingue. Only 160 of these women, men, and children made it alive to the port at Cap-Français. There, they were sold for 400 livres each. The others died in a valiant uprising on board one of the ships—Natchez people were determined to fight to their last breath for their liberty—and from sickness and abuse at sea.[69]

The barbarity of French practices of intergenerational chattel slavery was incomprehensible to Natchez people even as they endured these horrific fates. In January 1733, Bienville met with some of the enslaved Natchez leaders who had survived the Atlantic passage and at least a year of labor on St. Domingue. He reportedly spoke at length to St. Cosme, a preeminent man from Grand Village who had formerly served as a Natchez leader, and who was enslaved on a sugar plantation. St. Cosme attempted to assure Bienville that it was only the Natchez who had planned to take up arms against the French, and that the other Native nations had had no part in planning the conspiracy. Bienville reported that St. Cosme said "he hoped that they could return with me," and it is clear that this man believed his people might soon be able to go home to their lands on the Mississippi River. Within an Indigenous system of captivity, this option of return would have been an unlikely outcome, but it always remained a possibility, as did formal social integration. Within the racially stratified system of plantation labor in the French Caribbean, there was neither a chance for redemption or kinship. Bienville did not record how he responded to this heartbreaking question, but it is almost certain that none of these Natchez ever made it back to their fields and families.[70]

Other Natchez remained in vulnerable positions within Louisiana, either enslaved or pursued by enemies. Some sought to escape death and French enslavement by rebuilding their lives with the help of Indigenous allies and neighbors. For example, in December 1731, a group of Natchez from Flour Village once again sought refuge with the Tunicas. Some of the free Natchez who remained in the woods north of Natchez reached out to the Ofogoulas for aid in mediating between their people. Later that month, Dominique, one of the leaders of the Tunicas, also received this request for sanctuary through the enslaved daughter of the Flour Village leader. Dominique was returning from a mission to reclaim four Tunica women who had been captured by the Flour villagers during their attack against the Tunicas, so he ended up at Natchitoches alongside the other Natchez who were captured during the battle. Dominique engaged in diplomatic meetings to secure their release. He was presumably required to compensate the Nassitoches, who were holding these prisoners, for their return. After securing their release, Dominique and the women stopped by Juchereau de St. Denis's home, where they spoke with the enslaved daughter of the Flour Village's leader. St. Denis had evidently decided to keep this woman for his own use instead of sending her downriver to be sold with the majority of her kin. Although she was enslaved, the Flour Village leader's daughter managed to stay in communication with her free relatives, and even as an enslaved woman she continued to exercise her role as a representative for her people. She explained that the small band of Natchez who had escaped during this assault "were seeking a favorable opportunity to return to the Tunicas, and that they had been talking to Ofo[goulas] regularly [as] they are friends together." The Flour leader's daughter must have been incredibly persuasive and a very effective diplomat because, rather than dismissing her outright, Dominique entertained her request and told her that he would consider her proposal if the Natchez promised to surrender their arms before they sought refuge.[71]

The Flour Village woman did not manage to ensure sanctuary for her people again with the Tunicas, but several Natchez women did end up as captives, or possibly even as integrated and forced kin among the Tunicas in the years after the war. Tunica people captured a variety of Natchez men and women during the conflict. Indigenous Southerners often integrated women prisoners into their communities, either as captive and socially marginalized individuals or even as kin (albeit coercively), and Tunica people seem to have done the same thing with several of the Natchez women whom they obtained during and after the conflict. During the war, Lattanash, one of the younger Tunica leaders, caused a scandal among his community by maintaining an intimate relationship with a captive Natchez woman in the midst of the brutal violence. In the fall of 1731, Lattanash was living with this Natchez woman. Her presence and intimacy with this powerful Tunica man must have generated deep anger among the many Tunicas who had lost loved ones in the June attacks of that year. The records refer to her as a "slave," and it is possible that she was even taken captive by Lattanash. We know little of this relationship. Did the Natchez woman try to run away? Did she work to ingratiate herself to Lattanash as a way to protect herself from further harm? Whatever the case, it appears that this Natchez woman may have been able to regain her liberty. In December 1731, Lattanash caved in to pressure to leave her and return to his Tunica wife. After this point, the French records make no further mention of the Natchez woman except to say that she was no longer in the village. She may have been further trafficked, or she could have died. However, given that Lattanash did not turn her over to the French, and there is no record of her execution, it is also possible that she was able to use her relationship with Lattanash to gain covert passage out of Tunica territory and to liberty.[72]

It is similarly difficult to determine the fate of the daughter of the Flour Village leaders. She, like so many Natchez women, had been traumatized by the war, and was enslaved by St. Denis, the French commandant of Natchitoches, following the Natchez defeat in 1731. Her mother was publicly tortured to death by Tunicas and French in New Orleans and her father lost his life in the battle at Natchitoches. The war both stripped her of her kin and her freedom and left her exposed to the many brutalities of French colonial slavery.

However, instead of remaining enslaved by St. Denis, this woman may have ended up as a captive, slave, or forced kin of the Tunicas. In 1733 the Tunicas received two unnamed Natchez women from Périer as a gift for their service during the war. The enslaved women had belonged to St. Denis, and Governor Périer compensated the Natchitoches commandant for these women. While it was common for Petites Nations people to take Indigenous captives when they fought in war alongside the French, it was relatively unusual for Louisiana officials to gift Indigenous slaves to Native leaders in the 1730s. It is possible that, in 1733, Périer needed the help of the Tunicas and so these gifts were designed to generate goodwill, but it seems more likely that the Tunicas asked specifically for these enslaved women. Native nations sometimes requested the return of kin who were enslaved by Louisiana settlers as part of their diplomatic negotiations, so we might suspect that this was the case in this exchange. Given the Flour Village woman's prior conversations with Dominique and other Tunica leadership, it is possible that, after years of effort, the Flour Village leader's daughter finally managed to convince the Tunicas to acquire her and a relative so that she could escape French bondage and find a measure of peace or bodily safety. Alternatively, we might conclude that the Tunicas felt that possessing the Flour Village leader's daughter would finally cover the deep wound left by the destruction that her family wrought on the Tunicas during the June 1731 attack. The records of this exchange only tell part of the story. What is clear, however, is that women who were taken captive during the war often ended up forcibly integrated in a variety of unfree statuses within neighboring polities. Thus, the Natchez War, which was in many ways the result of Natchez efforts to prevent the exploitation of their lands and the enslavement of their people, concluded with massive loss of Natchez lives, lands, and liberty.[73]

The Natchez War was tremendously destructive, not just for the French and Natchez, but also for many of the Petites Nations. By the end of the conflict, Koroas, Tioux, Yazoos, and Natchez people had been chased from their homelands, enslaved, or killed; the Chaouachas had barely survived a genocidal campaign; the Ofogoulas had been displaced; and the Tunicas had suffered a catastrophic betrayal. The networks of economic exchange, intimate relations, and political alliances that had connected the Yazoo, Ofogoula, Tunica, Koroa, Chakchiuma, Natchez, and Tioux people since the late seventeenth century were shattered, and Tunica, Ofogoula, and Chakchiuma people continued to weather Natchez attacks throughout the 1730s.

With the Natchez dispersed and dispossessed, and the Louisiana colony in shambles, the Choctaws emerged as an even more dominant polity in the Lower Mississippi Valley. The war had clearly displayed the weakness of French imperial power, and the colony had been forced to beg for Choctaw support and to pay dearly for the Choctaws' services and alliance. If smaller nations like the Tunicas might have had trouble resisting Choctaw influence in the era before 1729, after the war the Choctaws were able to exert enormous pressure not only on the French but also on their Petites Nations allies. Of all the combatants, the Natchez War ended up best serving the political interests of the Choctaws.

This war did not lead to the collapse of Louisiana, but it did create a serious colonial crisis and substantially stymied the further development of France's empire on the Gulf Coast. In 1731 the Crown regained control of Louisiana, and the colony entered yet another era of underfunding and shortages. Fear of Indigenous violence also pushed many French settlers out of Indigenous spaces and back toward the centers of colonial settlements. So, while New Orleans continued to grow in the 1730s, and 1740s, many of the outposts remained small and thoroughly under Indigenous control.

Perhaps most critically, the war prevented the rapid transformation of the Lower Mississippi Valley into a plantation-based slave society. After 1731 only one more slave ship arrived in Louisiana during the era of French colonization, and that one did not come until 1743. Following the war at Natchez, the French Crown resumed control of the administration of Louisiana, and investment in the colony plummeted. The development of tobacco plantations and burgeoning settlements that had seemed so promising only two years prior now ground to a halt. So, although the Natchez had failed to defend their own people from slavery and exploitation, their violent response to French colonialism did halt the expansion of the French Empire and thwarted the enslavement of greater numbers of Africans on Indigenous lands.[74]

The Natchez War was such a catastrophe for French Louisiana that the imperial administration felt compelled to attempt to restore their reputation by pursuing a subsequent conflict with another one of their Native neighbors. Barely one year after Périer declared victory over the Natchez, he launched a fresh campaign against the Chickasaws. This deadly entanglement would lead to further losses for the Louisiana colony, and would once again force Petites Nations to find ways to protect their people in the midst of violent imperial conflicts in their homelands.

CHAPTER 6

Imperial Blunders and the Revival of Interdependency at Midcentury

In 1736 several Chakchiuma diplomats approached a senior Tunica leader with a covert proposition. They offered to include the Tunicas in a secret alliance with the Chickasaws. Together with the Chakchiumas and Nassitoches, this proposed partnership would grant the Tunicas access to British traders and the plentiful and high-quality merchandise they offered. However, this plan to rebuild economic relationships with the Chickasaws and British would only work if the Chakchiumas, Nassitoches, and Tunicas could prevent their French allies from learning of their designs. In the decade following the Natchez War, Louisiana was again desperately short on trade goods and gifts for its Indigenous allies, and this scarcity was only made worse by the French colonial governments' ongoing war with the Chickasaws. For the Tunicas, Nassitoches, and Chakchiumas, the potential for a relationship with the British and Chickasaws seemed to offer an alternative to the economic challenges their people were enduring and perhaps even the promise of greater political power through these eastern allies.[1]

The Chickasaw Wars that spanned the 1730s and exacerbated the economic hardships in Louisiana were a direct outgrowth of the Natchez War. Even after the Louisiana government declared victory over the Natchez in 1731, colonial officials remained committed to exterminating all the surviving Natchez in the Southeast. Governor Périer and his successor, Bienville, were determined to hunt down both the Natchez who remained in small groups in the Lower Mississippi Valley and those who had found refuge with Indigenous nations further east. Therefore, in 1732, on the basis that the Chickasaws were harboring Natchez refugees and thereby aiding enemies of the French colony, Périer asked Louisiana's Indigenous allies to attack the Chickasaws. This decision flagrantly violated Indigenous ethics of refugee sanctuary and warfare. It also had deadly consequences for both the Louisiana colony and the Chickasaws and once again embroiled Petites Nations and Choctaws in another costly imperial war.

French imperial anxiety during the 1730s and 1740s generated a series of violent conflicts in the Mississippi River Valley. As the Natchez War had demonstrated, the Louisiana colony was still relatively weak and Native politics and alliances would continue to determine the fate of the French Empire in the Gulf South. In Lower Louisiana, the dominance the Choctaws had secured via the collapse of the British Southeastern Indian slave trade and the Natchez War unnerved colonial administrators. Moreover, the Natchez survivors who resided across the Southeast continued to raid the Louisiana settlements. These raids served as harsh reminders of the settlers' vulnerability. Beyond the Gulf Coast, the Natchez War and the damage to France's relationships with Native nations had serious implications for the broader French imperial project in North America. This war, coupled with the failures and botched diplomacy of the French in the Illinois colony during the Meskwaki (Fox) Wars, generated resentment among Indigenous peoples across the continent. While Louisiana officials failed to appease their powerful Choctaw allies in the south, French officials to the north in Illinois likewise struggled to repair their relationships with the formidable Illinois Confederacy and Anishinaabeg leaders who sustained French political and economic influence in the midcontinent.

The pressure that Illinois, Natchez, Choctaw, Anishinaabeg, and Chickasaw peoples exerted on the French during the 1730s and 1740s led imperial administrators in both colonies to instigate wars with the Chickasaws and Choctaws that they hoped would reaffirm French power in eastern North America. These conflicts, which became known as the Chickasaw Wars and the Choctaw Civil War, aimed to neutralize the powerful Chickasaws, improve France's abysmal military reputation among the Indigenous peoples of the Mississippi River Valley, and channel the military might of France's powerful Native allies away from the Louisiana and Illinois colonies. Both were utter disasters.

Rather than restoring faith in the French Empire, these wars further antagonized Louisiana's larger Indigenous allies, and in Lower Louisiana the wars renewed settlers' reliance on the aid of the Petites Nations. So, for Petites Nations like the Ofogoulas, Mobilians, Tunicas, and Pascagoulas, the Chickasaw Wars and the Choctaw Civil War created opportunities and restored the close alliances that many smaller nations had held with the colony during its first two decades of establishment. These nations capitalized on Louisiana's need for military assistance, provisions, intelligence, protection, and other vital services. During this era of colonial vulnerability, the Petites Nations began again to be properly compensated for their services and resumed their roles as vital diplomatic allies of the colony. In practice, this meant that many Petites Nations were able to restore interdependent relationships with the Louisiana colony and that the settler fantasies of the 1720s, which imagined a future for the colony without the Petites Nations, became increasingly obsolete.

Unlike so many of their Petites Nations contemporaries, for the small nation of Chakchiumas, the Chickasaw Wars and the Choctaw Civil War created not opportunities but crises. For decades, the Chakchiumas had lived in the lands between the Chickasaw and Choctaw nations. Although these two larger nations were frequently at war, the Chakchiumas had managed to maintain political and personal relationships with both nations. Dual relationships with the Choctaws and Chickasaws protected the Chakchiumas and also enabled them to simultaneously access Choctaw, Chickasaw, French, and British economic and political networks. France's determination to go to war with the Chickasaws, which was born of Louisiana's anti-British policies and refusal to recognize Southeastern Indigenous codes of warfare and sanctuary, wrecked the carefully constructed web of alliances and relations that had protected the Chakchiumas throughout the first third of the century.

The Chakchiumas' participation in these conflicts profoundly shaped relationships among the Choctaws, Chickasaws, and French. The Chickasaw Wars and the Choctaw Civil War displaced the Chakchiumas from their homelands and forced the dispersal of their community. During the wars, they relied on the practices of multinational settlement and refugee acceptance to find sanctuary for their people in both the Choctaw and Chickasaws nations. Consequently, Chakchiuma refugees helped create and sustain diplomatic pathways even amid conflict. These displaced Chakchiumas would ultimately facilitate lasting peace among the Choctaws and Chickasaws even as their own people were forced to sacrifice political autonomy for long-term security.

The Natchez War Expands

The violence begun by the Natchez War radiated far beyond Natchez homelands throughout the 1730s. Louisiana's war with the Natchez did not simply end in 1731. Instead, by expanding the war to target the Chickasaws along with the Natchez, the French administration enlarged the conflict, drawing additional nations from both the Southeast and middle Mississippi River Valley into the fighting. Throughout the 1730s, France endeavored to keep its Indigenous allies engaged in continuous attacks on Chickasaw villages. In addition to financing and supporting these raids, in 1736 and again in 1739 French forces launched major campaigns against the Chickasaws. These two offenses are usually recognized by historians as the first and second Chickasaw Wars. The Chickasaw people managed to survive this colonial onslaught, and even to win several major victories against French forces, but the wars claimed many Chickasaw lives. If the Louisiana government was hoping that war with the Chickasaws would help repair its badly damaged image and restore faith in the French Empire, it had precisely the opposite effect. Both because of the way the French pursued this conflict, and because of their decision in 1736 to target the Chakchiumas along with the Chickasaws, by the conclusion of the Chickasaw Wars, France had once again been defeated and the relationships among Louisiana and their Choctaw allies were in tatters.[2]

The formal justification for the Chickasaw War was that the Chickasaws were harboring Natchez within their nation, but the French government's decision to pursue a full-fledged effort to "destroy" the Chickasaw nation during the 1730s was born of a wider variety of pressures and imperial designs from across the continent. Louisiana had been in intermittent conflicts with the Chickasaws throughout the first three decades of its existence. During the first half of this era, the Chickasaws had regularly attacked French settlers, and had also raided the Petites Nations and Choctaws for captives to sell in the slave markets of the British Atlantic. In response, the Louisiana government armed the Choctaws and supported their raids against the Chickasaws.

Weakening the powerful Chickasaws had long been a central component of Louisiana's diplomatic policy. In the decade after the Yamasee War, the Chickasaws repeatedly sought peace with Louisiana, but the colonial administration was neither willing nor able to make this happen. The merchandise shortages that plagued Louisiana throughout its existence meant that, even in the relatively prosperous 1720s, the colony was not able to supply the Chickasaws with enough trade goods. Therefore, even if the Chickasaws and French had managed to make peace, the Louisiana government would have been unable to provide sufficient economic support for the nation. Moreover, some French officials believed it would be more advantageous to keep the Choctaws and Chickasaws at war to prevent either of these polities from becoming too strong. Finally, France's alliance with the powerful Illinois Confederacy made peace with the Chickasaws impossible. In the early eighteenth century, both the Illinois and the Chickasaws were rapidly expanding their influence in the middle Mississippi River Valley, and the two nations fought for decades to secure control of the territory. So, in order to make peace, during the 1720s and 1730s, Chickasaws insisted that the French stop their Illinois allies from raiding their villages. They also requested the return of Chickasaw prisoners who were held within Illinois communities. The French were powerless to meet Chickasaw demands.[3]

The French were unable to force their Illinois to stop attacking the Chickasaws, and some officials ultimately came to see the ongoing Illinois and Chickasaw violence as an opportunity smooth over the blunders of the Natchez War in the south and the Meskwaki Wars in the north. Over the course of the second half of the seventeenth century, French officials and colonists forged alliances and settlements with Anishinaabeg polities of the Great Lakes (including Odawa, Ojibwe, Potawatomi, and other peoples) and the polities of the Illinois Confederacy in the Illinois River Valley (including Peorias, Kaskaskias, Tamaroa, Cahokias, and others). Settlers in the French colony in Illinois country did not live in quite as close proximity to Indigenous settlements during the eighteenth century as did their counterparts in Lower Louisiana, but they were similarly dependent on their Native allies. Consequently, when their Native neighbors sparred with other Indigenous polities, French settlers in Upper Louisiana could become caught in the fray. Such was the case when Anishinaabeg and Illinois Confederacy peoples clashed with the Meskwakis (Fox) and their Sauk, Kickapoo, and Winnebago allies in a series of violent conflicts that spanned from the late seventeenth century through the 1720s. These conflicts exposed French travelers to attacks, and they endangered French claims in the region. Therefore, in the decades around the turn of the eighteenth century, the French administration in Illinois worked hard to sustain alliances with all these Indigenous groups and to force Meskwakis and their allies into peace with the powerful Anishinaabeg polities and Illinois Confederacy.[4]

But the French could not make their desire for harmony among their Indigenous allies a reality. The settler governments in Illinois and Lower Louisiana did not have the power to force their Illinois and Anishinaabeg allies to stop raiding either the Chickasaws or the Meskwakis. Moreover, French desires to make peace in order to defend their empire from English incursions did not align with the political goals of the Anishinaabeg and Illinois. The dozens of Indigenous groups that made up the Illinois Confederacy and Anishinaabe polities were calibrating a series of geopolitical strategies that involved Dakota, Chickasaw, Haudenosaunee, Cherokee, and many other nations and factors beyond France's narrow focus on the contest between European powers. Additionally, Anishinaabeg and Illinois warriors were economically incentivized to continue their

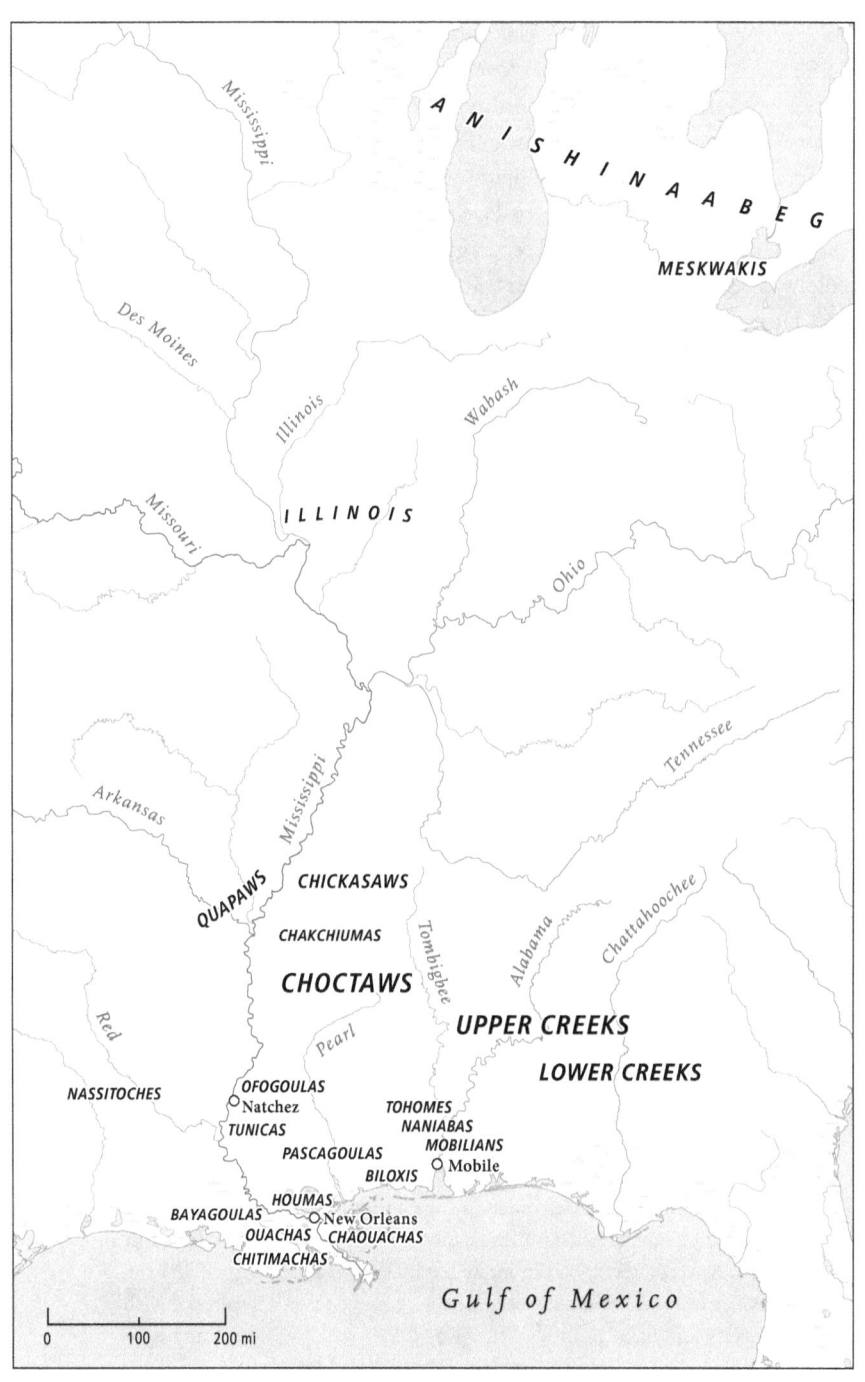

Figure 13. Selected nations circa 1734.

raids as colonists in Upper Louisiana and New France remained eager to purchase Meskwaki captives even as their governments formally pursued peace with these nations. Similarly, French colonists in Lower Louisiana continued to buy and sell captive Chickasaws. During the war, French soldiers captured Chickasaw women and children, and they dragged many of these Chickasaw prisoners back to New Orleans where they would be enslaved in colonial households. For all of these reasons, during the 1730s the French governments in Louisiana and the Illinois colony decided to wage an all-out war against the Chickasaws.[5]

During the early years of the Chickasaw conflict, Indigenous people, rather than the French army, did most of the fighting and bore the majority of the losses. While the French were not able to launch a full offensive until 1736, by 1732, Gov-

Figure 14. Painting of Indigenous people from a variety of nations in New Orleans in 1735 by Alexander de Batz. From left to right: an enslaved Meskwaki woman, visiting Illinois men, an enslaved African child, and an Ishak/Atakapa man. Alexander de Batz, *Desseins de Sauvages de Plusieurs Nations*, 1735, Peabody Museum, object 41-72-10/2. Reproduced with permission of the Peabody Museum of Archaeology and Ethnography, Harvard University, Cambridge.

ernor Périer was already mobilizing Petites Nations and Choctaws against the Chickasaws. In April of that year, the Choctaws attacked the Chickasaws and set their fields of corn ablaze. The Chickasaws quickly reached out to their Chakchiuma kin for help. They hoped that the Chakchiumas could intervene on their behalf and convince the Choctaws to make peace with their nation. However, when these diplomatic endeavors failed to produce results, the Chickasaws retaliated against both the Choctaws and the Chakchiumas, and in January 1733 joint Chickasaw and Natchez forces attacked the Chakchiuma villages.[6]

During the early phase of the Chickasaw conflict, the same Petites Nations that had been on the frontlines of the Natchez War continued to be key players in this next French imperial fight. As the Tunicas and Ofogoulas continued to track down surviving Natchez, by 1732 they also began to assist the French against the Chickasaws. In that year, combined groups of Chickasaws and Natchez raided the French settlement at Pointe Coupée, then passed into Tunica and Ofogoula homelands. So Tunicas and Ofogoulas were incentivized to join this fight to defend their people. Petites Nations not only supplied provisions and services to the French troops but they also contributed essential intelligence that helped the French commanders identify groups who were responsible for attacks on French and Petites Nations villages. For example, during a 1732 raid on Pointe Coupée and the Tunica villages, Natchez warriors left painted clubs bearing a declaration of war in a Tunica field. In this instance, Tunica assistance enabled French soldiers to read the marked clubs, so they understood that the Natchez intended to continue to fight, and that Pointe Coupée should be prepared for additional attacks.[7]

The Quapaws also provided essential support throughout both the Natchez and Chickasaw Wars, and they remained among France's most steadfast allies during this era. Like the Ofogoulas and Tunicas, they tracked down Natchez refugees in the lands north of Natchez after the war and led independent raids against Chickasaws in the 1730s. The Quapaws were committed to maintaining a French alliance as part of their foreign policy. In the 1730s, the French Empire also happened to be fighting several of its historical enemies.[8]

In response to the Quapaw and Petites Nations raids, Chickasaws targeted French and Petites Nations across the Lower Mississippi Valley. In 1732 Chickasaw raids into Mobilian, Naniaba, and Tohomes homelands drew many Mobile River nations into the conflict. At the end of March, Chickasaw raiders attacked Mobilian, Naniaba, and Tohome villages, as well as French settlements at Mobile, carrying off nine Tohome women and children. These Petites Nations worked quickly with their French allies to launch a retaliatory raid against the

Chickasaws and attempt to rescue their lost kin. In this attack, the combined Tohome, Mobilian, and Naniaba forces managed to both recover the captive women and children and kill twenty-two Chickasaws. The French lauded this assault as "une victoire complète!"[9] Throughout the 1730s, Mobilians, Naniabas, Tohomes, and other Mobile River nations continued to support the French fight against the Chickasaws in defense of their homelands and the multinational settlements at Mobile. They worked closely with the Chickasawhay Choctaws who had long been their allies, and continued to serve as guides, porters, and intelligence gatherers between the French and Choctaw nations. Petites Nations also directly supported French and Choctaw military endeavors. For example, during the French campaign against the Chickasaws in 1736, the Naniabas, Tohomes, Apalachees, Mobilians, and Chatots served alongside their Chickasawhay allies and French troops in a coordinated attack on Chickasaw villages.[10]

French settlers' and Petites Nations' mutual needs for support and defense during the Chickasaw conflict led to a renewal and improvement of diplomatic relationships among Petites Nations and their French allies across Lower Louisiana. The French officials were deeply grateful for the Petites Nations' assistance, and by the mid-1730s they again saw these nations as invaluable allies and integral parts of French settlements. The Petites Nations' support for French military endeavors and political initiatives during the 1730s indicated a remarkable change for many of the Mobile River nations' relationships with the Louisiana government from only a few years prior. As recently as 1729, the relationships among Mobilian, Naniaba, and Tohome leaders and the French were strained and fraying. By the end of the 1720s, the Mobilians, Naniabas, and Tohomes were all so frustrated with the French administration's treatment of their people and their failure to adequately respect or compensate them for their labor that some, like Tonty, the leader of the Mobilians, even refused to render small services to their French allies. Thus, while Mobilians, Naniabas, and Tohomes had remained engaged in interdependent economic exchange with their French neighbors, on the eve of the Natchez War the French were no longer treating them as essential diplomatic allies.[11]

Chickasaw attacks on the Mobile River settlements renewed both the French and Petites Nations' needs for military support, and this in turn revived Louisiana officials' commitments to treat these smaller nations as valuable diplomatic partners. This shift in attitudes is perhaps most visible when comparing Tonty's refusal in 1729 to provide porters for French officials with his military support and intelligence sharing with the French in the mid-1730s. In 1734 several Choctaw leaders approached the Mobilians and asked this Petite Nation to join an alliance with the Chickasaws. These Choctaws were working with the Chickasaws to oust the French from Mobile Bay, so they asked the Mobilians to assist them by attacking their French neighbors. This group of Choctaws sought to force the Mobilians to support their political strategy by threatening that if the Mobilians did not join their partnership with the Chickasaws and English, the Choctaws would fall on the settlements and attack both the Mobilians and the French. Choctaw towns enjoyed tremendous autonomy so not only could the four political divisions pursue separate diplomatic agendas but individual towns could also negotiate independently with foreign nations. Instead of giving in to this intimidation from the Chickasaw-allied Choctaws, Tonty refused their proposition and reported the incident to the commander of the Mobile Fort. This dire warning rightfully unnerved him, and the commander promptly ordered all the French inhabitants to be on their guard and to carry arms at all times. The very real threat of attacks from their powerful Chickasaw and Choctaw neighbors pushed Petites Nations and Louisiana settlers back into interdependent political relations.[12]

Still, not all Petites Nations benefited from bellicose French policies. French conflict with the Natchez and Chickasaws during the 1730s wrecked the fragile web of alliances that had buffered the Chakchiumas from the worst of the colonial violence of the first thirty years of the century. The war also forced the Chakchiumas into a closer partnership with the French. Following the breakdown of relations with the Chickasaws and their subsequent raid in 1732, Chakchiuma leaders reached out to both the Choctaws and French to ask for help defending their people. Their homelands along the upper Yazoo River had become a battleground and a dangerous place for Chakchiuma families. The military leader of the Western Division town of Coëchitto, whom the French knew by his official leadership title, Red Shoe (Soulier Rouge), offered the Chakchiumas sanctuary alongside his village.[13] Red Shoe had kin among the Chakchiumas and his town held an especially close relationship with this Petite Nation. However, Governor Bienville had other plans. Instead of having the Chakchiumas go to Coëchitto, where he feared the combined Chakchiuma and Coëchitto forces would be dangerous to French interests, he convinced the Chakchiumas and Choctaws that this Petite Nation should resettle further south along the Yazoo River near the site of the former Koroa and Yazoo towns and the French fort St. Pierre. From there, they would be able to monitor the river and gather intelligence for the French. Bienville also hoped that this location would allow the Chakchiumas to help defend French settlements further downriver at Natchez and Pointe Coupée. For several years, Bienville's plan worked, and the Chakchiumas even conducted raids against the Chickasaws. However, in 1736, just as the French were preparing for the first large-scale campaign by Louisiana and Illinois troops against the Chickasaws, the Chakchiuma and French alliance came crashing down.[14]

By the end of 1735, both the Chakchiumas and Chickasaws were tired of this incessant conflict, and the Chickasaws reached out to the French, Choctaws, and Chakchiumas to make peace. Even during the Chickasaw Wars, the Chickasaw diplomats had held out hope that they could negotiate an end to this conflict with the French. So, in early 1736, the Chakchiumas brought peace negotiations to the Tunicas and the Nassitoches, and they discussed the possibility of forming a trade partnership with the British and Chickasaws. The war had exacerbated Louisiana's shortages, and all three nations were eager for better access to European merchandise. However, the Tunica leadership was divided over how to respond to the Chakchiumas, and some Tunicas were wary of this scheme. While one of the senior Tunica leaders traveled to the Nassitoches to discuss this proposition, two junior military leaders traveled to New Orleans to inform Governor Bienville of the plan.

Bienville responded to the news of this trade alliance as though the Tunica leaders were reporting a heinous betrayal. Bienville was in the process of planning a large-scale assault on the Chickasaw villages, so the prospect of Chickasaws and British gaining access to the Pointe Coupée and Natchitoches posts risked destabilizing the whole upper region of the colony. In a letter to his superior back in France, Bienville confided that he believed this plot to be even "more dangerous than that of the Natchez," and demanded violent retribution for the Tunicas' and Chakchiumas' duplicity.[15]

The two Tunica leaders may well have regretted their decision to inform Bienville of the Chakchiumas' proposals. The governor responded to the Tunica leaders with a thinly veiled threat and demanded that the Tunicas attack their would-be Chakchiuma allies. He also offered to recognize both young leaders as the primary political representatives of their nation in lieu of the senior Tunica leader. He promised to forgive the Tunicas for their involvement in this affair if they were willing to demonstrate their loyalty by raiding the Chakchiuma villages. Implicit in this offer was the potential for the French to attack and enslave the Tunicas as they had the Chitimachas, Natchez, Chickasaws, and now Chakchiumas. The Tunicas accepted Bienville's offer, and returned home to the unenviable task of conveying to their fellow villagers the obligation they had just made on behalf of their nation. As the junior leaders explained to their people, they had to comply with this request or risk French vengeance. The Tunicas did ultimately carry out Bienville's orders with the support of the local commander at Pointe Coupée. In a deadly surprise assault, Tunica and French men killed half of the Chakchiuma men and carried off twelve children and women whom they gifted to the French as captives. The Tunicas' compliance with Bienville's orders ultimately helped ensure both better trade and better alliances between the French and the Tunicas. The attack reaffirmed French confidence in the nation and ushered in a period of economic prosperity and interdependence between the Tunicas and French at Pointe Coupée that sustained both peoples throughout the 1740s and 1750s. By contrast, this assault had devastating consequences for the Chakchiumas. Those who first fled to seek refuge with their old allies the Taposas, and then found more permanent refuge alongside the Coëchitto village of the Western Choctaws. Nevertheless, the Chakchiuma nation would never fully recover.[16]

Bienville's approach to punishing the Chakchiumas for their involvement in this trade alliance further strained Louisiana's relationship with the Western Choctaws. The French-orchestrated attack on the Chakchiumas was especially upsetting to the Choctaws of the Western Division town of Coëchitto. Like many Western Choctaws, the people of Coëchitto had long-standing relationships with the Chickasaws, and by 1736 they had grown resentful of continued French pressure to fight this neighboring nation. In fact, in that year Coëchitto was considering a plan to have the entire Chickasaw village of Ackia relocate to Choctaw homelands and settle alongside the Coëchittos. This proposition is remarkable not just because most of the Choctaws were at war with the Chickasaws but also because in the same months that the Coëchitto people considered offering refuge to these Chickasaws, other Choctaw leaders were planning a massive attack with the French on the Chickasaw village of Ackia (as well as Tchoukafalaya and Apeony).[17]

Red Shoe was furious and grief-stricken to learn of the attack on the Chakchiumas, and moved quickly to try to protect the survivors. In this moment of crisis, the Coëchitto Choctaws offered the Chakchiumas refuge alongside their village. After the Chakchiuma survivors were resettled, Red Shoe pursued the return of their enslaved kin who had been captured during the Tunica and French raid. Red Shoe made it clear that Coëchitto's support in the Chickasaw War hinged on the return of these women and children. The French and Tunicas had slain Red Shoe's Chakchiuma brother and uncle in the attack, and he felt compelled to respond to these killings. Either he could seek revenge by attacking Louisianans, or the French could cover the deaths of his kin by returning the other captives. Bienville realized that losing the support of the Western Choctaws had the potential to sabotage the French war effort. So he tracked down and purchased all twelve captives from the individual French settlers who held them in bondage, and returned these traumatized survivors to their families. While the Coëchittos remained deeply angry with the French, they complied with the bargain that Red Shoe had struck with the governor, and later that year they attacked the Chickasaw villages as promised.[18]

The year 1736 marked a significant turning point in the war. During this year, the Louisiana and Illinois governments launched the first major campaigns led by French troops against the Chickasaws. That spring, with the support of Illinois, Choctaw, Quapaw, Haudenosaunee, and Petites Nations allies, two forces, one from Lower Louisiana and one from Illinois, planned to converge in a multipronged attack on the Chickasaw villages. The Lower Louisiana military troops included French soldiers and free and enslaved Africans, as well as Apalachees, Chatots, Mobilians, Naniabas, Tohomes, and Chickasawhay Choctaws. However, poor communication and coordination between Bienville's troops and their Illinois counterparts led to disaster. The Illinois troops arrived too early and the formidable Chickasaw warriors cut down their army. The first wave of attackers also tipped off the Chickasaws off that there would be a second assault so the Chickasaws were well prepared for the arrival of Louisiana forces from the south. The women sung war songs to encourage the men, and the Chickasaw warriors ambushed the Louisiana forces, killing many French and dispersing their Indigenous allies. In this critical moment, the Chickasaws valiantly defended their homelands and villages from a massive, international military force, and they reveled in their triumph. The two major Chickasaw victories in 1736, along with the news that the Chickasaws had managed to capture and execute several prominent French commanders and soldiers, unnerved French settlers in Illinois and Louisiana. These epic blunders also infuriated France's Choctaw and Illinois allies who had sustained losses and devoted significant manpower to these campaigns. Indeed, Choctaw leaders like Red Shoe mocked the French for their inability to achieve victory in battle, especially since only a year prior, Choctaws had led an independent and highly successful campaign against a Chickasaw town in which they killed nearly fifty Chickasaws while losing only five men.[19]

The Chickasaw War strained the relationships among the four Choctaw divisions and left the polity divided about how to handle the Louisiana government's continuing appetite for war. While Choctaws from the Eastern, Western, and Chickasawhay divisions all supported the French, by 1735 some Choctaw towns and political leaders began to oppose this war and call for peace with the

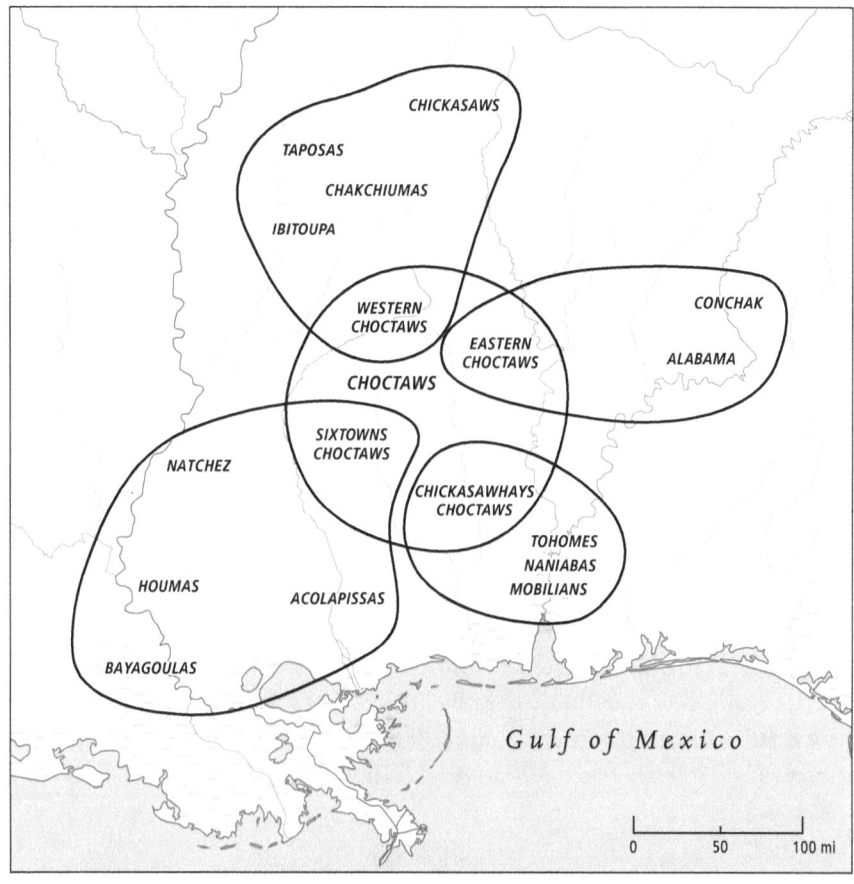

Figure 15. Four political divisions of the Choctaw nation and their allies. After Galloway, *Choctaw Genesis*, 313.

Chickasaws. As was the case with the Choctaw diplomats who approached the Mobilians in 1735 to ask them to sever their alliances with the French, some leaders even called for an outright break with Louisiana. After the French failures in 1736, these sentiments only grew stronger. In 1738 the Capinans and Biloxis near Mobile reported that groups of Choctaws were again planning to attack both of their nations and the French. This threat led the Biloxis and Pascagoulas to temporarily abandon their villages and relocate to the shelter of the small islands off the Gulf Coast. Similar concerns may have been the driving factor in motivating the Tohomes to leave their homes and seek refuge within the Eastern Division of the Choctaw nation during this era. Other Choctaw leaders decided to pursue independent negotiations with the Chickasaws. In 1738, while the French were formally still at war and in the process of orchestrating another large assault on the Chickasaws, Red Shoe was meeting with Chickasaw diplomats and trying to negotiate peace between Coëchitto and the Chickasaws.[20]

Red Shoe's relationship with Louisiana officials did not improve in the following years as the French continued to press on with the Chickasaw War and ask for Choctaw support for their campaigns. Bienville spent 1738 and 1739 recruiting Indigenous allies up and down the Mississippi River to join the French in the next wave of attacks on the Chickasaw villages. The French asked both their Choctaw and Illinois Confederacy allies to commit to long campaigns including a siege of the Chickasaw villages. This strategy required too much logistical support and too much time for a large international army without a strong supply chain. Choctaw and Illinois Confederacy warriors were tired of waiting and wasting time away from their villages, and many grew weary of the conflict. For the Chickasaws, the appearance of amassing forces convinced their leaders to again seek peace, and they reached out to the French troops to begin negotiations. Thus, what was supposed to be a major French offensive slowly ground to a halt when the Chickasaws and French, both exhausted by this decade-long conflict, negotiated a peace in 1740. Rather than being able to declare a grand victory, the Louisiana governor was instead left with an unceremonious draw and increasingly strained relationships with his Indigenous allies.[21]

The Choctaw Civil War

During the 1740s, the Chakchiumas were once again at the center of a violent conflict that was the result of hawkish colonial policies. The Choctaw Civil War of 1747–50 was partially caused by economic shortages, partly by imperial anxiety, and partly by Louisiana settlers' refusal to comply with the social and political ethics of the Native Southeast. From 1744 to 1748, the War of the Austrian Succession exacerbated trade shortages within the French colony. The scarcity made the Petites Nations even more vital suppliers of food and goods in the colony. However, these shortages also caused significant problems for both larger and smaller nations that relied on French networks to supply their people with tools, cloth, and weapons. To make matters worse, in the mid-1740s, Louisiana administrators increased the prices of Indian trade goods by upwards of 50 percent. For villages like Coëchitto, where Choctaws were already angered by France's conduct during the Chickasaw War and against their Chakchiuma allies, the increased economic pressure of the mid-1740s provided yet another incentive for their nation to reestablish trade relations with the British. As Red Shoe and other Western Choctaw leaders resumed relations with the British, French officials continued to insist on their rights to hold exclusive trade and political alliances with the Choctaws. The seeds of this discontent that had been sown in the Chickasaw conflicts of the 1730s, began to take root in the early 1740s as economic strain and French inflexibility exacerbated tensions among Western Choctaws and the Louisiana government. Ultimately this frustration grew into open war between the Western Choctaws who sought to expand their alliances with the British, and the Eastern Choctaws who were committed to supporting the French. This political split once again positioned the Chakchiumas in the center of a bloody transnational conflict. During this war, the decisions made by the Chakchiumas not only shaped the direction and expansion of this violence beyond the Choctaw homelands but also ultimately led to international agreements that promised to finally bring peace to the region.

The Chickasaw conflicts of the 1730s had done permanent damage to many of the Choctaw villages' relationships with the Louisiana settlers. During the war with the Chickasaws, the Louisiana government had demonstrated weakness, unskillful combat, and a willingness to use extreme violence toward their Indigenous enemies. The Choctaws were also troubled by the French administration's renewed drive to pursue conflict with the Chickasaws in the 1740s. Despite the peace agreements in 1740, Chickasaws continued to conduct small raids against Louisiana settlers, and French officials therefore called for the Choctaws to attack the Chickasaws in retribution. In reality, the end of the Chickasaw War brought a cession of formal hostilities, but it did not bring real peace to the Lower Mississippi Valley for either the French or the Chickasaws. Moreover, this war dealt a powerful blow to France's efforts to control the middle Mississippi River Valley.[22]

France's entanglement in two major imperial wars during the 1740s and 1750s added to the colonial officials' anxieties about the security of the Louisiana colony. Between 1744 and 1748, a conflict over the succession of the Austrian throne led France to join Spain in a war against the British and their Habsburg allies. Then, in 1756 France again entered into war with the British, this time as part of the major transatlantic conflict that became known as the Seven Years' War. Most of the fighting in the War of the Austrian Succession took place in Europe, but the Seven Years' War pulled Native nations into battles across eastern North America and required French administrations in New France to rely heavily on military support from their Anishinaabeg, Illinois, and other Indigenous allies. While none of the fighting in either of these conflicts occurred in the Lower Mississippi Valley, French officials were prepared for this possibility. During the entire course of their tenure in the Lower Mississippi Valley, the French administration received no more than 5,000 French troops, so they could not rely on Louisiana soldiers alone to defend the colony. Moreover, both the Louisiana and Illinois colonies continued to serve as buffers against British expansion, and this imperial strategy depended heavily on France's alliances with local Native nations. Unlike the British colonies along the Eastern Seaboard that had rapidly expanded during the eighteenth century, the populations in Illinois and Louisiana remained small. In fact, by the conclusion of the Seven Years' War in 1763, the entire colonial population of both enslaved and free inhabitants in the Lower Mississippi Valley was fewer than 10,000 people, while the population of the British-American colonies was closer to 1,500,000. So France's ability to hold these territories and defend French economic networks was entirely dependent on their relationships with both large and small Native nations. This reality made the French administration especially wary of British dealings with Louisiana's Native neighbors.[23]

In 1743 Red Shoe attempted to make peace with the Chickasaws independently and to bring his people into a trade alliance with the British. In response, the Louisiana governor, Pierre de Rigaud, marquis de Vaudreuil, actively worked to undermine Red Shoe and to isolate the leader within his nation. Red Shoe's growing influence within the Choctaw nation concerned the Louisiana officials, and when the War of the Austrian Succession began in 1744, the charismatic Choctaw leader's endeavors to forge alliances with France's enemies appeared even more insidious. By 1745 Vaudreuil had refused to recognize Red Shoe as a leader of the Western Choctaws or to supply his village with trade and diplomatic gifts. This strategy, which was designed to convince Red Shoe to cut off his trade with France's enemies and undermine the prominent leader, ultimately worked to the opposite effect and effectively forced Red Shoe and the Coëchittos into the arms of the British.[24]

The civil war that began among the Choctaw nation in 1747 was largely caused by political and economic pressures, but it was French insistence on their right to enact multiple forms of physical violence against Choctaws within the nation that provided the final catalysts for the war. First, in two different incidents in 1745, Choctaw leaders lodged complaints about French traders who had raped Choctaw women. In that year, one French trader had sexually assaulted a Chickasawhay woman and another raped Red Shoe's Coëchitto wife. The women and men of both Choctaw divisions demanded justice. In the matriarchal Choctaw villages, women had rights to bodily autonomy, and violence against women was a serious offense. Red Shoe likely felt obligated to seek retribution against the French for the sexual assault of his intimate partner. During this era, many enslaved Indigenous women were subject to sexual violence within colonial society, but the power of the Choctaw nation seems to have largely insulated free Choctaw women from this kind of harm and exploitation at the hands of colonizers. This offense was therefore neither common nor acceptable, and it engendered profound anger within the villages. In fact, when the Chakchiumas learned of the French trader's rape of their Coëchitto neighbor, they promptly sent diplomats to the Chickasaws to solicit support for the Coëchittos.[25]

The final sparks that set off the war came in 1746, when Red Shoe ordered the killing of three French traders who passed through his village and the French retaliated by ordering the assassination of this powerful Western Choctaw leader. During the previous year, French-allied Choctaws had killed two British traders, and Red Shoe's British allies desired revenge for their kinsmen's deaths. Additionally, several Eastern Choctaws had killed a Chickasaw diplomat and his wife as they traveled to the Western towns to confirm the peace agreements between the Chickasaws and Western Choctaws. Understandably, neither the Chickasaws nor the British wanted the Choctaws to assume that there would be no consequences for killing their men, and after being cut off from the French, Red Shoe could not afford to allow his relationship with the British to collapse. The archaeologist Patricia Galloway has argued that Red Shoe dealt with the British desire for vengeance in a way that allowed him to avoid seeking retribution against men of his own nation—by killing the Choctaws who had killed the British, which surely would have begun a cycle of internecine violence—and that still provided satisfaction to his trading partners. Therefore, instead of covering the deaths of the British and these Chickasaw diplomats with the deaths of other Choctaws, Red Shoe ordered the execution of these three French traders. The Louisiana governor responded to news of these killings by demanding the heads of three Choctaws and placing a bounty on the head of Red Shoe himself. These moves created a crisis, because the French officials would not accept alternative justice in lieu of deaths of more Choctaws, and they demanded that the Choctaws exact this unjust punishment on their own people. This was precisely what Red Shoe had sought to avoid. He understood the implications of these killings all too well, and when the French finally managed to convince the Choctaws to carry out this European-style punishment, the consequences were deadly. After several failed assassination attempts, in June 1747 Red Shoe was killed by a group of Eastern Choctaws.[26]

The combination of political and economic pressures and violent attacks—the French supply shortages and efforts to scuttle Western Choctaw and Chickasaw peace talks; the killing of the French traders, British traders, and of Chickasaw diplomats; the assassination of Red Shoe; and the sexual violence against Choctaw women—led to the outbreak of a brutal war among the Choctaws. In this war, the Eastern Choctaws, who were supported by the French and some of the Sixtowns and Chickasawhays, fought the Western Choctaws, who were supported by the British, Chakchiumas, other Chickasawhays, and the Chickasaws. This was an awful era for Choctaws. More than eight hundred Western Choctaw warriors died in the conflict, and the total number of dead was likely much higher. This war also led to the complete destruction of several Choctaw villages. In 1748 Eastern Choctaw warriors attacked Red Shoe's former home village of Coëchitto and the neighboring village of the Chakchiumas. These warriors burned the villages and killed or chased the inhabitants from their lands. Six Chakchiumas died in this assault, and the rest abandoned their homes and fled. These Chakchiumas reached out to their Chickasaw allies and through the practice of refugee sanctuary were again able to find safe haven and resettle their people alongside the Chickasaws.[27]

Chakchiumas played significant roles in the fighting of this war both while they lived alongside Coëchitto and once they took refuge with the Chickasaws. The Chakchiumas' decision to target not only Eastern Choctaws but also joint French and Petites Nations settlements expanded the conflict beyond the bounds of the Choctaw nation. During 1748 Chakchiumas and Coëchitto Choctaws jointly attacked French settlers at Natchez, outside of Mobile, and along the German Coast (a colonial settlement area along the lower western bank of the Mississippi). These attacks were not just about killing French or Petites Nations people. Rather, they seem to have been specifically designed to instill fear and provide a way for Chakchiumas to seek retribution for violence the French had orchestrated against their people. For example, during their raid against the Natchez post, Chakchiumas killed a French soldier who had been out fishing, then left his broken body along with painted clubs that identified their nation. This attack frightened the small force at the Natchez post and led them to rely more heavily on their Ofogoula allies for military support and provisions instead of venturing outside themselves. Reflecting back on the war in 1751, Vaudreuil remembered the destruction and fear caused by the Chakchiuma attacks against vulnerable French settlements. As he concluded, "This small number of Chakchiumas did us more harm during that war than the revolting Choctaws."[28]

Chakchiuma and Western Division Choctaw assaults on French settlers again provided opportunities for the Petites Nations. Following the spate of attacks in 1748, Vaudreuil reached out to Petites Nations across Louisiana for assistance. Some, like the Tunicas, offered their services to local French outposts when they heard of these raids. Many Petites Nations were also incentivized to support the French for fear of Choctaw attacks on their own villages. In response to their French allies' pleas for assistance, Biloxis and Pascagoulas patrolled the bayous outside of New Orleans, the Houmas watched over the German Coast, Tunicas and Ofogoulas defended the Pointe Coupée and Natchez posts, and Mobilians guarded the settlements near Mobile. The Louisiana governor was grateful for this support and ensured that the Petites Nations were compensated for their services. Perhaps more critically, Louisiana's military needs gave the Petites Nations bargaining leverage, and forced French officials to be flexible on policies like trade goods prices and punishment of French deserters who were returned by Petites Nations warriors.[29]

From their villages within the Choctaw nation, the Tohomes also provided essential aid to the Eastern Choctaw and French war effort. During the 1730s, many Tohomes left their Mobile homelands to live alongside Choctaw villages, remaining there during the 1740s. Traditionally, the Tohomes and other Mobile River nations had held the closest relationships with the Chickasawhays, but during the Choctaw Civil War, the Tohomes most closely allied with the Eastern Division. The Chickasaw conflicts of the 1730s had caused ruptures among the Chickasawhay leaders, and some had argued in favor of an alliance with the British, including Mongoulacha Mingo, a Chickasawhay leader with whom the Tohomes had been especially close. However, by the outbreak of the war in 1747, the Tohomes had decided to firmly align themselves with the Eastern Division, and a Tohome man even attempted to assassinate Red Shoe when the Louisiana government demanded his head. During the war itself, a man known as "The Grand Tohome" led Choctaw troops in an attack on the Western Division, and this Tohome leader also acted as a diplomat and attempted to recruit Alabamas, Tallapoosas, Cowetas, and Abhikas to the Eastern Division's cause.[30]

This war lasted for three years until, in 1750, the Western Division Choctaws, who were by then exhausted and had suffered heavy casualties, negotiated peace with the Eastern Choctaws. In order to bring the fighting to a close and renew their trade and political relationship with Louisiana, Choctaw representatives also signed peace accords with the French. Among the terms the French insisted on was one that obligated the Western Division Choctaws to ban all British traders from Choctaw villages, and another that Choctaws would "continue to make war against the Chickasaw until they are entirely destroyed."[31] By this point, France's wars with the Chickasaws had reduced the Chickasaw population to fewer than 2,500 people, so this demand was more about focusing the Choctaws' energies away from Louisiana than any serious threat from the Chickasaws. In effect, the brutal drive of the Louisiana government to use the Chickasaws to control their Choctaw allies and to wage a proxy war against the British continued throughout the entire period between 1730 and 1760.[32]

The highly destructive Chickasaw conflict and the Choctaw Civil War of the 1730s and 1740s destroyed the ability of the Chakchiumas to resume their former existence as an autonomous Petite Nation along the upper Yazoo River. In the decades after these wars, the Chakchiumas remained within the Chickasaw and Choctaw nations and their people were gradually incorporated into their adopted nations until, by the mid-nineteenth century, their descendants had lost most of their national distinction. It is possible to tell their story as a tale of destruction and disappearance, but to do so would be to miss the way that refugee acceptance and multinational settlement—including welcoming smaller polities into larger Native nations while still respecting their autonomy (as the Coëchitto Choctaws had with the Chakchiumas)—enabled many of the Chakchiuma people to survive this colonial violence and build new relations. This accounting would likewise ignore the story of how Choctaw and Chickasaw willingness to take in refugees in dire situations helped them rebuild their own communities after a series of brutal conflicts that left many destroyed villages and families missing kin.[33]

Beyond the importance of their physical presence and population within the Choctaws and Chickasaws, the political and social connections of the Chakchiumas turned out to have a significant impact on the futures and geopolitical relations of their adoptive nations in the decade after the Choctaw Civil War. By analyzing relationships among Chakchiumas, Choctaws, and Chickasaws, the historian Greg O'Brien has demonstrated that the inclusion of Chakchiumas within these polities was actually critical to the process by which these nations finally made peace in the late 1750s. In 1756, when France and Britain became involved in another transatlantic imperial war, the Choctaws were faced once again with serious trade shortages and vigorous encouragement from the French to resume their war with the Chickasaws. However, by the outbreak of the Seven Years' War, many Choctaws were tired of both France's shortages of trade goods and their lust for war, and they again desired access to British merchandise and peace with their Southeastern Indigenous neighbors. In the summer of 1758, during a raid against the Choctaws, several Chickasaws captured a man who they believed to be Choctaw, but who turned out to be Chakchiuma. Upon his arrival in the Chickasaw villages, this Chakchiuma man managed to reach out to several other Chakchiumas who lived with the Chickasaws, and they ensured that his life was spared. This man then had the opportunity to convey to his Chickasaw captors that he thought that the Choctaws would be willing to make peace with the Chickasaws and trade with the British again. This captive Chakchiuma man may have been successful in his efforts to convince the Chickasaws that the Choctaws would be open to peace, because that winter the Choctaws sent a Chakchiuma diplomat to the Chickasaws to negotiate peace among the two nations. Following the Chakchiuma diplomat's successful trip in 1759, delegations from the Eastern, Western, and Sixtowns Choctaws traveled to the Chickasaws' villages to formalize a peace. Later that same year, the Choctaws also signed a treaty and trade agreement with the British. Effectively, the Chakchiumas' unique position as the kin of both nations, and their long-standing work building alliances among both polities finally brought an end to more than two generations of conflict. After these agreements in 1759, the Chickasaws and Choctaws never fought again.[34]

While the Choctaws and Chickasaws settled their long-standing grievances, their colonial allies went to war in a conflict that would again reshape the political landscape of the continent. After decades of growing tension between Britain and France over control of American continental territories and waters, in 1754 the young British lieutenant George Washington and the Seneca/Mingo leader Tanaghrisson led the ambush of a small French force in contested territory in western Pennsylvania. The killing of these French soldiers was the spark that launched France and Britain into an all-out war that began in the American interior and ultimately expanded across Europe. In North America, both empires relied heavily on their Indigenous allies to wage war. Many Native Americans from across the eastern woodlands, including Haudenosaunee, Abenakis, Miamis, Weas, Anishinaabeg, and Shawnees agreed to fight with the British or the French. These Indigenous peoples joined the war for their own reasons. Many nations saw this conflict as a chance to halt the invasions of British settlers into their homelands, or to expand their territories or trade opportunities, and they fought in ways that suited their peoples' specific military and political aims. For example, in the South, Cherokees first fought with the British, but then in 1758, after Virginia settlers murdered a group of Cherokees, the Cherokees switched sides and began attacking settlements in Virginia and Carolina. Between 1758 and 1761, they waged a parallel war against the British that was intertwined in this larger conflict but motivated by a desire to protect their communities rather than their allegiance to France. Similarly, the Catawbas joined the war not so much to support the British, but because the war was a way for them to avenge the losses their people had suffered from their Haudenosaunee enemies, who were supporting the French. The Petites Nations were far from the center of this conflict, and while their people experienced the dramatic trade shortages and economic strains that came from another war which drained French coffers, they were not directly involved in the fighting.[35]

The war went dreadfully for France. Undersupplied, undermanned, and heavily reliant on Indigenous allies whom they had antagonized for decades, the French forces could not sustain the long war, and in 1763 the French Crown sued for peace. Even though Petites Nations did not fight in the conflict, Britain's ultimate victory, and the subsequent collapse of the French Empire in North America would have massive consequences for their people in the coming decades. Most significantly, France would give up its Louisiana colony, abandoning its Petites Nations allies. In the coming decades, Petites Nations would confront both the Spanish and British Empires and they would need to develop new relationships and strategies as fresh colonial administrations moved into their homelands. This war, which fundamentally reoriented not just colonial power but also Indigenous politics and populations across the American East, heralded a new era of British policy and laid the framework for the coming of the American Revolution in the South. All of these momentous changes would come to shape Petites Nations diplomacy in the 1760s and 1770s.

In many ways, the twilight years of France's tenure in the Lower Mississippi Valley closely resemble the early era of French settlement in terms of the colony's relationships with its Indigenous neighbors. In 1763, following their loss of the Seven Years' War, France was forced to cede its North American colonies to Spain and Britain. After more than six decades in the Gulf South, the Louisiana colony had never manifested the kind of success that the French Crown and imperial boosters had envisioned for the colony, and they were never able to dominate the region's Native polities. Through the end of French rule, Louisiana's population remained concentrated in New Orleans and along the coast. In the scattered outposts and smaller colonial settlements alongside Petites Nations at Natchitoches, Pointe Coupée, Natchez, Mobile, and along the German Coast, French settlers remained deeply dependent on the support of their Native neighbors. The conflicts of the 1730s and 1740s and French fears about the danger posed by the Choctaws, the Chickasaws, and the British, enabled Petites Nations to renew alliances that had soured during the colonial boom of the 1720s and they maintained these relationships through the 1750s. For many Petites Nations, this was an era of economic revitalization.

For nations, like the Chakchiumas, that suffered rather than profited from France's wars with the Natchez, Chickasaws, British, and Choctaws, the Southeastern Indigenous practices of refugee sanctuary and multinational settlement continued to serve as the critical lifelines that sustained their people thorough times of crisis. The protections offered by these political practices preserved Indigenous lives, and by the close of the 1760s the Chakchiumas too had found peace by seeking refuge amid their larger Native allies. While their story would no longer be defined by their full autonomy as a Petite Nation, their legacy instead would be the restoration of Choctaw and Chickasaw communities at a time of great loss and the creation of a lasting peace after decades of brutal conflict.

CHAPTER 7

Tunica Power After the Seven Years' War

In October 1772, Lattanash, who had become the primary leader of the Tunicas, journeyed down the Mississippi River to the British Fort Bute to clear up a misunderstanding. Charles Stuart, the deputy superintendent of Indian affairs, suspected that the Tunicas were thinking of reneging on the alliance they had forged with the British. Stuart was also deeply concerned that the Tunicas might relocate their village and set up a new residence on the western side of the Mississippi in Spanish-controlled Louisiana. The British official had good reason to question the Tunicas' loyalty to his nation. He knew that groups of Tunicas frequently left British West Florida and spent days across the river in Spanish Louisiana. Even more disturbing, Stuart had recently heard that the Tunica chief was engaged in political negotiations with Spanish officials on the other side of the river. Lattanash hoped that a council with the British superintendent would allow him to assuage Stuart's concerns and explain his motives for meeting with the Spanish at Pointe Coupée. While Lattanash intended to convince Stuart that the Tunicas desired British friendship and wished to remain allies of the British king, the Tunica leader did not plan to apologize for his people's regular border crossings, or for his attempts to win the favor of the Spanish. Rather, as he would explain, the Tunicas desired "to be friends with all the white people near us" in what the Europeans considered to be Spanish Louisiana and British West Florida.[1] For Lattanash, and for the rest of the Tunicas, this territory remained Tunica land, regardless of the new colonial powers in the region, and his people would continue to care for their lands and move freely across the Mississippi as they had for decades.

Following the conclusion of the Seven Years' War, the Petites Nations had adapted to a changed colonial landscape. France had lost the war, and in exchange for peace, the French king Louis XV surrendered his country's North American territories. In 1763, after six decades of French presence in the Lower Mississippi Valley, the Crown ceded control of their territory in the region and abruptly severed their alliances with the Native peoples of these lands. To placate France's Spanish allies, who had assisted France during the war, Louis XV gave Spain the western half of Louisiana and then ceded the eastern territory to victorious Britain. The settlement left Spain with a wide stretch of land along the Gulf Coast from New Orleans to Texas. Britain in turn claimed the territory south of the Yazoo River and east of the Mississippi and called the province West Florida. In transferring control of this territory, French officials assumed they could also seamlessly shift the alliances they had built with the local Native nations to Spain and Britain.

Figure 16. The Lower Mississippi Valley circa 1770.

The two decades following the Peace of Paris were a tense time for all the peoples of the Lower Mississippi Valley. Native Southerners were apprehensive about the arrival of new colonists, and the incoming Spanish and British were also concerned about their ability to control their new territories. Both imperial governments anticipated another European conflict and saw the American Southeast as a likely future battleground. British officials in West Florida and Spanish officials in Louisiana kept cautious watch over their imperial rivals as they were each convinced that the other was plotting to invade and conquer their territories. What neither British nor Spanish officials initially understood was that the vast majority of these lands remained firmly under Indigenous control. Further north, the British Empire also faced challenges from the powerful Native nations that lived in Illinois and along the Great Lakes. British officials who were tasked with taking possession of formerly French colonial claims in the midcontinent and implementing British rule in Anishinaabeg, Illinois, and Shawnee homelands were met with powerful, militant, and transnational Indigenous resistance. The Odawa leader Pontiac, who helped shape and lead this movement, was gaining ground in 1763. As British representatives entered the Lower Mississippi Valley, it appeared as though they might not be able to actually take possession of the Anishinaabeg, Shawnee, Lenape, and other northern territories the French had ceded in the peace accords. Gaining access to and control of the Mississippi River was therefore critical to British imperial strategies, and this made imposing British power in West Florida a priority.[2]

As British and Spanish colonists arrived in the Lower Mississippi Valley in the 1760s, they became aware of the fragility of their claims to the region. Neither Spain nor Britain had sufficient soldiers to defend these territories on their own, and local Indigenous peoples posed real threats to their political ambitions. Therefore, both empires sought to forge alliances with Native nations in order to support their colonial designs. Throughout the 1760s and 1770s, the defensive strategies of Spanish Louisiana and British West Florida were largely focused on building relationships with their Indigenous neighbors.

Alliances with Petites Nations like the Tunicas were key components of these British and Spanish defensive plans. By the 1760s, most of these Petites Nations lived near the Mississippi River, and consequently, directly along the new European border. In a 1767 official brief given to the Spanish Council of the Indies, King Carlos III of Spain described this river as a "fixed and definite boundary for his royal possessions in North America."[3] To enforce this "fixed and definite" border, both Spain and Britain relied on local Indigenous nations. From their perspectives, the Petites Nations who lived directly along the Mississippi

River were in ideal locations to help regulate and maintain this boundary. However, these plans would be successful only if the colonists could secure loyalty from the Petites Nations. Imperial administrators fretted that entangled Native diplomatic commitments could compromise their military utility. To avoid conflict, Spanish officials and British Indian agents agreed to deal only with the Native nations that resided on their respective sides of the border. However, this policy did not work out quite so cleanly in practice. As Lattanash's attempts to ally with "all the white people" illustrate, this division of Indigenous lands and alliances did not function as Spanish and British officials had hoped.[4] In reality, this policy was a profound failure. Lattanash and other Petites Nations leaders did not feel that their people should be bound by these imperial map lines or strong-armed into exclusive alliances, so they developed strategies that forced colonial officials to negotiate on their nations' terms.[5]

Even though their community had fewer than one hundred people by 1770, Tunica leaders managed to reject the exclusivity demanded by the British and make their own diplomatic policies. They were able to do this in large part because of their continued practices of multinational settlement and extensive alliance networks.[6] As Honored Man of the Tunicas Mingo Tallaija forcefully articulated in 1772, "If the French King has given away his right to his people's lands, what is it to me? He has not given away my lands or myself."[7] By that time, their nation had been forcing the British to negotiate on Tunica terms for nearly a decade and they were confident that both British West Florida and Spanish Louisiana were sufficiently vested in maintaining alliances with their people that they would continue to accept Tunica terms. Through strategic military action and by demonstrating the power of his nation's alliances, Mingo Tallaija and other Tunica leaders knew they had proven to both the Spanish and the British the value of their political support.

Although many Petites Nations had been able to determine the conditions of their relationships with the French during previous decades, it is perhaps surprising that, even with such small populations during the 1760s and 1770s, Petites Nations continued to be able to pressure colonial governments and exert political influence. Despite decades of declining Petites Nations populations, these nations still constituted a sizable portion of the regional population after the Seven Years' War, and this gave them critical leverage. Even after decades of colonization and epidemics, there were still about 32,000 Native Americans within the colonial territories claimed by Louisiana in 1763. Choctaws, Chickasaws, and Creeks made up about 25,000 of these people and constituted the majority of the region's population. Roughly 7,000 (about 22 percent) of the

Indigenous peoples in this region were not part of these larger nations and chose to remain as small polities. By comparison, the entire non-Indigenous colonial population, including enslaved people, was only 9,300 people, which meant that Petites Nations people made up roughly 17 percent of the total number of residents in the Lower Mississippi River Valley. Given that there were only 4,000 people of European descent in all of Lower Louisiana in 1763, Petites Nations collectively continued to outnumber European settlers in the region.[8]

The Tunicas' history is distinct from those of the many Native Southerners who lost diplomatic power in the decades after the Seven Years' War. Indigenous nations further east who were already confronting an onslaught of British settlers, and who were now isolated from the French and Spanish, faced challenging times. Small nations in North Carolina, South Carolina, Virginia, and along the Ohio River Valley struggled to exercise diplomatic power and retain their lands after this imperial transition. While nations like the Catawba and Delaware found creative ways to cope with new pressures and sustain their communities, they struggled to force colonial governments to negotiate on their terms as they had in prior generations. By contrast, in the continental interior, many Native groups actually benefited from this transition. In the Illinois and Arkansas River Valleys, Indigenous peoples capitalized on the British and Spanish colonial governments' fears that they could not control the midcontinent. Native groups—including the Kickapoos, Peorias, and Quapaws—were therefore able to build new relationships with these European governments that greatly benefited their people.[9]

France's cession of Louisiana destroyed many of the political and economic networks that Gulf Coast nations relied on, but also opened up new possibilities. Because Native nations like the Tunicas were able to develop highly effective diplomatic strategies, many Petites Nations were able to capitalize on this transition and rebuild their communities after decades of loss during the imperial wars. For the Tunicas, this decade was actually a high point of political power.[10] The Tunicas' extensive alliance networks and their creative political strategies revitalized their nation at a crucial moment and helped their people not merely survive but thrive in this turbulent era.

Transitions and Uncertainty in the 1760s

In the spring of 1763, Petites Nations women whispered disturbing news of their French allies' intentions to leave the Lower Mississippi Valley. That summer, Indigenous leaders flocked to New Orleans to confirm these troubling rumors with the colonial governor. The men returned with bad tidings. Not only were their Louisiana allies leaving but British and Spanish settlers would arrive in their stead. Would these newcomers buy the salt, peaches, pottery, and chickens that Petites Nations men and women produced? Could Petites Nations turn to them for defense against the Creeks or Choctaws? And why had the French worked out such an odd arrangement for inviting foreigners into Petites Nations' homelands? Jean-Jacque-Blaise d'Abbadie, governor of Louisiana, informed the Petites Nations that their lands along the Mississippi River would be split into two territories. The lands to the east would now be British, and the lands to the west would be Spanish. Communities to the east of the river that did not wish to build relationships with the British would therefore need to resettle to the west. These bold demands and economic uncertainties left Petites Nations peoples wondering how best they might prepare their communities for the coming years.[11]

The following year, in 1764, British troops and officials began to arrive in Petites Nations homelands. However, rather than rolling into the region as a powerful occupying force, these newcomers struggled to exercise authority. Not only were the British unable to take full control of the territory but they also found themselves threatened by Indigenous nations even within the coastal colonial cities. Just months after his troops' arrival at Mobile, in March 1764, the British major Robert Farmar reported to the secretary of war that he and his men were surrounded by large numbers of armed Native Americans. His powder and provisions had all been soaked and rendered useless, and the conditions of the fort at Mobile were deplorable. As he explained, "The fort and the garrison [are] so very weak as makes it impossible to be supported or kept teneable [sic] in case of Rupture, so that every means of support for the Troops are at present expos'd to the ravages of the Savages."[12] British efforts to take the land by force were going dismally. By entering this territory without first establishing relationships with Indigenous nations, British officials violated the sociopolitical systems that had organized shared Petites Nations and European spaces for the better part of the century. Consequently, large and small nations responded with shows of military force.

The Tunicas' efforts to negotiate the imperial transition began as they were forced to confront one of these British invasions. In February 1764, ominous reports of the approach of four hundred British gunmen began to circulate among the small Native polities of the Lower Mississippi Valley. The French governor had asked their peoples to be peaceful and welcoming to the incoming colonists, but no British officials had come to meet with Tunica leaders. If the British were sending gunmen rather than emissaries up the river, the Tunicas reasoned that it could only mean they intended to make war.[13]

The Tunicas were aware that their northern neighbors were taking up arms against the British instead of passively accepting British incursions into their homelands. As they considered their next moves, they must have taken into account that the military leader Pontiac and many of the Anishinaabeg polities of the Great Lakes were organizing a large transnational alliance and military strategy to oppose British imperialism. Pontiac and his followers had heard the Delaware spiritual leader Neolin's message warning of the dangers of close relationships with Europeans, and promising the transformative power of a cultural revival and restoration of the old ways. The many nations of the Great Lakes who had been confronting growing settler pressure and violence from British merchants and officials hoped that a strong military response would remove the British from their lands and restore peace and prosperity to their people. Their militant message wound its way down the curves of the Mississippi River in late 1763. The Petites Nations surely empathized with Pontiac and his followers' frustration at British efforts to assume control of their homelands. Although the traffic in Native captives in the Southeast had diminished after the Yamasee War, Pontiac's message of the threat of economic enslavement by the British would have resonated with Petites Nations people whose parents and grandparents remembered the violence of the Charleston-based Indian slave trade.[14]

As word spread of the imminent British arrival, many of the Petites Nations that lived in the Mobile Bay region began to migrate westward to get away from the settlers and out of the crosshairs of Creek and Choctaw warriors. Creeks and Choctaws had intermittently fought and raided each other's villages over the course of the eighteenth century, and after a lull in conflict during the Seven Years' War, Creek and Choctaw violence escalated again. This made Mobile, which stood between Choctaw and Creek territories, a dangerous place for Native families. In 1764 most of the Biloxis, Pascagoulas, Chatots, and Mobilians relocated their villages from Mobile to the western side of the Mississippi River where they would be safer from Creek attacks and British traders. These groups asked to resettle near the Tunicas and Ofogoulas, building their new homes in the lands between Pointe Coupée and Natchez. Some migrated even further and established villages along the Red River. This created an extended multinational settlement in the Tunicas' homelands, thereby strengthening all the nations' defenses. While many Mobilians moved west to Tunica homelands, others followed their Tohome neighbors and sought refuge with Choctaw allies alongside Chickasawhay villages. Some Mobilians and Chatots also chose to retreat into Choctaw territory but remain in a separate joint settlement along the Amite

River.¹⁵ The mass exodus of Petites Nations from the Mobile Bay region dispersed Indigenous communities and families, but it also greatly strengthened the nations whose lands they migrated into or alongside.

Bolstered by these new migrants, and even more convinced of the need to act with urgency, the Tunicas and Ofogoulas developed a bold plan. In 1764 the Tunicas held lands on both sides of the river by Pointe Coupée, while the Ofogoulas lived entirely on the eastern bank near Natchez. The Tunica leaders, Bride-les-Boeufs (Buffalo Tamer) and Lattanash, talked at length with Perruquier (Wig Maker), the charismatic leader of the Ofogoulas, and they carefully evaluated the possible outcomes of allowing the British fleet to pass through their territories. Both Bride-les-Boeufs and Lattanash had fought in the Natchez War and provided leadership through the Chickasaw and Choctaw conflicts of the 1730s and 1740s. Perruquier was likewise an established military leader, and his record was so impressive that the French gave him the nickname Perruquier—which was most likely a reference to how he dispensed with enemies in combat rather than a commendation of his hairstyling talents. All three were experienced political and military leaders and knew well the risks of taking on the British.¹⁶

Their best hope would be to attack the British as soon as they crossed into Tunica territory. They would aim to demonstrate their military might and force the British to recognize their territories. The Tunicas and Ofogoulas needed to make it clear that foreign nations would not be able to cross their lands without forging relationships with their people. Both the Ofogoulas and Tunicas called on their allies and recruited support for their assault. Then, in the early damp spring of 1764, a group of Ofogoula, Avoyelle, Tunica, and Choctaw leaders met to plan their attack.¹⁷

Tunica Land, Tunica Power

On March 15, 1764, fifty Tunica, Ofogoula, Avoyelle, and Choctaw warriors crouched in the thick brush along the Mississippi River. They waited, muskets in hand, as they peered through the cypress and moss at the muddy water. The British regiment led by Major Arthur Loftus slowly paddled into Tunica territory. It had taken the soldiers three weeks to fight their way upriver from New Orleans against the heavy current and arrive at the river bend at the place the French called "Davion's Bluff" on Tunica land.¹⁸ The further they paddled from New Orleans, the deeper they moved into Indigenous territory, and dozens of soldiers had already deserted in fear. Pontiac and his envoys had traveled through the region barely a week before the arrival of the British flotilla, spreading their message of Indigenous power and calls for military resistance. The Odawa leader had come to visit the French Fort Chartres in Illinois to ask the commander for munitions, and he met with Native nations upriver from the Tunicas to encourage them to take up arms.[19] Further unnerving the soldiers, a First Nations man, who was traveling with Loftus as a guide, had informed the company that they would be attacked before they reached Natchez.[20] By the time of their arrival in Tunica territory, the soldiers were exhausted and on edge.

Under the cover of riverine vegetation, the Tunica coalition loaded their muskets and waited for all twelve vessels to round the bend. Then they fired. Lead flew from both banks as the warriors rammed powder and shot into their muskets for a second volley. The Tunica coalition could hear the soldiers shouting as they fired wildly at their unseen attackers and attempted to maneuver away from the banks. The deft shots of the Tunica, Avoyelle, Ofogoula, and Choctaw warriors killed six and wounded four soldiers before the bulk of the fleet even made it around the bend. Surrounded, and fearing that this was only the beginning of a major assault on his troops, Major Arthur Loftus gave the order to retreat. The frightened British oarsmen splashed and frantically paddled away. Defeated, they let the pull of the muddy river take them all two hundred miles back to New Orleans. The Tunica, Ofogoula, Choctaw, and Avoyelle coalition had repelled the entire regiment without sustaining a single casualty.[21]

The Tunicas had managed to thwart the British advance into their territory and had gotten the colonial government's attention, but still they needed to use this momentum to forge a relationship with British West Florida. Lattanash and Bride-les-Boeufs had anticipated British retaliation, so they sought temporary refuge with the Pakanas at their town near Mobile immediately after the assault. Once again, refugee sanctuary helped protect this Petite Nation from violence. During the 1760s, the Pakanas chose to move away from the bulk of the emerging Creek Confederacy, effectively becoming a Petite Nation. While they maintained ties with their Creek relatives and allies, the Pakanas lived independently during this era. The Pakanas took in the Tunicas and sent one of their leaders with Bride-les-Boeufs to New Orleans to facilitate negotiations with the French. Lattanash and Brides-les-Boeufs' decision to seek refuge with the Pakanas was a careful strategic choice. The Tunicas knew that the British would be hesitant to attack an ally of the Creeks, so their people would likely be safe. They were correct, and the British did not pursue them.[22]

In 1764 the Spanish had not yet arrived to occupy Louisiana, so d'Abbadie was still acting as the transitional French governor when Bride-les-Boeufs arrived.

The Tunica leader expressed his people's desire to return to the western banks of the Mississippi. He reminded the governor of the Tunicas' long record of service and alliance with the French and he explained that he now needed help to avoid British retribution. D'Abbadie offered the Tunicas and Pakanas the use of lands alongside the Acolapissas in the bayous of southern Louisiana until he was able to acquire a permanent land grant for them along the Red River. Bride-les-Boeufs and the Pakana leader agreed to this proposition and both of their nations crossed the Mississippi to seek refuge alongside the Acolapissas, safely out of the reach of British soldiers.[23] Lest French aid to the Tunicas create political turmoil, Governor D'Abbadie arranged for a meeting among the Tunicas, Ofogoulas, and British officials later that summer.

On a sweltering July day, the two Tunica leaders—Lattanash and Bride-les-Boeufs—and the Ofogoula leader Perruquier, met with the British captain Philip Pittman and d'Abbadie in New Orleans. Lattanash, Bride-les-Boeufs, and Perruquier confidently approached d'Abbadie and Pittman, their copper and shell bracelets and anklets gently clinking as they advanced. They stood proudly, displaying their French medals of alliance on ribbons around their necks and the prestigious tattoos that covered their arms, chests, and faces.[24] This imposing group listened calmly as d'Abbadie began by admonishing the leaders for the attack and explaining that it was the wish of their great French father that they befriend the British.[25] However, even in the presence of their French allies and this British official, Lattanash, Bride-les-Boeufs, and Perruquier refused to apologize for attacking Loftus. The leaders emphasized that this was Tunica and Ofogoula territory, and the British could not trespass without their consent. Perruquier went even further, defending their collective action. As he passionately explained, "The English have always destroyed the nations.... When I knew that they were coming into our territory I said: they will make us die, it is better to kill them."[26] Together, these three leaders were so impressive that Pittman chose to avoid demanding retribution, and instead sought alliances with these nations on behalf of the British Crown.

For the Tunicas, their military strategy and diplomatic aid from the Pakanas, Ofogoulas, Choctaws, French, Avoyelles, and Acolapissas resulted in tremendous success. From the safety of New Orleans, and with the backing of their French allies, they had so convincingly persuaded Pittman that the British needed Tunica friendship that he not only established nation-to-nation relations with the Tunicas but also solicited their nation to move back to their homelands east of the Mississippi and act as British emissaries in the region. The Tunicas accepted the offer and, by the end of that summer, they had returned to their eastern lands.

In December they received generous gifts from the British and affirmations of alliance.[27]

The successes of 1764 marked the beginning of this new phase of delicate diplomacy for the Tunicas. Although the British were less in need of quotidian provisions and services than the French had been, they still turned to Petites Nations for help with tracking down criminals, illegal traders, and other outlaws in the backwoods.[28] Even more importantly, the new positions of Petites Nations like the Tunicas on the border between Louisiana and West Florida provided them with considerable leverage. Since the Tunicas were one of the few nations who chose to move back to British-claimed territory after the partition, the British were eager to maintain their relationship with the Tunicas and hoped they could use this Petite Nation's political influence to their advantage.[29]

In addition to British concerns about the stability of the border and the potential for the Spanish to mobilize the Petites Nations against their settlements, British officials recognized that even small nations presented serious challenges to colonial security and development in a region. Just one year after the Tunicas repelled Loftus, John Thomas, the British Indian agent in the region, was forced to flee from the British Fort Iberville when a coalition of Alabamas and Houmas attacked in 1765. These Petites Nations and Creek warriors destroyed Thomas's possessions and stalled the construction of the military outpost. The damage they wrought made a compelling and disturbing statement about Houma and Alabama territorial control and their sentiments toward the British. As one officer recorded, "the Indians came, destroyed the stockades, and rolled the cannon into the river, this put an end to the undertaking." Construction could not proceed until the British satisfied their diplomatic obligations. Ultimately, British officials decided it would be both safer and less expensive to negotiate with the Petites Nations that controlled the region than to attempt to fight them.[30]

The Spanish required less convincing of the value of alliances with the Petites Nations, but they still struggled to develop workable relationships with the region's Native nations. Unlike in Florida or Texas, the Spanish did not attempt to establish missions or *encomiendas* in Louisiana. Rather, they assessed that the most effective policy for retaining possession of the less densely settler-populated lands was to continue the practices of their French predecessors of managing territorial control via Indigenous alliances.[31]

However, maintaining these relations required substantial investments of time and money. Within a year of his arrival in 1768, the first Spanish governor of Louisiana, Antonio de Ulloa, was already complaining about the cost of these relationships. Negotiating on Petites Nations' terms was not how he had envisioned managing Spain's empire in the Lower Mississippi Valley. He insisted that the "Indians cannot be despotic in their demands, and that they must not be given everything they are minded to ask for." The Gulf Coast nations were well aware of how desperately these weak colonial governments needed their support, and they capitalized on European dependency. Drawing on the regional customs of diplomatic hospitality, the Indigenous representatives arrived at British and Spanish forts to speak with the commanders and expected to be received, fed, and given gifts. Native leaders exploited this practice and sometimes remained for days at European posts. Ulloa felt trapped by these tactics. and he particularly resented their "threats of attack if they are not gratified every time they come to the forts."[32] So, while he continued to insist that these practices must cease, Ulloa's complaints should be read as evidence of his powerlessness to do anything other than comply with the expectations and demands of Spain's Native allies.

In essence, the combination of imperial competition and pressure from local Indigenous nations forced Spanish officials to acknowledge their reliance on Indigenous nations to preserve the colony and protect their international border.[33] Just one year after Ulloa's initial insistence that excessive generosity was bad policy, the next Spanish governor, Alejandro O'Reilly, reversed Ulloa's approach to diplomatic gift giving. O'Reilly recognized the value of Native nations' military alliances. In addition to diplomacy with the Choctaws, Osages, and Quapaws, between September and October 1769, O'Reilly hosted deputations of Tunicas, Tensas, Pakanas, Houmas, Bayagoulas, Ofogoulas, Chaouachas, Ouachas, Chatots, Biloxis, Pascagoulas, Mobilians, and Chitimachas. He gifted medals of alliance and secured formal trade and diplomatic relationships with these Petites Nations. At these meetings, the Tunica leaders received an abundance of gifts, and Tunicas stand out among records of Spanish imperial expenditures. In 1769 the Tunicas were listed as receiving twice as many presents as similarly sized nations, and from 1770 to 1777 they consistently ranked among the top Spanish expenditures for smaller nations in the Arkansas and Mississippi River Valley region.[34] For a nation that had only around one hundred people by the 1760s, these gift records indicate the outsized political power that the Tunicas wielded during this era.[35]

However, not all of the Petites Nations were so eager to develop relationships with the British newcomers, and after their joint military maneuver in 1764, the Ofogoulas' political strategies diverged from those of the Tunicas. Ofogoula objections to British colonization continued throughout the 1760s and 1770s and critically shaped their international relations during this era. When Perruquier told Pittman in 1764 that the British "will make us die," he was not speaking metaphorically. Shortly after the arrival of the British in the region, a deadly wave of smallpox broke out across the Lower Mississippi Valley.[36] The infectious disease killed many Ofogoulas, and Perruquier was still grieving these losses when he met with the French commandant of Pointe Coupée shortly after the attack in March 1764. During their meeting, Perruquier emphasized that the Ofogoulas had lived alongside the French for many years at their fort at Natchez with no such problems, and he accused the British of intentionally poisoning his people. As he lamented, "the English have scarcely arrived and they have caused nearly all our children to die by the smallpox they have brought."[37] This virulent disease wiped out an entire generation of Ofogoulas, and by 1771 the nation had fewer than fifty people.[38] The epidemic convinced Perruquier of the need to halt British expansion. The Ofogoulas subsequently moved to the west of the river, refused to meet with the British, and implored their neighbors to do the same.

In October 1771, the British Indian agent John Thomas traveled upriver to meet with the leaders of the Petites Nations near Pointe Coupée. Thomas was on a mission to reaffirm British alliances with the small nations. He was also still trying to convince these peoples to return to their former homes on the eastern bank of the river. By his estimates, the Petites Nations in this region, including the Tensas, Biloxis, Pascagoulas, Mobilians, Pakanas, Alabamas, and Chatots could supply 298 gunmen, and in 1777 another British official estimated that the Petites Nations west of the Mississippi could field 1,500 warriors. Their alliances would be essential for British colonial security.[39]

Thomas considered his mission to be a success. First, on October 24 he met with the Tunicas. The following day, he stopped on the bank of the river just north of Pointe Coupée across from the villages of the Biloxis, Ofogoulas, Pascagoulas, Mobilians, and Chatots. He invited these nations to cross the river and feast with him so that he could distribute their annual gifts and discuss their alliances. Thomas reported to his superior that he had met with many nations and was successfully convincing them to build alliances with Britain. Some, he reported, were even considering resettling on the eastern bank of the river. As he delightedly explained, "The Tonica [sic] chief and his warriors have been here and gave me a dance the eagles tail and calumet of peace. Likewise the pascagoulas, choctoes, alibamons, pakana, and tansa [sic]."[40]

Thomas was nonetheless distressed to learn that Perruquier was undermining his efforts. The Ofogoula leader had convinced the Biloxis not to meet with the British Indian agent, and Thomas saw this as an ominous development. He knew that he should not expect the attendance of the Ofogoulas at the diplomatic ceremony since he considered Perruquier "a Frenchman in his heart and an enemy to the English," but Mathaah Cush, the leader of the Biloxis, had also skipped the October 24 feast.[41]

Mathaah Cush and his people wrestled with whether they should accept a British alliance. The lived close to and shared much with their Ofogoula neighbors. Both groups were Siouan-speaking peoples and Mathaah Cush greatly respected the guidance of Perruquier. The Biloxis also remembered the British slave traders and colonial officials who, for many decades, had instigated other nations to attack their people. Now, the British promised peace and trade, and many of their contemporaries found their alliances fruitful. After abstaining from the October 24 feast, Mathaah Cush shifted tactics and decided to meet with Thomas. Some of the Biloxi men had attended the meal, presumably to scout out the situation, and midway through the meeting they rowed back across the river to tell Mathaah Cush they thought he should come. When they did finally meet, Mathaah Cush placated the British official by promising to consider moving back to the eastern side of the river, and the two men were able to forge an alliance. The Biloxi leader also apologized for missing the first meeting, attributing his absence to Perruquier's influence.

Perruquier and the Ofogoulas' stridently anti-British policy made them outliers among the Petites Nations near Pointe Coupée as most nations did ultimately form alliances with both the Spanish and British. Like the Biloxis, many communities avoided making firm commitments to one nation or the other, and pursued policies that allowed them to benefit from loose alliances with both empires. The settlements on Tunica homelands along the European border strengthened the collective power of these Petites Nations and provided individual leaders and nations with additional leverage to use with Spanish and British diplomats. Critically, the protection provided by this multinational settlement and alliance network also enabled each nation to pursue separate and even opposing diplomatic strategies, as did the Tunicas and Ofogoulas after 1764. So, even as Perruquier used the insulation of other Petites Nations' alliances to shield his people from British retribution, the Tunicas were able to use these same networks to usher in a highpoint in Tunica political power.

Negotiating on Tunica Terms

During the ten months preceding Lattanash's 1772 visit to Fort Bute to meet with Charles Stuart, relations between English and Spanish colonial officials had become especially strained as the Tunicas flexed their political muscle. Since 1764 the Tunicas had taken full advantage of the prestige they had gained from the Loftus assault. They marketed themselves as regional power brokers among the Petites Nations and maintained a steady presence on both sides of the border.[42] Although the Tunicas technically lived on the eastern bank of the river, like most of the Petites Nations near Pointe Coupée, they planted, hunted, and traded on both the eastern and western shores, so maintaining good relations with both Spain and Britain was essential to maintaining their lands on both sides of the river.[43] Moreover, the Tunicas' rejection of the border was shared by most of the other nations. As Stuart reported in 1772, the Biloxis, Pascagoulas, and Tunicas all lived on the western side of the river, but planted and tended their cornfields to its east. In fact, he lamented, "The Alibamons [sic] I found to be the only Indians at present residing on one side of the river." British and Spanish efforts to restrict Native travel and to carve up Indigenous homelands were going very badly indeed.[44]

Maintaining these dual alliances was difficult, and by the early 1770s both British and Spanish officials were frustrated by their inability to secure the exclusive alliance of the Tunicas. The situation was not improved by Lattanash's habit of flaunting his people's multiple alliances by simultaneously wearing both his Spanish and British medals. In December 1771, Lattanash reported to John Thomas, the British Indian agent at Fort Bute, that Bathazar de Villiers, the commanding officer of the Spanish fort across the river at Pointe Coupée, had attempted to wrest his British medal from his neck while he was on a diplomatic visit. The Spanish officer aimed to pressure Lattanash to sever his ties with Britain and relinquish his British medal. Given the severity of this gesture, John Thomas recognized it as nothing less than an international provocation.[45]

British and Spanish officials exchanged a flurry of correspondence over the incident. Villiers accused Lattanash of lying and manipulating Thomas. Thomas threatened to encourage other Indian nations to relocate to British West Florida. The British deputy superintendent Charles Stuart berated Thomas for risking pitching British West Florida and Spanish Louisiana into conflict over the incident, and ultimately both Stuart and Lattanash had to travel to Fort Bute to straighten things out in person."[46]

By the 1770s, the value of the alliances of the nations along the Mississippi River were at a premium, and the Tunicas were in an ideal position to exploit the anxieties of the Spanish and English colonists.[47] Concerns about the possibility of war between England and Spain over the Falkland Islands reenergized Spanish and English efforts to court local nations of all sizes along the border.[48]

Then, in the mid-1770s, as a possible rupture between England and its Atlantic colonies loomed, Spanish and British officials again readied for a multitheater confrontation.

Regardless of British hopes and Spanish fears, Lattanash had no intention of agreeing to an exclusive relationship with the British. Why should he? Colonial governments had long held conflicting alliances with multiple Native nations, and his own people had maintained relationships with a wide variety of Indigenous and European polities for decades. In October 1772, at Fort Bute, he approached the British—surrounded by his Pascagoula, Biloxi, Choctaw, and Alabama allies—and calmly addressed the issue. Turning to Stuart, he said, "I heard you [were] angry at my having this Medal [and a Spanish flag]. why would you be angry at that[?] I had the medal before the English [came] here.... We want to be friends with all the White People near us, as we live amongst them, and are we not free to go to which side of the River we please[?] are not the lands our Own?"[49]

Indeed, the lands belonged to the Tunicas, and so too did they possess the extensive webs of relations to the land and to the surrounding nations that enabled them to hold and maintain these territories. British and Spanish officials certainly did not like it that Lattanash layered his medals, allowing them to jostle and clank against one another in a visual and auditory show of his powerful connections, and they were frustrated that Tunicas refused to respect the European boundary. But they also did not have the might to stop him or the other Petites Nations. Instead, they were forced to negotiate on Petites Nations terms and recognize Native sovereignty in Indigenous homelands.[50]

Through the 1770s, not only the Tunicas but also the Alabamas, Pascagoulas, Chitimachas, Houmas, and Biloxis had mastered the diplomatic tactics needed to maintain dual European alliances and were thereby able to maintain their sovereignty and caretaking obligations to lands, people, and nonhumans on both sides of their river. The Petites Nations were always crossing the river, always mentioning that they were considering moving over to the British side, and always arriving at Spanish forts looking for presents.[51] Petites Nations also strategically explained their webs of alliances in ways that were palatable to their European allies. During talks with colonial officials, these Petites Nations simultaneously portrayed themselves as tiny, weak, and dependent and then used this image of powerlessness to reaffirm their need for multiple relationships. To the Spanish officials, the Petites Nations stressed that they needed access to more trade goods, as Spanish officials were unable to compete with the plentiful and inexpensive goods offered by British traders. To British officials, they emphasized their need to be able to cross the river and stay on the Spanish side to protect themselves from Creek raids. The British knew that they were unable to either control the Creeks or offer the Petites Nations adequate military protection. Thus, the Petites Nations leaders argued that, in order to be able to protect their poor, tiny communities, they must continue to hold dual European alliances.[52]

Despite their strategic rhetoric of weakness, the Tunicas clearly did not think that they were powerless or at the mercy of colonial officials. Instead, throughout the 1760s and 1770s, Tunicas pursued bold diplomatic and military strategies that mirrored the broader trends of Indigenous resistance to European incursions across eastern North America. By forging extensive alliance networks and relying on the same practices of refugee sanctuary, community mobility, and multinational resettlement that had sustained their people for generations, they managed to overcome these new colonial challenges and thrive during this era. In many ways, the imperial transition actually generated a high point of Tunica power. For Pakanas, Mobilians, Ofogoulas, and others, the ability to count on migration and multinational settlements enabled them to weather the upheavals of this colonial transformation and preserve their communities, and in some cases, even their lands. These same practices of building transnational relationships and living arrangements, and the ability to move quickly in response to European threats, would become critical in the coming decades as settler immigration began to transform the region.

CHAPTER 8

The Beginnings of Marginalization

The arrival of the European new year seemed to augur disaster and bloodshed for the Tunicas. They were less than a week into 1771, and their Choctaw allies were demanding that the Tunicas execute one of their own. Lattanash knew he must avert war with the Choctaws, or many of his people would die, but the killing of a kinsman was bad business. Spilling a fellow Tunica's blood was not something his people would do if they could find any means to avoid it. In January 1771, Lattanash gathered with Tunica elders to discuss the dire situation. Right after the turn of the new year, a group of Choctaws, who were visiting Tunica territory, discovered the remains of several slain Choctaw youths. They suspected that Tunicas had killed these young men, and they demanded recompense. The Tunica leadership must deliver a head, they insisted, or there would be war. Lattanash and the other community leaders needed to find a solution, and fast.[1]

The previous year had been a difficult one for the Tunicas and their French and Spanish neighbors at Pointe Coupée. Throughout 1770, large groups of Choctaws had taken to making lengthy diplomatic visits to the Tunicas, and they used these trips as opportunities to intimidate the nearby Petites Nations and the surrounding European settlers alike. The Spanish military at Pointe Coupée, as well as the French and Spanish families who lived on small farms near the post, still depended heavily on their Tunica allies for food, services, and defense, and the visiting Choctaws destabilized the balance of the interdependent Petites Nations and settler relationships. Hungry Choctaw guests devoured most of the food the Tunicas would normally have traded with settlers at the post, and their presence consumed much of the Tunica men's and women's time and labor. The large numbers of visiting Choctaws made the settlers uneasy, as they strained the vital supply chains that supported both Indigenous and settler communities in Tunica homelands.

As Lattanash complained to Jean-François Allain, the Spanish commander of the post, the Tunicas simply could not get rid of their Choctaw guests. Since the Choctaws and the Tunicas were allies, the Tunicas were obligated to receive and host these visitors for as long as the Choctaws desired to stay. Anything less would have been regarded as akin to an open declaration of hostility. The Choctaws also remained the most powerful nation in the region, so both the Spanish and the Tunicas were determined to maintain good relationships with this polity even when their diplomatic obligations created financial strain on the Tunica or Spanish governments. Nonetheless, by the end of 1770, Lattanash and the leading Tunica men and women were unsure of how they would continue to withstand the economic and social burdens of these extended Choctaw visits. Their visitors consumed huge quantities of the Tunicas' provisions and they required continual entertainment. When the Tunicas finally ran out of meat, the Choctaws raided the fields of nearby Spanish and French settlers. By winter, both the Tunicas and the Spanish had become resentful of their powerful guests. In this tense situation, a group of settlers or of Tunicas may have been angry enough to come to blows with the ill-fated Choctaw youths they met walking the woods at the water's edge.

The discovery of slain Choctaw youths brought the simmering tensions over Indigenous hospitality obligations, Choctaw intimidation, and imperial anxiety to a head. This killing demanded a response from the Tunicas, and a resolution of the unsustainable situation at Pointe Coupée. The Spanish commander fretted that if the Tunicas did not resolve the crisis, and the conflict turned into a full-blown war, then their post could be left without vital Tunica support or even come under Choctaw attack. The Tunicas knew that a conflict with the powerful Choctaws would go dreadfully for their people, so they were highly motivated to make peace. The Choctaws needed to use this political moment to remind the Tunicas and the Spanish alike of the might of their nation and that both groups were fundamentally dependent on their relationships with the Choctaws to hold their lands along the Mississippi River. These pressures created a toxic brew that increased friction among the Choctaws and the Petites Nations and imperiled the security of colonial settlements in both British West Florida and Spanish Louisiana.

During the 1770s, increasing immigration of Euro-American settlers into the Gulf South strained and sometimes ruptured the diplomatic alliances between the Choctaws and the Petites Nations. While the Choctaws had always been heavy-handed in their diplomatic and social relationships with Petites Nations, in prior decades their support had protected many of these nations from

Creek raiders, European soldiers, and colonists who sought to encroach on their lands. Petites Nations that shared particularly strong alliances with the Choctaws, like the Tohomes, Mobilians, and Naniabas, also gained economic opportunities and military support through these relationships. However, the dual pressures of a growing settler invasion and the erosion of Choctaw support for Petites Nations near Pointe Coupée placed many Petites Nations in vulnerable positions. These geopolitical shifts heralded a new era during which the Petites Nations lost both large pieces of their homelands and regional influence.

The final third of the eighteenth century was a period of intense political and demographic change in the Lower Mississippi Valley. During the 1760s and 1770s, rising tensions among the Creeks and Choctaws led to an escalation of violence in the buffer zone in the lands between the Alabama and Tombigbee Rivers that had traditionally separated Creek and Choctaw territory. The rise of violence in their homelands further encouraged many Petites Nations that had lived along the Mobile Bay to migrate west. Then, during the 1770s, Petites Nations witnessed fresh conflict and imperial turmoil as Spain ejected Britain from the Gulf Coast during the Revolutionary War. Following the conclusion of the American Revolution, Americans began to flood into the Mississippi Delta and Native nations were faced with yet another massive demographic transformation. As these colonial empires reorganized and vied for political power, Native Southerners' homelands underwent momentous social and political changes.[2]

In this era, both Mobile and Pointe Coupée were transformed by settler immigration. Unlike New Orleans, which was the center of colonial power, or an Indigenous town like Concha, which was within Choctaw territory and remained fully under Choctaw control and influence, in the 1760s Pointe Coupée and Mobile were zones of mixed settler and Indigenous populations and places of layered and overlapping sovereignties. These borderlands were home to French, British, and Spanish settlers living under colonial legal codes, but they were also still Tunica, Ofogoula, Mobilian, and Apalachee homelands where Indigenous people retained authority over lands and waters. Both multinational settlements were also on the peripheries of Choctaw territory and thereby within the sphere of Choctaw influence but not under Choctaw dominion. During the 1770s and 1780s, thousands of settlers moved into these Indigenous homelands, and their arrival drove many Petites Nations off of their territories near Mobile and Pointe Coupée, converting the borderlands that had provided refuge for so many Petites Nations into colonial domains.

The Tunicas, Mobilians, Apalachees, and many other Petites Nations fought to preserve their communities and to hold their nations together as they confronted this settler invasion. These nations' strategies for navigating the onslaught of British and Spanish settlers into their homelands were varied. Some nations— like the Mobilians, Tohomes, and Naniabas—were forced to give up their autonomy and amalgamate with the Choctaws. Others migrated to new lands and formed new multinational communities in order to avoid settler violence. Almost all the Petites Nations lost large portions, if not the entirety, of their homelands during the 1770s, but despite these dispossessions, many nations managed to survive as autonomous polities. Even as Petites Nations became peripheral players in a settler-dominated Gulf, the systems of refugee acceptance, migration, and multinational settlement that had protected their ancestors for generations continued to be the social glue and political strategy that helped preserve their communities in the wake of widespread dispossession.

Strained Alliances at Pointe Coupée

On the eve of the American Revolution, Spanish and British settlers in the Lower Mississippi Valley remained dependent on their relationships with large and small Indigenous nations. Partnerships with local Native people remained essential for the Spanish and British governments largely because, despite some growth during the 1760s, the settler populations of British West Florida and Spanish Louisiana had remained relatively small throughout the decade. The 1769 Spanish census indicates that the total colonial population of Louisiana was only 11,344 persons, including enslaved persons, free people of color, and white settlers. With nearly 4,000 people in New Orleans alone, the remaining settler population was spread thinly across the territory. In the mid-1760s, the population of British West Florida was even smaller, as it contained only 2,000 settlers, and most of these colonists were clustered along the coast and near Mobile.[3]

Pointe Coupée was a settlement of average size for Spanish Louisiana in the 1770s. In 1769 it had about 550 people. Pointe Coupée's colonial population was similar in size to the French and Spanish settlements along the Acadian coast, in the Atakapas and Opelousas districts, and St. Louis in Illinois, and it was about two-thirds the size of Natchitoches. During the 1760s and 1770s, the region between Pointe Coupée and Natchez was also home to the Petites Nations of Tunicas, Ofogoulas, Biloxis, Mobilians, Pakanas, Alabamas, and Chatots. While Tunicas and Ofogoulas had lived in the region for generations, the Biloxis, Mobilians, Pakanas, Alabamas, and Chatots were all recent migrants. In 1771 these small nations collectively numbered between 1,050 and 1,500 people.[4] Pointe Coupée was located on Tunica land, and at the beginning of the 1770s, there were only about half as many settlers as Indigenous people in the surrounding area. So, in 1771 Pointe Coupée was a small node of the Spanish Empire within a territory that was controlled by the Tunicas and their allies, and one that was beginning to come under greater pressure from the Choctaws as they were forced west.

In the years before the American Revolution, British colonists who illegally settled beyond the formal boundaries of Virginia and Carolina invaded Creek and Choctaw homelands in increasing numbers, and some Choctaws began to push further west into the Lower Mississippi Valley to escape the violence these settlers brought to their lands. In the spring of 1770, Allain began complaining about the near-constant presence of Choctaws at the Tunica village alongside the Spanish post at Pointe Coupée. The Choctaws sometimes came in groups of one hundred people, which was roughly equivalent to the entire Tunica population. Entertaining their guests placed immense labor burdens on Tunica women, who were responsible for feeding their visitors, and it prevented Lattanash and other tribal representatives from traveling to conduct normal diplomatic business.

As far as Allain was concerned, the presence of Choctaws at Pointe Coupée brought nothing but trouble. He blamed the Choctaws for enticing the Tunicas across the river to meet with the English, for bringing rum and disorder to Petites Nations villages, and for fomenting a plot that involved the Tunicas and Choctaws jointly attacking Pakanas and Alabamas—presumably as an extension of the ongoing Creek and Choctaw violence—that never came to fruition. During their visits to the Tunicas, Choctaws killed settlers' cattle, demanded food from the Spanish and French farmers, and ate all the Tunicas' provisions. Feeding the Choctaws meant the Tunicas had less produce and meat to sell to the settlers, and the Choctaws' very presence terrified European families. Local inhabitants witnessed these groups of Tunicas and Choctaws crossing the Mississippi to trade with their British adversaries on the other side of the river in West Florida. They circulated frenzied rumors of British plots to send Choctaws to assault the post. Sometimes they even feared that "the normally docile Tunicas will be goaded into hostilities by the Grand Nation [Choctaws]."[5] In the tense years between the Seven Years' War and the American Revolution, the threat of another imperial war loomed large in the minds of these borderlands settlers. As the inhabitants of Pointe Coupée lived right along this interimperial division, they were wary of what might happen if the British managed to seduce away their Native allies. This would leave the post undefended, or worse, full of British-aligned Indigenous mercenaries. By 1770 the French and Spanish inhabitants were deeply anxious about the activities of their Native neighbors. Allain had also become skittish, and he repeatedly issued orders requiring that settlers carry firearms at all times. However, beyond instructing the settlers to be on guard, and hoping Lattanash could resolve this crisis, he could do little except complain to the colonial governor.[6]

Although Allain did not record the Choctaws' explanations for their extended visits to the Tunicas, their actions suggest that they were seeking to intimidate the Spanish and send a forceful political message; and they were successful. The Choctaws' extended stays at Pointe Coupée can be understood as part of a strategy to create diplomatic leverage and remind the Spanish of Choctaw military might. Their decisions to slaughter cattle, demand food, and to play stickball unceasingly were not merely the product of desperation created by pressure from border conflicts with the Creeks and English settlers. Nor were they random acts of banditry by rogue individuals. Rather, it seems that these symbolic demonstrations of military might were part and parcel of Choctaw diplomatic strategies during the Revolutionary Era.[7]

The forced hospitality, "theft," and even the stickball the Choctaws played at Pointe Coupée were potent, symbolic statements of military and political power. Native Southerners referred to stickball as "the younger brother of war" and they took this often-violent game very seriously. As the players chased each other up and down the field, sticks colliding and their shoulders slamming into the ribs of their adversaries, they demonstrated agility, determination, and the muscle of the Choctaw nation. By playing stickball, the Choctaws were performing their military capability on the doorstep of the Spanish settlement. In this light, the Choctaws' strategy to intimidate the colonists and remind them of their people's capacity to enact real violence were highly effective.[8]

Likewise, the act of killing cattle had symbolic meaning and had long been used by Native people as a tactic to assert territoriality. At Natchez, just upriver from Pointe Coupée, the Natchez had repeatedly attacked settlers' cattle in the 1720s to communicate their frustration with French human and animal trespasses and mistreatment of their lands. When the French failed to heed these warnings, the Natchez turned their attacks from the cows to the settlers themselves, launching a war to destroy the French settlements in their territories. Similarly, by demanding or taking food from French and Spanish settlers, the Choctaws were also forcing the residents of the region to act in a diplomatically acceptable way, requiring their European political partners to be generous in order to maintain these alliances.[9]

The Tunica leaders seemed to have been able to work out a resolution that assuaged Choctaw grief and restored the alliance among their peoples. While the extant colonial correspondence from Pointe Coupée does not describe the specific resolution of this dispute, there is also no report of a war. Given that the Tunicas were able to remain as allies of the Choctaws and in their village for the next decade, we can infer that the two nations did not come to blows. Considering the need to cover the death of the Choctaw youth, it is likely that the Tunicas either delivered a human life or a substantial payment to the Choctaws to settle the matter. Whether or not the Tunicas believed that this murder was justified, they absolutely could not afford to alienate the Choctaws as they recognized that their ability to exercise regional power—and remain in their homelands—depended on maintaining good relationships with the Choctaws. Lattanash may have resented the fact that he had been unable to travel down to New Orleans to receive his annual gifts from the Spanish governor in 1770 because he was too busy hosting Choctaw visitors, but he was also absolutely aware that his relationship with the Choctaws was a significant part of the reason he was receiving presents from the colonial governor at all.[10]

Choctaws similarly used raiding tactics to apply pressure to the British government in West Florida. Regular small-scale Choctaw raids kept British settlers in fear. Colonists near Mobile and New Orleans felt continuously under siege and were often unable to protect their property from Indigenous raiders. The British officials' failure to secure good relations with the Choctaws in West Florida plagued their settlers and made them question their safety even in the metropoles of the Gulf South. In 1768 a group of Sixtowns Choctaws raided settlements just outside of New Orleans. They killed cattle, stole goods, and terrified the settlers.[11] Three years later, in 1771, the Citizens' Council of Mobile met to compose a letter to the governor of West Florida pleading for more assistance protecting themselves against the Choctaws. The Choctaws had been plundering homes outside of Mobile and the citizens were afraid the city might be next. Compounding these fears, the panicked inhabitants had also heard rumors that the Choctaws had just been in New Orleans receiving presents from the Spanish, and they therefore imagined that the Spanish were coordinating a full-scale assault on the city.[12]

Their impressive military reputation sometimes enabled Choctaws to protect Petites Nations people from encroaching settlers. In December 1771, John Thomas asked his supervisor for assistance settling a land dispute with Mr. Canty, a British settler. Canty claimed that he had been given a land grant to settle on the "old fields" of the Petites Nations near Pointe Coupée and was anxious to begin planting on the fields that had been previously cultivated by Native women. Thomas knew that, although many of the Petites Nations lived on the western side of the river, they still used and owned these fields. So Thomas was afraid that Canty would attack the Native owners when they returned to use the land and tend their peach trees. As he explained, if Canty claimed title and attempted to enforce possession of these lands with violence, "in firing on the Indians it would probably be the means of an Indian War. It is true the Nations of Indians are but small. It ought to be Considered that such Rash proceedings would alarm the Great Chactaw [sic] Nation as those Little tribes are in great Friendship with them."[13] Thomas was therefore forced to advise against Canty's efforts to claim title. So, even as the Tunicas resented the Choctaws' heavy-handed approach, they recognized that their alliance was invaluable and provided them with critical support in their dealings with colonial governments.

Despite the best efforts of both Tunicas and Choctaws to limit dispossession, by the mid-1770s, English hunger for land at Pointe Coupée began to lead to real land losses, and this encouraged the Tunicas to consider relocating their community away from white settlers. In March 1772, Mr. Blomart, a British settler, attempted to take possession of a portion of the Tunicas' fields on the eastern shore of the river. Blomart insisted that he had secured the lands from the estate of another local settler (who had claimed but not tended the land) after the man's death. Further complicating matters, the British Indian agent John Thomas had paperwork indicating that the governor of Pensacola had granted the same tract of land to another British settler "one Fairchild." Meanwhile, the Tunicas insisted to both their Spanish and British allies that the land was theirs and rightfully had been for years. Thomas was concerned about the implications of this triple-layered land conflict, and he urgently wanted to ensure that the Tunicas received satisfaction for this injustice. However, unlike Canty's claim years earlier, in Blomart's case, Thomas proposed to compensate the Tunicas for their land in order to ensure proper title. As Thomas reported, "Mr. Blomart has taken possession of late Fergy's land which is beyond all doubt the Tonicas' [sic] property.... An extensive piece of this ground has been cleared and planted with peach trees (now in perfection) by the Tonicas [sic] who say they are not willing to hurt their brothers the English, at the same time they are determined to take possession or to have some consideration for the purchase; but I think that piece of ground should be purchased with all the land useful to the Crown that the Tonicas [sic] may be entitled to and willing to dispose of."[14] By 1772 the Tunicas no longer believed that they were in a position to militarily confront British colonists, and they were instead shifting toward a strategy that would enable them to maintain peaceable relationships with their European neighbors and protect what land and community they had remaining.

By 1788 the colonial population at Pointe Coupée topped 2,000 people, and there were twice as many colonists and enslaved Africans as there were Tunicas, Ofogoulas, Chatots, Biloxis, and Avoyelles. The region as a whole was likewise being transformed by settler immigration. By 1785 the Lower Mississippi Valley contained 30,471 white and Black inhabitants, and the population of non-Indigenous people in the region had nearly doubled in less than two decades.[15] The termination of the Revolutionary War therefore roughly coincided with the end of the era during which the Choctaws and Tunicas relied on similar strategies of violence, raids, and formal diplomacy to protect their communities.

The Choctaw nation was so large and so diverse that it is difficult to characterize a single strategy that Choctaws employed to confront European and American empires, but it is clear that Choctaws continued to rely on military power to achieve their diplomatic aims. The strategies of Choctaw towns during this era can be broadly described as a combination of strategic violence; an expansion of Choctaw networks and presence west of the Mississippi; and continued formal diplomatic negotiations with imperial powers. During the American Revolution, the Choctaws were aggressively courted by both the British and Spanish. As in previous conflicts, Choctaws were not united in their decisions about whether to intervene in this European war, so Choctaws served on both sides of the American War of Independence. After the revolution, Choctaws maintained relationships with both the Spanish in Louisiana and Florida and the new United States representatives in order to again secure access to trade and political support. In 1784 the Choctaws met with representatives from the state of Georgia to discuss an economic partnership, and in 1785 and 1786 they negotiated an alliance with the United States. The 1786 Treaty of Hopewell—which Choctaws, Creeks, and Cherokees all signed with the new United States—forced these Southeastern nations to cede significant portions of their southern territories, but it promised to enable trade among the Choctaws and United States and to protect Choctaws from squatters and invading settlers. Specifically, Article 4 of the treaty promised that if citizens of the United States trespassed and attempted to hunt or settle on Choctaw land, "such person shall forfeit the protection of the United States of America, and the Indians may punish him or not as they please." While the Choctaws lost land after the American Revolution, they did obtain written recognition of their sovereignty in the eyes of the United States. This recognition came with a promise of protection for their territory, which was something that none of the Petites Nations had initially managed to achieve.[16]

In 1784 Choctaw leaders signed a treaty with Spain that formally permitted them to travel west of the Mississippi, and by the 1790s, Choctaw migrants, traders, and hunters were ranging as far as the Sabine River. Not surprisingly, Caddos and Osages did not take kindly to Choctaw invasions of their territories. Under pressure from both east and west, and facing shortages of access to hunting grounds and provisions, Choctaws increasingly exploited their Petites Nations allies to sustain themselves. Similar to events that Allain recorded in the 1770s at Point Coupée, the lieutenant governor of the Red River district complained in 1796 that the Petites Nations of the Tensas, the Apalachees, and the Pascagoulas in the district "attract the Choctaws who remain for some months consuming all their food and finally abusing them."[17]

Small-scale raids on colonial settlements became a critical mode by which Choctaws expressed power and enforced territory during this era. From 1760 to 1800, the Choctaws expanded the scope of their raids and targeted communities from Natchez to Lafourche and Mobile to Adayes. Relying on the same tactics they used at Pointe Coupée in 1770, the Choctaws sought to extend their influence even further west in eastern Texas during the 1790s. Their continued use of symbolic and performative violence and theft not only garnered badly needed supplies but, as one American official at Natchez put it in 1798, it also reminded the settlers that "we live here only upon sufferance and their good will." Therefore, when Choctaw diplomats met to negotiate treaties with Spain in 1784, 1792, and 1793, with Georgia in 1784, and with the United States in 1786 and 1792, they entered these discussions against the backdrop of settlers' fear and their recognition of colonial vulnerability.[18]

By the 1780s, Tunicas and Choctaws were pursuing different approaches to confronting settler incursions in the Gulf South. In the last decades of the century, the Choctaws would continue to negotiate with diplomatic representatives, to militarily confront the expanding United States, and to pursue international strategies in much the same way they had in previous years. For the Tunicas, the onslaught of settlement and the strain on the Choctaws meant that they ceased to be as politically and militarily threatening as they had been in previous generations. Instead, Lattanash and his people would spend the next decades carefully cultivating relationships and economic strategies that would allow his people to survive and find new lands using more discreet tactics than they had employed in the 1760s.

Pressure at Mobile

Petites Nations near Mobile experienced the impact of settler immigration both earlier and more intensely than the Choctaws or Petites Nations at Pointe Coupée. By 1785 the colonial population of the Lower Mississippi Valley had increased to 30,471 with 13,076 white settlers and 16,248 enslaved people. By 1788 Mobile had nearly 1,500 colonial inhabitants. Although the Native population of the Lower Mississippi Valley continued to recover during the Revolutionary Era, the growth of Indigenous populations was far outpaced by the growth of settler populations in the region. In the final decades of the eighteenth century, more and more colonists arrived, and by 1800 there were 50,000 colonial and enslaved settlers in the Lower Mississippi Valley compared to 40,000 Indigenous people.[19]

This demographic shift, along with the increasing strain that Choctaws were experiencing, left Petites Nations with few options for leveraging political power, so many Petites Nations had little choice except to leave the colonial settlements that had once been their homelands. In the 1770s, 1780s, and 1790s, Petites Nations pursued several strategies that helped their people survive as communities even as they were pushed off of their lands by encroaching settlers. Some polities joined larger Indian nations, and many others migrated to geographically remote locations or into difficult terrain where there were smaller numbers of settlers. A few communities also attempted to integrate themselves directly into colonial settlements and to take advantage of the economic opportunities that expanding European settlements provided.

Many Petites Nations communities moved multiple times and through different series of multinational settlements as they sought security and new futures away from the colonial crush in their homelands. Prior to 1763, Mobile was home to the Tensas, Pascagoulas, Biloxis, Chatots, Mobilians, Naniabas, Tohomes, and Apalachees, with the Pakanas living nearby. During the 1760s, as Creek and Choctaw conflict escalated and the British moved into the region, nearly all of these nations fled west. The Pakanas, some of the Mobilians, and some of the Biloxis joined the settlement of Tunicas, Ofogoulas, and Avoyelles at Pointe Coupée, so they too witnessed the rising tension at Pointe Coupée in the 1770s. Meanwhile, the Chatots, Pascagoulas, and some of the Biloxis moved west to the Red River and formed joint settlements with the Yowani Choctaws (a Choctaw town that had decided to leave the nation and relocate west independently). West of the Mississippi, these groups were safer from Creek raids, and the groups at the Pointe Coupée post were strategically positioned on an imperial border that gave them both diplomatic power and multiple trade opportunities.[20]

The only group that attempted to stay in Mobile after 1763 were the Apalachees, and only part of their community decided to remain. The Apalachees had migrated from northern Florida to Mobile in 1706 to escape Creek slave raids. In Florida, they had lived within Spanish missions and embraced Catholicism, so they settled at Mobile in part because their location there afforded them access to some of the few Catholic priests in Louisiana. Many community members were loath to leave their congregations and relocate to destinations where they would have had no access to Catholic institutions and community. Even with the growing settler population and the threat of Creek and Choctaw violence, a group of devout Apalachees chose to stay at Mobile in order to observe their faith. Like most Southeastern nations, Apalachee social organization allowed for dissent within the community and for groups to pursue different courses of action. So, in the 1760s, the Apalachee community split into multiple communities. While their relatives remained at Mobile, a second Apalachee group migrated to the Red River to seek refuge alongside Tensas, Mobilians, Alabamas, and other displaced Petites Nations.[21]

In this other multinational settlement, located in a region that was less densely settled by Europeans, the Apalachees were better able to exercise power and defend their lands. Perhaps their experiences of colonial violence and dispossession—first from their homelands in northern Florida by English and Creek raiders in 1704, and then from Mobile by British settlers in the 1760s—conditioned the creative Apalachee responses to settler expansions along the Red River. Even there, they were not fully free of European incursions and land theft.

In April 1768, several Apalachees and Alabamas came into conflict with a local French settler named Vincent. In the spring of that year, some Apalachees were helping their Alabama neighbors clear a patch of land south of their village for a new field. When Vincent insisted that they stop because the lands they were clearing were his, the Apalachees and Alabamas took this complaint to the commander of Rapides Parish Valentine Layssard. Layssard failed to intervene or remedy this dispute, permitting Vincent to continue using the disputed territory. The Alabamas and Apalachees took bold action to stop this theft. Instead of waiting for a resolution, or for Vincent to be able to finish his planting, the Apalachee leader Martin brought his entire village to Layssard's home. Once there, the Apalachees not only forcibly stopped several enslaved Africans from laboring to clear the commander's own fields but they also began cutting down the trees on Layssard's property, as though they intended to plant this land themselves. When the commander confronted the Apalachees to ask what they were doing and why they were on his property, Martin responded by explaining that "since Vincent had taken some of their land, they could take some of Layssard's."[22] Martin's logic was brutal, witty, and flawless. Clearly, by the late 1760s, this group of refugee Apalachees believed that encroaching settlers could only be stopped by forceful, nonviolent action.

While the Tensas, Chatots, Biloxis, Pascagoulas, some of the Mobilians and Apalachees, and individual Pakana and Alabama villages chose to relocate west, the three other Mobile-based Petites Nations, the Naniabas, Tohomes, and the remainder of the Mobilians, chose to seek protection by settling alongside their longtime Choctaw allies. The Mobilians, Naniabas, and Tohomes had long been closely allied with the Chickasawhay Choctaws, and during the Choctaw Civil War they had forged close connections with Eastern Choctaws. This was not the first time that Mobile Bay Petites Nations had sought refuge with the Choctaws during moments of crisis. During the 1730s and 1740s, groups of Mobilians and Tohomes intermittently lived within the Choctaw Nation, and French correspondence from 1748 indicates that at least some groups of Tohomes remained with the Choctaws "for several years" at a time. In the late 1740s, some Eastern Choctaws in turn sought refuge among the Naniaba and Tohome settlements at Mobile in order to escape the violence of the Choctaw Civil War.[23] This intimate relationship and the mobility of Indigenous towns help illustrate why the Naniabas and Tohomes appear to periodically drop out of French colonial correspondence for years at a time. Moreover, this pattern suggests that the Mobile nations' relocations were not meant to be permanent integrations, but were rather primarily ways to secure refuge for their people during dangerous times.

Naniabas, Mobilians, and Tohomes' continued caretaking of their homelands during the 1760s and 1770s indicates that they intended their stay with the Choctaws to be temporary. Even while the Naniabas lived in the Choctaws' territory, they still tended their fields at Mobile and collected their harvests each year. This pattern of land use indicates an ongoing relationship with the land, and this labor probably helped reify Naniaba territoriality in the eyes of their Indigenous neighbors. Many Petites Nations performed similar caretaking work on their lands, even during periods of time when they were unable to live in their territories. British officials recorded that, during the 1770s, nearly all the groups who resettled at Pointe Coupée continued to cultivate their lands on the eastern side of the river, and that they brought back bountiful harvests of peaches and corn. It therefore seems abundantly clear that the three Petites Nations fully intended to return to their homes at Mobile.[24]

However, once the Mobile-based Petites Nations moved into Choctaw lands, the British strove to find a way to acquire title to these territories. In 1765 the Choctaws ceded portions of their territories to West Florida in exchange for alliance with the British and the promise of annual gifts and steady trade to their nations, and British officials attempted to force the Choctaws to cede Petites Nations lands as well as their own.[25] When the British pushed the Choctaws to give them larger portions of land near Mobile and along the Mississippi River, the Choctaw leaders responded by emphasizing that they had no right to cede those lands, and that those territories belonged to the Petites Nations.

In April 1765, during one of these conversations about cessions of the lands near Mobile, the Choctaw leaders were careful to clarify that these lands specifically belonged to the Naniabas and Tohomes. Even though the nations had sought refuge with the Choctaws, and were living with the Chickasawhays during this time, both they and the Choctaws recognized their continuing claims to the lands on both sides of the junctions of the Mobile and Coosa Rivers. As the superintendent of Indian affairs explained in 1770, "I had my information from the Choctaws themselves and from my deputies sent to the banks of the Mississippi, inhabited by various small tribes entirely distant from and not connected with the Choctaw nation; in actual possession of the lands which has been deemed their property from time immemorial. The Choctaws in settling their boundary line with us declared the lands on the Mississippi to belong to the small nations living on them; and ceded his majesty 'lands to the westward of the Pascagoula as far as they had any claim or right to cede them' which indicates their consciousness of having no just claim to the lands on the Mississippi." Apparently, in the midst of this conference, the Choctaw leader Tomatly Mingo of the Sixtowns Division stood up and declared that "the Lands from the Nameaba [Naniaba] to Old Tomé [Tohome] were excepted in their cession made to the white people and reserved for the Nameaba and Mobillian Indians."[26] This emphasis on their having "no just claims" and the recognition of Naniaba, Tohome, and Mobilian rights to these territories are testaments to the power of the Mobilians, Tohomes, and Naniabas alliances with the Choctaws. Given how fiercely the Choctaws and Creeks fought for control of the lands between the Alabama and Tombigbee Rivers, their willingness to give up portions of their own lands, and not the Petites Nations' claims, illustrates that the Choctaws valued these relationships and continued to see these smaller nations as significant allies.

When the British failed to secure Mobilian, Naniaba, and Tohome lands via treaties with the Choctaws, colonial officials turned to less scrupulous tactics. During a conference with Creek representatives at Pensacola in 1771, British officials pressured the Creek leaders to relinquish title to these lands. In effect, British representatives bypassed both the Petites Nations and the Choctaws by recognizing Creek control over these lands, and then pressured the Creeks to cede the territory. When the Creeks initially resisted their attempts to obtain this cession, the British Indian agent John Stuart argued that, since the Creeks and British were allies, would not the Creeks let the British use the lands as they permitted the Naniabas and Tohomes to?[27] Upon receiving news of this land theft, the Naniaba chief promptly came and met with Stuart to protest the cession. The Naniaba leader "as well as the Choctaw chiefs insists that the Creeks have not the least right or claim to the lands ceded to his Majesty by the Choctaws in 1765 lying in the fork above the confluence of Tombecby [sic] and Alabama or Coosa Rivers ... said land having time immemorial been possessed by and deemed the property of the Tome's, [sic] Naniabas, and Mobilians, now incorporated with the Chickasawhays and belonging to their district."[28] Although the Choctaws verbally supported the Naniabas' claims in diplomatic meetings, they chose not to assert the Naniabas' claims with military force. Altogether, the Naniabas, Tohomes, and Mobilians numbered only about 350 people in the 1760s, so they would not independently have been able to defend their lands from the powerful Creeks or from British settlers. Therefore, despite their protestations, and those of their Choctaw allies, the British were able to steal the Mobilians, Naniabas, and Tohomes' homelands and open them up to settlers.[29] While the Tohome, Naniaba, and Mobilian communities survived, and they almost certainly maintained town-level autonomy and separate cultural identities at least for a time, in saving their communities they lost both their lands and political independence. Following this era, they gradually transformed from Petites Nations into part of the "Grand Nation" of Choctaws.

The onslaught of settlement in the Lower Mississippi Valley from 1770 through the 1790s pushed the Petites Nations out of their prerevolutionary homelands. As settler pressure intensified on Choctaws and Creeks as well, the Petites Nations found themselves confronting the threat not just of violence from Spanish, British, and American settlers but also of coercion from Creeks and Choctaws who had been forced west and were grappling with a new and expanding American Empire. While some nations, like the Biloxis and the Pakanas, pursued autonomy by migrating further away from settlers, others, like the Tohomes, sought refuge within the Choctaw nation. Even the Tunicas, with their extensive webs of connections and Lattanash's visionary leadership, were eventually pressed out of their lands, and in the 1780s left Pointe Coupée to go seek new lives in western Louisiana and Texas.

Although the Petites Nations' actions during this era demonstrate none of the diplomatic dominance of the 1760s, and they wielded less political influence than they had during the French colonial era, they continued to survive using their old strategies of migrating, seeking and providing refuge, forging new relationships, incorporating new groups into multinational settlements, and reinventing their economic strategies. By the 1780s, the histories of the Petites Nations had turned from those of small polities exercising outsized power in the borderlands to ones of survivance and creative resilience on the edges of empire. So the arrival of American settlers represented not the end of the Petites Nations' stories, but rather a turning point. In the coming decades, the Petites Nations would fully weaponize the inaccessibility of their territories, carve out niches within the expanding nineteenth-century market economy, and continue their long fight against dispossession.

CHAPTER 9

Remembering, Forgetting, and Mythologizing the Petites Nations

In Jackson County, Mississippi, the Pascagoula River sings. According to local legend, long ago, a beautiful, young Biloxi princess named Miona fell in love with a dark-eyed Pascagoula prince called Olustee. Miona's father, however, had already promised her to another Biloxi man, so she was forbidden from following her heart. In spite of her betrothal, Miona and Olustee decided to run away and marry in secrecy. When Miona's father, the chief of the Biloxis, discovered their wedding plans, he became enraged. If they wed, the Biloxi chief threatened to kill all the Pascagoulas as retribution. The young couple heard of Miona's father's plans and despaired. In their grief, they swore to drown themselves before they would be torn apart, so they plunged headlong into the nearby river, taking their own lives. The Pascagoulas were so heartbroken by the loss of their prince and his beloved that the whole tribe followed them into the water, singing their death songs until they too were taken by the current. Or so this folk legend claims. A version of this story that was published in 1935 in the *Biloxi Daily Herald* recounted their fabled end: "Now the sound of the Singing Waters softly whispers, / This weird chanting song of victory, / In memory of the valiant Pascagoulas, / And plighted love's enduring constancy."[1] Thus, as the tale goes, the noble Pascagoulas vanished from the region, leaving only their name on the river and their voices in its current.[2]

This story is a condensed version of the popular myth of the disappearance of the Pascagoulas and the origins of the famous gurgling river in Mississippi. Forbidden love, tragic demise, savage violence, and ghostly haunting: this southern legend has it all. One can even imagine a teller of this story crying "Olustee! My Love" with ingenuous earnestness. This folktale appears to have originated in the nineteenth century, and more than a century later it still compels visitors of the Gulf South who are looking for the region's ancient charm and romantic tales of a haunted Indian past. In fact, this legend is so tied to the regional identity of the town of Pascagoula that, in the 1930s, the federal government commissioned the artist Lorin Thompson to render a monumental mural depicting the fabled mass suicide of the Pascagoulas in the Pascagoula River for the local Mississippi post office. Although the painting was taken down in the 1980s, it was returned to its "rightful place" in 2010 and once again hangs in the Pascagoula post office today. The story of the singing river is even featured on the landing page of the Pascagoula city government website where it serves to welcome tourists to the city and simultaneously to remind visitors of the inevitable demise of these mythical Southeastern Indians.[3]

Gulf Coast mythology is full of legends of vanishing Indians, and the city of Pascagoula is hardly unique in celebrating and commemorating an ancient Indigenous past. The Deep South is saturated with Native place names and rivers that draw their titles from Indigenous languages, yet there is a striking absence of representation of contemporary Native people alongside these mythic histories. Stories like the tale of the singing river help make sense of the seeming dissonance between the South's fabled Native past and the absence of a Native present. Regional lore tells of star-crossed lovers, intertribal conflict, and the dramatic melting away of small Native nations into the natural surroundings.[4] These stories are convenient. They help explain how places like Bayou Goula and the Mobile, Tensaw, Biloxi, Pascagoula, and Tangipahoa rivers got their names,

Figure 17. *Legend of the Singing River*, by Lorin Thompson. Smithsonian National Postal Museum.

as well as how these nations conveniently disappeared to make room for subsequent American settlers.

Narratives of the inevitable demise and vanishing of Native peoples fit seamlessly within our national mythos of American expansion into an untamed and empty wilderness. Rarely do we stop to question the settler logic that suggests a tragic mass suicide is a reasonable explanation for what happened to an entire Indigenous nation. Furthermore, narratives like this one, which present destruction and disappearance as something that happened in time immemorial, remove any traces of settler complicity in these violent processes of removal, so they comfort us by not forcing Americans to reconcile with a landscape that is inscribed with so many markers of Indigenous dispossession.[5]

To unsettle these colonial narratives, we must return to the 1790s and critically examine their origins and the supposed disappearance of Native peoples as a precursor to American expansion. In order to solidify American land claims in the newly acquired Louisiana territory, settlers in the 1780s and 1790s insisted, much as they had for the past century, that the small Native polities of the Gulf Coast were either gone or on the verge of destruction, even as so many of these Native groups remained in the Mississippi Delta. By placing European and American reports of Native disappearance in conversation with Indigenous accounts of the same eras, it becomes clear that, although settlers increasingly failed to recognize Native peoples and land claims, the people themselves did not disappear. Instead, Petites Nations continued to rely on the practices of migrant welcome and multinational settlement to help them forge new communities or strengthen their existing nations and protect their people from the novel colonial challenges of the U.S. era. Throughout the 1790s and first decades of the nineteenth century, Native nations continued to be integrally connected to the development of the colonial South, and they developed innovative strategies that helped them both evade removal and retain community in the shadows of an expanding American Empire.

Removals and Erasures

The erasure of the Petites Nations' lives and land claims occurred alongside the larger processes of dispossession that reshaped the Indigenous South in the last decades of the eighteenth century. In this era, the Gulf South was transformed from an Indigenous-dominated borderland into the territory of a settler state. Likewise, the informal exchange economies and small colonial settlements that had defined French, Spanish, and British colonization transitioned into an agriculturally intensive plantation economy that relied on the labor of enslaved Africans. These pressures made the region less hospitable to small Native nations and pushed many of the Petites Nations to migrate to new territories on the margins of the American republic.

Between the 1780s and the 1820s, the onslaught of American settlers, the expansion of U.S. territorial claims, then the transfer of local governmental jurisdictions transformed the region. The influx of settlers after the American Revolution raised the colonial population of the Lower Mississippi Valley to 30,471 by 1785, and by 1820, the non-Indigenous population of Louisiana skyrocketed to over 150,000. The massive migrations of American settlers accelerated the process of Indigenous dispossession, transforming the Mississippi Delta into a predominantly non-Native place. While the Louisiana Purchase in 1803 did not immediately convert these Indigenous homelands into territories controlled by the Mississippi Territory government, and Native people continued to evade and contest state power through the 1820s (and beyond), this transfer did lay the framework for the forcible incorporation of this land and its people into the United States. Furthermore, during the first decades of the nineteenth century, it became increasingly clear that, although the southern states and the federal government were anxious to incorporate Native property and lands, they envisioned no future for Indigenous peoples within the American nation. For many Native Southerners, these nineteenth-century experiences of forcible incorporation into the United States resulted in violent and coerced removals westward to territories in modern-day Oklahoma.[6]

In the wake of the American Revolution, Native people east of the Mississippi River were faced with new challenges from this rapidly expanding nation. As Woody Holton, Colin Calloway, and others have demonstrated, many British subjects, especially in the southern colonies, supported the American Revolution because they believed that a new and independent government would allow them to lay claim to Native lands west of the Appalachian Mountains.[7] Indeed, in the 1790s the federal government launched and financed a military campaign to conquer the Ohio River Valley and dispossess the region's Native inhabitants so that they could open up this land for American settlement. Shawnees, Delawares, Miamis, Anishinaabeg, Kickapoos, Odawas, Potawatomis, and the other Native nations that lived in this region refused to relinquish their lands, and in the 1790s organized a massive multinational coalition to fight the invading army of this nascent American republic. In 1790 and 1791, this multinational Indigenous coalition won two battles that are still considered to be the largest Native American victories over the United States Army. However, the tremendous military successes of this international Indigenous coalition also generated an overwhelming military response from the federal government. By 1795 a brutal U.S. military campaign forced these Native nations to cede their territories in the Ohio River Valley and relocate westward. With this endeavor, the federal government illustrated to Native people across the eastern portion of the continent that it would not respect Indian land claims, and that it was willing to mobilize tremendous resources to remove Native people by force from their homelands.[8]

While some Southern nations also turned to armed resistance in the 1790s and again in the 1810s, in the first decades of the nineteenth century, the largest Southern Native nations also dedicated considerable effort toward another approach to maintaining their territory. Between the 1790s and 1830s, Creeks, Choctaws, Chickasaws, Cherokees, and Seminoles embraced aspects of the U.S. government's civilization program. Many among these nations believed that by strategically embracing some of the trappings of settler society and rendering their territories and political structures legible to U.S. officials, they would be able to stay on their lands and could have futures alongside Southern settlers. Between 1810 and 1830, many Cherokees, Creeks, Chickasaws, and Choctaws wrote constitutions, printed newspapers, embraced Christianity, fenced their properties, implemented patriarchal governance structures, and owned and exploited enslaved Africans.[9]

However, the federal government ultimately refused to acknowledge the sovereignty of Native nations. Instead of recognizing them as fellow, modern nations, as Native Southerners had hoped, Americans instead mobilized a racial logic of inherent biological inferiority to argue that Native people did not have the capacity to be citizens and that their savage ways meant that they did not deserve to hold land in the American South, Midwest, or Great Lakes regions. Therefore, in order to avoid conflict with encroaching white settlers, and under a thin veneer of benevolence, the federal government decided that Native people should be removed to Indian Territory where they would be able to "civilize" at their own pace. Between 1820 and 1840, more than sixty thousand Native people were forcibly removed from the Southeast.[10]

In addition to this physical assault on Native lands and bodies, American settlers were launching another kind of ideological attack that also sought to destroy Native claims to territory. Part of the logic of Native dispossession and the U.S. civilization program was the expectation that Native people would ultimately simply cease to be. If they were not physically killed by settlers, Native people could be made un-Indian by being civilized (and losing their distinctive culture) or by reproducing outside of their nations (and thereby reducing the amount of biological Indianness of each generation). In theory, then, as their Indigeneity was bled out and they were culturally transformed, Native peoples' claims to land and sovereign status would also be liquidated. This is what is so brilliant and insidious about the logic of blood quantum and the judicial transformation of sovereign native nations into a racial minority within the expanding American Empire. This ideology rendered a Native future with sovereign territories in North America an impossibility, and promised the gradual dissolution of Native people's "biological Indianness" and thereby their political status as citizens of foreign nations.[11]

The processes of the racialization of Native nations and Indian dispossession are fundamental components of the U.S. settler colonial framework. The term "settler colonialism" signifies ideologies and processes that seek to dispossess and eliminate Native people, to found new societies on their land, and to envision nation-states with no future for the original inhabitants. This settler logic undergirded the well-known process of Indian removal in the American Southeast, but it is also central to understanding what happened to the Petites Nations and all the other Native nations whose stories do not mirror these better-known histories.[12]

Although Indian Removal dominates our national memory and popular understanding of the histories of Native people in the Southeast, many people, including many of the Petites Nations, managed to avoid this process. The crush of settlers into the American Southeast at the turn of the nineteenth century presented Native people with a daunting challenge, and they responded in a wide variety of ways. Even among the largest nations, not all Native people chose to pursue "civilization" as a path to maintain their autonomy. For example, while many Choctaws labored to create a centralized nation-state, other Choctaws split with the nation and pursued independent strategies to avoid dispossession.[13]

As in earlier eras, coalescence remained a multidirectional process and groups of Choctaws continued to choose to separate from the larger Choctaw nation when they found that they were politically at odds with the national leadership. Around 1800, for example, a group of Choctaws chose to leave their people and homelands and to migrate west across the Mississippi River. Following the paths of some of the smaller nations, like the Biloxis and Apalachees who had sought refuge on the Red River in the 1790s, this group of Choctaws migrated west, and settled alongside Alabama and Coushatta communities on Bayou Rapide. These Alabamas and Coushattas had formerly lived as part of the Creek nation, but they too had chosen to split with the larger Creek Confederacy (and their entanglement with U.S. civilization schemes) in order to migrate west and seek their futures in places with less settler pressure.[14]

As they had for more than a century, Southeastern Native groups continued to rely on refugee acceptance to help them migrate to places of safety and find sanctuary alongside other Native nations. Stories like those of the Creek and Choctaw communities that broke off from their nations and pursued alternative paths in less-accessible parts of the Southeast complicate narratives of Native nation-building and removal which insist that this era was defined by increasing political centralization and hierarchy within Native polities. However, they also make the stories of the Petites Nations appear to be less anomalous and illustrate the diversity of strategies pursued by Native Southerners in the early nineteenth century.

For obvious reasons, the continued presence of Native nations in the American Southeast after both the Louisiana Purchase and the era of Southeastern removal complicated U.S. claims to Southern territories. If Native peoples and nations remained in these lands, then presumably their titles were not extinguished, and these lands could not be claimed by white settlers. Therefore, Native peoples who avoided centralizing into bordered nation-states that were legible to U.S. government officials in the first decades of the nineteenth century had to navigate dual pressures. If they were perceived to be large, powerful, and threatening, like the Cherokees or Choctaws, they risked violence and forced removal. So, while large nations sought legibility and prominence, many smaller nations moved to the margins of American settlements and to spaces where they were beyond the gaze of settler society and the reach of state power. They did this by drawing on the centuries-old strategies of joint settlements and refugee acceptance. Second, even as they sought to make themselves illegible to the state, Native people had to simultaneously confront American narratives that portrayed them as vanishing or extinct, or that did not recognize them as Native people. Stories like those of the vanishing Pascagoulas do just this kind of ideological work of dispossession by assigning Biloxi and Pascagoula peoples to an ancient and mythological past in ways that render their descendants unrecognizable in the present. Vanishing narratives are therefore the counterparts of forced physical removal. These folk stories and popular imaginings of Native people help illustrate how so many Southerners came to insist that the Petites Nations people had disappeared or were in decline by the turn of the nineteenth century even as their communities remained in the South.

From Petites Nations to Wandering Savages

The absence of small Native polities in American records, even as local populations remained acutely aware of Indians' presence in the Mississippi Delta, is jarring. Only two decades prior, the Petites Nations were using the Spanish and British imperial border to exert outsized political influence in the region. Barely twenty years later, the small nations' complete exclusion from diplomatic negotiations must have been acutely felt within their communities.

Compared to the 1760s and 1770s, the Spanish colonial records and American territorial papers from the 1790s and 1800s contain only sporadic references to the Petites Nations. The extensive reports detailing the Petites Nations' political maneuverings that were common among British and Spanish diplomatic correspondence no longer appeared in the reports of their American successors. Likewise, the territories and villages of Native nations also began to vanish from regional maps.[15] Travelers and new settlers in the region did not perceive these nations to be mighty diplomatic rivals, but rather wandering and scattered peoples who were the dying remnants of their former selves.

The accounts left by contemporary travelers and officials present a curious combination of recognition that Native people continued to live in the region and refusal to acknowledge them as nations. In 1804, for example, the French observer Paul Alliot recorded that "some hundreds of savages live on the outskirts of New Orleans, and live apart in the huts which they have constructed on the vacant lands." He explained that Native people sold meat, baskets, wood, and produce in the city at excellent prices and presented these Indigenous traders as critical parts of the markets of New Orleans. Likewise, Alliot stressed that the Native people who lived further from New Orleans were also important contributors to the growing American settlements as they guided travelers through the region and provided them with provisions for their journeys. By treating Native people as mere individuals, who were primarily useful to the growing settlements, Alliot conveniently sidestepped any discussion of territorial rights and sovereignty. However, Alliot could not fully ignore the political power of these nations, and he was well aware that these "savages" continued to present a threat to Spanish territorial claims west of the Mississippi. Even in this late era, Spanish officials were concerned about the ramifications if they failed to live up to their obligations to their Native allies.[16] As Alliot explained, "A score of times has the Spanish government tried to violate the treaty which binds those nations. A score of times has it been conquered; and the proprietors living far away from New Orleans have been pillaged, devastated, and murdered. Ill betide the Spaniard who would insult a savage!"[17] In essence, even as Alliot described the lands around New Orleans as "vacant," the strategic raids of Choctaws and Petites Nations that enforced their control of these territories tell a very different story about enduring Native authority over these lands.

Pierre-Louis Berquin-Duvallon, a French sugar planter who fled the Haitian Revolution in the 1790s and resettled in New Orleans, likewise insisted in 1802 that the destruction of all the Native nations of the region was nigh. As he put it, "Their race has been thinned and will probably soon become extinct. The small pox and spirituous liquors have committed unexampled devastations among the tribes. The vicinity of the whites will accelerate the blow: to civilize them is not practicable; they visit New Orleans to trade and receive presents; they behold with indifference the grandest performances of art or frigidly exclaim 'That is pretty.'"[18] Berquin-Duvallon understood the destruction of Native inhabitants in the Lower Mississippi Valley as part of the larger process of Native demise that was taking place across the Southeast. Native people were indeed facing dramatic population declines and losses of land at the turn of the nineteenth century, however, their destruction was far from realized or inevitable. By stressing that disease and alcoholism were primarily responsible for their downfall, Berquin-Duvallon suggested that Native people themselves, not settlers, were responsible for their own demise.

American territorial records portray a similar story of tribal decline and a seemingly inevitable march toward extinction. Thomas Hutchins's 1784 account of Louisiana is typical of the eighteenth-century versions of these narratives. As he explains, "About 60 miles from New Orleans are the villages of the Humas [sic] and Alibamas [sic]. The former were once a considerable nation of Indians, but are reduced now to about 25 warriors; the latter consists of about 30." Of the Tunicas he writes that, "on the East side of the river, and opposite to the upper plantations of Pointe Coupée, is the village of the Tonicas, formerly a numerous nation of Indians; but their constant intercourse with the white people, and immoderate use of spirituous liquors, have reduced them to about twenty warriors."[19] Similarly, American territorial papers from 1803 describe the Petites Nations as existing in communities of 50 to 100 persons like the "Wanderers of the tribes of Bilexis [sic] & Choctaws on Bayou Crocodile which empties into the Teche, about 50 Souls."[20] Here again, by calling these groups "wanderers" the

American state official emphasized that these groups had no fixed land claims and therefore would present no impediment to American settlement and territorial sovereignty in the region.

This ability to see Indian people while refusing to recognize Native polities as sovereign nations with territorial rights was a critical part of the project of Native erasure and dispossession. By refusing to acknowledge that the land on which their "huts" stood and where their mothers grew crops and their uncles and brothers hunted was their rightful territory, American settlers reconceptualized these Petites Nations not as sovereign polities, but as stateless savages. Without territory, these autonomous political groups could not constitute nation-states. Therefore, from the perspectives of the settlers and local officials, the Petites Nations were something less than independent foreign nations with whom the government must recognize international relationships and foreign boundaries. While this lack of acknowledgment did not mean that these Native polities were suddenly no longer sovereign nations, this perception of statelessness did lead to a completely different series of Petites Nations experiences with Spanish and American colonial governments than those of the Choctaws or other larger nations whose bordered territories forced the federal government to continue to treat them as foreign nations.

While the Petites Nations slide out of the documentary record during the 1780s and 1790s, larger native nations—like the Creeks, Choctaws, and Chickasaws—continued to feature prominently in Spanish and American diplomatic records. Through the last decades of the eighteenth century, these large confederacies continued to meet in international councils, to maintain pressure with low levels of violence, and to negotiate boundaries and land cessions, so they still appear frequently in diplomatic documents. Thanks to their savvy political leadership and military prowess, these nations also continued to form critical pieces of both Spanish and American diplomatic strategies.

In contrast, the Petites Nations were not able to exercise the same level of regional influence as they had over the past century, so they no longer featured prominently in imperial reports after the 1770s. Their fall from diplomatic power and the rise in language that depicted the Petites Nations as wandering, impoverished, and marginalized groups has led historians to describe this era as defined by the process of Petite Nations' slide into alcoholism and disappearance. As F. Todd Smith argued in his aptly titled 2005 book, *From Dominance to Disappearance: The Indians of Texas and the Near Southwest, 1786–1859*, the Petites Nations were overwhelmed by settlers during this era, and the collective numerical advantage that small nations had previously enjoyed was gone by the 1780s.[21] Anthropologists and historians have also frequently portrayed this as an era of both political and cultural decline or as a time when assimilation began to strip them of their Indigeneity.[22] Smith is correct in his assessment of the loss of Petites Nations' diplomatic power and the crucial role of population shift. However, analyses that focus primarily on the military and political might of these nations elide the profound stories of the resilience of Petites Nations that increasingly embraced obscurity and inaccessibility as strategies of survivance.[23]

More than two centuries on, the enduring power of these narratives has had devastating consequences for the Pointe-au-Chien and other Native Southerners who avoided removal. Around the turn of the nineteenth century, small groups of Ishak/Atakapas and Biloxis fled settler expansion and sought refuge with groups of Chitimachas in the southern bayous. Because these groups were successful in avoiding invading Spanish and American colonists, there are only sparse archival records of their history during this era. This paucity of documentary records, coupled with the overwhelming perception that the Petites Nations were all but destroyed by the late eighteenth century, has hindered the Pointe-au-Chien Indian Tribe's contemporary efforts to secure federal acknowledgment. Even though there is strong archival, oral, and archaeological evidence of Indigenous communities in the marshy southern lands that are now Terrebonne and Lafourche Parishes both before and after the decades around the turn of the nineteenth century, the Bureau of Indian Affairs' Branch of Acknowledgment and Research has concluded that the tribe has not demonstrated sufficient evidence of the existence of the Pointe-au-Chien community before 1830. So, for Pointe-au-Chien, as for their Houma, Biloxi, and Choctaw neighbors, these histories of erasure, marginalization, and invisibility are not confined to the late eighteenth century, but rather have fundamentally shaped their community's experiences for centuries. Their ancestors' survival and ability to build new communities in the wake of dispossession have therefore come at a very high cost.[24]

Hearing Tunica and Biloxi Histories

The Tunicas' and Biloxis' descendants also tell very different stories about this tumultuous era than those of their settler neighbors. Their own nations' histories neither suggest that they crumbled in the wake of the American Empire, nor vanished into the bayous leaving nothing but their names on the landscape of the Gulf South. Instead, they understand this era as a time of reorganization and migration. By the 1780s, the multinational settlement near Pointe Coupée where both the Tunicas and Biloxis had lived was shattering. Like the Mobilians, Naniabas, and Tohomes who lived near Mobile, the Tunicas found that the crush of settlers into the region was making their lives untenable in their homelands. With a new, burgeoning American population, the Petites Nations could no longer hold on to this prime riverine territory, so they developed new strategies to protect their communities from further violence.

In 1933 Sesostrie Youchigant, a former chief and a fluent Tunica speaker, spoke to the California linguist Mary Haas about his people's origins. Of his many stories, two refer specifically to this era. The first explains the demise of the Petite Nation of Avoyelles (who were the Tunicas' distant neighbors), and the second describes the Biloxis' migrations and the continued importance of refugee acceptance.[25]

Youchigant began his telling of "The Tunica and the Spanish Defeat the Avoyelle" with an account of how the Tunicas and Avoyelles had historically been great allies. To open the tale, Youchigant recounted how the Avoyelles once joined the Tunicas in an assault against the English. Presumably, Youchigant was referring to Lattanash and Perruquier's stunning defeat of the British navy in 1764 and the joy the Tunicas and Ofogoulas felt in protecting their lands and forcing the British to beg for an alliance. "The Tunica where the ground on he used to hunt. Now the Englishman came. Now they fought. Now the Mississippi he was coming down. The river where he came and he settled. Now Indians they got together, they came to fight him. Now half they killed them."[26] He tells this history as if he were witnessing the event unfold "now," before his very eyes. His style captures the listener's attention, making each development sound urgent and immediate, and it also emphasizes the enduring power of the community memories of these histories.

Youchigant then explained how the Tunicas were guided by a flock of buzzards to relocate their people across the river after the battle. A group of buzzards led the Tunicas to the Avoyelles' village. This sequence of events seems to refer to the migration of the Tunicas from Pointe Coupée to a village in Avoyelles Parish in the 1780s. "Now the buzzards were crossing. Now he was (sitting) looking [at] his people. He spoke, 'where the buzzards, where they're going, [he] was watching.' He said. Now, his people, he sent right straight, 'if you all are going where straight land is there,' he told them. Now the boat they took, they were going [to] the island, where they crossed, they found (the land.) Now the Avoyelle were there. Now there was great danger, there were too many. Now back they turned and went again to their home, when they came, the chief, they spoke to him. Now the land they found it (again) but the Avoyelle were there. Now there was great danger, there were too many."[27]

With both the Tunicas and Avoyelles desiring to live on this beautiful, "straight" land, the Tunica leader was nervous. Presumably, this land was further away from the white settlers and it promised to nourish their people and provide safety. But, as Youchigant recalled, "There was great danger, there were too many" people who all wanted to live there. Settler land pressure created exacerbated conflicts among Native neighbors, even those who had been longtime allies, and the Avoyelles responded to this overcrowding by attempting to kick the Tunicas off the land. They launched a surprise attack against their old Tunica allies and killed the Tunica leader. Youchigant recollected that the Tunicas went to their Spanish allies for help, and that the combined Spanish and Tunica force returned to seek vengeance against the Avoyelles. The battle was long and gruesome. As he explained, the Tunica women were mourning and making mounds in the earth while blood ran "up to their waists."[28] Ultimately, the Tunicas emerged victorious and were able to claim the land for their people.

A close analysis of this story suggests that the Tunicas relied on traditional patterns of diplomacy, multinational settlement, violence, and forced adoption to rebuild their communities during the Spanish era. In his descriptions, Youchigant included many details that reference older patterns of Lower Mississippi Valley diplomacy and social practices. For example, before launching into the account of the major battle, he described the Avoyelles and the Tunicas sharing a meal in traditional diplomatic fashion. "Something you didn't cook? ... hominy not cooked?" the Tunica chief asked the leader of the Avoyelles. At any major international summit, Petites Nations people would have been expected to feed their guests, so the Tunica leader was likely waiting for the Avoyelle women to begin the multinational gathering by presenting stewed corn. After this meal, the leaders did begin discussing their alliance, or as Youchigant put it, "now the chief the both friends they made." Without warning, at least in Youchigant's telling, the Avoyelles suddenly went from feasting and honoring their allies and guests to attacking them.[29]

Youchigant's description of shared ritual meals, leaders discussing international relationships, a sudden, violent betrayal, and then the complete destruction of the nation, all describe parts of the methods that Petites Nations commonly used to both integrate and sever multinational settlements in times of crisis. With so many people living on the same lands, and no unifying judicial or political superstructure between nations, it was very difficult to peacefully sever relationships or resolve disputes between autonomous groups. This pressure

Figure 18. Photo of Sesostrie Youchigant in 1939. Mss.Ms.Coll.94, Haas Papers, Tunica Series, box 179, Graphics: 8059, APS. Reproduced with permission of the American Philosophical Society, Philadelphia.

only became worse as multinational settlements had access to smaller and smaller territories as their Spanish and American neighbors gobbled up the surrounding lands. In the incident between the Avoyelles and the Tunicas, Youchigant makes it clear that the shortage of land was the central issue that led to conflict. The Avoyelle chief insisted that the land belonged to *his* people. Perhaps after eating corn and reaffirming their friendship, the Tunica leader refused to leave. As settlers had overwhelmed his people's homelands, he did not have a place he could return to. Youchigant's story does not describe the conversation between the Avoyelle and Tunica leaders, so we are left to speculate about how their negotiations transpired. Ultimately, however, the Avoyelles turned to violence to force their former allies out.

At least some of the surviving Avoyelles seem to have been integrated into the Tunica community. Perhaps some of them were taken captive during this battle and made into forced kin, or perhaps they chose to join the Tunicas when their own nation fractured after this bloody conflict. Although the Avoyelles vanish from the documentary records by the turn of the nineteenth century, many contemporary Tunica-Biloxi tribal members recall that they had Avoyelle ancestors, and there were members of their community who maintained Avoyelle identities through the twentieth century.[30]

The documentary record of the Avoyelles during the eighteenth century is sparse and vague, and it suggests that this nation prioritized alliances with Native nations over Europeans and aimed to keep their distance from French, English, and Spanish colonists. Because colonial officials did not regularly deal with the Avoyelles, they often misidentified their people so sometimes they appear in the records as the Little Tensas, sometimes as part of the Natchez, sometimes by other names like Tassengoula. At times, they were even confused with the Tunicas.[31] Tunica and other Indigenous historical records are therefore essential to reconstructing their fragmented history. The ethnologist John Swanton translated the Tunicas' name for the Avoyelles, the *shi' xkal-tīni*, as meaning "Flint[arrow]-point-people," while the Choctaw called them the "people of the stones." Given these titles, and their historic location along the Red River near groups that specialized in salt or bear grease, it seems probable that the Avoyelles had developed a specialized niche economy manufacturing and trading crafted flint points. While they lived along the Red River, their economic enterprises meant that individual Avoyelles frequently circulated through the Pointe Coupée region.[32]

As they had with many other Petites Nations, French colonists were eager to proclaim the demise of the Avoyelles. In 1758 the French governor Louis

Kerlérec declared that the Avoyelle nation, along with the Chaouacha, Ouacha, Acolapissa, and Bayagoula nations had been destroyed by their proximity to the French and by alcohol.[33] Governor Kerlérec must have been deeply surprised eight years later to receive the news that these supposedly deceased Indians had partnered with the Tunicas and mounted a formidable attack on the British navy. Even more disturbingly, this allegedly vanished nation had helped the Tunicas, Choctaws, and Ofogoulas mount a crushing blow against the British Empire. After their joint victory, the Tunicas, Ofogoulas, and Choctaws appear frequently in local British documents, but the Avoyelles do not. The commanders at the British fort near Pointe Coupée recorded continual diplomatic negotiations, exchanges of services with the Tunicas, and receipts for the generous gifts the British paid to the Tunica nation to maintain their alliance and stave off another humiliating military defeat. However, neither the Avoyelles nor the Ofogoulas appear as recipients of British gifts. Both the Ofogoulas and the Avoyelles lived on the western side of the river and unlike Lattanash, their leaders seemed to have no desire to form alliances with the British. Perhaps the charismatic Perruquier had convinced the Avoyelles to avoid these dangerous colonists.

Although the British had no relationships with the Avoyelles, their people frequently circulated near Pointe Coupée throughout the early 1770s. In the spring of 1770, as the prolonged Choctaw visits were raising tensions among Tunica and Spanish settlers near the Tunica villages, the Spanish commander Jean-François Allain was also working with the Ofogoula leader, Perruquier, and two Avoyelle leaders, St. André and Noucache, to gather intelligence on the movements of the Chickasaws and Choctaws in the lands to the north. In April the leaders met with Allain and informed him that they had nothing unusual to report, aside from the fact that both groups were gathering in great numbers. This singular reference provides good evidence of both the endurance of the Avoyelle nation and the continuance of their strategy of minimizing their interactions with European settlers.[34]

On the few occasions when the Avoyelles did appear in colonial correspondence, they were often described as negotiating with European officials alongside the Tunicas. In both 1771 and 1777, the Avoyelles appeared at Spanish posts with the Tunicas and the two nations received gifts in joint ceremonies. The formidable Lattanash received personal gifts along with the larger tribute to his nation and to the Avoyelles, but there is no mention of the Avoyelles' leader(s). Usually, each Petite Nation would receive their own gifts from colonial officials. So it is puzzling that the Avoyelles who, according to the colonial records, lived further up the Red River and operated independently of the Tunicas, received joint gifts with the Tunicas who were living alongside the Spanish and British near Pointe Coupée. Based on these records, it seems likely that in this era the Avoyelles had split and that some of their people lived alongside the Tunicas while another group resided on the Red River. Even though the Tunicas and Avoyelles lived as neighbors in a multinational settlement and accepted a single set of gifts, they still maintained separate political and social entities. So the Spanish referred to them as the discrete nations of the "Tonicas y Avoyelles."[35] Perhaps this same small group of Avoyelles encouraged or facilitated the Tunicas' move to Avoyelle territory when they were pushed out by Spanish and American settlers. In any case, the Tunicas had good reason to believe they would be welcome in Avoyelle homelands in their time of need, and the ultimate forced integration of the two nations through the bloody fight permanently fused these old allies.

The present-day Tunica-Biloxi Tribe—which is composed of the descendants of the Ofogoulas, Biloxis, and Tunicas—also recognizes the Avoyelles as an important part of their ancestry. If we can read "along the bias grain" of later ethnographic work, it is possible to see further evidence of Tunica and Avoyelle integration. As she worked with the Tunica community in the 1930s, Mary Haas somehow managed to conclude that not only the Avoyelles but also the Tunicas were rapidly dying, and both nations would soon be destroyed. As she put it, "Near the end of the nineteenth century the Indian village near Marksville was inhabited by the *remnants of at least three rapidly dying tribes: Tunica, Ofo, and Avoyelles*."[36] The once again allegedly deceased Avoyelles had apparently been resurrected so they could die yet again at the turn of the following century. The ethnologist John Swanton likewise confirmed the survival of at least some of the Avoyelles within this community—even as he worked to salvage and record the culture of these "dying" peoples. During his trip to Louisiana to research the Tunica tribe in 1908, John Swanton found that one of his Tunica informants had an Avoyelle grandmother.[37] Thus, despite insistence that the Avoyelles had been destroyed in the 1750s, at least some of the Avoyelles were clearly alive and maintaining close relationships with the Tunicas through the mid-nineteenth century.

While the Tunicas and Avoyelles merged, other Petites Nations communities split apart and migrated to regions that were under less pressure from settlers. Youchigant's second story, "The Origins of Indian Bayou," explains how the Biloxis came to settle near the Tunicas during the U.S. era. In this account, he recalls that, while "the American Governor gave them land there," the Biloxis sold their land and "his people all every which way they go live."[38]

Beyond Youchigant's description of the story as taking place during the time of the "American Governor" (presumably the governor of the Mississippi Territory), his discussion of disease also helps situate this story in the late eighteenth century. Youchigant described a terrible illness that struck the Biloxis. As he recalled, "Now the people every day died." The Biloxis sought to remedy this plague by removing dangerous spirits from the waters near their homes.[39] Between 1778 and 1779, the smallpox epidemic that had wracked the revolutionary army spread through the Southeast and arrived in the Lower Mississippi Valley where it took an especially high toll on the Native population.[40] As more and more settlers flooded into the region in the 1780s and 1790s, they carried with them influenza, fever, and other deadly viruses. The spread of these diseases may have prompted the Biloxis to seek more secluded regions further from the centers of colonial settlement and disease transmission. At least some of the Biloxis sought temporary refuge with the Tunicas during the first years of the nineteenth century.

It further seems that the Biloxis did continue to "go every which way" after leaving their homelands near Mobile in the 1760s. First, they sought safe haven for their communities by migrating to Pointe Coupée to live near the Tunicas in the 1760s and early 1770s, then they moved further west to the Red River and into Texas in the late 1770s and 1780s. In 1806 the Indian agent John Sibley reported that the group of Biloxis who had been living with the Tunicas in Avoyelles Parish moved out of their village.[41]

Youchigant's stories also discuss the Biloxis who went to "Long/Grand Island" and to Pinewood, Louisiana. Today, the land near Grand Isle, Louisiana, is largely underwater due to coastal erosion, but within the adjacent Terrebonne and Lafourche Parishes, the Isle de Jean Charles Band of Biloxi-Chitimacha-Choctaw Tribe, the Grand Caillou/Dulac Band of Biloxi-Chitimacha-Choctaw, the Bayou Lafourche Band of Biloxi-Chitimacha Indians, and the Pointe-au-Chien Indian Tribe all trace their lineages to Biloxi ancestors. Youchigant's recollections of Biloxi migrations line up with Pointe-au-Chien community memory of the movement of Biloxis into Chitimacha communities during this era. The bayous of Lafourche and Terrebonne were difficult terrain even before coastal erosion and the damage done by oil pipeline infrastructure dragged much of this land back into the sea. These marshlands protected the small migrant communities of Biloxis and Chitimachas, as well as larger groups of Houmas who also sought refuge on the peripheries of the growing settler empire. Until the twentieth century, these Biloxi, Chitimacha, and Houma descendants were largely undisturbed by either white settlers or the federal government. In the bayous they fished, hunted, grew sugarcane, and traveled up to New Orleans to sell their fish and baskets and to buy essentials. By building lives and communities beyond the gaze of their settler neighbors, these small nations were rendered invisible or marginal in the eyes of the state and able to peacefully retain autonomous territories out of the way of the exploding colonial population.[42]

Youchigant's stories directly challenge the narratives of Biloxi and Pascagoula disappearance that legends like the "singing river" popularized. In his telling of "The Origins of Indian Bayou," he identifies Pinewood as a destination of a Biloxi group during the 1770s. Spanish records indicate that in 1775 there were some Biloxis living in Rapides Parish (about sixty miles east of Pinewood) with their old Pascagoula allies. In the 1780s, a segment of the Biloxis were living at Bayou Boeuf (thirty miles north and east), which was also known as Indian Creek, and had settled in close proximity to a group of Choctaws. By 1805 at least some of this Rapides group had relocated further east again to the area near Marksville in close proximity to the Tunicas.[43] Thus, rather than participating in some tragic, mass suicide, the Biloxis rebuilt communities with the Pascagoulas and vanished not into a river, but into Texas.

Tracing out the histories of the Tunicas and Biloxis in detail illustrates the stark divergences between settler accounts of Indigenous disappearance and destruction and Native people's stories of survival and community reinvention. Furthermore, by putting these histories in conversation, it becomes clear that Native explanations of this turbulent era are absolutely essential to understand this past. The records of the Tunicas and Biloxis are some of the clearest for the Petites Nations, but they are by no means exceptional. Instead, the processes of migration and integration, and the devastating losses they describe, are indicative of broader trends across many of the Petites Nations as they struggled to survive the transition of the Lower Mississippi Valley from an Indigenous-dominated borderland to a settler state.

Throughout the 1780s and 1790s, the Petites Nations continued to relocate and to seek new multinational settlements. Many of them chose new homes in remote lands in western Louisiana or in the difficult bayou terrain of southern Louisiana, or they looked for locations that were under less pressure from settlers, but that also gave them access to trade with Spanish settlers. In Avoyelles Parish, the Tunicas and their Ofogoula and Avoyelle allies made themselves integral parts of the local economies. Instead of supplying provisions and labor to the colonial fort at Pointe Coupée, they provided meat and services to settlers, and they cultivated a reputation as both harmless and valuable Native neighbors. Nations like the Chitimachas and Houmas, who lived further from colonial settlements, brought meat, fish, and baskets to trade in New Orleans and they migrated seasonally between the city and the bayous. Further west, the Atakapas, who were more insulated from the brunt of colonial expansion, participated in a black-market exchange of stolen horses and cattle with Louisiana settlers.[44]

Many Petites Nations that lived in proximity to colonial settlements sustained relations with Euro-American settlers by providing intelligence and services in addition to trade. Sometimes these services even functioned to uphold the exploitative plantation societies that had dispossessed their communities. Occasionally, Petites Nations people served as informants or slave catchers for plantation owners, or worked on plantations themselves. For example, in 1784 Acadian settlers in Lafourche Parish paid twelve Houma men to help them track down several enslaved people who had fled into the bayou. Likewise, in 1796 two Tunica women reported an alleged slave revolt at Pointe Coupée. This conspiracy has become one of the most infamous incidents in Spanish Louisiana history. As Gwendolyn Midlo Hall has demonstrated, the enslaved Africans near Pointe Coupée were influenced by the rhetoric and promise of liberty of the French and Haitian Revolutions and engaged in heated debates about their potential paths to freedom. While their actual plans are unclear from the records, French settlers' fear of an armed slave insurrection led them to crack down on all the enslaved who were reportedly involved in this liberation movement. Between May and June 1795, fifty-seven enslaved Africans and three white settlers were convicted of participating in the conspiracy, and twenty-three enslaved Africans were brutally executed.

The two Tunica women, Madeleine and Françoise, who are both identified as "sauvagesse" in court documents, and who both lived on the Riché estate near Pointe Coupée, provided key testimony in these trials. They explained that they had learned of this planned slave revolt when bad weather forced them to stop in the *cyprèere* (swamp) behind Widow LaCour's plantation. They reported to French authorities that Chika, another Tunica woman, who was living on Widow LaCour's plantation, told them of the enslaved men and women's plans to revolt. It is not clear if these Tunica women were working as free or coerced laborers, but they were obviously not being treated like the enslaved Africans held on these estates because they could freely leave the plantations as they chose. It is also impossible to gauge from the records whether these women believed that the enslaved Africans really were planning to overthrow their masters and murder Chika along with the plantation owners, or if these women were trading this information to their own ends.[45] In either case, these records suggest that at least some Petites Nations peoples' labor supported plantation regimes in the Deep South. While both African and Indigenous people challenged the power of white settlers during this era, their struggles to protect themselves and their communities did not always overlap, and some Indigenous peoples labored in ways that upheld structures of white supremacy and plantation slavery. These small sections of testimony also illustrate that Tunica people worked in a variety of spaces and capacities for settlers during the 1790s, and that they continued to capitalize on their ability to trade intelligence as a way to maintain relationships with their white neighbors.

These combinations of migration to distant or difficult terrains and sustained economic connections with white settlers provided the Petites Nations communities with relative autonomy on the margins of colonial society. The Petites Nations had thrived for generations by positioning their people geographically on the edges of larger confederacies and nations. These borderlands helped them maintain their independence and accumulate power by giving them options to forge connections with a wider range of polities. As many nations buckled in the face of the expanding American Empire, the Petites Nations again sought independence on the peripheries of a large nation, but this time being beyond the limits of state power meant being on the extreme margins of a single, dominant nation.

Dangers of Life on the Margins

Petites Nations peoples who lived in remote territories during the nineteenth century managed to obtain some security and independence, however the combination of repeated migrations, difficult terrain, and the power of settler rhetoric that insisted these groups were stateless and uncivilized meant that the limited protections afforded to the Native nations that had formal relationships with the U.S. government were not available to the Petites Nations. In contrast to their French, Spanish, and British predecessors, when U.S. territorial officials moved into what they called "Mississippi Territory" after the Louisiana Purchase, these representatives did not seek diplomatic relationships with the Petites Nations.[46] Unlike in the 1760s when Lattanash had been able to force the British to enter into an alliance with his people via military resistance, by 1800 these small communities were in no position to take on the U.S. Army, so an armed response was no longer a viable option.

Not having treaties created problems for many of the Petites Nations, as this meant that they lacked formal recognition of their territories or sovereignty by the federal government. Without state-sanctioned claims of territorial sovereignty, the Petites Nations had limited options for seeking recourse against settlers who trespassed or committed crimes on their lands. For example, in 1807 an American settler murdered a Coushatta man near Natchitoches, Louisiana, and the Coushattas found themselves caught in a jurisdictional bind. The Coushattas lived in far western Louisiana, in an area that twenty years prior would have been considered a remote village along the Sabine River. During the 1760s, as the Naniabas and Tohomes moved into the Choctaw nation to seek refuge from settler pressure and the Choctaw and Creek war, the Coushattas took a different approach and opted to leave the Creek nation.[47] The same fears of violence along the Choctaw and Creek front drove all three nations to migrate and embrace dramatic political changes, but they all pursued different strategies. While the Tohomes and Naniabas sought safety in numbers, the Coushattas desired the mobility and flexibility offered by a smaller population and migrated west across the Mississippi River. Unfortunately for the Coushattas, their efforts to escape frontier violence and encroaching settlers did not last long.

By the turn of the century, American settlers flooded as far west as the Sabine River, and unlike their Creek relatives in the East who had treaties with the U.S. government, the Coushattas had no formal claims to their lands or recognition of their jurisdictional sovereignty. Therefore, they found it difficult to manage trespassers on their lands. When a Coushatta man was murdered in 1807 by a white settler, several Coushatta leaders and some of his relations sought out the American Indian agent John Sibley. Like most other Southeastern nations, the Coushattas believed that it was the responsibility of the kin of the victim of a murder to seek restitution for their loved one, so this man's family hoped that Sibley would help them fulfill their duty. It is important to note that rather than seeking to kill another American they instead chose to go to a U.S. representative and seek restitution in a way that would be socially acceptable to their American neighbors. This alternative means of justice would cover their relative's death and rebalance the spiritual forces that had been disturbed by his murder, without necessitating more bloodshed. In essence, by bringing Sibley into this process of restitution the Coushatta family members were seeking to adapt their long-standing strategies for regulating violence to the new contexts of this settler era.

Sibley could not or would not cover the death with gifts or punish the murderer, so the Coushattas returned to their traditional approach and sought to avenge this murder on their own. After several Coushattas (possibly the slain man's kin) killed two Americans, the territorial governor escalated the matter to the U.S. secretary of war. The case helped convince the American territorial governor William Claiborne that this type of violence would continue to be an issue, and he recommended that the United States enter into formal relationships with the Native nations as soon as possible. As he put it, "My own opinion is, that differences between the Frontier Settlers, and the Small tribes West of the Mississippi, will frequently arise until Treaties are entered into with them. The Conchattas [Coushattas] consider themselves a Separate Nation; they are not bound by Treaty to surrender a murderer and was the demand made on the present occasion, it would no doubt be refused."[48]

In 1826, as discussion over Southern Indian removal was reaching a fever pitch, the Tunicas too sought federal protection for their lands. While the Cherokees, Choctaws, and Creeks fought to defend their lands through the U.S. court system and by signing additional treaties with the federal government, the Tunicas similarly aimed to use the local courts and the power of federal recognition to hold their lands. In 1826 a settler named Celestin Moreau attempted to force one of the Tunica villages off of their lands near present-day Goudeau, Louisiana. Moreau had acquired written title to the land through the local land office, and thereby claimed that the land was now his rightful property. The Tunicas contracted a lawyer to pursue their case. However, the Tunicas had no treaty with the federal government guaranteeing them this land, and when they presented their case to the registrar of the lands, he refused to uphold the Tunicas' claims. In fact, the registrar was explicit in his decision that, as uncivilized peoples, the Tunicas had no legal rights to any of their lands. As he put it, "The spirit and intentions of the law does not exclude them as Indians, but it certainly does as savages."[49] The combination of the lack of treaties and the ideological might of stereotypes of Indians as stateless barbarians enabled the dispossession of a nation that had been among the most powerful of the Petites Nations merely fifty years prior.

For the next century and a half, the Tunicas continued to fight to preserve their community and to obtain federal acknowledgment before finally receiving federal recognition. In the twentieth century, the Tunicas again sought the strength of international tribal alliances. In the 1920s, the Tunica chief Earl Barbry assessed that there was again an advantage to being part of a multinational Indigenous group so he invited the Biloxi Choctaws of Indian Bayou to apply with the Tunicas for joint federal recognition.[50] Through all the relocation and turmoil of the nineteenth century, the Tunicas had maintained their relationships with their Biloxi and Choctaw allies and neighbors. In the early twentieth century, the Biloxis, Choctaws, and Tunicas all lived in close proximity to Marksville, Louisiana. The three nations gathered regularly to dance and play stickball and to catch up with their kin and friends. Even after more than a century, the groups still had to communicate with one another in Mobilian (the regional Indigenous trade language) because, despite their close proximity, the Tunicas still spoke Tunica, the Biloxis still spoke Biloxi, and the Choctaws still spoke Choctaw, as their ancestors had done for generations.[51] Their multinational settlement preserved local political autonomy and culture, sustained alliances among these nations for more than a century, and prepared the nations for their next battle against a colonial government. Only this time it would be waged with documents, anthropologists, and genetic samples rather than with flintlocks and pirogues.

Their road to recognition was long and arduous, but in 1981 the Tunica-Biloxi Tribe of Louisiana finally acquired recognition from the federal government. In part, this process was made more difficult by the pervasive myth that all the "real Indians" of the Gulf South had been removed, assimilated, or had vanished into the rivers and mists of time.[52] In 1978 the Tunica chief Earl Barbry recalled the Tunica-Biloxi tribal frustration with the long and crushing colonial process of obtaining recognition of his people as both authentic Native Americans and as a rightful sovereign nation. As he put it, "I guess there was a reason for it, but to us, it seemed rather ridiculous. You know, we knew we existed as a tribe, we knew who we were. And it's kind of frustrating that Indians are the only ones to have to prove who they are, where they came from.... It's rather insulting when the Spanish, French, and British governments recognized our tribe—were allies of the Tunica-Biloxi—for years. And there's documentation to that effect: letters written by those governments acknowledging that the tribe existed as a nation and should be treated as such, with respect. Yet the United States government didn't see fit to recognize us—recognize our existence—until the 1980s."[53]

As Chief Barbry explained, there remains a fundamental disconnect between the way settler Southerners and Indigenous Southerners understand the histories and trajectories of the Gulf Coast's small Native nations. According to colonial records and American myths, Petites Nations have been destroyed and/or have been continually on the brink of vanishing for the last three hundred years. These settler narratives have warped our understanding of the Lower Mississippi Valley's Indigenous history and of Native peoples' relationships to Louisiana as a colony, state, and territory. They also continue to harm contemporary Native Southerners. Still, the resilience and stubbornness of the Petites Nations' descendants—who continue to tell their own stories, defend their own lands, and proudly claim their Native American identities—have prevented these settler dreams and stories of Indigenous disappearance from becoming reality. The living descendants of these small Native nations know that their people have always been here, living in multinational settlements, preserving their distinctive cultures, and embracing new kin as their ancestors have done for centuries. Or, as John D. Barbry, the current director of the Language and Cultural Revitalization Program of the Tunica-Biloxi tribe more succinctly puts it, "'*Tayoroni-Halayihku Hihchi 'Ɔnta!*' The Tunica-Biloxis remain here!"[54]

* * *

Beginning in the 1760s for the Mobile River groups, and in the late 1770s for the nations near Pointe Coupée, the Petites Nations steadily moved away from colonial settlements. These migrations form part of the larger story of forced removals and relocations of Native peoples east of the Mississippi in the sixty years after the Revolutionary War. However, the Petites Nations' relocation processes are distinct from those of the Choctaw Nation or their larger Native neighbors. By staying in such small communities, Petites Nations peoples were able to move into areas with more limited resources and form new multinational settlements or defend their existing communities in areas of unhospitable terrain. In essence, although American settler pressure forced the dispossession of the Petites Nations, their relocations were orchestrated not by the U.S. government, but rather independently or in collaboration with other Native groups. Even hundreds of years later, many of the descendants of the Petites Nations still maintain these multinational communities and identities. As we can see from the Alabama-Coushatta, the Tunica-Biloxi, the Pointe-au-Chien, the Isle de Jean Charles Band of Biloxi-Chitimacha-Choctaw Tribe, the Grand Caillou/DuLac Band of Biloxi-Chitimacha-Choctaw, the Bayou Lafourche Band of Biloxi-Chitimacha Indians, and other multinational tribal groups, these small settlements continued to make space for people of different national backgrounds and provided a way to preserve distinct cultural identities. In these names and the way these nations have held on to their multiple national and ethnic origins, we can see the longevity of the refugee acceptance practice and the continuing power of this system to help the Petites Nations navigate the nineteenth century.

The American-era histories of Petites Nations are not stories of power and dominance and daring military maneuvers, but they do form compelling narratives of how the Tunicas, Biloxis, Chitimachas, and others managed to avoid the crushing engine of the American settler empire. Thus, while the closing of the Lower Mississippi Valley borderlands forced the Petites Nations to the margins of colonial society, many of these communities found ways to once again adapt and protect their communities in the face of seemingly insurmountable obstacles.

Similar to the stories of so many Native peoples who lived through the periods during which their homelands were overrun by non-Native settlers, the stories of the Petites Nations at the turn of the nineteenth century are marked by the tragedies of land loss and violence. In spite of this, they are not fundamentally narratives of social decay and declension. For more than a century, Petites Nations peoples had navigated violence, dislocation, and political upheavals wrought by colonial networks. The conversion of the Gulf South from an Indigenous borderland to a plantation economy was radically different from the upheavals of the eighteenth century in that the Petites Nations were confronting a new expanding settler state and a new set of racial ideologies. However, for those who were able to employ the strategies they had developed over the past century, including migration, economic reinvention, refugee acceptance, and multinational settlements, they were able not just to survive, but in many cases to hold on to their lands and cultures through to the present century. Their survival demands that we look more critically at narratives that insist on Southern Indigenous erasure or totalizing removal, and listen to the stories of the many Native nations and their descendants who remain in the homelands of their ancestors. Today, the Pascagoula River may sing, but so too do the Tunica-Biloxi, in the Tunica language, on their sovereign tribal lands in the Mississippi River Delta.[55]

AFTERWORD

As I finished writing this book, Hurricane Ida tore through Louisiana's southern bayous. On Sunday, August 29, 2021, I sat in my tiny apartment in New York City sending frantic emails and text messages and feeling helpless as the powerful category 4 hurricane made landfall first near Port Fourchon, Louisiana, and then a second time at Pointe-aux-Chênes, Louisiana. The storm seemed to pause interminably over Terrebonne and Lafourche Parishes where the tribal homelands of the Pointe-au-Chien, United Houma Nation, the Grand Caillou/Dulac Band of Biloxi-Chitimacha-Choctaw, the Bayou LaFourche Band of Biloxi-Chitimacha Indians, and the Isle de Jean Charles Band of the Biloxi-Chitimacha-Choctaw Tribe are all located. The eye of the storm stalled over these Indigenous communities, generating tornadoes and flood waters that wreaked havoc on the land. Salt-soaked sustained winds of more than 150 miles per hour and sheets of pounding rain tore off roofs, dragged away chunks of marshland and aquatic life, and flung fishing boats and tree limbs across the sodden ground. The scene left behind is that of a disaster zone. Most of the homes at Pointe-aux-Chênes have been destroyed and their contents—patterned dishes passed down from grandmothers, photographs of weddings and men brandishing a bountiful day's catch, tribal regalia, and soaked and mangled furniture—still dot the landscape. As the storm curved north and east it toppled power lines in New Orleans, leaving much of the city without power for weeks. Days later, the largely spent storm swept through my New York neighborhood flooding subways and basement apartments.[1]

The scope of the destruction is hard to comprehend. Not only have the already vulnerable and vanishing wetlands of the southern bayou been dealt another crushing blow but so too have the Indigenous communities who rely on these lands to make their homes and livelihoods. Mercifully, most of the folks who live in Pointe-aux-Chênes were able to evacuate, but it took Pointe-au-Chien tribal members days, and in some cases weeks or months, before they were able to return. Downed trees and immense piles of wreckage blocked the roads, and state and federal aid has been slow to arrive. The first tribal members to return began to clear the roads, and over the coming weeks extraordinary Louisianians and local organizations worked with the community to begin to remove the debris. Donald and Theresa Dardar, Pointe-au-Chien tribal members and longtime community advocates, were among the first on the scene, hauling wood and assessing the damage. As Theresa explains, "Most everyone wants to come back home. They say they will rebuild because they want to hang on to this community." The Dardars and others in their community have set up a relief station at the Pointe-au-Chien Indian Tribe Community Center. This building is mercifully intact, and they have used the space to distribute food, paper goods, and other essentials to neighbors in need.[2]

Two months later, in late October, the situation remains materially the same for the Pointe-au-Chien Indian Tribe. Patty Ferguson tells me that the Tribe is struggling to get assistance from the parish, state, or federal governments, and Laura Kelley explains with grief that "homes are just totally demolished." FEMA has yet to arrive, so many in the community have been left without trailers, electricity, and running water for months. Of the eighty homes in lower Pointe-aux-Chênes, only twelve are currently livable. The inhabitants are relying on the heroic efforts of community members and friends to clean up the wreckage and to find temporary shelter. Among them, Patty has been helping organize recovery efforts from afar and Laura repeatedly heads down to the bayou with busloads of Tulane University students to haul debris and clear the ground.[3]

Although Pointe-au-Chien tribal members are determined to rebuild their community, without substantial federal or state financial assistance the road to restoration will be long and difficult. Patty Ferguson stresses to me that the rebuild must be sustainable, and therefore the construction and restoration of homes must be designed to withstand category 5 hurricanes and to meet the increased elevation requirements for anticipated future flooding. As of October 25, 2021, the Tribe has raised just over $140,000 in donations to support the recovery. This is barely 10 percent of the estimated $1,380,000 the Tribe anticipates it will need to rebuild and repair the roads, homes, and watercraft that support this community.

The Pointe-au-Chien Indian Tribe, whose ancestors have sought refuge in the bayous for hundreds of years, is facing an existential threat. Without federal recognition, tribal members have been forced to apply for emergency recovery aid and seek insurance payouts as individuals and families, rather than as a nation. This process leaves them at the whim of private, state, and federal bureaucracies whose decisions will mean the difference between returning and rebuilding or not. In essence, the same invisibility that left their nineteenth-century ancestors without legal protections for their lands again threatens to dispossess the Pointe-au-Chien and imperil the future of their community.

It is too easy to say that Indigenous peoples are resilient and point to the unspeakable horrors that our peoples have endured or to reflect that we have been displaced and have recovered many times before. We could look at the historical movements of the Pointe-au-Chien's ancestors and the stories of how Petites Nations peoples survived repeated colonial crises by migrating, adapting, and remaking their lives. Indeed, there is comfort in remembering the strength of our ancestors and the powerful love for our nations that has sustained generations of Native peoples. But our modern world offers the Petites Nations' descendants no easy or bountiful alternative location where they can migrate and resettle alongside other Indigenous nations while the community recovers. Moreover, this land, which has sheltered and provided for generations of Pointe-au-Chien families, remains at the heart of their identities, spiritualities, and foodways. Even in its broken and damaged state, this place is still the center of tribal life.

Way down the Mississippi River, people talk about what it means to be "bayou strong," and you can feel the toughness and the love for these wetlands in the Pointe-au-Chien Tribe. There is an almost palpable connection between tribal members and the marsh waters and grasses that have sustained their people for generations. I have no doubt that, even if they must haul every splintered plank of wood themselves, this community will rebuild and recover. But theirs is an uphill struggle that will only become more difficult as severe weather events and climate change make life along the marshy coast increasingly precarious. Events like Hurricane Ida highlight in painful resolution the way that the lack of federal recognition leaves already marginalized Indigenous communities in perilous circumstances and makes it hard for them to build a future for their peoples.

For the Pointe-au-Chien and for their United Houma Nation, Grand Caillou/Dulac Band of Biloxi-Chitimacha-Choctaw, Bayou LaFourche Band of Biloxi-Chitimacha Indians, and Isle de Jean Charles Band of the Biloxi-Chitimacha-Choctaw Tribe neighbors, the coming months hold uncertainty. It is not clear how many families will be able to return. The Pointe-au-Chien are planning to resubmit their petition for federal recognition this winter (they are appealing the decision that denied them acknowledgment in 2008), but with the turmoil caused by Hurricane Ida it is unclear whether they will be able to keep to this timeline. Whether the federal government steps in to provide relief and whether they decide to grant federal acknowledgment to the Pointe-au-Chien and their neighbors will critically shape the lives of Indigenous communities in

Louisiana's bayous for generations. While the government deliberates over their appeals for aid, they will continue to care for each other as they have always done and to rebuild their communities as their ancestors have so many times before. As the sea rises and their claims are weighed against the Office of Federal Acknowledgment's criteria, their future hangs in the balance.

NOTES

INTRODUCTION

1. Patricia Ferguson, Pointe-au-Chien Indian Tribe, "Our Community: Yesterday, Today, Tomorrow," Pointe-au-Chien Indian Tribe tribal website, accessed August 15, 2021, https://www.pactribe.com/history.

2. Christine Baniewicz, "Coastal Louisiana Tribes Team Up with Biologist to Protect Sacred Sites from Rising Seas," *Southerly Magazine*, September 2, 2020; Kirsten Vinyeta, Kyle Powys Whyte, and Kathy Lynn, "Climate Change Through an Intersectional Lens: Gendered Vulnerability and Resilience in Indigenous Communities in the United States" (Corvallis, OR: U.S. Department of Agriculture, Forest Service, Pacific Northwest Research Station, 2015), 22–24, 35–36; Harrison Golden, "Fighting Coastal Erosion, a Louisiana Tribe Banks on Oyster Shells," February 7, 2019, BRProud, https://www.brproud.com/news/fighting-coastal-erosion-a-louisiana-tribe-banks-on-oyster-shells/; Anne Spice, "Indigenous Relations Against Pipelines," *Environment and Society* 9, no. 1 (2018): 40–56; Andy Horowitz, *Katrina: A History, 1915–2015* (Cambridge, MA: Harvard University Press, 2020), 21–43; Monique Verdin, *Return to Yakni Chitto: Houma Migrations*, ed. Rachel Breulin (New Orleans, LA: University of New Orleans Press, 2019), 66, 74–79.

3. Office of the Governor of Louisiana, "Federal and State Tribal Contact List," 2018, Indian Affairs programs, https://gov.louisiana.gov/assets/Programs/IndianAffairs/LouisianaTribes.pdf; James Scott, *The Art of Not Being Governed: An Anarchist History of Upland Southeast Asia* (New Haven, CT: Yale University Press, 2009); Summary Under the Criteria and Evidence for Amended Proposed Finding Against Federal Acknowledgment of the Biloxi, Chitimacha Confederation of Muskogees, Inc., May 22, 2008, BCCM #56a—Proposed Finding, Bureau of Indian Affairs, U.S. Department of the Interior, 1–64.

4. Ferguson, "Our Community."

5. Brian DeLay, ed., *North American Borderlands* (New York: Routledge, 2013), 9; Juliana Barr, "Geographies of Power: Mapping Indian Borders in the 'Borderlands' of the Early Southwest," *William and Mary Quarterly* 68, no. 1 (2011): 6–11; Cary Miller, *Ogimaag: Anishinaabeg Leadership, 1760–1845* (Lincoln: University of Nebraska Press, 2010), 23–28; Kathleen DuVal, *The Native Ground: Indians and Colonists in the Heart of the Continent* (Philadelphia: University of Pennsylvania Press, 2007), 8–9; Lauren Benton, *A Search for Sovereignty: Law and Geography in European Empires, 1400–1900* (Cambridge: Cambridge University Press, 2010), 1–11; Josh Reid, *The Sea Is My Country: The Maritime World of the Makahs, and Indigenous Borderlands People* (New Haven, CT: Yale University Press, 2015), 11–52; Jeffrey Erbig Jr., *Where Caciques and Mapmakers Met: Border Making in Eighteenth-Century South America* (Chapel Hill: University of North Carolina Press, 2020), 40, 48.

6. Emily Riddle, "Mâmawiwikowin: Shared First Nations and Métis Jurisdiction on the Prairies," *Briarpatch Magazine*, September 10, 2020, https://briarpatchmagazine.com/articles/view/mamawiwikowin.

7. Coulthard describes Indigenous people's relationships with the land as based in systems of "reciprocal relations and obligations" and "grounded normativity" as "the modalities of Indigenous land-connected practices and longstanding experiential knowledge that inform and structure our ethical engagements with the world and our relationships with human and non-human others over time." Glen Coulthard, *Red Skin, White Masks: Rejecting the Politics of Recognition* (Minneapolis: University of Minnesota Press, 2014), 13; Leanne Betasamosake Simpson, "Indigenous Resurgence and Co-Resistance," *Critical Ethnic Studies* 2, no. 2 (2016): 22–23; Lisa Brooks, *Our Beloved Kin: A New History of King Philip's War* (New Haven, CT: Yale University Press, 2018), 29–30.

8. Daniel Usner's pathbreaking work on the Lower Mississippi Valley illustrates how Petites Nations people shaped the development of colonial Louisiana and intersected with other Native people, African peoples, and European settlers during the eighteenth century. This work's framing of the stories of the Petites Nations is deeply influenced by Usner's scholarship. Daniel Usner, *Indians, Settlers, and Slaves in a Frontier Exchange Economy* (Chapel Hill: University of North Carolina Press, 1992).

9. Denis Diderot and Jean le Rond d'Alembert, eds., *Encyclopédie: Ou dictionnaire raisonné des sciences, des arts, et des métiers* (Paris: Samuel Faulche, 1765), 11:36.

10. Nancy Shoemaker, *A Strange Likeness: Becoming Red and White in Eighteenth-Century North America* (New York: Oxford University Press, 2004), 6; Erbig, *Where Caciques and Mapmakers Met*, 15–18, 58–59.

11. Eric Besson, "SE Texas' Atakapa Tribe Seeking Federal Designation," *Beaumont (TX) Enterprise*, September 24, 2014, https://www.beaumontenterprise.com/news/article/SE-Texas-Atakapa-tribe-seeking-federal-5722475.php; John. D. Barbry, "'*Tayoroni-Halayihku Hihchi 'Onta!'* The Tunica-Biloxis Remain Here!," in *The Tunica-Biloxi Tribe: Its Culture and People*, ed. Brian Klopotek, John D. Barbry, Donna M. Pierite, and Elisabeth Pierite-Mora, 35–40, 2nd ed. (Marksville: Tunica Biloxi Tribe of Louisiana, 2017), 35; Jacques Godchot, "Nation, patrie, nationalisme, et patriotisme en France au XVIII siècle," *Annales historiques de la Révolution française* 43, no. 206 (1971): 483–484; Shoemaker, *Strange Likeness*, 5–8; Benton, *Search for Sovereignty*, 1–11.

12. Elman R. Service, "Origins of the State and Civilization: The Process of Cultural Evolution," (New York: W. W. Norton, 1975), 14–16, 47–49, 146–148; Juliana Barr, "The Red Continent and the Cant of the Coastline," *William and Mary Quarterly* 69, no. 3 (2012): 521–526; Richard White, *The Middle Ground: Indians, Empire, and Republics in the Great Lakes Region, 1650–1815* (New York: Cambridge University Press, 1991), 1–20.

13. Peter H. Wood, "The Changing Population of the Colonial South," in *Powhatan's Mantle: Indians in the Colonial Southeast*, ed. Gregory A. Waselkov, Peter H. Wood, and Tom Hatley, 60–61, 92–106, 2nd ed. (Lincoln: University of Nebraska Press, 2006), 60, 94, 96–97; John R. Swanton, *Indian Tribes of the Lower Mississippi Valley and Adjacent Coast of the Gulf of Mexico*, Bureau of American Ethnology, Bulletin 43 (Washington, DC: Smithsonian Institution, 1911), 40–43; Daniel Usner, *American Indians in the Lower Mississippi Valley: Social and Economic Histories* (Lincoln: University of Nebraska Press, 1998), 35.

14. Usner, *Indians, Settlers, and Slaves*, 108, 113, 279; Jeffrey Brain, George Roth, and Willem de Reuse, "The Tunica, Biloxi, and Ofo," in *The Handbook of North American Indians*, vol. 14, *The Southeast*, ed. Raymond Fogelson (Washington, DC: Smithsonian, 2004), 14:139.

15. David Davis, "A Case of Identity: Ethnogenesis of the New Houma Indians," *Ethnohistory* 48, no. 3 (2001): 473–494.

16. Both the Jena Band of Choctaw Indians and the Tunica Biloxi Tribe of Louisiana went through this acknowledgment process during the twentieth century in order to secure recognition.

Sara Sneath, "Louisiana Tribes Say Federal Recognition Will Help to Face Threat of Climate Change," *Nola*, July 26, 2018, https://www.nola.com/archive/article_e26d68a2-c6cb-5809-9ef8-f7cf6f13fofc.html; Jeremy Shapiro, "Local Tribes Marking Official State Recognition," *HoumaToday*, June 29, 2004, https://www.houmatoday.com/story/news/2004/06/29/local-tribes-marking-official-state-recognition/26822028007/; Naomi King, "Feds Reject Two Local Indian Tribes," *HoumaToday*, June 11, 2008, https://www.houmatoday.com/story/news/2008/06/11/feds-reject-two-local-indian-tribes/26773017007/; Angela Gonzales and Timothy Evans, "The Imposition of Law: The Federal Acknowledgment Process and the Legal De/Construction of Tribal Identity," in *Recognition, Sovereignty Struggles, and Indigenous Rights in the United States*, ed. Amy E. Den Ouden and Jean M. O'Brien (Chapel Hill: University of North Carolina Press, 2013), 37–63; Mark Moberg and Tawnya Sesi Moberg, "The United Houma Nation in the U.S. Congress: Corporations, Communities, and the Politics of Federal Acknowledgment," *Urban Anthropology and Studies of Cultural Systems and World Economic Development* 34, no. 1 (2005): 85–124; Courtney Rivard, "Archival Recognition: The Pointe-au-Chien's and Isle de Jean Charles Band of the Biloxi-Chitimacha Confederation of Muskogees' Fight for Federal Recognition," *Settler Colonial Studies* 5, no. 2 (2015): 117–127; Tristan Ahtone, "Tribal Nations Are Tired of Waiting for Uncle Sam to Recognize Them, *Al Jazeera*, January 17, 2014; Brian Klopotek, *Recognition Odysseys: Indigeneity, Race, and Federal Tribal Recognition Policy in Three Louisiana Indian Communities* (Durham, NC: Duke University Press, 2011); Denise Bates, *Basket Diplomacy: Leadership, Alliance-Building, and Resilience Among the Coushatta Tribe of Louisiana, 1884–1984* (Lincoln: University of Nebraska Press, 2020); Daniel Usner, *Weaving Alliances with Other Women: Chitimacha Indian Work in the New South* (Athens: University of Georgia Press, 2015).

17. Jana-Rae Yerxa, "Gii-kaapizigemin manoomin Neyaashing: A Resurgence of Anishinaabeg Nationhood," *Decolonization: Indigeneity, Education and Society* 3, no. 3 (2014): 159–166; Zoe Todd, "Refracting the State Through Human-Fish Relations: Fishing, Indigenous Legal Orders and Colonialism in North/Western Canada," *Decolonization: Indigeneity, Education and Society* 7, no. 1 (2018): 60–75; Karl Gardner and Richard Peters (Giibwanisi), "Toward the 8th Fire: The View from Oshkimaadziig Unity Camp," *Decolonization: Indigeneity, Education and Society* 3, no. 3 (2014): 167–173; N. Bruce Duthu, *Shadow Nations: Tribal Sovereignty and the Limits of Legal Pluralism* (Oxford: Oxford University Press, 2013), 6–22.

18. Steve Cheramie to Ada Deer, April 22, 1996, "Letter of Intent," Bureau of Indian Affairs, U.S. Department of the Interior; Carl J. Artman, "Summary Under the Criteria and Evidence for Amended Proposed Finding Against Federal Acknowledgment of the Pointe-au-Chien Indian Tribe," May 22, 2008, Proposed Finding, PACIT (#56b)—Proposed Finding, Bureau of Indian Affairs, U.S. Department of the Interior, 1–11.

19. Philip J. Deloria, *Indians in Unexpected Places* (Lawrence: University Press of Kansas, 2004).

20. DuVal, *Native Ground*; Heidi Bohaker, "'Nindoodemag': The Significance of Algonquian Kinship Networks in the Eastern Great Lakes Region, 1600–1701," *William and Mary Quarterly* 63, no. 1 (2006): 23–52; Jacob Lee, *Masters of the Middle Waters: Indian Nations and Colonial Ambitions Along the Mississippi* (Cambridge, MA: Harvard University Press, 2019); Brian DeLay, *War of a Thousand Deserts: Indian Raids and the U.S.-Mexico War* (New Haven, CT: Yale University

Press, 2008); Pekka Hämäläinen, *The Comanche Empire* (New Haven, CT: Yale University Press, 2008); Theda Perdue, *Cherokee Women: Gender and Culture Change, 1700–1835* (Lincoln: University of Nebraska Press, 1998); Jason Baird Jackson, ed., *Yuchi Indian Histories Before the Removal Era* (Lincoln: University of Nebraska Press, 2012); Laura Keenan Spero, "'Stout, Bold, Cunning and the Greatest Travellers in America': The Colonial Shawnee Diaspora" (PhD diss., University of Pennsylvania, 2010); Michael Witgen, *An Infinity of Nations: How the Native New World Shaped Early North America* (Philadelphia: University of Pennsylvania Press, 2012); Francis Jennings, *The Ambiguous Iroquois Empire: The Covenant Chain Confederation of Indian Tribes with English Colonists from Its Beginnings to the Lancaster Treaty of 1744* (New York: W. W. Norton, 1984); Michael McDonnell, *Masters of Empire: Great Lakes Indians and the Making of America* (New York: Hill and Wang, 2016).

21. Testimony of R. Lee Fleming, director, Office of Federal Acknowledgement, for the Hearing Before the Committee on Indian Affairs, United States Senate on the Federal Acknowledgement Process, May 11, 2005, U.S. Department of the Interior, Office of Congressional and Legislative Affairs, https://www.doi.gov/ocl/federal-acknowledgement; Federal Acknowledgment of American Indian Tribes, A Rule by Indian Affairs Bureau, July 1, 2015, *Federal Register*, 80 FR 37861, no. 2015-16193, https://www.federalregister.gov/documents/2015/07/01/2015-16193/federal-acknowledgment-of-american-indian-tribes; Testimony of Bryan Newland, senior policy advisor, Office of the Assistant Secretary for Indian Affairs, U.S. Department of the Interior to the Committee on Indian Affairs, United States Senate Oversight Hearing on Federal Acknowledgment: Political and Legal Relationship Between Governments, July 12, 2012, U.S. Department of the Interior, Office of Congressional and Legislative Affairs, https://www.doi.gov/ocl/hearings/112/FederalTribalRecognition_071212; Artman, "Summary Under the Criteria and Evidence for Amended Proposed Finding Against Federal Acknowledgment of the Pointe-au-Chien Indian Tribe," May 22, 2008, Proposed Finding, PACIT (#56b)—Proposed Finding, Bureau of Indian Affairs, U.S. Department of the Interior, 1–11.

22. Despite multiple attempts to improve and clarify procedures and requirements, federal recognition remains a deeply flawed process. In recent years, many Native American and Indigenous studies scholars and legal theorists have contributed to a strident critique of federal recognition as a whole. Indigenous scholars like Brian Klopotek, Bruce Duthu, Jean O'Brien, Joanne Barker, Malinda Maynor Lowery, Glen Coulthard, and many, many others have emphasized the inconsistency, anti-Blackness, and colonial frameworks embedded in this federal process. Moreover, Native people across both the United States and Canada have long critiqued the larger ideological violence of allowing settler governments to define what it means to be a First Nations or Native American person or nation. Within the United States, the modern definitions of nationhood, which undergird the logic of the federal recognition process, are grounded in Westphalian concepts of bordered nation-states, sovereignty based primarily on autonomous territorial possession and sole political control, exclusionary logics of citizenship, and blood-based belonging. See Klopotek, *Recognition Odysseys*; Malinda Maynor Lowery, *Lumbee Indians in the Jim Crow South: Race, Identity, and the Making of a Nation* (Chapel Hill: University of North Carolina Press, 2010); Jean M. O'Brien, *Firsting and Lasting: Writing Indians Out of Existence in New England* (Minneapolis: University of Minnesota Press, 2010); Coulthard, *Red Skin, White Masks*; Joanne Barker, *Native Acts: Law, Recognition, and Cultural Authenticity* (Durham, NC: Duke University Press, 2011); N. Bruce Duthu, *American Indians and the Law* (New York: Penguin Books, 2009); Lisa Ford, *Settler Sovereignty: Jurisdiction and Indigenous People in America and Australia, 1788–1836* (Cambridge, MA: Harvard University Press, 2010); Kevin Bruyneel, *The Third Space of Sovereignty: The Postcolonial Politics of U.S.-Indigenous Relations* (Minneapolis: University of Minnesota Press,

2007); Samuel R. Cook, "The Monacan Indian Nation: Asserting Tribal Sovereignty in the Absence of Federal Recognition," *Wicazo Sa Review* 17, no. 2 (2002): 91–116; Mishuana Goeman, *Mark My Words: Native Women Mapping Our Nations* (Minneapolis: University of Minnesota Press, 2013), 28–37; Allogan Slagle, "Unfinished Justice: Completing the Restoration and Acknowledgement of California Indian Tribes," *American Indian Quarterly* 13, no. 4 (1989): 325–345; Lorinda Riley, "When a Tribal Entity Becomes a Nation: The Role of Politics in the Shifting Federal Recognition Regulations," *American Indian Law Review* 39, no. 2 (2014–2015): 451–505; David Nichols, "Treaties and Sovereign Performances, from Westphalia to Standing Rock," *Origins* 10, no. 5 (2017), http://origins.osu.edu/print/4403; Simpson, "Indigenous Resurgence and Co-Resistance," 22–23.

23. Jeffrey Ostler, *Surviving Genocide: Native Nations and the United States from the American Revolution to Bleeding Kansas* (New Haven, CT: Yale University Press, 2016).

24. Witgen, *Infinity of Nations*; Usner, *Weaving Alliances with Other Women*; N. Bruce Duthu, "The Houma Indians of Louisiana: The Intersection of Law and History in the Federal Acknowledgment Process," *Louisiana History* 38, no. 4 (1997): 409–436; Malinda Maynor Lowery, "Telling Our Own Stories: Lumbee History and the Federal Acknowledgment Process," *American Indian Quarterly* 33, no. 4 (2009): 499–522; Theda Perdue, "American Indian Survival in South Carolina," *South Carolina Historical Magazine* 108, no. 3 (July 2007): 215–234; Arica Coleman, "Denying Blackness: Anthropological Advocacy and the Remaking of the Virginia Indians," in *That the Blood Stay Pure: African Americans, Native Americans, and the Predicament of Race and Identity in Virginia* (Bloomington: Indiana University Press, 2013), 122–148: Joshua Piker, *Okfuskee: A Creek Indian Town in Colonial America* (Cambridge, MA: Harvard University Press, 2004); Mikaëla Morgan Adams, *Who Belongs: Race Resources, and Tribal Citizenship in the Native South* (New York: Oxford University Press, 2016); Jane Dinwoodie, "Beyond Removal: Indians, States, and Sovereignties in the American South, 1812–1860" (PhD thesis, University of Oxford, 2017).

25. Many southeastern Native communities continue to refer to themselves as *Indian* and prefer the term to *Indigenous* or *Native American*. My own community predominantly uses the word *Indian*, and I use *Indian* here to emphasize the racial significance of this identity within the historically segregated South. Lowery, *Lumbee Indians in the Jim Crow South*, 81–119; Davis, "Case of Identity," 478; Klopotek, *Recognition Odysseys*, 209–222; Verdin, *Return to Yakni Chitto*, 8, 58–59.

CHAPTER I

1. Jean-Baptiste-Louis Franquelin, *Carte de la Louisiane ou des voyages du Sr. De La Salle*, 1901 [original, 1684], no. 2001620469, Geography and Map Division, Library of Congress, Washington, DC.

2. Antoine-Simon Le Page du Pratz, *Histoire de la Louisiane* (Paris, 1758), 3:89.

3. Du Pratz, *Histoire de la Louisiane*, 3:90.

4. Du Pratz, *Histoire de la Louisiane*, 3:91.

5. Alejandra Dubcovsky, *Informed Power: Communication in the Early South* (Cambridge, MA: Harvard University Press, 2016), 11–41.

6. Du Pratz, *Histoire de la Louisiane*, 3:90–91.

7. The printed margin notes accompanying Du Pratz's account of Moncacht-Apé's adventures label these bearded, white men as Japanese. Du Pratz, *Histoire de la Louisiane*, 3:118–129;

Claudio Saunt, *West of the Revolution: An Uncommon History of 1776* (New York: W. W. Norton, 2014), 34–53.

8. Jean-François-Benjamin Dumont de Montigny, *Mémoires historiques sur la Louisiane, contenant ce qui y est arrivé de plus mémorable depuis l'année 1687 jusqu'à présent; avec l'établissement de la colonie françoise dans cette province de l'Amérique Septentrionale sous la direction de la Compagnie des Indes; le climat, la natur & les productions de ce pays; l'origine & la religion des sauvages qui l'habitent; leurs murs & leurs coutumes, &c* (Paris, 1753), 2:246–253; Du Pratz, *Histoire de la Louisiane*, 3:103–118, 129.

9. Dumont de Montigny, *Mémoires historiques sur la Louisiane*, 2:246–254.

10. Juliet Morrow, "The Sacred Spiro Landscape, Cahokia Connections, and Flat Top Mounds," *Central States Archaeological Journal* 51, no. 2 (2004): 112–114; Cameron Lacquement, "Recalculation Mound Volume at Moundville," *Southeastern Archaeology* 29, no. 2 (2010): 352; William Iseminger, "Cahokia: A Mississippian Metropolis," *Central States Archaeological Journal* 24, no. 1 (1977): 117–124; Timothy R. Pauketat, *Cahokia: Ancient America's Great City on the Mississippi* (New York: Viking, 2009), 25–35, 69–84; Charles Hudson, *Knights of Spain, Warriors of the Sun: Hernando de Soto and the South's Ancient Chiefdoms* (Athens: University of Georgia Press, 1997), 220–225; Charles Hudson and Carmen Chaves Tesser, introduction to *The Forgotten Centuries: Indians and Europeans in the American South, 1521–1704*, ed. Charles Hudson and Carmen Chaves Tesser, 1–14 (Athens: University of Georgia Press, 1994), 2–10; Megan Kassabaum, *A History of Platform Mound Ceremonialism: Finding Meaning in Elevated Ground* (Gainesville: University of Florida Press, 2021), 10–11, 18–22, 65–87, 158–183; John H. Blitz, "Mississippian Chiefdoms and the Fission-Fusion Process," *American Antiquity* 64, no. 4 (1999): 577–592; Patricia K. Galloway, *Choctaw Genesis, 1500–1700* (Lincoln: University of Nebraska Press), 110–111.

11. This region featured a convergence of Mississippian, Coles Creek, and Caddoan influences. Jeffrey P. Brain, "Late Prehistoric Settlement Patterning in the Yazoo Basin and Natchez Bluffs Regions of the Lower Mississippi Valley," in *Mississippian Settlement Patterns: Studies in Archaeology*, ed. Bruce D. Smith (New York: Academic Press, 2014), 331–365; Ian W. Brown, "Plaquemine Architectural Patterns in the Natchez Bluffs and Surrounding Regions of the Lower Mississippi Valley," *Midcontinental Journal of Archaeology* 10, no. 2 (1985): 251–305; Tristram R. Kidder, "Ceramic Chronology and the Culture History of the Southern Ouachita River Basin: Coles Creek to the Early Historic Period," *Midcontinental Journal of Archaeology* 15, no. 1 (1990): 61–67; John Scarry, "The Late Prehistoric Southeast," in Hudson and Chaves Tesser, *Forgotten Centuries*, 17–35, 20–30; Juliana Barr, "There's No Such Thing as 'Prehistory': What the Longue Durée of Caddo and Pueblo History Tells Us About Colonial America," *William and Mary Quarterly* 74, no. 1 (2017): 203–240.

12. Ian Brown and Vincas Steponaitis, "The Grand Village of the Natchez Indians Was Indeed Grand: A Reconsideration of the Fatherland Site Landscape," in *Forging Southeastern Identities: Social Archaeology, Ethnohistory, and the Folklore of the Mississippian to Early South*, ed. Gregory A. Waselkov and Marvin T. Smith, 182–204 (Tuscaloosa: University of Alabama Press, 2017), 184–185, 197; William H. Sears, "The Sociopolitical Organization of Pre-Columbian Cultures on the Gulf Coastal Plain," *American Anthropologist* 56, no. 3 (1954): 339; Lettre du P. le Petit, sur les Sauvages du Mississipi, et en particulier les Natchez, et relation de leur entreprise sur la colonie française, en 1729, July 12, 1730, Archives nationales d'outre-mer (Aix-en-Provence) (hereafter cited as ANOM), 04DFC 40, 2–20; Jean-François-Benjamin Dumont de Montigny, *The Memoir of Lieutenant Dumont, 1715–1747*, ed. Gordon M. Sayre and Carla Zecher, trans. Gordon M. Sayre (Chapel Hill: University of North Carolina Press, 2012), 186; Lettre de l'abbé Barthellon au ministre qui fait la relation des villages sauvages qui habitent le fleuve St Louis

depuis la Balise jusqu'aux Illinois, January 13, 1731, ANOM, 04DFC 42, 3–4; Du Pratz, *Histoire de la Louisiane*, 2:223; Thomas Nairne, *Nairne's Muskhogean Journals: The 1708 Expedition to the Mississippi River*, ed. Alexander Moore (Jackson: University of Mississippi Press, 1988), 75–76; Jean-Baptiste-Bénard de La Harpe, *The Historical Journal of the Establishment of the French in Louisiana*, ed. Glenn Conrad, trans. Joan Cain and Virginia Koenig (Lafayette: University of Southwestern Louisiana, 1971), 17; André Pénicaut, *Fleur de Lys and Calumet: Being the Pénicaut Narrative of French Adventure in Louisiana*, trans. and ed. Richebourg McWilliams (Tuscaloosa: University of Alabama Press, 1988), 177; George Edward Milne, *Natchez Country: Indians, Colonists, and the Landscapes of Race in French Louisiana* (Athens: University of Georgia Press, 2015), 29–41; Galloway, *Choctaw Genesis*, 308.

13. Quiz Quiz was a larger Mississippian chiefdom that was located near present-day Memphis and was one of the polities that de Soto encountered. Jeffrey P. Brain, *Tunica Archaeology* (Cambridge, MA: Harvard University Press, 1988), 21–25; H. Edwin Jackson, *The Ables Creek Site: A Protohistory in Southeast Arkansas* (Fayetteville: Arkansas Archaeological Survey, 1992), 113–114; Ian Brown, "Historic Indians of the Lower Mississippi Valley: An Archaeologists View," in *Towns and Temples Along the Mississippi*, ed. David H. Dye and Cheryl Anne Cox, 227–238 (Tuscaloosa: University of Alabama Press, 1990), 231; Hudson, *Knights of Spain, Warriors of the Sun*, 277–284; Charles R. Cobb, "Mississippian Chiefdoms: How Complex?," *Annual Review of Anthropology* 32 (2003): 76–78; Tristram R. Kidder, "The Koroa Indians of the Lower Mississippi Valley," *Mississippi Archaeology* 23, no. 2 (1988): 12–13; Charles R. Cobb and Brian M. Butler, "The Vacant Quarter Revisited: Late Mississippian Abandonment of the Ohio River Valley," *American Antiquity* 67, no. 4 (2002): 636–638.

14. Robbie Ethridge, "Introduction: Mapping the Mississippian Shatter Zone," in *Mapping the Mississippian Shatter Zone: The Colonial Indian Slave Trade and Regional Instability in the American South*, ed. Robbie Ethridge and Sheri M. Shuck-Hall, 1–62 (Lincoln: University of Nebraska Press, 2009), 2; Du Pratz, *Histoire de la Louisiane*, 3:87–105; Hudson and Chaves Tesser, introduction, 1–13.

15. Stephen A. Kowalewski, "Coalescent Societies," in *Light on the Path: The Anthropology and History of the Southeastern Indians*, ed. Thomas Pluckhahn and Robbie Ethridge, 94–122 (Tuscaloosa: University of Alabama Press, 2006), 104–105.

16. Hudson, *Knights of Spain, Warriors of the Sun*, 423–426; Adam King, "The Historic Period Transformation of Mississippian Societies," in Pluckhahn and Ethridge, *Light on the Path*, 179–195, 181; Jeffrey P. Brain, Alan Toth, and Antonio Rodriguez-Buckingham, "Ethnohistoric Archaeology and the De Soto Entrada into the Lower Mississippi Valley," in *The Conference on Historic Site Archaeology Papers 1972*, vol. 7, ed. Stanley South, 232–289 (1974), book 8, 254, 263–264, 283; Kidder, "Koroa Indians of the Lower Mississippi Valley," 3–6, 26–27; François Jolliet de Montigny, letter of Mr. De Montigny, January 2, 1699, in *Early Voyages Up and Down the Mississippi by Cavelier, St. Cosme, Le Sueur, Gravier*, ed. John Gilmary Shea (Albany, NY: Joel Munsell, 1861), 75–76, 80; Nicholas de Fer, "Les Costes aux environs de la rivière de Mississipi: Découverte par Mr. de La Salle en 1683 et reconnues par Mr. Le Chevallier d'Iberville en 1698 et 1699," 1701, Cartographic Collections, Newberry Library, Chicago; Guillaume de L'Isle, *Carte des environs du Missisipi*, 1701, Louis C. Karpinski Map Collection, Newberry Library, Chicago; Swanton, *Indian Tribes of the Lower Mississippi Valley*, 42; Robbie Ethridge, *Chicaza to Chickasaw: European Invasion and the Transformation of the Mississippian World, 1540–1715* (Chapel Hill: University of North Carolina Press, 2010), 135.

17. Brain, Toth, and Rodriguez-Buckingham, "Ethnohistoric Archaeology and the De Soto Entrada," book 8, 7:283; Stephen Williams, "On the Location of the Historic Taensa

Villages," in *The Conference on Historic Site Archaeology Papers, 1965–1966*, vol. 1, 3–13 (1967), 3–11; Tristram R. Kidder, "Ceramic Chronology," 56–73; Tristram R. Kidder, "Excavations at the Jordan Site (16MO1), Morehouse Parish, Louisiana," *Southeastern Archaeology* 11, no. 2 (1992): 109.

18. For spiritual as well as political reasons, American Indians across the Southeast felt compelled to avenge the deaths of their kin. Unless these deaths were "covered"—meaning that the families of the dead were compensated by the killer with gifts and material support for the loss of their loved ones—the death of kin required blood vengeance. The "crying blood" of the dead demanded that the killer or one of his kin be killed in order to restore spiritual balance. Wayne E. Lee, *Barbarians and Brothers: Anglo-American Warfare, 1500–1865* (Oxford: Oxford University Press, 2011), 136–138, 164–166; Christina Snyder, *Slavery in Indian Country: The Changing Face of Captivity in Early America* (Cambridge, MA: Harvard University Press, 2010), 80–100; Witgen, *Infinity of Nations*, 36–39; Daniel Richter, *Before the Revolution: America's Ancient Pasts* (Cambridge, MA: Harvard University Press, 2011), 131–133, 147–151; Daniel Richter, "Ordeals of the Longhouse: The Five Nations in Early American History," in *Beyond the Covenant Chain: The Iroquois and Their Neighbors in Indian North America, 1600–1800*, ed. Daniel Richter and James Merrell, 11–27(Syracuse, NY: Syracuse University Press, 2011), 11–27.

19. White, *Middle Ground*, 1–5; William A. Fox, "Events as Seen from the North: The Iroquois and Colonial Slavery," in Ethridge and Shuck-Hall, *Mapping the Mississippian Shatter Zone*, 63–80, 63–75; Jennings, *Ambiguous Iroquois Empire*, 10–24.

20. Marvin D. Jeter, "Shatter Zone Shock Waves Along the Lower Mississippi," in Ethridge and Shuck-Hall, *Mapping the Mississippian Shatter Zone*, 365–387, 374–376; Richard L. Haithcock, "The Ohio River Valley Sioux and the Siouan, Monacna, Mannahoac and the Siouan Piedmont Catawba of the Virginia, Carolina Piedmont," in *The Mosopelea Ofo Ganatchi and Occaneechi*, 1999, unnumbered, Special Collections, Newberry Library, Chicago; Emily J. Blasingham, "The Depopulation of the Illinois Indians," *Ethnohistory* 3 (1956): 373–377; Jacques Marquette, *Carte de la nouvelle découverte, que les pères Jésuites ont fait en l'année 1672; et continuée par le P. Jacques Marquette de la mesme compagnie,1850*, VAULT drawer Ayer MS map 47, Edward E. Ayer Collection, Newberry Library, Chicago; Franquelin, *Carte de la Louisiane*; Charles A. Hanna, *The Wilderness Trail: Or the Ventures and Adventure of the Pennsylvania Traders on the Allegheny Path, with Some New Annals of the Old West, and the Records of Some Strong Men and Some Bad Ones* (New York: G. P. Putnam's Sons, 1911), 96–101; Ethridge, *Chicaza to Chickasaw*, 123–124; Jacques Marquette, *Carte de la nouvelle découverte que les RR. Pères Jésuites ont fait en l'année 1672 et continuée par le R. Père Jacques Marquette, de la mesme compagnie, accompagné de quelques François en l'année 1673, qu'on pourra nommer la Manitounie, à cause de la statue qui s'est trouvée dans une belle vallée et que les sauvages vont recon[n]oistre pour leur Divinité, qu'ils appellent Manitou, qui signifie Esprit, ou Génie* (1673), CPL GE C-5014 (RES), Département cartes et plans, Bibliothèque nationale de France.

21. Nicolas de La Salle, *The La Salle Expedition on the Mississippi River: A Lost Manuscript of Nicolas de La Salle, 1682*, ed. William Foster, trans. Johanna Warren (Austin: Texas State Historical Association, 2003), 106; Swanton, *Indian Tribes of the Lower Mississippi Valley*, 136, 260–265; Gabriel Gravier, *Découvertes et établissements de Cavelier de La Salle de Rouen dans l'Amérique du Nord* (Rouen: L. Deshays, 1870), 187–189; Henri de Tonti, *Relation of Henri de Tonty Concerning the Explorations of La Salle from 1678 to 1683*, trans. Melville B. Anderson (Chicago: Caxton Club, 1898), 103–105; Ethridge, *Chicaza to Chickasaw*, 123–124, 137; Elizabeth Ellis, "The Natchez War Revisited: Violence, Multinational Settlements and Indigenous Diplomacy in the Lower Mississippi Valley," *William and Mary Quarterly* 77, no. 3 (2020): 450.

22. John Sibley, "Historical Sketches of the Several Indian Tribes in Louisiana, South of the Arkansas River, and Between the Mississippi and River Grande," Annals of Cong., 9th Cong., 2d Sess., December 1, 1806–March 3, 1807 (Washington, DC, 1852), 1085–1088; Ian Brown, "The Calumet Ceremony in the Southeast and Its Archaeological Manifestations," *American Antiquity* 54, no. 2 (1989): 313–315; Bienville to Antoine de la Mothe, Sieur de Cadillac, June 23, 1716, *Mississippi Provincial Archives: 1704–1743, French Dominion*, vol. 3 ed. Dunbar Rowland and Albert Godfrey Sanders, trans. Dunbar Rowland (Jackson, MS: Press of the Mississippi Department of Archives and History, 1924), 3:214 (hereafter cited as *MPA:FD*); Baron de Lahontan, *New Voyages to North America*, ed. Reuben Gold Thwaites (Chicago: A. C. McClurg, 1905), 423–424; Christopher Rodning, "Cherokee Towns and Calumet Ceremonialism in Eastern North America," *American Antiquity* 79, no. 3 (2014): 425–443; Ethridge, *Chicaza to Chickasaw*, 131; Lee, *Masters of the Middle Waters*, 31–32.

23. Dumont de Montigny, *Memoir of Lieutenant Dumont*, 341–342; Jean-François-Benjamin Dumont de Montigny, Poème en vers touchant l'établissement de la province de la Louisianne connue sous le nom du Missisipy, avec tout ce qui s'y est passé depuis 1716 jusqu'à 1741, le massacre des François au poste des Natchez, les mœurs des sauvages, leurs danses, leurs religions, enfin ce qui concerne le pays en général, Arsenal MS-3459, fol. 142, Bibliothèque nationale de France.

24. Pénicaut, *Fleur de Lys and Calumet*, 171–180; James F. Barnett, *The Natchez Indians: A History to 1735* (Jackson: University Press of Mississippi, 2007), 24–25; Ethridge, *Chicaza to Chickasaw*, 130–131.

25. Swanton, *Indian Tribes of the Lower Mississippi Valley*, plate 1; Frederick Hodge, ed., *Handbook of American Indians North of Mexico* (Washington, DC: U.S. Government Printing Office, 1910), 2:108; l'Abbé François de Montigny à Saint-Vallier, August 25, 1699, *Les missions du Séminaire de Québec dans la Vallée du Mississippi, 1698–1699*, ed. Noël Baillargeon (Quebec: Musée de la Civilisation, 2002), 77.

26. De Montigny à Saint-Vallier, August 25, 1699, *Les missions du Séminaire de Québec*, 78–79; Ethridge, *Chicaza to Chicasaw*, 140–142; James Brooks, *Captives and Cousins: Slavery, Kinship, and Community in the Southwest Borderlands* (Chapel Hill: North Carolina University Press, 2002), 4–5, 17–18, 30–36; DuVal, *Native Ground*, 69, 73, 92.

27. I am using the term *Indian* here intentionally. Although no Native nations in the Lower Mississippi Valley conceptualized themselves through the racialized category of Indian in the early eighteenth century, the term is useful here because the mass enslavement of Native people was central to producing the concept of Indians and an Indian race. When Native people were trafficked into British colonies, they were listed on bills of sale and in court documents as "Indian" slaves rather than as people of specific Native nations. While, in later centuries, many Native people would go on to claim the term *Indian* as a meaningful racial and cultural identity, in this context the word serves to highlight the racial component of commodification of human beings.

28. Fox, "Events as Seen from the North," 65–72; Eric E. Bowne, *The Westo Indians: Slave Traders of the Early Colonial South* (Tuscaloosa: University of Alabama Press, 2005), 49–52; Maureen Myers, "From Refugees to Slave Traders: The Transformation of the Westo Indians," in Ethridge and Shuck-Hall, *Mapping the Mississippian Shatter Zone*, 81–103, 90.

29. Joel Martin, "Southeastern Indians and the English Trade in Skins and Slaves," in Hudson and Chaves Tesser, *Forgotten Centuries*, 304–326, 306–312; Jerald Milanich, "Franciscan Mission and Native Peoples in Spanish Florida," in Hudson and Chaves Tesser, *Forgotten Centuries*, 276–303, 286.

30. Ethridge, *Chicaza to Chickasaw*, 91, 97–98; Bowne, *Westo Indians*, 37–38; Paul Kelton, *Epidemics and Enslavement: Biological Catastrophe in the Native Southeast, 1492–1715*, (Lincoln:

University of Nebraska Press, 2009), 102–120; John Stewart to her majesty Queen Anne of Great Britain, Humbly laying down some Observations on American Indians, 1711, Colonies C13 Louisiane (Washington, DC: Foreign Copying Program, Library of Congress), digitized microfilm, C-13 C2, reel 2, fol. 80; Rebecca Anne Goetz, "The Nanziatticos and the Violence of the Archive: Land and Native Enslavement in Colonial Virginia," *Journal of Southern History* 85, no. 1 (2019): 33–60; Hayley Negrin, "Possessing Native Women and Children: Slavery, Gender, and English Colonialism in the Early American South, 1670–1717" (PhD diss., New York University, 2018), 128–132; Martin, "Southeastern Indians and the English Trade in Skins and Slaves," 306–313.

31. Snyder, *Slavery In Indian Country*, 51–54, 61; Patricia Galloway, "Colonial Transformations in the Mississippi Valley: Dis-integration, Alliance, Confederation, Playoff" in *Transformation of the Southeastern Indians: 1540–1760*, ed. Robbie Ethridge, 225–247 (Jackson: University of Mississippi Press, 2002), 242–243; Usner, *American Indians in the Lower Mississippi Valley*, 35.

32. Ethridge, *Chicaza to Chickasaw*, 101; Frank F. Schambach, "Spiro and Tunica: A New Interpretation of the Role of the Tunica in the Cultural History of the Southeast and Southern Plains," in *Arkansas Archaeology: Essays in Honor of Don and Phyllis Morse*, ed. Robert Mainfort Jr. and Marvin D. Jeter, 169–224 (Fayetteville: University of Arkansas Press, 1999), 202; Robbie Ethridge, "Creating the Shatter Zone: Indian Slave Traders and the Collapse of Southeastern Chiefdoms," in Pluckhahn and Ethridge, *Light on the Path*, 207–218, 215; de la Salle to Monseigneur, April 1, 1702, Colonies C13 Louisiane (Washington, DC: Foreign Copying Program, Library of Congress), digitized microfilm, C-13 C2, reel 2, fol. 35.

33. Susan Sleeper-Smith, *Indigenous Prosperity and American Conquest: Indian Women of the Ohio River Valley, 1690–1792* (Chapel Hill: University of North Carolina Press, 2018), 160–180; Ethridge, *Chicaza to Chickasaw*, 216–217, 233–35; Brett Rushforth, *Bonds of Alliance: Indigenous and Atlantic Slaveries in New France* (Chapel Hill: University of North Carolina Press, 2012), 4–6.

34. Pénicaut, *Fleur de Lys and Calumet*, 159–160; Ethridge, *Chicaza to Chickasaw*, 137–139, 216–217, 233–35.

35. Snyder, *Slavery in Indian Country*, 67–74; Ethridge, *Chicaza to Chickasaw*, 185; La Harpe, *Historical Journal*, 76; Ethridge, *Chicaza to Chickasaw*, 215–217.

36. Ethridge, *Chicaza to Chickasaw*, 216–217; Marcel Giraud, "L'Exacte Description de la Louisianne' d'Étienne Véniard de Bourgmont," *Revue Historique* 217, no. 1 (1957): 36.

37. These numbers exclude those slaves taken by the Spanish or French and deaths from related factors, such as movement of disease and violence across the Southeast. Furthermore, Robbie Ethridge posits that the slave trade could account for up to half of the total population losses of the Southeast during this same era, suggesting that the destruction wrought on the Southeast by the slave trade was roughly equal in magnitude to that of the waves of epidemics that are so often blamed for depopulating the Southeast and paving the way for a new eighteenth-century political order. Iberville suggests that, by 1702, 500 Choctaws had been enslaved by the Chickasaws and that 1,800 had been killed by the violence, meaning that the numbers of those who were actually enslaved could represent only about 20 percent of total casualties for all who were the victims of slave trade–related violence. Alan Gallay, *The Indian Slave Trade: The Rise of the English Empire in the American South, 1670–1717* (New Haven, CT: Yale University Press, 2002), 150, 296–297; Ethridge, *Chicaza to Chickasaw*, 175, 218–219, 237; Swanton, *Indian Tribes of the Lower Mississippi Valley*, 40–43; Wood, "Changing Population of the Colonial South," 99–112; Pénicaut, *Fleur de Lys and Calumet*, 159–60.

38. The Mobile River Petites Nations of Mobiles and Tohomes were each reduced from populations of roughly one thousand each in 1650 to populations of about six hundred by 1702. Jay Higginbotham, *The Mobile Indians* (Mobile, AL: Sir Rey's, 1966), 80.

39. Excerpt from the Tale of the Fighting Eagles recorded by Mary Haas. This tale explains how these two chiefs became eagles, and the Tunica-Biloxis use this story to explain how their people came to identify with the emblem of the eagle. Mary R. Haas, "Fighting Eagles," in *Tunica Texts* (Berkeley: University of California Press, 1950), 75.

40. John D. Barbry, director of development and programing, Language and Culture Revitalization Program at the Tunica-Biloxi Tribe of Louisiana, personal correspondence with author, January 15, 2015; *Hichut' una Awachihk' unanahcb: Fighting Eagles* (Marksville: Tunica-Biloxi Tribe of Louisiana, 2011), 9.

41. Stephen Warren, *The Worlds the Shawnees Made: Migration and Violence in Early America* (Chapel Hill: University of North Carolina Press, 2014), 83, 149; Jean-Baptiste Le Moyne, Sieur de Bienville, to Jérôme de Pontchartrain, February 25, 1708, *MPA:FD*, 3:113–114; Kelton, *Epidemics and Enslavement*, 42, 113; La Harpe, *Historical Journal*, 147; Martin, "Southeastern Indians and the English Trade in Skins and Slaves," 309.

42. Vernon James Knight, "The Formation of the Creeks," in Hudson and Chaves Tesser, *Forgotten Centuries*, 373–392, 376, 385–387; Patricia Galloway, "Confederacy as a Solution to Chiefdom Dissolution: Historical Evidence in the Choctaw Case, in Hudson and Chaves Tesser, *Forgotten Centuries*, 393–420, 393, 406–407; James H. Merrel, *The Indians' New World: Catawbas and Their Neighbors from European Contact Through the Era of Removal* (Chapel Hill: University of North Carolina Press, 2009), 113–116; George Milne, "Picking Up the Pieces: Natchez Coalescence in the Shatter Zone," in Ethridge and Shuck-Hall, *Mapping the Mississippi Shatter Zone*, 388–417, 390–391; Stephen Warren, "Reconsidering Coalescence: Yuchi and Shawnee Survival Strategies in the Colonial Southeast," in *Yuchi Indian Histories Before the Removal Era*, ed. Jason Baird Jackson, 155–188 (Lincoln: University of Nebraska Press, 2012), 156–159, 163–164.

43. Robbie Ethridge, *Creek Country: The Creek Indians and Their World* (Chapel Hill: University of North Carolina Press, 2003), 24.

44. Jenny Davis, *Talking Indian: Identity and Language Revitalization in the Chickasaw Renaissance* (Tucson: University of Arizona Press, 2018), 9–12, 20–22; David A. Nichols, "The Enterprise of War: The Military Economy of the Chickasaw Indians, 1715–1815," in *The Native South: New Histories and Enduring Legacies*, ed. Tim Alan Garrison and Greg O'Brien, 33–46 (Lincoln: University of Nebraska Press, 2017), 34; James R. Atkinson, *Splendid Land, Splendid People: The Chickasaw Indians to Removal* (Tuscaloosa: University of Alabama Press, 2004); Ethridge, *Chicaza to Chickasaw*, 74–75; Usner, *American Indians in the Lower Mississippi Valley*, 35.

45. LeAnne Howe, "Ohoyo Chishba Osh: Woman Who Stretches Way Back," in *Pre-Removal Choctaw History: Exploring New Paths*, ed. Greg O'Brien, 26–47 (Norman: University of Oklahoma Press, 2008), 32; Kelton, *Epidemics and Enslavement*, 137; Galloway, *Choctaw Genesis*, 2–4, 28–29, 350–358; James Taylor Carson, *Searching for the Bright Path: The Mississippi Choctaws from Prehistory to Removal* (Lincoln: University of Nebraska Press, 1999), 8–27; William Brescia Jr., "Choctaw Oral Tradition Relating to Tribal Origin," in *The Choctaw Before Removal*, ed. Carolyn Keller Reeves, 3–16 (Jackson: University Press of Mississippi, 1985), 6–13; Isaac Pistonatubbee, "The Choctaw Creation Legend," in *The Listening Wind: Native Literature from the Southeast*, ed. Marcia Haag and H. S. Halbert, 13–14 (Lincoln: University of Nebraska Press, 2016), 13–14; Vernon Knight Jr., "The Symbolism of Mississippian Mounds," in Waselkov, Wood, and Hatley, *Powhatan's Mantle*, 421–434, 423–424; Michelene Pensatubbee, *Choctaw Women in a Chaotic World: The Clash of Cultures in the Colonial Southeast* (Albuquerque: University of New Mexico Press, 2005), 10; Galloway, "Confederacy as a Solution to Chiefdom Dissolution," 406–409.

46. Jack Martin, *A Grammar of Creek (Muskogee)* (Lincoln: University of Nebraska Press, 2011), 3–5; Thomas Foster II, "Evidence of Historic Creek Indian Migration from a Regional and Direct Historic Analysis of Ceramic Types," *Southeastern Archaeology* 23, no. 1 (2004): 66–68; Mary R. Haas, "Dialects of the Muskogee Language," *International Journal of American Linguistics* 11, no. 2 (1945): 69–70.

47. Michael Green, *The Politics of Indian Removal: Creek Government and Society in Crisis* (Lincoln: University of Nebraska Press, 1985), 5–12; Claudio Saunt, *A New Order of Things: Property, Power, and the Transformation of the Creek Indians, 1733–1816* (Cambridge: Cambridge University Press, 1999), 19–22; Sheri M. Shuck-Hall, "Alabama and Coushatta Diaspora and Coalescence in the Mississippian Shatter Zone," in Ethridge and Shuck-Hall, *Mapping the Mississippian Shatter Zone*, 250–271, 260–267; Kowalewski, "Coalescent Societies," 94–122; Ned Jenkins, "Tracing the Origins of the Early Creeks, 1050–1700 CE," in Ethridge and Shuck-Hall, *Mapping the Mississippian Shatter Zone*, 188–249, 188–236; Usner, *Indians, Settlers, and Slaves*, 19; Piker, *Okfuskee*, 4–10; Ethridge, *Creek Country*, 22–31, 92–116; Kathryn Holland Braund, *Deerskins and Duffels: The Creek Indian Trade with Anglo-America, 1685–1815*, 2nd ed. (Lincoln: University of Nebraska Press, 2008), 3–12; Gallay, *Indian Slave Trade*, 140.

48. Neil Whitehead, "Tribes Make States and States Make Tribes: Warfare and the Creation of Colonial Tribes and States in Northeastern South America," in *War in the Tribal Zone: Expanding States and Indigenous Warfare*, ed. R. Brian Ferguson and Neil Whitehead, 127–150 (Santa Fe, NM: School of Advanced Research, 1992), 130–132; Piker, *Okfuskee*, 4–10, 16–17; Galloway, "Confederacy as a Solution to Chiefdom Dissolution," 408.

49. Tim Alan Garrison, *The Legal Ideology of Removal: The Southern Judiciary and the Sovereignty of Native American Nations* (Athens: University of Georgia Press, 2002), 34–46; Tiya Miles, *The House on Diamond Hill: A Cherokee Plantation Story* (Chapel Hill: University of North Carolina Press, 2010), 175–177; Theda Perdue, *Slavery and the Evolution of Cherokee Society, 1540–1866* (Knoxville: University of Tennessee Press, 1979), 55–57; Melanie K. Yazzie and Cutcha Risling Baldy, "Introduction: Indigenous Peoples and the Politics of Water," in *Decolonization: Indigeneity, Education and Society* 7, no. 1 (2018): 1–3; Kim Tallbear, "Dossier: Theorizing Queer Inhumanisms: An Indigenous Reflection on Working Beyond the Human/Not Human," *GLQ: A Journal of Lesbian and Gay Studies*, 21, nos. 2–3 (2015): 232–235; Enrique Salmón, "Kincentric Ecology: Indigenous Perceptions of the Human-Nature Relationship," *Ecological Applications* 10, no. 5 (October 2000): 1327–1329; Simpson, "Indigenous Resurgence and Co-Resistance," 22–25; Coulthard, *Red Skin, White Masks*, 60–62; Nick Estes, *Our History Is the Future* (New York: Verso, 2019), 14–16; Noura Erakat, *Justice for Some: Law and the Question of Palestine* (Redwood City, CA: Stanford University Press, 2019).

50. DeLay, *North American Borderlands*, 9; Barr, "Geographies of Power," 6–11; Miller, *Ogimaag*, 23–28; DuVal, *Native Ground*, 8–9; Ellis, "Natchez War Revisited," 440–452.

51. Another traveling missionary similarly described the Bayagoula and Mugulasha settlement. The Jesuit priest Father Gravier remarked that the Petite Nation of Mugulashas "formed a village with the Baiougoula (Bayagoula) as the Pioüaroüa (Peoria) do with the Kaskaskia." By drawing a comparison to his experience in the Illinois country, Gravier indicates that this is not an unusual village arrangement, but rather that this practice of joining villages was common throughout the eastern woodlands. Jacques Gravier, "Journal of Father Gravier's Voyage," in Shea, *Early Voyages Up and Down the Mississippi*, 115–163, 150; de Montigny à Saint-Vallier, August 25, 1699, in *Les missions du Séminaire de Québec*, 80.

52. Laurence M. Hauptman, "Refugee Havens: The Iroquois Villages of the Eighteenth Century," in *American Indian Environments: Ecological Issues in Native American History*, ed.

Chirstopher Vecsey and Robert W. Venables, 128–139 (Syracuse, NY: Syracuse University Press, 1980), 129–132; Pierre Margry, *Découvertes et établissements des Français dans l'ouest et dans le sud de l'Amérique Septentrionale (1614–1754)* (Paris: Jouaust, 1880), 4:180.

53. Jacques Marquette, *American Journeys Collection: The Mississippi Voyage of Joliet and Marquette, 1673* (Madison: Wisconsin Historical Society, 2003), 250–253; Gilles Havard and Cécile Vidal, *Histoire de l'Amérique française* (Paris: Flammarion, 2006), 104–108.

CHAPTER 2

1. Kelton, *Epidemics and Enslavement*, 112, 137–156; letter of Mr. Thaumur de la Source, in Shea, *Early Voyages*, 81; Ethridge, *Chicaza to Chickasaw*, 141–142; Paul Kelton, "Shattered and Infected," in Ethridge and Shuck-Hall, *Mapping the Mississippian Shatter Zone*, 312–332, 314.

2. Usner, *Indians, Settlers, and Slaves*, 25; Mathé Allain, "In Search of a Policy, 1701–1731," in *The Louisiana Purchase Bicentennial Series in Louisiana History*, vol. 1, *The French Experience in Louisiana*, ed. Glenn R. Conrad, 86–105 (Lafayette: University of Southwestern Louisiana, 1995), 86–87, 90–92; Alejandra Dubcovsky, *Informed Power: Communication in the Early American South* (Cambridge, MA: Harvard University Press, 2016), 117–118; Michael James Forêt, "Red Over White: Indians, Deserters, and French Colonial Louisiana," *Proceedings of the Meeting of the French Colonial Historical Society* 17 (1993): 79–82; Havard and Vidal, *Histoire de l'Amérique française*, 125–126.

3. Old Mobile, also known as first Mobile, was constructed at 27-mile bluff. Severe flooding led the French to move the location of their fort and settlement further inland, and in 1711 this second Mobile was constructed close to the site of present-day Mobile, Alabama. Local Native peoples referred to the base of the Mississippi River, where New Orleans would later be built, as "Balbancha." Jeffrey U. Darensbourg, "Hunting Memories of the Grass Things: An Indigenous Reflection on Bison in Louisiana," *Southern Cultures* 27, no. 1 (2021): 14–24; Du Pratz, *Histoire de la Louisiane*, 1: 141; John Brice Harris, *From Old Mobile to Fort Assumption* (Nashville, TN: Parthenon Press, 1959), 16; Usner, *Indians, Settlers, and Slaves*, 28–31; Marcel Giraud, *A History of French Louisiana*, vol. 1, *The Reign of Louis XIV, 1698–1715*, trans. and ed. Joseph C. Lambert (Baton Rouge: Louisiana State University Press, 1974), 1:101; Relation de la Louisianne, 1735, 5–14, VAULT Ayer MS 530, Edward E. Ayer Collection, Newberry Library, Chicago (hereafter cited as Ayer Collection, Newberry Library); Étienne Véniard de Bourgmont, "Exact Description of Louisiana," doc. no. AJ-093, *American Journeys Collection*, ed. Marcel Giraud, trans. Max Myers (Madison: Wisconsin Historical Society Digital Library and Archives, 2003), 10–12.

4. Although Iberville identified these groups as the "Annochy" and "Moctoby" archaeologists, Bonnie Gums and Cameron Gill have identified these as groups of Biloxis and Capinans. Bonnie Gums and Cameron Gill, "The La Pointe-Krebs Plantation Archaeology Project," in *Archaeology at La Pointe-Krebs Plantation on the Mississippi Gulf Coast*, ed. Bonnie L. Gums and Gregory Waselkov, 1–23 (Jackson: Mississippi Department of Archives and History, 2013), 7–9; Guillaume de L'Isle, *Carte des environs du Misisipi*, 1701, Louis C. Karpinski Map Collection, Newberry Library, Chicago; N. de Fer, *Les costes aux environs de la rivière de Misisipi*, 1701, Louis C. Karpinski Map Collection, Newberry Library, Chicago; Pierre Le Moyne d'Iberville, *Iberville's Gulf Journals*, ed. Richebourg Gaillard McWilliams (Tuscaloosa: University of Alabama Press, 1981), 5–7, 44–49; La Harpe, *Historical Journal*, 9–10; Pierre Le Moyne d'Iberville, "The Iberville Journal," in *A Comparative View of French Louisiana, 1699 and 1762: The Journals of Pierre Le Moyne d'Iberville and Jean-Jacques-Blaise d'Abbadie*, ed. and trans. Carl A. Brasseux, 11–76 (Lafay-

ette: University of Southwestern Louisiana, 1981), 31–46; Nellis M. Crouse, *Lemoyne d'Iberville: Soldier of New France* (Baton Rouge: Louisiana State University Press, 2001), 1–3, 55–62, 207–212.

5. Giraud, *History of French Louisiana*, 1:58–59; Mathé Allain, *Not Worth a Straw: French Colonial Policy and the Early Years of Louisiana* (Lafayette, LA: Center for Louisiana Studies, 1989), 47–54; Iberville, Mémoire sur l'éstablissement de la mobile et du misisipy, June 20, 1702, Colonies C13 Louisiane (Washington, DC: Foreign Copying Program, Library of Congress), digitized microfilm, C13 C2, reel 2, fols. 48–65; de La Salle to Monseigneur, April 1, 1702, Colonies C13 Louisiane (Washington, DC: Foreign Copying Program, Library of Congress), digitized microfilm, C-13 C2, reel 2, fols. 36–37.

6. Michael Witgen, "The Rituals of Possession: Native Identity and the Invention of Empire in Seventeenth-Century Western North America," *Ethnohistory* 54, no. 4 (2007): 640–642, 646–648; White, *Middle Ground*, 105, 142–149; Havard and Vidal, *Histoire de l'Amérique française*, 122–124.

7. In the Mobilian trade language *Mongoula* simply means, "my friend," so Mugulasha was likely not the formal name of this nation, but rather a French misunderstanding of the Bayagoulas' introduction of their neighboring nation as "my friends." David Wheat, "My Friend Nicolas Mongoula: Africans, Indians, and Cultural Exchange in Eighteenth-Century Mobile," in *Coastal Encounters: The Transformation of the Gulf South in the Eighteenth Century*, ed. Richmond Brown, 117–131 (Lincoln: University of Nebraska Press, 2007), 117–118; Elizabeth Reitz, Kevin Gibbons, and Maran Little, "Animal Remains from La Pointe-Krebs Plantation," in Gums and Waselkov, *Archaeology at La Pointe-Krebs*, 166–220, 111–114.

8. Iberville, *Comparative View*, 32–35, 43; James O. Dorsey and John R. Swanton, *A Dictionary of the Biloxi and Ofo Languages: Accompanied with Thirty-One Biloxi Texts and Numerous Biloxi Phrases* (Washington, DC: U.S. Government Printing Office, 1912), 6; Swanton, *Indian Tribes of the Lower Mississippi Valley*, 41; Margry, *Découvertes*, 4:153–155.

9. Usner, *Indians, Settlers, and Slaves*, 13; Ethridge, *Chicaza to Chickasaw*, 174–175; James F. Barnett, *Mississippi's American Indians* (Jackson: University Press of Mississippi, 2012), 73; Margry, *Découvertes*, 4:155; Jacques Gravier, *Relation ou Journal du voyage du r.p. Jacques Gravier, de la Compagnie de Jésus, en 1700 depuis le pays des Illinois jusqu'à l'embouchure du Mississipi*, Sabin Americana (New York, 1859), 55, 57; Iberville, "Journal of the Badine," in *Iberville's Gulf Journals*, 7.

10. Henri Abraham Chatelain, *Atlas historique, ou nouvelle introduction a l'histoire, à la chronologie, et à la géographie ancienne et moderne* (Amsterdam, 1719), 93.

11. Iberville estimated that there were about 170 homes and 250 men in the Bayagoula villages. Using the conservative multiplier of 3.5, this would suggest that the total Bayagoula population should have been around 875 people. Iberville, *Comparative View*, 48–50; Margry, *Découvertes*, 4:164, 171.

12. Iberville, *Comparative View*, 45; Kim Tallbear, "Making Love and Relations Beyond Settler Sex and Family," in *Making Kin Not Population*, ed. Adele Clarke and Donna Haraway, 145–164 (Chicago: Prickly Paradigm Press, 2018), 145–166; Salar Mohandesi and Emma Teitelman, "Without Reserves," in *Social Reproduction Theory: Remapping Class, Recentering Oppression*, ed. Tithi Bhattacharya, 37–67 (London: Pluto Press, 2017), 39–40; Sedef Arat-Koç, "Whose Social Reproduction? Transnational Motherhood and Challenges to Feminist Political Theory," in *Social Reproduction: Feminist Political Economy and Challenges to Neo-Liberalism*, ed. Kate Bezanson and Meg Luxton, 75–92 (Montreal: McGill-Queen's University Press, 2006), 85–88.

13. Alan Taylor, *The American Colonies* (New York: Viking, 2001), 292–293; Evan Haefli and Kevin Sweeney, *Captives and Captors: The 1704 French and Indian Raid on Deerfield* (Amherst: University of Massachusetts Press, 2005), 35.

14. In 1708 the entire population of French colonial Louisiana consisted of 180 men bearing arms, 27 French families, and 60 French men living dispersed among Native nations. Gregory A. Waselkov, "French Colonial Archaeology at Old Mobile: An Introduction," in "French Colonial Archaeology at Old Mobile: Selected Studies," ed. Gregory A Waselkov, special issue, *Historical Archaeology* 36, no. 1 (2002): 4–6; Pénicaut, *Fleur de Lys and Calumet*, 106; Bienville to Pontchartrain, June 6, 1704, *MPA:FD*, 3:25; Savole to Pontchartrain, August 1, 1701, *Mississippi Provincial Archives: 1701–1729, French Dominion*, vol. 2 ed. Dunbar Rowland and Albert Godfrey Sanders, trans. Dunbar Rowland (Jackson, MS: Press of the Mississippi Department of Archives and History, 1929), 2:12; Peter J. Hamilton, *Colonial Mobile: An Historical Study Largely from Original Sources of the Alabama-Tombigbee Basin and the Old South West from the Discovery of the Spiritu Santo in 1519 Until the Demolition of Fort Charlotte in 1821* (Tuscaloosa: University of Alabama Press, 1976), 65; Usner, *Indians, Settlers, and Slaves*, 25–27; "Census of Louisiana by Nicolas de la Salle," 1708, *MPA:FD*, 2:19.

15. Over the past two decades, scholarship on early Native American history has increasingly emphasized the roles of Native women in shaping colonial encounters and early American societies. Scholars including Christina Snyder, Kathleen DuVal, and James Brooks have revolutionized how we understand the role of captive women in forging international relationships, and Theda Perdue, Susan Sleep Smith, Michelene Pensatubbee, and Juliana Barr have brilliantly illustrated how women exercised power through kinship connections. Historians have also correctly emphasized Native peoples' understandings of gender complementarity—the belief that men and women should have distinct social, political, and labor roles but that each of men's and women's contributions to society were equally valuable—shaped societies as diverse as the Cherokees, Iroquois, Choctaws, and Apaches. Even as historians have increasingly recognized the influence of elite ruling women within the Southeast, most of the scholarship on diplomacy in the Lower Mississippi Valley still tends to be focused on the roles of men, with people who are gender nonbinary overlooked almost entirely. Although historians of the Lower Mississippi Valley have sometimes recognized the role of women leaders among the Natchez, there has been almost no exploration of the role of women's political leadership within Petites Nations' societies. The practice of women assuming roles of paramount political leadership within Southeastern polities stretches at least as far back as the 1540s when a powerful female leader ruled the Mississippian polity of Cofitachequi. In the early eighteenth century, the majority of the highest ranking political leaders of Southeastern nations were men, but women continued to play crucial roles in international and internal politics. Susan Schroeder, introduction to *Indian Women of Early Mexico*, ed. Susan Schroeder, Stephanie Wood, and Robert Haskett, 3–35 (Norman: University of Oklahoma Press, 1997), 15; Juliana Barr, *Peace Came in the Form of a Woman: Indians and Spaniards in the Texas Borderlands* (Chapel Hill: University of North Carolina Press, 2007); Snyder, *Slavery in Indian Country*; Brooks, *Captives and Cousins*; Perdue, *Cherokee Women*; "Nouvelle relation de la Louisiane," *Le Nouveau Mercure*, September 1717, in *Le Plus Beau Païs du Monde*, ed. May Rush Gwin Waggoner (Lafayette: Center for Louisiana Studies, 2005), 40; Paul A. Kunkel, "The Indians of Louisiana, About 1700: Their Customs and Manner of Living," in Conrad, *French Experience in Louisiana*, 248–268, 252–253; DuVal, *Native Ground*, 20, 63, 73; Carl J. Ekberg, *Stealing Indian Women: Native Slavery in the Illinois Country* (Urbana: University of Illinois Press, 2007); Milne, "Picking Up the Pieces," 387–412; Perdue, *Slavery and the Evolution of Cherokee Society*, 9; Charles Hudson, *Knights of Spain, Warriors of the Sun: Hernando de Soto and the South's Ancient Chiefdoms* (Athens: University of Georgia Press, 1997),174–175; James Taylor Carson, "Molly Brant: From Clan Mother to Loyalist Chief," in *Sifters: Native American Women's Lives*, ed. Theda Perdue, 48–59 (New York: Oxford University Press, 2001), 48–58; Martha W. McCartney, "Cockacoeske,

Queen of the Pamunkey: Diplomat and Suzerain," in Waselkov, Wood, and Hatley, *Powhatan's Mantle*, 243–265, 243, 254–255; Pensatubbee, *Choctaw Women in a Chaotic World*, 10–31.

16. Margry, *Découvertes*, 4:166; Barr, *Peace Came in the Form of a Woman*, 33–35; Christian Crouch, *Nobility Lost: French and Canadian Martial Cultures, Indians, and the End of New France* (Ithaca, NY: Cornell University Press, 2014), 72–74.

17. Howe, "Ohoyo Chishba Osh," 28–29.

18. Sibley, "Historical Sketches of the Several Indian Tribes in Louisiana," 1085–1088; Ian Brown, "Calumet Ceremony in the Southeast," 313–315; Bienville to Antoine de la Mothe, Sieur de Cadillac, June 23, 1716, *MPA:FD*, 3:214; Baron de Lahontan, *New Voyages to North America*, ed. Reuben Gold Thwaites (Chicago: A. C. McClurg, 1905), 2:423–424; de Montigny "Poème en vers touchant l'établissement de la province de la Louisianne," 320, 400; David H. Dye, *War Paths, Peace Paths: An Archaeology of Cooperation and Conflict in Native Eastern North America* (Lanham, MD: Altamira Press, 2009), 158, 164–165; Fred B. Kniffen, Hiram F. Gregory, and George Stokes, *Historic Indian Tribes of Louisiana: From 1542 to the Present* (Baton Rouge: Louisiana State University Press, 1987), 294; Henri Joutel, *Cavalier de La Salle à la recherché du Mississipi: Le journal de survivant Rouennais Henri Joutel*, ed. Étienne Taillemite (Rouen: ASI Editions, 2003), 186; La Harpe, *Historical Journal*, 9–10; Iberville, "Journal of the Badine," 5–7, 44–49.

19. Pénicaut, *Fleur de Lys and Calumet*, 6–7.

20. Pénicaut, *Fleur de Lys and Calumet*, 6–7; Margry, *Découvertes*, 4:176; Iberville, "Journal of the Badine," 44; Pierre Margry, ed., *Journal of the Frigate "Le Marin" (September 5th, 1698–July 2nd, 1699): 275th Anniversary, Biloxi Bay Colony* (Ocean Springs, MS: Bossman Printing, 1974), 38–39, 49–50; Dumont de Montigny, *Memoir of Lieutenant Dumont*, 343; Joseph Patrick Key, "The Calumet and the Cross: Religious Encounters in the Lower Mississippi Valley," *Arkansas Historical Quarterly* 61, no. 2 (2002): 154, 157–158; Donald J. Blakeslee, "The Origin and Spread of the Calumet Ceremony," *American Antiquity* 46, no. 4 (1981): 759–760, 766; Tracy Neal Leavelle, *The Catholic Calumet: Colonial Conversions in French and Indian North America* (Philadelphia: University of Pennsylvania Press, 2012), 2–3; Pekka Hämäläinen, "The Western Comanche Trade Center: Rethinking the Plains Indian Trade System," *Western Historical Quarterly* 9, no. 4 (1998): 509–510; Witgen, *Infinity of Nations*, 226–229; Patricia K. Galloway, "'So Many Little Republics': British Negotiations with the Choctaw Confederacy, 1765," *Ethnohistory* 41, no. 4 (1994): 520; Kathleen DuVal, "'A Good Relationship, and Commerce': The Native Political Economy of the Arkansas River Valley," *Early American Studies* 1, no. 1 (2003): 69; Juliana Barr, "A Diplomacy of Gender: Rituals of First Contact in the 'Land of Tejas,'" *William and Mary Quarterly* 61, no. 3 (2004): 393–434; Michelle LeMaster, *Brothers Born of One Mother: British-Native American Relations in the Colonial Southeast* (Charlottesville: University of Virginia Press, 2012), 19–22, 32–38.

21. Haas, *Tunica Texts*, 133; Atkinson, *Splendid Land, Splendid People*, 13–14; LeMaster, *Brothers Born of One Mother*, 68–72.

22. Sauvole de la Villantray, *The Journal of Sauvole: Historical Journal of the Establishment of the French in Louisiana*, ed. Jay Higginbotham (Mobile, AL: Colonial Books, 1969), 25, 28, 40–41; Margry, *Découvertes*, 4:166–167, 172–75.

23. *Journal of the Frigate "Le Marin,"* 40–41.

24. *Journal of Sauvole*, 23–24; Iberville, "Journal of the Badine," 79.

25. *Journal of Sauvole*, 23; Margry *Découvertes*, 4:448; Iberville, *Comparative View*, 50; Vernon J. Knight and Sherée L. Adams, "A Voyage to the Mobile and Tomeh in 1700, with Notes on the Interior of Alabama," *Ethnohistory* 28, no. 2 (1981): 182.

26. *Journal of Sauvole*, 23.

27. Margry, *Découvertes*, 4:448.

28. This is likely a title rather than a personal name. For example, in the 1720s, the Natchez also referred to women leaders as "women of valor" and there is good indication that Choctaw people also used this title to refer to esteemed women. Jean-Bernard Bossu, *New Travels in North America*, trans. and ed. Samuel Dorris Dickinson (Natchitoches, LA: North Western State University Press, 1982), 92; Relation de la Louisiane, 1735, 65–66, 144–146, Ayer Collection, Newberry Library; Pensatubbee, *Choctaw Women in a Chaotic World*, 24.

29. Bossu, *New Travels in North America*, 92–96.

30. Bossu, *New Travels in North America*, 92–94.

31. Relation de la Louisiane, 1735, 65–66, Ayer Collection, Newberry Library; Diron d'Artaguiette, Journal, September 1, 1722–September 10, 1723, ANOM, C13 C2, fols. 188, 222; Pierre-François-Xavier de Charlevoix, *Histoire et description generale de la nouvelle France avec le Journal historique d'un voyage fait par ordre du roi dans l'Amérique Septentrionnale* (Paris, 1744), 3:420–423; Perdue, *Cherokee Women*, 36; Tiya Miles, "'Circular Reasoning': Recentering Cherokee Women in the Anti-Removal Campaigns," *American Quarterly* 61, no. 2 (2009): 224–227; Milne, *Natchez Country*, 126–130; Douglas R. White, George P. Murdock, and Richard Scaglion, "Natchez Class and Rank Reconsidered," *Ethnology* 10, no. 4 (1971): 373–374; Lettre du P. le Petit, 1730, sur les Sauvages du Mississipi, et en particulier les Natchez, et relation de leur entreprise sur la colonie française, en 1729, July 12, 1730, ANOM, 04DFC 40, 14–16.

32. De Montigny à Saint-Vallier, August 25, 1699, *Les missions du Séminaire de Québec*, 83–86; Swanton, *Indian Tribes of the Lower Mississippi Valley*, 41; M. L'Abbé Amédée Gosselin, "Les sauvages du Mississippi (1698–1708)," in *Quinzième Session du Congrès International de Américanistes* (Quebec: Dussault et Proulx, 1907), 41.

33. De Montigny à Saint-Vallier, August 25, 1699, *Les missions du Séminaire de Québec*, 79.

34. One of Montigny's Tensa guides died several days after passing through the Houmas' village, presumably of disease. De Montigny à Saint-Vallier, August 25, 1699, *Les missions du Séminaire de Québec*, 83.

35. Gravier, *Relation ou Journal du voyage*, 42–43.

36. The archaeologists who uncovered this burial at Angola—the Louisiana State Penitentiary farm—concluded that it indicates that "at least one member of society other than the chief wore articles of European clothing. This was probably true of many tribal members, including women, by the second or third decade of the eighteenth century." These conclusions, however, are not supported by documentary evidence from this time period. French explorers repeatedly recorded and placed tremendous import on the fact that Cahura-Joligo, the Tunica chief during this era, dressed in a European waistcoat and carried a gold-headed cane. It would be surprising if European observers placed so much emphasis on these sartorial choices if they were common among the Tunicas and we might also expect to see more discussion of this in French records. Moreover, archaeologists did not find evidence of European clothing in any of the other burials at Angola. Men, women, and children who were interred in these graves were buried with copper bangles, metal pots, guns, and other European items, but not European clothing. Even the burials that contained the greatest wealth of material objects do not appear to contain any European clothing (excluding jewelry). Therefore, it does not seem that frock coats and trousers were common items. Le Page du Pratz, *The History of Louisiana, or of the Western Parts of Virginia and Carolina: Containing a Description of the Countries That Lie on Both Sides of the River Mississippi with an Account of the Settlements* (London, 1774), 312; Pierre François Xavier de Charlevoix, "Historical Journal of Father Pierre François Xavier de Charlevoix: in letters addressed to the Dutchess of Lesdiguières," in *Historical Collections of Louisiana*, ed. and trans. Benjamin F. French, 119–196

(New York: 1851), 174; Alexander de Batz, *Sauvage matachez en Guerrier*, 1759, Peabody Museum of Archaeology and Ethnography at Harvard University; Brain, *Tunica Archaeology*, 152–177; Sophie White, *Wild Frenchmen and Frenchified Indians: Material Culture and Race in Colonial Louisiana* (Philadelphia: University of Pennsylvania Press, 2013), 128, 194.

37. In another burial at the Angola farm site, archaeologists recorded uncovering a grave containing a female person buried with a flintlock gun. Scant additional evidence indicates a deeper Mississippian tradition of burying extraordinary females with typically male items and weapons of war. At the late Mississippian King cite in northern Georgia, David Hally has analyzed a burial (possibly two burials) of females who were interred with implements of war, and in a manner like the male burials at the site rather than the female interments. Hally has suggested that this could either suggest that these interred females were warrior women, or that they were identified with or gendered as men or masculine. Brain, *Tunica Archaeology*, 158, 170; David Hally, *King: The Social Archaeology of a Late Mississippian Town in Northwestern Georgia* (Tuscaloosa: University of Alabama Press, 2008), 339–344.

38. Jeffrey P. Brain, Alan Toth, and Antonio Rodriguez-Buckingham, "Ethnohistoric Archaeology and the De Soto Entrada into the Lower Mississippi Valley," in *The Conference on Historic Site Archaeology Papers 1972*, vol. 7, ed. Stanley South (1974), book 8, 262; Patricia K. Galloway "'This nation . . . is very brave and has always served the French well'—Tunicas Under the French Regime, 1676–1763," in *The Tunica-Biloxi Tribe: Its Culture and People*, ed. Faye Truex and Patricia Q. Foster, 20–32 (Marksville, LA: Tunica-Biloxi Indians of Louisiana, 1987), 20–32; Dumont de Montigny, *Memoir of Lieutenant Dumont*, 185–186.

39. While the modern term *two-spirit* falls short of conveying the complexity of nonbinary individuals within Natchez and Petites Nations, considering historical Indigenous terminology for these identities may shed further light on Native conceptions of sexuality and gender in the early modern era. For example, in addition to words for men and women, in Anshinaabemowin (the Anishinaabe/Ojibwe language), the words *ikwekaazo* and *ininiikaazo* mean "one who endeavors to be like a woman" and "one who endeavors to be like a man," respectively. Likewise, Diné (Navajo) people speak of those who embrace aspects of other genders as *Nádleehí*, meaning "one who is transformed," and Lakota speakers use *winkté* to indicate that, although the person is male, they behave as a woman. In all cases, these words do not mean simply man, woman, or transgender, but rather indicate specific cultural and social roles and gender identities that have no equivalents in English or in contemporary Euro-American gender ideologies. Niigaan Sinclair, "Returning to Ourselves: Two Spirit Futures and the Now," in *Love Beyond Body, Space, and Time: An Indigenous LGBT Sci-Fi Anthology*, 12–19 (Winnipeg: Bedside Press, 2016), 14; Joseph Gilley, *Becoming Two-Spirit: Gay Identity and Social Acceptance in Indian Country* (Lincoln: University of Nebraska Press, 2006), 8–15, 25–34; Jen Manion, "Transgender Representations, Identities, and Communities," in *The Oxford Handbook of American Women's and Gender History*, ed. Ellen Hartigan-O'Connor and Lisa Materson, 311–331 (Oxford: Oxford University Press, 2018), 314–315; Joanne Barker, introduction to *Critically Sovereign: Indigenous Gender, Sexuality, and Feminist Studies*, ed. Joanne Barker, 1–44 (Durham, NC: Duke University Press, 2017), 12–13; Andrew Jolivette, *Indian Blood: HIV and Colonial Trauma in San Francisco's Two-Spirit Community* (Seattle: University of Washington Press, 2016), 9–11, 16–19; Jenny Davis, "More Than Just 'Gay Indians': Intersecting Articulations of Two-Spirit Gender, Sexuality, and Indigenousness," in *Queer Excursions: Retheorizing Binaries in Language, Gender, and Sexuality*, ed. Lal Zimman, Jenny Davis, and Joshua Raclaw, 62–80 (New York: Oxford University Press, 2014), 63–78; Roger Carpenter, "Womanish Men and Manlike Women: The Native American Two-Spirit as Warrior," in *Gender and Sexuality in Indigenous North America, 1400–1850*, ed. Sandra Slater and Fay Yar-

brough, 146–164 (Columbia: University of South Carolina Press, 2011), 146–161; Leanne Betasamosake Simpson, *As We Have Always Done: Indigenous Freedom Through Radical Resistance* (Minneapolis: University of Minnesota Press, 2017), 119–127; Marie Laing, *Urban Indigenous Youth Reframing Two-Spirit* (New York: Routledge, 2021), 26–29, 46–53, 61–73, 90–117; Duane Brayboy, "Two Spirits, One Heart, Five Genders," *Indian Country Today*, September 7, 2017, https://newsmaven.io/indiancountrytoday/archive/two-spirits-one-heart-five-genders-9UH _xnbfVEWQHWkjNnorQQ/; Anton Truer, *The Assassination of Hole in the Day* (St. Paul, MN: Borealis Books, 2011), 27.

40. Père le Maire, Mémoire sur la situation présente de la Louisianne, January 15, 1714, ANOM, C13 C2, fols. 109, 128.

41. Vallette de Laudun, *Journal d'un voyage à la Louisiane, fait en 1720* (Paris, 1768), 263–264.

42. De Montigny notes that it is possible that other nations may have similar practices, but he is careful to only discuss nonbinary Natchez people because he is unsure whether these practices are the same among other nations. Laudun, *Journal d'un Voyage à la Louisiane*, 263–264; Dumont de Montigny, *Mémoires historiques sur la Louisiane*, 1:247–249.

43. Giraud, *History of French Louisiana*, vol. 2, *Years of Transition: 1715–1717*, trans. Brian Pierce (Baton Rouge: Louisiana State University Press, 1993), 2:15–17.

44. The early evidence of two-spirit people in the Southeast may be slim, but there is good evidence that nonbinary people were important constituents of Mississippian societies. In the mid-sixteenth century, a French traveler in what is now Florida recorded descriptions of Timucua healers he observed to be male, but who wore women's clothing and served as diplomats and healers for the Timucua polity. These Timucuans were serving in essential and prestigious social roles, and it is clear that their gender made them valuable social members. In the early eighteenth century, a French soldier traveling among the Illinois people described seeing men who wore women's clothing. Further, he explained, these "men" embrace all aspects of feminine dress and behavior as "they are tattooed on their cheeks like the women and also on the breast and the arms, and they imitate their accent, which is different than of the men. They omit nothing that can make them like the women." Although the soldier was shocked by this behavior, he recorded that these women were accepted and valued within their nations. White, *Wild Frenchmen and Frenchified Indians*, 86, 102–103; Will Roscoe, "Sexual and Gender Diversity in Native America and the Pacific Islands," in *LGBTQ America: A Theme Study of Lesbian, Gay, Bisexual, Transgender, and Queer History*, ed. Megan E. Springate, 9:1–29(Washington, DC: National Parks Service, 2016), 9:2–29; Carpenter, "Womanish Men and Manlike Women," 150.

45. Du Pratz, *History of Louisiana*, 367.

46. According to Jeffrey Brain's estimates, the Tunicas numbered only five hundred in 1719. Combined with the Ofo and Yazoo communities, their settlement on the Yazoo River in 1699 was home to two thousand individuals. Brain, *Tunica Archaeology*, 316; Paul Kelton, "The Great Southeastern Smallpox Epidemic," in Ethridge, *Transformation of the Southeastern Indians*, 21–38, 35.

47. The Natchez, for example, tolerated the presence of missionaries within their villages but certainly never embraced their influence. St. Cosme, who was stationed among the Natchez, complained that he did not have enough muscle to enforce his conversion of the Natchez, and that he was maltreated and occasionally attacked by Natchez villagers. Barnett, *Natchez Indians*, 49; Brain, *Tunica Archaeology*, 316–317; Milne, *Natchez Country*, 45–49; Ethridge, *Chicaza to Chickasaw*, 180; La Harpe, *Historical Journal*, 60; letter of Mr. De Montigny, January 2, 1699, in Shea, *Early Voyages*, 75, 78; de Montigny à Saint-Vallier, August 15, 1699, *Les missions du Séminaire de Québec*, 77.

48. Milne, *Natchez Country*, 199; Galloway "'This nation ... is very brave,'" 20–32; Du Pratz, *History of Louisiana*, 312; Charlevoix, *Historical Journal*, 174; White, *Wild Frenchmen and Frenchified Indians*, 77–78, 86–87.

49. Gums and Gill, "La Pointe-Krebs Plantation Archaeology Project," 7–9.

50. Patricia Galloway suggests that Concha is likely referring to the Creek town of Coosa and that "Pinisca" may be a misreading of Apsicas for Abihka. Ives Goddard, Patricia Galloway, Marvin D. Jeter, Gregory A. Waselkov, and John E. Worth, "Small Tribes of the Western Southeast," in Fogelson, *Handbook of North American Indians*, 14:178–179; Willard B. Walker, "Creek Confederacy Before Removal," in Fogelson, *Handbook of North American Indians*, 14: 373–375; *Journal of Sauvole*, 45.

51. Sauvole, *Journal of Sauvole*, 45–46, 48; "Carte pour donner une idée de la positions des villages sauvages ou l'on voit par une ligne ponctuée en rouge la séparation des Sauvages qui tiennent pour nous d'avec ceux qui tiennent pour les Englois," Louis C. Karpinski Map Collection, Newberry Library, Chicago; Higginbotham, *Mobile Indians*, 43.

52. Gravier, *Relation ou journal du voyage*, 66–67.

53. A combination of poor planning, lack of regulation, wars in Europe, and the distance between France and Louisiana meant that shipments of crucial food, supplies, and trade goods arrived sporadically and were often loaded with unusable provisions. Colonial officials complained repeatedly that shoddy packaging and handling meant that wine arrived soured, olive oil leaked, meat turned rancid, and flour rotted before they reached Louisiana. Food shortages were a constant struggle for the Louisiana settlers throughout France's tenure in the Lower Mississippi Valley. Waselkov, "French Colonial Archaeology at Old Mobile," 10; Pénicaut, *Fleur de Lys and Calumet*, 106; Hubert to the Council, October 26, 1717, *MPA:FD* (1929), 2:240; Périer and De La Chaise to the Directors of the Company of the Indies, July 31, 1728, *MPA:FD*, 2:576; Bienville to Pontchartrain, June 6, 1704, *MPA:FD*, 3:25; Savole to Pontchartrain, August 1, 1701, *MPA:FD*, 2:12; Hamilton, *Colonial Mobile*, 65; Usner, *Indians, Settlers, and Slaves*, 35–40.

54. Sauvole, *Journal of Sauvole*, 159; Giraud, "L'Exact Description de la Louisianne' d'Étienne Véniard de Bourgmont," 34–36; Père Raphaël à l'abbé Raguet, May 18, 1728, Colonies C13 Louisiane (Washington DC: Foreign Copying Program, Library of Congress), digitized microfilm, C-13 A11, reel 18, fols. 264, 268; Michael Farmer, *Sacramental Records of the Roman Catholic Church of the Archdiocese of Mobile* (Mobile, AL: Archives of Mobile, 2002), 57; Usner, *Indians, Settlers, and Slaves*, 13–43.

55. Eric E. Bowne, "Southeastern Indian Polities of the Seventeenth Century," in *Native American Adoption, Captivity, and Slavery in Changing Contexts*, ed. Max Carocci and Stephanie Pratt, 65–78 (New York: Palgrave MacMillan, 2012), 66, 73, 75, 77; Ethridge, "Introduction: Mapping the Mississippian Shatter Zone," 34, 37; Ethridge, *Creek Country*, 24; Kelton, *Epidemics and Enslavement*, 189, 200; Usner, *Indians, Settlers, and Slaves*, 45; George E. Lankford, *Cultural Resources Reconnaissance Study of the Black Warrior–Tombigbee System Corridor, Alabama* (Mobile: Department of Geology and Geography, University of South Alabama), 17.

56. Lankford, *Cultural Resources*, 5–45; John R. Swanton, "The Tawasa Language," *American Anthropologist* 31, no. 3 (1929): 439.

57. Bienville to Pontchartrain, February 25, 1708, *MPA:FD*, 3:115. Here, "Choctaws" is definitely a misspelling of "Chatots," a smaller Native nation that migrated from Pensacola to Mobile between 1704 and 1706.

58. Usner, *Indians, Settlers, and Slaves*, 25; Usner, *American Indians in the Lower Mississippi Valley*, 35; Laudun, *Journal d'un Voyage à la Louisiane*, 269; Jay Higginbotham, *Old Mobile Fort*

St. Louis de la Louisiane (Tuscaloosa: University of Alabama Press, 1991), 358; Bienville to Pontchartrain February 20, 1707, *MPA:FD*, 3:38.

59. Galloway "'So Many Little Republics,'" 516–517.

60. Lankford, *Cultural Resources*, 11, 35; Monsieur de Beauchamps, "Journal of Visit to the Choctaws," 1746, in *Travels in the American Colonies*, ed. Newton D. Mereness, 259–300 (New York: Macmillan, 1916), 262–268; Pénicaut, *Fleur de Lys and Calumet*, 163; Nicolas Henri, Succession of Antoine Bunel, September 13, 1735, French Colonial Records, 10143–10187, box 2, folder 22, Notarial Archives Research Center, Office of the Clerk of Civil District Court for the Parish of Orleans, State of Louisiana, New Orleans; Père Raphaël à l'abbé Raguet, May 18, 1728, ANOM, C13 A11, reel 18, fols. 264, 268; Régis, Journal du vouyage que j'ai fait dans la nation des Chactas, l'année 1729, ANOM, C13 A12-1, reel 19, fols. 67, 70–71.

61. Higginbotham, *Old Mobile*, 189–193, 216; Lankford, *Cultural Resources*, 17, 45, 65–67.

62. Bienville to Pontchartrain, June 6, 1704, *MPA:FD*, 3:19.

63. Jean Baptiste Le Moyne Sieur de Bienville served as the governor of Louisiana four different times and for a total of thirty years during the French tenure in the Lower Mississippi Valley. Although he was repeatedly accused of corruption and malfeasance in office, Bienville is largely considered to be Louisiana's most adept colonial governor. He held the office first from 1701 to 1713, then for a short stint from 1716 to 1717, again after a brief interlude from 1718 to 1725, and finally from 1733 to 1743. Duclos to Pontchartrain, June 17, 1716, *MPA:FD*, 3:205–211; Joseph G. Dawson III, ed., *The Louisiana Governors: From Iberville to Edwards* (Baton Rouge: Louisiana State University Press, 1990), 7–17; Bienville to Pontchartrain, February 25, 1708, *MPA:FD*, 3:113–114; Brad Raymond Lieb, "The Natchez Indian Diaspora: Ethnohistoric Archaeology of the Eighteenth-Century Refuge Among the Chickasaws" (PhD diss., University of Alabama, 2008), 222.

64. La Harpe, *Historical Journal*, 46.

65. Bienville to Pontchartrain, June 6, 1704, *MPA:FD*, 3:20–22; Hamilton, *Colonial Mobile*, 65.

66. Higginbotham, *Mobile Indians*, 80; Wood, "Changing Population of the Colonial South," 74; Margry, *Découvertes*, 4:602; Usner *Indians, Settlers, and Slaves*, 19–20.

67. Although other scholars have suggested that this plague may have been yellow fever, Paul Kelton suggests that this is unlikely given the longer incubation period before the Mobilians and Tohomes began to exhibit symptoms. Either way, this "plague" caused terrible losses in the Mobilian and Tohome communities. When their sick warriors returned home, they spread the illness among their villages and "almost annihilated" their entire nation. Kelton, *Epidemics and Enslavement*, 191. Years later, when Bienville recorded this expedition in his memoir, he recalled that the 1704 plague had reduced this nation by roughly 90 percent. He estimates that in that year the smaller Tohome settlement, called the "Little Tohomes," lost 270 of their 300 warriors. "Bienville's Memoir of Louisiana, 1725–1726," *MPA:FD*, 3:537; Higginbotham, *Old Mobile*, 201.

68. Margry, *Découvertes*, 4:171, 408; La Harpe, *Historical Journal*, 24; Paul du Ru, *Journal of Paul du Ru, February 1 to May 8, 1700, Missioniary Priest to Louisiana*, trans. Ruth Lapham Butler (Chicago: Caxton Club, 1934), 5–7; *Journal of the Frigate "Le Marin,"* 43; Gravier, "Journal of Father Gravier's Voyage," in Shea, *Early Voyages Up and Down the Mississippi*, 150.

69. Pénicaut, *Fleur de Lys and Calumet*, 106–108.

70. Pénicaut, *Fleur de Lys and Calumet*, 106–115.

71. Pénicaut, *Fleur de Lys and Calumet*, 145–146.

72. Shortly before the Acolapissas first met the French in 1699, they had suffered a terrible raid by British and Chickasaw slavers. These raiders burned two of the Acolapissas' towns and took

fifty women and children. The Acolapissas consolidated their six towns and moved off the Pearl River to the east bank of the Mississippi, about forty-five miles north of present-day New Orleans. Some of the Acolapissas also sought refuge independently with the Bayagoulas. By 1702 the Acolapissas had only 250 families in their settlement. Kelton, *Epidemics and Enslavement*, 192–193; La Harpe, *Historical Journal*, 14; Margry, *Découvertes*, 4:429, 602.

73. Pénicaut, *Fleur de Lys and Calumet*, 146.

74. Pénicaut, *Fleur de Lys and Calumet*, 146.

CHAPTER 3

1. Excerpt from a speech from a Chitimacha diplomat to Governor Bienville in 1718. Du Pratz, *Histoire de la Louisiane*, 1:112–113; Swanton, *Indian Tribes of the Lower Mississippi Valley*, 133, 341.

2. Snyder, *Slavery in Indian Country*, 46–79; Gallay, *Indian Slave Trade*, 1–19, 288–314; William L. Ramsey, *The Yamasee War: A Study of Culture, Economy, and Conflict in the Colonial South* (Lincoln: University of Nebraska Press, 2008), 34–53; Ethridge, *Chicaza to Chickasaw*, 194–231; Usner, *Indians, Settlers, and Slaves*, 16–24; John E. Worth, "Razing Florida: The Indian Slave Trade and the Devastation of Spanish Florida, 1659–1715," in Ethridge and Shuck-Hall, *Mapping the Mississippian Shatter Zone*, 295–311, 295–309.

3. Three years after they issued this request, in 1712, there were a mere twenty enslaved Africans in colonial Louisiana. The numbers of enslaved Africans remained extremely low until 1719, when the transition of the title of Louisiana to the Scottish financier John Law increased French investment and attention to Louisiana. The continual inability of the French settlers to provide for themselves exacted devastating tolls from Louisiana's enslaved Black population. Daniel H. Usner, "From African Captivity to American Slavery: The Introduction of Black Laborers to Colonial Louisiana," in Conrad, *French Experience in Louisiana*, 183–200, 183–197; Jennifer M. Spear, *Race, Sex, and Social Order in Early New Orleans* (Baltimore: Johns Hopkins University Press, 2009), 20, 54–57; Allain, *Not Worth a Straw*, 84–87; Higginbotham, *Old Mobile*, 143, 163; White, *Wild Frenchmen and Frenchified Indians*, 195–198; Elizabeth Ellis, "Dismantling the Dream of 'France's Peru': Indian and African Influence on the Development of Early Colonial Louisiana," in *The World of Colonial America: An Atlantic Handbook*, ed. Ignacio Gallup-Diaz, 355–372 (New York: Routledge, 2017), 360.

4. Usner, *Indians, Settlers, and Slaves*, 25–27; "Census of Louisiana by Nicolas de la Salle," 1708, *MPA:FD*, 2:19.

5. By the second half of the 1720s, the increased importation of enslaved Africans into colonial Louisiana resulted in far less demand for Indian captives. The 1721 census of Louisiana lists 161 Indian slaves and 680 African slaves. Five years later, the census from 1726 lists the colony as having 159 Indian slaves, suggesting no increase in the number of Native laborers, while the number of African slaves had nearly tripled to 1,385. However, the number of unfree Native laborers was likely higher than this figure as census takers often did not include coureurs de bois or count captive Native women who had "married" their captors. Kathleen DuVal, "Indian Intermarriage and Métissage in Colonial Louisiana," *William and Mary Quarterly* 65, no. 2 (2008): 273; Gallay, *Indian Slave Trade*, 310–311; "Census of Louisiana by Nicolas de la Salle," 1708, *MPA:FD*, 2:19–20; Juliana Barr, "Captives to Slaves: Commodifying Indian Women in the Borderlands," *Journal of American History* 92, no. 1 (2005): 29; Ekberg, *Stealing Indian Women*, 14–21; Sophie White, *Voices of the Enslaved: Love, Labor, and Longing in French Louisiana* (Chapel Hill: University of North Carolina Press, 2019), 108–112.

6. The exact numbers of male and female slaves in Louisiana are unclear in part because census takers did not always include the same areas of Louisiana in their records. The census of 1727, for example, includes only the settlements of Louisiana between New Orleans and Pointe Coupée (it does not count either Biloxi or Mobile) and it lists only 75 Indian slaves. Likewise, the census of 1731 only includes settlements along the Lower Mississippi River below Pointe Coupée. In 1731 these settlements are recorded as containing only 47 Indian slaves who were not differentiated by sex. Bill Baron, *Census of Pointe Coupee Louisiana, 1745* (New Orleans, LA: Polyanthos, 1978), 18–21; Jaqueline K. Voorhies, comp. and trans., *Some Late Eighteenth-Century Louisianans: Census Records, 1758–1796* (Lafayette: University of Southwestern Louisiana, 1973); Charles Maduell, *The Census Tables for the French Colony of Louisiana from 1699–1732* (Baltimore: Genealogical Publishing, 1972), 81; Stephen Webre, "The Problem of Indian Slavery in Spanish Louisiana, 1769–1803," *Louisiana History* 25, no. 2 (1984): 117–135; "Segun los padrones del año 1769 en los papeles remitidos por el Estimado Señor O'Reilly . . . ," Combined Censuses of 1769 and 1777, legajo 2359, Special Collections, Newberry Library, Chicago; Jean-Jacques Blaise d'Abbadie to Minister, January 10, 1764, in *The Critical Period*, ed. Clarence W. Alvord and Clarence E. Carter (Springfield: Trustees of the Illinois State Historical Library, 1915); Wood, "Changing Population of the Colonial South," 103; Farmer, *Sacramental Records*, 1–343.

7. Du Pratz, *Histoire de la Louisiane*, 1:84, 120; Pierre Heinrich, *La Louisiane sous la Compagnie des Indes, 1717–1731* (New York: Burt Franklin, 1970), 54; Usner, *Indians, Settlers, and Slaves*, 180–181, 229–230; LaSonde v. Coupart, August 14, 1724, no. 1724-08-14-1, 3, Superior Council Records, Louisiana Historical Center, New Orleans.

8. Sarah Deer, *The Beginning and End of Rape: Confronting Sexual Violence in Native America* (Minneapolis: University of Minnesota Press, 2015), 61–64; Sharon Block, *Rape and Sexual Power in Early America* (Chapel Hill: University of North Carolina Press, 2012), 16–18; Gregory Waselkov, *Old Mobile Archaeology* (Tuscaloosa: University of Alabama Press, 2005), 38, 46; La Mothe Cadillac to Pontchartrain, October 26, 1713, *MPA:FD*, 2:169; Bienville to Pontchartrain, February 25, 1708, *MPA:FD*, 3:124; Abstracts of letter from Cadillac, Diron, and Bienville to Crozat, October 1713, *MPA:FD*, 3:176–178; Ekberg, *Stealing Indian Women*, 29; Usner, *Indians Settlers, and Slaves*, 57–59; Jennifer Morgan, *Laboring Women: Reproduction and Gender in New World Slavery* (Philadelphia: University of Pennsylvania Press, 2004), 18–21, 73–86.

9. Jean Delanglez, *The French Jesuits in Lower Louisiana* (Washington, DC: Catholic University of America, 1935), 393–398; White, *Wild Frenchmen and Frenchified Indians*, 112–147, 177–184; Spear, *Race, Sex, and Social Order*, 17–51; Jennifer M. Spear, "Colonial Intimacies: Legislating Sex in French Louisiana," *William and Mary Quarterly* 60, no. 1 (2003): 84–88.

10. Delanglez, *French Jesuits*, 398; le R.P. Tartarin, Considérations sur le mariage des Français et des sauvagesses, 1738, ANOM, C13 A23, reel 31, fols. 241, 241–243; Périer et de la Chaise to the directors of the Company of the Indies, March 25, 1729, ANOM, C13 A11, reel 19, fols. 322, 332.

11. Memoir of D'Artaguette to Pontchartrain, September 8, 1712, *MPA:FD*, 2:72.

12. Farmer, *Sacramental Records*, 3, 21, 28, 36, 39, 44, 46, 69; "Le Code Noir ou recueil des reglements rendus jusqu'a present" (Paris, 1767), trans. John Garrigus, Societé d'Histoire de la Guadeloupe (1980); Jessica Johnson, *Wicked Flesh: Black Women, Intimacy, and Freedom in the Atlantic World* (Philadelphia: University of Pennsylvania Press, 2020), 128–132.

13. Council Minutes, September 1, 1716, *MPA:FD*, 2:218; Mémoire sur la Louisiane, 1726, ANOM, C13 A10, reel 17, fols. 143, 156; Périer à l'abbé Raguet, May 12, 1728, ANOM, C13 A11, reel 18, fols. 7–8; Bienville to Pontchartrain, February 25, 1708, *MPA:FD*, 3:124; DuVal, "Indian Intermarriage and Métissage," 275; Morgan, *Laboring Women*, 1–11.

14. Brett Rushforth, "'A Little Flesh We Offer You': The Origins of Indian Slavery in New France," *William and Mary Quarterly* 60, no. 4 (2003): 800; White, *Middle Ground*, 78–79, 203–204; Rushforth, *Bonds of Alliance*, 11, 64.

15. "Le Code Noir," 1767, trans. Garrigus.

16. Whether this was the law in practice, or not, in the Mascarene Islands, it certainly was not common in Louisiana. I have only found one record of a Frenchman in the Lower Mississippi Valley, Louisiana, who liberated his enslaved Native woman once she had his child. In 1721 an enslaved Indian woman recorded only as Marianne gave birth to a son, Jean François. Three years later, in 1724, Jean François's father, François Alvin, had this child baptized. There is a note that says both Marianne and Jean François were declared free. Winston de Ville, *Gulf Coast Colonials: A Compendium of French Families in Early Eighteenth Century Louisiana* (Baltimore: Genealogical Publishing, 1968), 17.

17. Sophie White has traced the connections between French Louisiana and the Mascarene Islands and illustrated the connections between the 1685 Code Noir (slave code), the 1723 slave code for the Mascarene Islands, and the 1724 slave code for Louisiana. She has argued that La Vente and other colonial officials were already developing racialized ideas about identity at the turn of the eighteenth century and connecting these ideas about race and enslavement to their experiences in Louisiana. White, *Wild Frenchmen and Frenchified Indians*, 230; White, *Voices of the Enslaved*, 28–32.

18. Bienville to Pontchartrain, October 27, 1711, *MPA:FD*, 3:160; Margry, *Découvertes*, 4:516–517, 561; Rushforth, *Bonds of Alliance*, 240–243.

19. Although early scholarship claimed that only a negligible number of Indian peoples were enslaved by the French in Louisiana, it is now generally accepted that the French did enslave Native peoples in considerable numbers during the eighteenth century. Natchez and Chickasaws, whose nations were intermittently engaged in conflicts with the Louisiana colony, were also enslaved in considerable numbers. Patricia Dillon Woods, "The French and Natchez Indians: 1700–1731," in Conrad, *French Experience in Louisiana*, 278–295, 289; Waselkov, "French Colonial Archaeology at Old Mobile," 5; DuVal, "Indian Intermarriage and Métissage," 273; Barr, "Captives to Slaves," 24; Hamilton, *Colonial Mobile*, 78–79, 111; Robert Morrissey, *Empire by Collaboration: Indians, Colonists, and Governments in the Colonial Illinois Country* (Philadelphia: University of Pennsylvania Press, 2015), 125–126; White, *Wild Frenchmen and Frenchified Indians*, 107.

20. Diron, Recensement des habitants du fort Louis de la Mobile et des villages circonvoisins, June 28, 1721, BAC, Archives/Collections and Fonds, MG1-G1, reel C-10206, F-804, item no. 2319130; Usner, *Indians, Settlers, and Slaves*, 48–49.

21. Recensement par Diron du Fort Saint-Jean-Baptiste des Natchitoches, May 1, 1722, BAC, Archives/Collections and Fonds, MG1-G1, reel C-10206, F-804, item no. 2319133; Helen Sophie Burton and F. Todd Smith, *Colonial Natchitoches: A Creole Community on the Louisiana-Texas Frontier* (College Station: Texas A&M University Press, 2008), 142; Declaration par le Sr. Pery, October 22, 1738, no. 1738-10-22-03, Superior Council Records, Louisiana Historical Center, New Orleans.

22. Rushforth, *Bonds of Alliance*, 11–13; Barr, "Captives to Slaves," 20; Perdue, *Cherokee Women*, 66–68.

23. De Montigny à Saint-Vallier, August 25, 1699, *Les missions du Séminaire de Québec*, 78–79; DuVal, *Native Ground*, 74–75.

24. Robert Neitzel, *Archeology of the Fatherland Site: The Grand Village of the Natchez*, Anthropological Papers of the American Museum of Natural History, vol. 51, pt. 1 (1965): 71, 90; James

Mooney, "The End of the Natchez," *American Anthropologist* 1, no. 3 (1899): 510; William MacLeod, "Natchez Political Evolution," *American Anthropologist* 26, no. 2 (1924): 212; Relation de la Louisianne, 1735, 101–102, Ayer Collection, Newberry Library; Du Pratz, *Histoire de la Louisiane*, 2:213; Kidder, "Ceramic Chronology," 70.

25. Thaumur de la Source records that the Tensas only killed thirteen when their leader died in 1699. Letter of Mr. Thaumur de la Source, 1699, in Shea, *Early Voyages*, 82; Swanton, *Indian Tribes of the Lower Mississippi Valley*, 154; letter of Mr. De Montigny, January 2, 1699, in Shea, *Early Voyages*, 78; de Montigny à Saint-Vallier, August 25, 1699, *Les missions du Séminaire de Québec*, 87; Ethridge, *Chicaza to Chickasaw*, 135–138.

26. Letter of Mr. De Montigny, January 2, 1699, in Shea, *Early Voyages*, 76; de Montigny à Saint-Vallier, August 25, 1699, *Les missions du Séminaire de Québec*, 83; Barnett, *Natchez Indians*, 38, 50.

27. Ethridge, *Chicaza to Chickasaw*, 139; Margry, *Découvertes*, 1:556–569.

28. Tristram Kidder, "The Ouachita Indians of Louisiana: An Ethnohistorical and Archaeological Investigation," *Louisiana Archaeology* 12 (1985): 180–183.

29. De Montigny à Saint-Vallier, August 25, 1699, in *Les missions du Séminaire de Québec*, 73–90.

30. Snyder, *Slavery in Indian Country*, 62.

31. Gravier, *Relation ou Journal du voyage*, 34; Pénicaut, *Fleur de Lys and Calumet*, 29; Ross Phares, *Cavalier in the Wilderness: The Story of the Explorer and Trader Louis Juchereau de St. Denis* (Baton Rouge: Louisiana State University Press, 1952), 17–19; La Harpe, *Historical Journal*, 22–23; Margry, *Découvertes*, 4:414; Carson, *Searching for the Bright Path*, 20–22.

32. In 1704 the Chickasaws sold at least twelve Tensas to the British at Carolina. Ethridge, *Chicaza to Chickasaw*, 214; Snyder, *Slavery in Indian Country*, 66.

33. The Tunicas negotiated not only with the French but also with British and Chickasaw representatives during this era. In 1700 the Tunicas received a deputation of Chickasaw diplomats into their villages and attempted to negotiate an alliance with them in order to stop their continuous raiding. Still, Chickasaw raiders continued to attack their people. So, in 1704 they attempted to bypass the Chickasaws and make a direct alliance with the Chickasaws' British allies. During their 1704 meeting, the Tunicas provided the British with a gift of Tensa captives. Perhaps they intended to convey that they too could provide the British with slaves. Although the British were geographically distant, the Tunicas made efforts to sustain this relationship, with the Tunicas receiving British traders in their villages in 1708 and 1714. La Harpe, *Historical Journal*, 68; Brain, *Tunica Archaeology*, 299; Barnett, *Mississippi's American Indians*, 104–105; Higginbotham, *Old Mobile*, 357–358.

34. Snyder, *Slavery in Indian Country*, 62.

35. Snyder, *Slavery in Indian Country*, 66; Swanton, *Indian Tribes of the Lower Mississippi Valley*, 265–279.

36. Ethridge, *Chicaza to Chickasaw*, 239.

37. Bienville to Pontchartrain, October 12, 1708, *Mississippi Provincial Archives: 1729–1740, French Dominion*, vol. 1 ed. Dunbar Rowland and Albert Godfrey Sanders, trans. Dunbar Rowland (Jackson, MS: Press of the Mississippi Department of Archives and History, 1927).

1:39; Nairne, *Nairne's Muskhogean Journals*, 75–76.

38. Even as they met with British and other traders, the Tensas maintained relations with the French at Mobile. In 1711 the Tensas met with the French governor to reaffirm their alliance. Hamilton, *Colonial Mobile*, 249.

39. Hamilton, *Colonial Mobile*, 64, 99; Farmer, *Sacramental Records*, 18.

40. Margry, *Découvertes*, 6:316; Farmer, *Sacramental Records*, 18.

41. In addition to recording most of the Indian captives without their tribal affiliations, or without their first names, some of the records of early Mobile families simply give no indication of who the mothers of French men's children might be. De Ville, *Gulf Coast Colonials*, 20–25, 48, 51, 57; M. Scott Heerman, *The Alchemy of Slavery: Human Bondage and Emancipation in the Illinois Country, 1730–1865* (Philadelphia: University of Pennsylvania Press, 2018), 26.

42. Farmer, *Sacramental Records*, 23, 39; Hortence Spillers, "Mama's Baby, Papa's Maybe: An American Grammar Book," *Diacritics* 17, no. 2 (1987): 74, 76.

43. Farmer, *Sacramental Records*, 41, 61, 126.

44. Farmer, *Sacramental Records*, 41, 126.

45. De Ville, *Gulf Coast Colonials*, 17, 18, 21, 22, 26, 36–37, 44, 45, 52; Farmer, *Sacramental Records*, 21–23, 36, 39, 60–70, 80, 85, 87, 97, 118, 126, 137, 178, 200, 217, 235, 247, 288, 308, 343; Shannon Speed, *Incarcerated Stories: Indigenous Women Migrants and Violence in the Settler Capitalist State* (Chapel Hill, N.C.: University of North Carolina Press, 2019), 10–11.

46. LeBoeuf owned multiple Indian slaves, and during the 1710s, while he lived with Marguerite, he also owned at least one enslaved Chitimacha. Higginbotham, *Old Mobile*, 456; Hamilton, *Colonial Mobile*, 99; Farmer, *Sacramental Records*, 22, 40, 42, 43, 44; Jennifer L. Morgan, "Periodization Problems: Race and Gender in the History of the Early Republic," *Journal of the Early Republic* 36, no. 2 (2016): 356–357; Negrin, "Possessing Native Women and Children," 99; L. H. Roper, "The 1701 'Act for the Better Ordering of Slaves': Reconsidering the History of Slavery in Proprietary South Carolina," *William and Mary Quarterly* 64, no. 2 (2007): 398–401; Guillaume Aubert, "'The Blood of France': Race and Purity of Blood in the French Atlantic World," *William and Mary Quarterly* 61, no. 3 (2004): 458–459; Spear, *Race, Sex, and Social Order*, 40–42; Shannon Lee Dawdy, *Building the Devil's Empire: French Colonial New Orleans* (Chicago: University of Chicago Press, 2008), 154–156; DuVal, "Indian Intermarriage and Métissage in Colonial Louisiana," 271–273.

47. Gravier, *Relation ou Journal du voyage*, 29; Morgan, *Laboring Women*, 18–21; Marc-Antoine Caillot, *A Company Man: The Remarkable French-Atlantic Voyage of a Clerk for the Company of the Indies; A Memoir*, ed. Erin M. Greenwald (New Orleans, LA: Historic New Orleans Collection, 2013), 97–98.

48. Père le Maire, Mémoire sur la situation présente de la Louisiane, January 15, 1714, ANOM, C13 C2, fols. 109, 128; Shelbi Nahwilet Meissner and Kyle Whyte, "Theorizing Indigeneity, Gender, and Settler Colonialism," in *The Routledge Companion to the Philosophy of Race*, ed. Paul Taylor, Linda Martín Alcoff, and Luvell Anderson, 209–227 (New York: Routledge, 2017), 209–227; Simpson, *As We Have Always Done*, 105–111; Bossu, *New Travels in North America*, 94–95.

49. Relation de la Louisiane, 1735, 78–79, Ayer Collection, Newberry Library.

50. Dumont de Montigny, *Memoir of Lieutenant Dumont*, 349–350; Kristen Gremillion, "Archaeobotany at Old Mobile," *Historical Archaeology* 36, no. 1(2002): 126–127; White, *Voices of the Enslaved*, 70.

51. Andrea Krüsi, Thomas Kerr, Christina Taylor, Tim Rhodes, and Kate Shannon, "'They won't change it back in their heads that we're trash': The Intersection of Sex Work–Related Stigma and Evolving Policing Strategies," *Sociology of Health and Illness* 38, no. 7 (2016): 1138–1143; Yasmin Jiwani and Mary Lynn Young, "Missing and Murdered Women: Reproducing Marginality in News Discourse," *Canadian Journal of Communication* 31, no. 4 (2006): 899–900; Robyn Maynard, "Fighting Wrongs with Wrongs? How Canadian Anti-Trafficking Crusades Have Failed

Sex Workers, Migrants, and Indigenous Communities," *Atlantis: Critical Studies in Gender, Culture, and Social Justice* 37, no. 2 (2015): 41–47.

52. Hamilton, *Colonial Mobile*, 100, 115, 116; Farmer, *Sacramental Records*, 51, 55.

53. After the 1710s, records of the Capinans appear only infrequently in the documentary record. This man's decision to identify himself as "Capinan" suggests that he may have been a Capinan man who ultimately integrated himself into Chatot society, or that a group of Capinans might still have been living at Mobile alongside the Chatots during this era. The Chatots who migrated to Mobile were predominantly Catholic, so if this man was in fact Chatot instead of Capinan, it seems more likely that he and his enslaved partner requested a baptism for their daughter versus the baptisms of the children of enslaved non-Catholic parents at Mobile. The relationships that crossed the boundaries of freedom and slavery and involved Christian Native Americans also deeply troubled the French priests at Mobile, who refused to recognize these unions. Alexander Huvé, the priest who baptized Marie, later added a comment on the record of this baptism to happily note that Capinan had left this enslaved woman and found another woman to replace her. Hamilton, *Colonial Mobile*, 112–114; Margry, *Découvertes*, 1:196–197, 602; Pénicaut, *Fleur de Lys and Calumet*, 98; Johnson, *Wicked Flesh*, 176–180.

54. "Minutes of the Superior Council of Louisiana," July 23, 1723, *MPA:FD*, 3:356–357; Vaudreuil to King Louis XV, February 10, 1744, *Mississippi Provincial Archives: 1729–1748, French Dominion*, vol. 4 ed. Patricia K. Galloway, Dunbar Rowland and Albert Godfrey Sanders, trans. Dunbar Rowland (Baton Rouge: Louisiana State University Press, 1984), 4:213; Margry, *Découvertes*, 4:408; La Harpe, *Historical Journal*, 24.

55. Hamilton, *Colonial Mobile*, 110, 114; Farmer, *Sacramental Records*, 38, 59, 62; Ekberg, *Stealing Indian Women*, 42–43, 71–72.

56. Robert A. Brightman, "Chitimacha," in Fogelson, *Handbook of North American Indians*, 14:642.

57. Tracy Neal Leavelle, *The Catholic Calumet: Colonial Conversions in French and Indian North America* (Philadelphia: University of Pennsylvania Press, 2012), 7; Robert A. Williams Jr., *Linking Arms Together: American Indian Treaty Visions of Law and Peace, 1600–1800* (New York: Routledge, 1999), 46–47.

58. Guillaume de L'Isle, *Carte de la Louisiane et du cours de Mississipi*, 1730, Everett D. Graff Collection of Western Americana, Newberry Library, Chicago; Guillaume de L'Isle, *Carte de la Louisiane et du cours de Mississipi*, 1718, Roger S. Baskes Collection, Newberry Library.

59. As late as the 1730s, the French were still hesitant to establish relationships with the Ishak/Atakapas because they believed the rumors that this nation would capture and eat trespassers into their territory. In his terse commentary on the Opeloussa and Ishak/Atakapa nations to the west of the Mississippi River, Bienville was sure to include, along with a population tally and that they were successful fishermen, that the Atkapas "eat their prisoners." "Bienville's Memoir of Louisiana 1725–1726," *MPA:FD*, 3:529; Le Contrôleur general à Pèrier, November 1, 1730, ANOM, C13 A12, reel 20, fols. 338, 345; Lyle Campbell, *American Indian Languages: The Historical Linguistics of North America* (New York: Oxford University Press, 1997), 145–146; Swanton, *Indian Tribes of the Lower Mississippi Valley*, 360.

60. These are John Swanton's figures, and he seems to have included the Yakni-Chitos in his estimate of the Chitimacha population. Swanton, *Indian Tribes of the Lower Mississippi Valley*, 45.

61. Swanton, *Indian Tribes of the Lower Mississippi Valley*, 338.

62. La Harpe, *Historical Journal*, 60; Higginbotham, *Old Mobile*, 93.

63. In multiple narratives, this boy is listed as a *slave*, yet this term does not appropriately convey the relationship of the Natchez boy to the French travelers. Given that St. Cosme was traveling from the Natchez village where he had been working to spread Christianity, it is likely that the boy was given to the French missionary to act as an emissary and laborer. Much like the cabin boys that French officials left among their Native allies to learn their languages and facilitate relationships, the Natchez had probably loaned this boy to the missionary as a gesture of friendship and alliance. These children might be expected to labor, but they also maintained their connections to their communities. Both the Mobilians and Tohomes, for example, gave children to the French settlers at Mobile as a way to foster connections between the two nations. Bienville had two Mobilian "slaves" who taught him to speak Mobilian so that he could communicate with the nations of the region. Although the French expected these children to serve them and occasionally listed them as "slaves," their experiences were markedly different from those of captives taken in war. La Harpe, *Historical Journal*, 77; Snyder, *Slavery in Indian Country*, 5–8; Giraud, *History of French Louisiana*, 1:84–85; Higginbotham, *Old Mobile*, 205.

64. Although the Chitimacha murder of St. Cosme has most commonly been told as an act of random and senseless Native violence, it is evident that the Chitimachas had good reason to feel threatened by the French presence in their lands, and they wanted to send a clear message to potential slave raiders. Many contemporary and historical accounts of this story suggest that St. Cosme's end was purely bad luck. In these versions, a war party of Chitimachas was out in search of their enemies the Bayagoulas. When the enraged Chitimachas were unable to find an opportunity to attack the Bayagoulas, they instead turned their wrath on the guileless St. Cosme and his party, who happened to cross their path. Dana Bowker Lee has offered one of the best accounts of this war and one of the few that connects St. Denis's slave raids to the outbreak of war in 1706. Dana Bowker Lee, "Captives to Kin: Indian Slavery and the Changing Social Identities on the Louisiana Colonial Frontier," in Carocci and Pratt, *Native American Adoption, Captivity, and Slavery in Changing Contexts*, 79–96, 80–85; Hamilton, *Colonial Mobile*, 50–51; La Harpe, *Historical Journal*, 54; Swanton, *Indian Tribes of the Lower Mississippi Valley*, 337; Barnett, *Mississippi's American Indians*, 103; Père le Maire, Mémoire sur la situation présente de la Louisiane, January 15, 1714, ANOM, C13 C2, fols. 109, 127.

65. The killing of St. Cosme was not the first killing of a French priest by a nation with which the French claimed alliance. In 1702 several Koroas had slain a French missionary and his three compatriots along the Yazoo River. The French were enraged by this murder, but four years later they still had been unable to exact revenge or punish the Koroas for this incident. Although various French traders had been killed in the backwoods, including one by the Alabamas just two years prior to the St. Cosme murder, and allegedly twelve by the Chitimachas between 1700 and 1707, the deaths of the two priests troubled French officials in a way that the deaths of the coureurs de bois had not. As Louisiana missionaries operated in effect as state-sanctioned emissaries, there could be no suggestion that the murder of a priest was an isolated or meaningless incident; rather, both the French and the Chitimachas understood these killings as conveying much larger political messages. Bienville to Pontchartrain, June 6, 1704, *MPA:FD*, 3:22; Bienville to Pontchartrain, February 20, 1707, *MPA:FD*, 3:38–40; Barnett, *Natchez Indians*, 50–51; Giraud, *History of French Louisiana*, 1:207; Delanglez, *French Jesuits*, 34; Père le Maire, Mémoire sur la situation présente de la Louisiane, January 15, 1714, ANOM, C13 C2, fols. 109, 127.

66. Swanton, *Indian Tribes of the Lower Mississippi Valley*, 337.

67. Pénicaut, *Fleur de Lys and Calumet*, 100–102.

68. Usner, *Indians, Settlers, and Slaves*, 24; La Harpe, *Historical Journal*, 5; Sophie Burton and F. Todd Smith, "Slavery in the Colonial Louisiana Backcountry: Natchitoches, 1714–1803," *Louisiana History* 52, no. 2 (2011): 140.

69. Hamilton, *Colonial Mobile*, 64.

70. Bienville to Cadillac, June 23, 1716, *MPA:FD*, 3:214; Pénicaut, *Fleur de Lys and Calumet*, 216–217; Swanton, *Indian Tribes of the Lower Mississippi Valley*, 339; Usner, *Indians, Settlers, and Slaves*, 62.

71. The French were aware of the developments of the Yamasee War as the conflict sent Indigenous refugees fleeing across the Southeast, at least some of whom ended up seeking refuge with the nations around Mobile. Gregory Waselkov has argued that the Tohome man who murdered the British trader Price Hughes was acting in concert with the other Southeastern Indian nations that killed British traders in their territories and therefore should be understood as part of the Yamasee War. Hamilton, *Colonial Mobile*, 111; William L. Ramsey, "Something Cloudy in Their Looks: The Origins of the Yamasee War Reconsidered," *Journal of American History* 90, no. 1 (2003): 44–57; Bienville to Pontchartrain, September 1, 1715, *MPA:FD*, 3:187–189; La Harpe, *Historical Journal*, 65; Gregory A. Waselkov and Bonnie L. Gums, *Plantation Archaeology at Rivière aux Chiens ca. 1725–1848* (Mobile: University of South Alabama Center for Archaeological Studies, 2000), 19; Steven Hahn, "The Long Yamasee War: Reflections on Yamasee Conflict in the Eighteenth Century," in *The Yamasee Indians: From Florida to South Carolina*, ed. Denise Bossy 191–218 (Lincoln: University of Nebraska Press, 2018), 192–197.

72. Swanton, *Indian Tribes of the Lower Mississippi Valley*, 342.

73. Farmer, *Sacramental Records*, 14, 21, 40, 44, 46, 50–52, 56, 62, 68, 74–76, 80, 96; Extrait des Registres de Baptêmes, a la paroisse ND des Cas, depuis le mois de mai, 1723 jusqu'à le mois de mai 1724, le 2 mai 1724, Dépôt des Papiers Publics des Colonies, Section 1DPPC2866: Louisiane 1720–1734, ANOM, 2.

74. *Le Nouveau Mercure* (Paris, 1717), 183–184.

75. Du Pratz, *History of Louisiana*, 21–22, 77, 316; Gordon M. Sayre, *Indian Chief as Tragic Hero: Native Resistance and the Literatures of America, from Moctezuma to Tecumseh* (Chapel Hill, NC.: University of North Carolina Press, 2005), 207.

76. Du Pratz, *Histoire de la Louisiane*, 84–86; Sydney Brownstone, "How Naked Burt Reynolds Ended Up in a Native Art Gallery in Seattle," *KUOW*, September 7, 2018, https://www.kuow.org/stories/how-naked-burt-reynolds-ended-up-in-a-native-art-gallery-in-pioneer-square.

77. Du Pratz, *Histoire de la Louisiane*, 1:120–122.

78. Ethridge, *Chicaza to Chickasaw*, 141; Reitz, Gibbons, Little, "Animal Remains from La Pointe-Krebs Plantation," in Gums and Waselkov, *Archaeology at La Pointe-Krebs Plantation*, 107–120; Relation de la Louisianne, 1735, 219, Ayer Collection, Newberry Library; Diron d'Artaguiette, Journal, September 1, 1722–September 10, 1723, FR ANOM, C13 C2, fols. 188, 219.

79. Jon Sensbach, "Black Pearls: Writing Black Atlantic Women's Biography," in *Biography and the Black Atlantic*, ed. Lisa Lindsay and John Wood Sweet, 93–107 (Philadelphia: University of Pennsylvania Press, 2014), 93–100; Marisa Fuentes, *Dispossessed Lives: Enslaved Women, Violence, and the Archive* (Philadelphia: University of Pennsylvania Press, 2016), 1–12, 48–49, 137–143.

80. Du Pratz, *Histoire de la Louisiane*, 112–116.

81. Snyder, *Slavery in Indian Country*, 5–8; Kathleen DuVal, *Independence Lost: Lives on the Edge of the American Revolution* (New York: Random House, 2015), xxi–xxii.

82. Du Pratz, *Histoire de la Louisiane*, 116.

83. Patricia Galloway has written extensively about how the French and Native people frequently used this language of "French fathers" to talk about French settlers' relationships to Native people, but as she has made clear, they meant very different things by employing this term. Galloway, "The Chief Who Is Your Father: Choctaw and French Views of Diplomatic Relations," in Waselkov, Wood, and Hatley, *Powhatan's Mantle*, 345–370, 345–365.

84. In the sources and secondary literature, this Chitimacha woman has been referred to as Du Pratz's slave, concubine, and spouse. As Gordon Sayre points out, it is difficult to tell what the nature of this relationship was and whether this Chitimacha woman bore Du Pratz's children. Gordon M. Sayre, "Natchez Ethnohistory Revisited: New Manuscript Sources from Le Page Du Pratz and Dumont de Montigny," *Louisiana History* 50, no. 4 (2009): 416–417.

85. Du Pratz, *Histoire de la Louisiane*, 90–91.

86. For the most in-depth analysis of this Chitimacha woman's life and her relationship with Du Pratz, see Patricia Galloway's chapter, "Natchez Matrilineal Kinship: Du Pratz and the Woman's Touch," in Patricia Galloway, *Practicing Ethnohistory: Mining Archives, Hearing Testimony, Constructing Narrative* (Lincoln: University of Nebraska Press, 2006), 99–107.

87. Du Pratz, *Histoire de la Louisiane*, 118–120.

88. Higginbotham, *Old Mobile*, 444–445.

89. Archaeological records from Dauphin Island indicate that the early French settlers were engaged in illicit exchanges with traders from Veracruz, Mexico, and other Caribbean travelers. The archaeologist George Shorter posits that English pirates may have been able to lead a successful raid and bypass the French colony's defenses in 1710 in part because the inhabitants of Dauphin were engaged in illegal commerce and receiving unauthorized ships at Dauphin. George W. Shorter Jr., "Status and Trade at Port Dauphin," *Historical Archaeology* 36, no. 1 (2002): 135–141.

90. Recensement par Diron du Fort Saint-Jean-Baptiste des Natchitoches, May 1, 1722, BAC, Archives/Collections and Fonds, MG1-G1, reel C-10206, F-804, item no. 2319133, 1–3; Katherine Bridges and Winston De Ville, "Natchitoches and the Trail to the Rio Grande: Two Early Eighteenth-Century Accounts by the Sieur Derbanne," *Louisiana History* 8, no. 3 (1967): 239–259; Burton and Smith, "Slavery in the Colonial Louisiana Backcountry," 133–188.

91. La Harpe, *Historical Journal*, 10–11.

92. D'Artaguiette, "Journal of Diron d'Artaguiette," in Mereness, *Travels in the American Colonies*, 15–94, 42.

93. Herman Moll, "North America, According to ye Newest and most Exact Observations," in *Atlas Geographicus*, 1712, Ayer Collection, Newberry Library; Guillaume de L'Isle, *Carte de la Louisiane et du cours de Mississipi*, 1718, Roger S. Baskes Collection, Newberry Library, Chicago; Guillaume de L'Isle, *Carte des environs du Missisipi*, 1701, Louis C. Karpinski Map Collection, Newberry Library; Sieur de Beauvilliers, *Carte Nouvelle de la partie de l'oest de la Province de la Louisiane sur les observations & découvertes du Sieur Bernard de La Harpe*, 1720, Louis C. Karpinski Map Collection, Newberry Library.

94. Ethridge, *Chicaza to Chickasaw*, 175.

95. Higginbotham, *Old Mobile*, 445; Lee, "Captives to Kin," 83–85.

96. It was not uncommon for enslaved Native people at Mobile to appear in parish records with their tribal identity listed as their last name. For example, in 1746 Marguerite Panyoussa was buried in Mobile and in 1713 Marguerite Tanca gave birth to a son Claude. Panyoussa and Tanca are almost certainly French spellings for Panioucha and Tensa. De Ville, *Gulf Coast Colonials*, 21, 45.

97. Swanton, *Indian Tribes of the Lower Mississippi Valley*, 337; Campbell, *American Indian Languages*, 145–146.

98. It seems clear that the Yakni-Chitos were able to maintain separate political identities even if the French largely failed to recognize this after the Chitimacha War. In two separate Spanish records from 1777, the "Chitimachas de la Grande Tierra" and the "Chetimachas de la grande terre," show up as political entities who received gifts from the Spanish government. Like so many of the alleged destructions or disappearances of the Petites Nations, the disappearance of the Yakni-Chitos is better understood as a story of political transformation than community destruction. Baron de Crenay, *Carte de partie de la Louisiane*, 1733, Louis C. Karpinski Map Collection, Newberry Library, Chicago; Nicolas de Fer, *Partie meridionale de la rivière Misisipi, et sus environs, dans l'Amérique Septentrionale*, 1718, Ayer Collection, Newberry Library; Henri Abraham Chatelain, *Atlas historique, ou nouvelle introduction à l'histoire, à la chronologie, et à la géographie ancienne et moderne* (Amsterdam: Chez L'Honore et Chatelain Libraires, 1719), 93; Bernardo de Gálvez to José de Gálvez, September 15, 1777, microfilm no. 246, reel 1, 197, Mississippi Provincial Archives: Spanish Dominion, John C. Pace Library, University of West Florida, Pensacola; Libro de Los Regalos que se debe hacer annualmente a los naciones de Indios por Reglamento del exelentisimo Senor Don Alejandro O'Reilly, January 9, 1777, microfilm no. 246, reel 1, 48–50, Mississippi Provincial Archives: Spanish Dominion, John C. Pace Library, University of West Florida, Pensacola.

99. Burton and Smith, "Slavery in the Colonial Louisiana Backcountry," 136, 140.

CHAPTER 4

1. Jean-Paul Masclary, Réflexions sur l'établissement général de la Louisiane avec un projet d'établissement particulier à peu de frais dans cette colonie présentées à Messieurs les Inspecteurs syndics et Directeurs généraux de la Compagnie des Indes, September 1725, ANOM, Bibliothèque et Archives Canada (hereafter cited as BAC), MG1-DFC, 5–10, 34–35; Jean Paul Masclary, Counseiller au Conseil supérieur de la Louisiane, 1722, Secrétariat d'État à la Marine, personnel colonial ancien, ANOM, COL E 305, 200–203; Henri Abraham Chatelain, *Atlas historique, ou Nouvelle introduction a l'histoire, à la chronologie, et à la géographie ancienne et moderne* (Amsterdam, 1719), 93; Ellis, "Dismantling the Dream of 'France's Peru,'" 361.

2. Laudun, *Journal d'un voyage à la Louisiane*, 235, 238, 246.

3. Recensement par Diron du Fort Saint-Jean-Baptiste des Natchitoches, May 1, 1722, ANOM, BAC, MG1-G1, reel C-10206, F-804, item no. 2319133, 1–5; Dawdy, *Building the Devil's Empire*, 25–32.

4. Gallay, *Indian Slave Trade*, 288–292; John Stewart to her majesty Queen Anne of Great Britain, Humbly laying down some Observations on American Indians, 1711, ANOM, C13 C2, fols. 80, 73–75; Père le Maire, Mémoire sur la situation presente de la Louisianne, January 15, 1714, ANOM, C13 C2, fols. 109, 126; Ethridge, *Chicaza to Chickasaw*, 204–216.

5. Matthew J. Jennings, "Violence in a Shattered World," in Ethridge and Shuck-Hall, *Mapping the Mississippian Shatter Zone*, 272–294, 285–286; Worth, "Razing Florida," 299–306; Ellis, "Dismantling the Dream of 'France's Peru,'" 355, 358–359.

6. David H. Thomas, *Fort Toulouse: The French Outpost at the Alabamas on the Coosa* (Tuscaloosa: University of Alabama Press, 1989), 1–14.

7. Braund, *Deerskins and Duffels*, 34–37; Ramsey, *Yamasee War*, 134–142; Gallay, *Indian Slave Trade*, 73–74; Thomas, *Fort Toulouse*, 1–14.

8. Wood, "Changing Population of the Colonial South," 94–97.

9. Wood, "Changing Population of the Colonial South," 94–97; Cécile Vidal, *Caribbean New Orleans: Empire, Race, and the Making of a Slave Society* (Chapel Hill: University of North Carolina Press, 2019), 121.

10. In the late seventeenth and early eighteenth centuries, there were likely more than these six towns. Some accounts list as many as nine Natchez towns. However, by the 1720s it is clear there were primarily six political units at Natchez. Four of these were Natchez towns, and two were immigrant Tioux and Grigra towns. Nairne, *Nairne's Muskhogean Journals*, 75–76; Pénicaut, *Fleur de Lys and Calumet*, 159, 160–163; Ethridge, *Chicaza to Chickasaw*, 216–217, 235; James F. Barnett, "The Yamasee War, the Bearded Chief and the Founding of Fort Rosalie," *Journal of Mississippi History* 74, no. 1 (2012): 2–9, 15–22; Neitzel, *Archaeology of the Fatherland Site*, 56; Karl G. Lorenz, "A Re-Examination of Natchez Sociopolitical Complexity: A View from the Grand Village and Beyond," *Southeastern Archaeology* 16, no. 2 (1997): 97–112; Iberville, "Journal of the Badine," 73; Galloway, "Colonial Transformations in the Mississippi Valley," 244; Barnett, *Natchez Indians*, xv–xvi, 17–18, 41–44; Marvin T. Smith, "Aboriginal Population Movements in the Postcontact Southeast," in Ethridge, *The Transformation of the Southeastern Indians*, 3–20, 17–18; Milne, "Picking Up the Pieces," 397–400; Swanton, *Indian Tribes of the Lower Mississippi Valley*, 186–193; Usner, *American Indians in the Lower Mississippi Valley*, 20; Ian W. Brown, "An Archaeological Study of Culture Contact and Change in the Natchez Bluffs Region," in *La Salle and His Legacy*, ed. Patricia K. Galloway, 176–193 (Jackson: University Press of Mississippi, 1982), 178–179.

11. Milne, *Natchez Country*, 57–66.

12. Barnett, "Yamasee War," 11, 21; Milne, *Natchez Country*, 57–66; Ellis, "Natchez War Revisited," 458–460.

13. Vidal, *Caribbean New Orleans*, 50–53; Allain, "In Search of a Policy, 1701–1731," 91–98.

14. "A la Nouvelle Orleans, Province de la Louisiane sur le Mississipi, le 5 novembre 1718," *Le Nouveau Mercure*, March 1719, 184; Carl A. Brasseaux, "The Image of Louisiana and the Failure of Voluntary French Emigration, 1683–1731," in Conrad, *French Experience in Louisiana*, 153–162, 153–160.

15. Gwendolyn Midlo Hall, *Africans in Colonial Louisiana: The Development of Afro-Creole Culture in the Eighteenth Century* (Baton Rouge: Louisiana State University Press, 1992), 5, 7; James D. Hardy, "The Transportation of Convicts to Colonial Louisiana," *Louisiana History* 7, no. 3 (1996): 208–212; Emily Clark, *Masterless Mistresses: The New Orleans Ursulines and the Development of a New World Society, 1724–1834* (Chapel Hill: University of North Carolina Press, 2007), 36, 38, 83; Vidal, *Caribbean New Orleans*, 53–57; Yevan Terrien, "Exiles and Fugitives: Labor, Mobility, and Power in French Colonial Louisiana" (PhD diss., University of Pittsburgh, 2020), 29–58; Ellis, "Dismantling the Dream of 'France's Peru,'" 361.

16. Hall, *Africans in Colonial Louisiana*, 43; Spear, *Race, Sex, and Social Order*, 54–69; Daniel Usner, "From African Captivity to American Slavery: The Introduction of Black Laborers to Colonial Louisiana," *Louisiana History* 20, no. 1 (1979): 30–32; Dawdy, *Building the Devil's Empire*, 194–200; Vidal, *Caribbean New Orleans*, 79–81; Johnson, *Wicked Flesh*, 86–87, 107, 123, 174; Terrien, "Exiles and Fugitives," 108–131; Ellis, "Dismantling the Dream of 'France's Peru,'" 362.

17. Usner, *American Indians in the Lower Mississippi Valley*, 35; Milne, *Natchez Country*, 83.

18. Usner, *Indians, Settlers, and Slaves*, 35–36; Thomas N. Ingersoll, *Mammon and Manon in Early New Orleans: The First Slave Society in the Deep South, 1718–1819* (Knoxville: University of Tennessee Press, 1999), 9; Relation de la Louisianne, 1735, 12, Ayer Collection, Newberry Library; Maduell, *Census Tables*, 50; Shannon Lee Dawdy, "La Nouvelle-Orléans au XVIIIe siècle:

Courants d'échange dans le monde caraïbe," *Annales: Histoire, Sciences Sociales* 62, no. 3 (2007): 666; Terrien, "Exiles and Fugitives," 138–141.

19. Registre de ceux qui sont morts au vieux fort de Biloxi pendant l'administration de M. Damon depuis le 8 août 1720, May 9, 1727, BAC, Archives/Collections and Fonds, MG1-G1, reel F-597, item no. 2318744; Brasseaux, "Image of Louisiana," 159; Maduell, *Census Tables*, 16, 50; Hall, *Africans in Colonial Louisiana*, 43; Usner *Indians, Settlers, and Slaves*, 36; no. 145. Concessions Deucher, Coetlogon, Sainte-Catherine, Lettre de Faucon Dumanoir aux directeurs de la concession Sainte-Catherine, July 18, 1721, ANOM, COL G1, 465, 3, 6–7.

20. Périer and de la Chaise to the Directors of the Company of the Indies, July 31, 1728, *MPA:FD*, 2:576.

21. Périer and de la Chaise to the Directors of the Company of the Indies, July 31, 1728, *MPA:FD*, 2:584; Périer and de la Chaise to the Directors of the Company of the Indies, November 3, 1728, *MPA:FD*, 2:601.

22. The combination of shortages and restrictive trade policies of the Company of the Indies fostered the development of large-scale informal economies in Louisiana. Throughout France's tenure, Louisiana settlers dealt in stolen goods and with forbidden Spanish and British merchants. Diana DiPaolo Lauren, "Threads: Collecting Cloth in the North American French Colonies," *Archaeologies* 4, no. 1 (2008): 57; Bénard de La Harpe, "Exploration of the Arkansas River by Bénard de La Harpe, 1721–1722: Extracts from His Journal and Instructions," trans. and ed. Ralph A. Smith, *Arkansas Historical Quarterly* 10, no. 4 (1951): 343; Périer and de la Chaise to the Directors of the Company of the Indies, November 2, 1727, *MPA:FD*, 2:554–555, 580, 612–613; Hubert to the Council, October 26, 1717, *MPA:FD*, 2:238–249; Committee of Louisiana to the Directors of the Company, November 8, 1724, *MPA:FD*, 2:404; Sophie White, "Slaves and Poor Whites' Informal Economies in an Atlantic Context," in *Louisiana: Crossroads of the Atlantic World*, ed. Cécil Vidal, 89–102 (Philadelphia: University of Pennsylvania Press, 2013), 89–102; Dawdy, "La Nouvelle-Orléans au XVIIIe siècle," 677–681.

23. DuVal, *Native Ground*, 98–100; Usner, *Indians, Settlers, and Slaves*, 26–27; Bienville to Pontchartrain, October 27, 1711, *MPA:FD*, 3:160; Vaudreuil to Maurepas, February 12, 1744, *MPA:FD*, 4:216; LeMaster, *Brothers Born of One Mother*, 40–43; Patricia Galloway, "Choctaws at the Border of the Shatter Zone," in Ethridge and Shuck-Hall, *Mapping the Mississippian Shatter Zone*, 333–364, 345–359; Périer and de la Chaise to the Directors of the Company of the Indies, July 31, 1728, *MPA:FD*, 2:580.

24. Hubert to the Council, October 26, 1717, *MPA:FD*, 2:249.

25. Minutes of the Superior Council of Louisiana, December 22, 1724, *MPA:FD*, 3:463; Vaudreuil to Rouille, May 10, 1751, *Mississippi Provincial Archives: 1749–1763, French Dominion*, vol. 5 ed. Patricia K. Galloway, Dunbar Rowland and Albert Godfrey Sanders, trans. Dunbar Rowland (Baton Rouge: Louisiana State University Press, 1984), 5:93; Bienville to Pontchartrain, September 1, 1715, *MPA:FD*, 3:188–189; Hubert to the Council, October 26, 1717, *MPA:FD*, 2:240; de la Chaise to the Directors of the Company of the Indies, September 6, 1723, *MPA:FD*, 2:312–315; LeMaster, *Brothers Born of One Mother*, 68–72.

26. Bienville to Pontchartrain, October 27, 1711, *MPA:FD*, 3:159; Bienville to Chateaugué, Mémoire sur la Louisiane, 1726, ANOM, C13 A10, reel 17, fols. 138, 138–140.

27. Diron au Ministre, October 17, 1729, ANOM, C13 A12-1, reel 19, fols. 148, 149; Périer a Régis du Roullet, September 21, 1729, Instruction pour le voyage que velui-ci doit effectuer aux Chactas, ANOM, C13 A12-1, reel 19, fols. 65; Diron au Ministre, December 9, 1728, ANOM, C13 A11, reel 18, fols. 174, 172–176; Bienville sur les Sauvages, March 25, 1734, ANOM, C13 A18, reel 26, fols. 217; Bienville au Ministre, February 10, 1736, ANOM, C13 A21, reel 29, fols. 122, 122–132;

Journal des Operations Saites dans la Louisianne par M. de Regis, in Documents on French Colonial Louisiana, Acadia, the Antilles, and the Yucatan (manuscripts) ca. 1760, ed. Chrétien Guillaume de Lamoignon de Malsherbes, 1–7, #419, Rudy Lamont Ruggles Collection, Newberry Library; Maurepas to Vaudreuil, April 25, 1746, LO 64, Pierre de Rigaud, marquis de Vaudreuil Papers, 1740–1753, box 2, 1746–1747, 46 MSS, Loudoun Papers: Americana, Huntington Library, San Marino, CA; Marcel Giraud, *A History of French Louisiana*, vol. 5, *The Company of the Indies, 1723–1731*, trans. Brian Pearce (Baton Rouge: Louisiana State University Press, 1991), 5:363.

28. Some Petites Nations also took the threat seriously. In 1729 the Apalachees, Chatots, and Tawasas relocated their villages to the west of Mobile Bay in order to distance themselves from the Choctaws. The Pascagoulas and Biloxis likewise returned to their lands on the far side of Lake Pontchartrain. These actions lent credibility to this threat. Diron au Ministre, October 17, 1729, ANOM, C13 A12-1, reel 19, fols. 148, 148–154.

29. Dean Itsuji Saranillio, *Unsustainable Empire: Alternative Histories of Hawai'i Statehood* (Durham, NC: Duke University Press, 2018), 10–11.

30. Réflexions [de Masclary] sur l'établissement général de la Louisiane, 35; Patrick Wolfe, "Settler Colonialism and the Elimination of the Native," *Journal of Genocide Research* 8, no. 4 (2006): 387–409; Eve Tuck and K. Wayne Yang, *Decolonization: Indigeneity, Education and Society* 1, no. 1 (2012): 4–9; Lorenzo Veracini, *Settler Colonialism: A Theoretical Overview* (London: Palgrave Macmillan, 2010), 2–12; Allan Greer, "Settler Colonialism and Empire in Early America," *William and Mary Quarterly* 76, no. 3 (2019): 387–390.

31. Pierre Charlevoix, Letter 30, January 10, 1722, *Letters to the Dutchess of Lesdiguieres: Giving an account of a voyage to Canada, and travels through that vast country, and Louisiana, to the Gulf of Mexico* (London, 1763), 330.

32. Charlevoix, Letter 32, April 5, 1722, *Letters to the Dutchess of Lesdiguieres*, 330, 343.

33. *Carte du cours du Mississipi depuis La Nouvelle Orléans jusqu'au grand gouffre, 1719* (?), CPL GE DD-2987 (8831), Département des Cartes et plans, Bibliothèque nationale de France; *Carte du cours du fleuve St Louis depuis son embouchure jusqu'au poste des Natchez, avec partie des Rivière rouge, R. Noire et des Taenças, 1732*, Ge SH 18 pf 138 bis div 3 p 10, Département des Cartes et plans, Bibliothèque nationale de France; Diron d'Artaguiette, *Fleuve St Louis cy devant Mississipy relevé à la boussole par le Sieur Diron l'an 1719 depuis la Nouvelle-Orléans en montant jusqu'au village sauvage Cahokia, 1719*, Service hydrographique, Bibliothèque nationale de France, C 4040-13, Louis C. Karpinski Map Collection, Newberry Library; Valentin Devin, *Carte de la côte de la Louisiane depuis la Baye St. Joseph, jusqu'à celle de St. Bernard où tous les ports et bons mouillages sont marquez par des ancres; avec la quantité de piés d'eau que l'on y trouve, 1726*, Ayer MS map 30, sheet 78, Ayer Collection, Newberry Library; *Carte des costes de la Louisiane depuis la baie de l'Ascension jusques à celle de Ste Rose, où les nouvelles habitations sont marquées, avec les isles, ports et brasses d'eau etc*, Ge SH 18 pf 138 bis div 1 p 13 D, Département des cartes et plans, Bibliothèque nationale de France; de Beauvilliers, *Coste de la Louisiane, 1721*, Service historique de la Défense, Département de l'Armée de Terre, Etat Major 7C 209, Louis C. Karpinski Map Collection, Newberry Library.

34. "Nouvelle Relation de la Louisianne," *Le Nouveau Mercure*, September 1717, 137.

35. Réflexions [de Masclary] sur l'établissement général de la Louisiane, 35; Bienville's memoir of Louisiana 1725–1726, *MPA:FD*, 3:519–527.

36. Bienville's memoir of Louisiana 1725–1726, *MPA:FD*, 3:527, 535, 536; Caillot, *Company Man*, 82–84; Usner, *American Indians in the Lower Mississippi Valley*, 38.

37. Quotes from first three sources, in order of citation. Kelton, *Epidemics and Enslavement*, 189, 200; Alan Taylor, *American Colonies*, 389; Bowne, "Southeastern Indian Polities of the Sev-

enteenth Century, 77; Lankford, *Cultural Resources*, 65–67; Giraud, *History of French Louisiana*, 1:30–42, 73, 76, 77.

38. Maduell, *Census Tables*, 62–64.

39. I am using the very conservative multiplier of 3.5 people per warrior to calculate populations. If I were instead to use the common 5x multiplier, Bienville's estimate signifies that there were 200 Biloxis and Barthellon's suggests 800. Mémoire sur l'état de la Colonie de la Louisiane en 1746, ANOM, C13 A30, reel 38, fols. 242, 259–260; Lettre de l'abbé Barthellon au ministre qui fait la relation des villages sauvages qui habitent le fleuve St Louis depuis la Balise jusqu'aux Illinois, January 13, 1731, ANOM, 04DFC 42, 4–5; Bienville's memoir of Louisiana 1725–1726, *MPA:FD*, 3:535.

40. Bienville's memoir of Louisiana 1725–1726, *MPA:FD*, 3:535–537; Margry, *Découvertes*, 4:602; Higginbotham, *Mobile Indians*, 80; Kelton, *Epidemics and Enslavement*, 189–192; Usner, *American Indians in the Lower Mississippi Valley*, 35; Usner, *Indians, Settlers, and Slaves*, 40–44, 50–51; Loubuey au Ministre, November 28, 1738, ANOM, C13 A23, reel 31, fols. 169, 171; Lettre de l'abbé Barthellon au ministre qui fait la relation des villages sauvages qui habitent le fleuve St Louis depuis la Balise jusqu'aux Illinois, January 13, 1731, ANOM, 04DFC 42, 4–5; Ignace-François Broutin, *Carte de la Louisiane dressée d'apres les plans et mémoires des ingénieurs qui ont eté a la Louisiane, 1764*, VI-A-6, Archivo del Museo Naval, Madrid.

41. Bienville's memoir of Louisiana, 1725–1726, *MPA:FD*, 3:535; Père Le Maire, Mémoire sur la Loüisiane, 1718, ANOM, C13 C2, fols. 153, 163; Erbig, *Where Caciques and Mapmakers Met*, 131–132.

42. Du Pratz, *Histoire de la Louisiane*, 1:124–128; Milne, *Natchez Country*, 83–88.

43. In 1723 there were 22 horses and 58 livestock at Natchez. There were also five enslaved Indigenous people within the French settlements at Natchez. Milne, *Natchez Country*, 93–95; Recensement par Diron des habitants et des ouvriers des concessions Le Blanc et Sainte-Catherine aux Natchez, January 19,1723, ANOM, COL G1 464.

44. Longraye, Relation de la Guerre que les Natchés ont fait sur l'habitation a St. Catherine situé lieu des Natchez, November 4, 1722, ANOM, COL G1 465, no. 147, 17.

45. Barnett, *Natchez Indians*, 85–87; Lettre de Guenot, Mustel, Litant, Saint-Hilaire, officiers sur la concession Sainte-Catherine: Procès-verbal d'u ne attaque des Natchez contre la concession and Lettre de Berneval, commandant le fort, aux officiers de la concession Sainte-Catherine: Offre de secours armé contre les Natchez, ANOM, COL G1 465, no. 146, 146–147; Longraye, Relation de la Guerre, November 4, 1722, ANOM, COL G1 465, no. 147, 1–16; Journal de la guerre des Natchez, October 1722, ANOM, 04DFC 29, 1, 7; La Loire Flaucourt, Relation de la guerre des Natchez avec les Français, June 6, 1723, ANOM, 04DFC 31, 1–2, 7–10.

46. Relation de la guerre des Natchez, 1723, ANOM, 04DFC 30, 5–15; Numéro 148, Concessions Deucher, Coetlogon, Sainte-Catherine, Lettre de Des Longrais à Faucon Dumanoir, Compte-rendu des ravages exercés journellement par les Natchez à l'encontre de la concession Sainte-Catherine, May 11, 1723, ANOM, COL G1, no. 456; Relation de la guerre des Natchez, 1723, ANOM, 04DFC 30, 13–18.

47. It is difficult to determine the population of the Natchez polity, but estimates generally range between 3,000 and 4,000 people during the 1720s. In 1708 Thomas Nairne reported that the Natchez had 800 warriors, while Pénicaut suggested that in 1714 the Natchez had 1,200 men. Le Page du Pratz estimated that in the 1720s the combined populations of the Natchez, Grigras, and Tioux were about 1,200 men as well. An anonymous French manuscript that breaks down the Natchez settlements into eight separate villages, rather than the usual six, estimates that, including the Grigra, the Natchez settlements had 700 warriors, or about 2,450 people. Usner,

Indians, Settlers, and Slaves, 29; Du Pratz, *Histoire de la Louisiane,* 2:223; Nairne, *Nairne's Muskhogean Journals,* 75–76; La Harpe, *Historical Journal,* 17; Pénicaut, *Fleur de Lys and Calumet,* 177; Mémoire sur le Mississippi et la Rivière de la Mobile, ANOM, C13 C2, fols 166, 173–175; Ian Brown and Vincas Steponaitis, "The Grand Village of the Natchez Indians Was Indeed Grand: A Reconsideration of the Fatherland Site Landscape," in *Forging Southeastern Identities: Social Archaeology, Ethnohistory, and the Folklore of the Mississippian to Early South,* ed. Gregory A. Waselkov and Mavin T. Smith, 182–204 (Tuscaloosa: University of Alabama Press, 2017), 184–185; Ian W. Brown, "Natchez Indians and the Remains of a Proud Past," *Natchez Before 1830,* ed. Noel Polk, 8–28 (Jackson: University of Mississippi Press, 1989), 8, 15–16; Milne, *Natchez Country,* 15; Patricia D. Woods, "The French and Natchez Indians in Louisiana, 1700–1731," *Louisiana History* 19, no. 4 (1978): 414–415.

48. Relation de la guerre des Natchez, 1723, ANOM, 04DFC 30, 1–5, 8, 11.

49. Relation de la guerre des Natchez, 1723, ANOM, 04DFC 30, 7–15.

50. Minutes of the Council of War, November 23, 1723, *MPA:FD,* 3:385; de la Chaise to the Directors of the Company of the Indies, October 18, 1723, *MPA:FD,* 2:374; Relation de la guerre des Natchez, 1723, ANOM, 04DFC 30, 17.

51. Minutes of the Council of War, November 23, 1723, *MPA:FD,* 3:385–387.

52. Relation de la guerre des Natchez, 1723, ANOM, 04DFC 30, 17–18.

53. Letter from Father du Poisson, Missionary to the Arkansas, to Father [?], October 3, 1727, in *Jesuit Relations and Allied Documents: Travels and Explorations of the Jesuit Missionaries in New France, 1610–1791,* ed. Reuben Gold Thwaites (Cleveland, OH: Burrows Brothers, 1900), 67:279–303.

54. Father du Poisson to Father [?], October 3, 1727, in Thwaites, *Jesuit Relations,* 67:279–303.

55. It is unclear whether the Chitimachas or the Natchez were responsible for these attacks. The Tunicas informed Bienville that they believed it was the Chitimachas who were responsible. However, Bienville concluded it was likely that the Natchez had committed these murders. Memoir of the King to Serve as Instruction for Sieur de Bienville, the governor of the province of Louisiana, February 2, 1732, *MPA:FD,* 3:555; Bienville to Maurepas, August 10, 1733, *MPA:FD,* 3:625.

56. Regis du Roullet to Maurepas, 1729, *MPA:FD,* 1:21–54; Regis du Roullet to Périer, March 16, 1731, *MPA:FD,* 4:65.

57. Régis, Journal du vouyage que j'ai fait dans la nation des Chactas, l'année 1729, ANOM, C13 A12-1, reel 19, fols. 67, 69–71; Audra Simpson, *Mohawk Interrruptus: Political Life Across the Borders of Settler States* (Durham, NC: Duke University Press, 2014), 2–10.

CHAPTER 5

1. L'officier de Laye, Relation du massacre des Français aux Natchez et de la guerre contre ces sauvages, June 1, 1730, ANOM, 04DFC 38, 4.

2. Ellis, "Natchez War Revisited," 462.

3. As George Milne has shown, the escalating conflict between the French and the Natchez helped unify the competing Natchez towns into a powerful military and political force. Milne, *Natchez Country,* 159–177; Swanton, *Indian Tribes of the Lower Mississippi Valley,* 221–225; Usner, *Indians, Settlers, and Slaves,* 26–27; Barnett, *Natchez Indians,* 105; Diron au Ministre, March 20, 1730, ANOM, C13 A12, reel 20, fols. 371, 371–372; "Extrait d'une letter contenant la

relation de la défait des Natches par M. Périer, Commandant General à la Loüisianne, au mois de Janvier 1731," September 1731, *Mercure de France, dédié au Roy* (Paris, 1731), 2086; Ellis, "Natchez War Revisited," 446–447.

    4. It is difficult to determine the exact number of soldiers who were in Louisiana in December 1729. Marcel Giraud suggests that the number was no more than 325. During 1730 France sent an additional 242 soldiers to defend the colony. However, Giraud suggests that these reinforcements were functionally useless as they overwhelmingly arrived sick, malnourished, and unadjusted to the Louisiana climate. So Louisiana had roughly the military capacity of a single Petite Nation. In 1723, six years before this conflict, French officials estimated that the Houmas had roughly 300 warriors, the Acolapissas had 150, and the Tunicas had 200. The Tohomes and Mobilians could field an army of 140 warriors in 1730. D'Artaguiette, "Journal of Diron d'Artaguiette," in Mereness, *Travels in the American Colonies*, 42–44; Giraud, *History of French Louisiana*, 5:403–404, 409; Wood, "Changing Population of the Colonial South," 74; Higginbotham, *Old Mobile*, 180–194; Dumont de Montigny, *Mémoires historiques sur la Louisiane*, 2:131–146; Usner, *Indians, Settlers, and Slaves*, 66; Périer au Ministre, December 29, 1731, ANOM, C13 A13, reel 21, fols. 207, 207–208; Lusser to Maurepas, January 25, 1730, *MPA:FD*, 1:100–110; Périer to Ory, November 15, 1730, *MPA:FD*, 4:53–55; Regis du Roullet to Périer, March 16, 1731, *MPA:FD*, 4:65–66; Dumont de Montigny, *Mémoires historiques sur la Louisiane*, 2:188–190; Extrait de la lettre de M. Périer à Le Pelletier, March 18, 1730, ANOM, C13 A12, reel 20, fols. 295; Diron au Ministre, March 20, 1730, ANOM, C13 A12, reel 20, fols. 371, 373–375.

    5. Milne, *Natchez Country*, 112–119, 160–174.
    6. Duclos to Pontchartrain, June 7, 1716, *MPA:FD*, 3:211.
    7. Ellis, "Natchez War Revisited," 471.
    8. Du Pratz, *Histoire de la Louisiane*, 1:204.
    9. Milne, *Natchez Country*, 120–122; Karl G. Lorenz, "A Re-Examination of Natchez Sociopolitical Complexity: A View of the Grand Village and Beyond, *Southeastern Archaeology* 16, no. 2 (1997): 102–103; Andrew Albrecht, "Indian-French Relations at Natchez," *American Anthropologist* 48, no. 3 (1946): 341–349; Minutes of the Council of War, January 7, 1724, *MPA:FD*, 3:386; Dumont de Montigny, *Mémoires historiques sur la Louisiane*, 2:118–120.

    10. Regis du Roullet to Maurepas, abstracts of journal, 1729–1733, *MPA:FD*, 1:176.

    11. Simpson, *As We Have Always Done*, 105–106, 42–44, 75, 113; Milne, *Natchez Country*, 104–105, 164–165; Relation de la guerre des Natchez, 1723, ANOM, 04DFC 30, 7, 11–12, 13–15; Jennifer Nez Denetdale, "'No Explanation, No Resolution, and No Answers': Border Town Violence and Navajo Resistance to Settler Colonialism," *Wicazo Sa Review* 31, no. 1 (2016): 113–114, 127; Speed, *Incarcerated Stories*, 35.

    12. Ibrahima Seck, "The Relationships Between St. Louis of Senegal, Its Hinterlands, and Colonial Louisiana," in *French Colonial Louisiana and the Atlantic World*, ed. Bradley G. Bond, 265–290 (Baton Rouge: Louisiana State University Press, 2005), 269–270; Hall, *Africans in Colonial Louisiana*, 60; Maduell, *Census Tables*, 56–57; Ira Berlin, *Many Thousands Gone: The First Two Centuries of Slavery in North America* (Cambridge, MA: Harvard University Press, 2000), 82–83; Barnett, *Natchez Indians*, 56–57; Snyder, *Slavery in Indian Country*, 1–45.

    13. De Laye, Relation du massacre, June 1, 1730, ANOM, 04DFC 38, 30; Beauchamps, "1746 Journal of Visit to the Choctaws," in Mereness, *Travels in the American Colonies*, 266–267; Mémoire sur la Louisiane, 1726, ANOM, C13 A10, reel 17, fols. 143, 156; Relation de la guerre des Natchez, 1723, ANOM, 04DFC 30, 12–14, 17.

    14. Relation de la Louisianne, 1735, 65, Ayer Collection, Newberry Library.

15. Relation de la Louisianne, 1735, 65, Ayer Collection, Newberry Library; Milne, *Natchez Country*, 150–174; Du Pratz, *Histoire de la Louisiane*, 1:180; Barnett, *Natchez Indians*, 84–98.

16. Du Pratz, *Histoire de la Louisiane*, 3:231–232; Milne, *Natchez Country*, 164.

17. De Laye, Relation du massacre, June 1, 1730, ANOM, 04DFC 38, 21; Arnaud Balvay, *La Révolte des Natchez* (Paris : Editions du Felin, 2008), 133.

18. Du Pratz almost certainly did not hear this speech firsthand, as he would not have been invited to attend such private Natchez deliberations. Nonetheless, the speech that Du Pratz recorded draws together what he learned both before and after the November attack about Natchez perceptions of the French and their decision to resort to violence. Du Pratz, *Histoire de la Louisiane*, 3:238–239.

19. Milne, *Natchez Country*, 170–174.

20. Governor Étienne Périer claimed that not just the Natchez but also the Choctaws and "all of the Petites Nations had entered into the plot," and that there was a "general conspiracy against the French." Extrait de la lettre de M. Périer à Le Pelletier, March 18, 1730, ANOM, C13 A12, reel 20, fols. 288, 290; Extrait de la lettre de M. Périer à Le Pelletier, March 18, 1730, ANOM, C13 A12, reel 20, fols. 295, 283; Lettre du P. le Petit, 1730, sur les Sauvages du Mississippi, et en particular les Natchez, et relation de leur entreprise sur la colonie française, en 1729, July 12, 1730, ANOM, 04DFC 40, 49–54; Broutin to the Company, August 7, 1730, *MPA:FD*, 1:131; Dumont de Montigny, *Mémoires historiques sur la Louisiane*, 2:135; Balvay, *La Révolte des Natchez*, 151–160.

21. De Laye, Relation du massacre, June 1, 1730, ANOM, 04DFC 38, 1.

22. Milne, *Natchez Country*, 181.

23. Milne, *Natchez Country*, 154–162, 180–181; Johnson, *Wicked Flesh*, 108–113.

24. De Laye, Relation du massacre, June 1, 1730, ANOM, 04DFC 38, 5–6.

25. De Laye, Relation du massacre, June 1, 1730, ANOM, 04DFC 38, 5–6, 62; Milne, *Natchez Country*, 149–174; Lettre du P. le Petit, 1730, sur les Sauvages du Mississippi, et en particulier les Natchez, et relation de leur entreprise sur la colonie française, en 1729, July 12, 1730, ANOM, 04DFC 40, 30.

26. Milne, *Natchez Country*, 199.

27. Diron d'Artaguiette, Journal, September 1, 1722 to September 10, 1723, ANOM, C13 C2, fols. 188, 221; Maduell, *Census Tables*, 29.

28. De Laye, Relation du massacre, June 1, 1730, ANOM, 04DFC 38, 10.

29. LisaMarie Malischke, "Heterogeneity of Early French and Native Forts, Settlements, and Villages: A Comparison to Fort St. Pierre (1719–1729) in French Colonial Louisiana" (PhD diss., University of Alabama, 2015), 89, 180–181, 311; Bienville to Pontchartrain, June 6, 1704, *MPA:FD*, 2:22; Bienville to Pontchartrain, August 20, 1709, *MPA:FD*, 2:136; Bienville to Pontchartrain, February 25, 1708, *MPA:FD*, 2:113–115; Pénicaut, *Fleur de Lys et Calumet*, 100; DuVal, *Native Ground*, 91; Swanton, *Indian Tribes of the Lower Mississippi Valley*, 204.

30. Delanglez, *French Jesuits*, 447.

31. Lettre du P. le Petit, 1730, sur les Sauvages du Mississipi, et en particulier les Natchez, et relation de leur entreprise sur la colonie française, en 1729, July 12, 1730, ANOM, 04DFC 40, 60–72; Giraud, *History of Louisiana*, 5:382–384, 400; Malischke, "Heterogeneity of Early French and Native Forts," 337–339; White, *Wild Frenchmen and Frenchified Indians*, 105; Diron au Ministre, February 9, 1730, ANOM, C13 A12, reel 20, fols. 362, 364; *Journal de Vaugine de Nuisement*, ed. Steve Canac-Marquis et Pierre Rézeau (Quebec: Les Presses de l'Université Laval, 2005), 26; Dumont de Montigny, *Mémoires Historiques sur la Louisiane*, 2:160–164.

32. Several Ofogoulas killed three Frenchmen as they traveled down the river. Lusser to Maurepas, January 25, 1730, *MPA:FD*, 1:99–100.

33. Dumont de Montigny, *Memoir of Lieutenant Dumont*, 189.

34. Galloway, *Practicing Ethnohistory*, 264.

35. Before the Natchez War, the Chaouchas were located only three leagues downriver from New Orleans on the eastern bank. Pénicaut, *Fleur de Lys and Calumet*, 219–220.

36. Périer to Maurepas, November 28, 1729, *MPA:FD*, 1:64.

37. Extrait de la lettre de M. Périer à Le Pelletier, March 18, 1730, ANOM, C13 A12, reel 20, fols. 283–284, 295; Périer, Relations du Massacre des Natchez, March 18, 1730 and April 10, 1730, ANOM, C13 A12-1, reel 19, fols. 40–41, 47.

38. It is difficult to tell exactly how many Chaouachas died in this assault. Périer claimed that he destroyed the nation, however this is primarily because he wanted to proclaim the expedition a success. Dumont de Montigny says they killed "eight or nine Indian men as well as some women." Like many nations the French claimed to have destroyed, the survivors sought refuge with an ally and established a new joint settlement. Following this assault, the Chaouachas fled to the Ouachas and took up residence at their village. In 1739 the Chaouachas and Ouchas together numbered about 105 people and in 1758 the Ouachas alone numbered roughly 35–40 people. Swanton, *Indian Tribes of the Lower Mississippi Valley*, 42; Goddard et al., "Small Tribes of the Western Southeast," in Fogelson, *Handbook of North American Indians*, 14:189; Balvay, *La Révolte des Natchez*, 135–136; Milne, *Natchez Country*, 180–185; Hall, *Africans in Colonial Louisiana*, 102; Maduell, *Census Tables*, 81; Périer à l'abbé Raguet, May 12, 1728, ANOM, C13 A11, reel 18, fols. 7, 8; Extrait de la lettre de M. Périer à Le Pelletier, March 18, 1730, ANOM, C13 A12, reel 20, fols. 295, 283–284; Périer au Ministre, April 10, 1730, ANOM, C13 A12, reel 20, fols. 300–302; Dumont de Montigny, *Memoir of Lieutenant Dumont*, 250.

39. Swanton, *Indian Tribes of the Lower Mississippi Valley*, 337.

40. Pénicaut, *Fleur de Lys and Calumet*, 159–160.

41. The Houmas, Bayagoulas, and Acolapissas were also very unlikely to have sympathized with the Natchez. In 1723 a Natchez diplomat came to a village of the Acolapissas to try to convince them to join the Natchez in their war against the French. The Acolapissas not only declined this offer but they also held the Natchez diplomat hostage at their village and informed the French of this plan. Additionally, during this 1723 conflict, more than two hundred warriors from the Petites Nations, including the Houmas, traveled to Natchez to provide their services to the French. All three nations had long-standing trade relationships with the French and had assisted them greatly during the early years of settlement. Each of these nations also participated in the 1729 Natchez War and ultimately supported the French and Choctaws. D'Artaguiette, "Journal of Diron d'Artaguiette," in Mereness, *Travels in the American Colonies*, 30–36; Relation de la guerre des Natchez, 1723, ANOM, 04DFC 30, 1; Caillot, *Company Man*, 150.

42. Périer au Ministre, April 1, 1730, ANOM, C13 A12, reel 20, fols. 352, 354.

43. Milne, *Natchez Country*, 188–190; Galloway, "'So Many Little Republics,'" 516.

44. Boisbriant aux directeurs de la Compagnie, January 12, 1727, ANOM, C13 A10, reel 17, fol. 252.

45. Diron au Ministre, October 17, 1729, ANOM, C13 A12-1, reel 19, fols. 148, 149–154.

46. Diron au Ministre, February 9, 1730, ANOM, C13 A12, reel 20, fols. 362, 363.

47. De Laye, Relation du massacre, June 1, 1730, ANOM, 04DFC 38, 30; Ellis, "Natchez War Revisited," 464–466.

48. Giraud, *History of French Louisiana*, 5:409; Broutin to the Company, August 7, 1730, *MPA:FD*, 1:131–132.

49. By my calculations, the Atakapas, Chitimachas, Bayagoulas, Biloxis, Chaouachas, Houmas, Tohomes, Mobilians, Opelousas, Ouchas, Chakchiumas, Ibitoupas, Taposas, Tensas, and

Tunicas could field a combined force of 1,775 warriors in the mid-1720s. Together these nations' populations included roughly 6,213 people. According to Daniel Usner's estimates, in 1725 the total Indian population of the Lower Mississippi Valley (as far north as the Quapaws, as far west as the Red River, and as far east as the Mobile River) was 35,000. Not including the Choctaws, Chickasaws, or Creeks, this puts the total population of smaller nations, including the Natchez and Quapaws, at 10,600, of which the aforementioned Petites Nations made up roughly 59 percent. Based on my population estimates for the fifteen aforementioned Petites Nations, these nations made up roughly 18 percent of the total Indigenous population of the region and thus their support in the war would have been essential. If the total number of Petites Nations warriors had arrived to support the initial French endeavors, they would have more than doubled the number of Choctaws involved in the fighting. Usner, *American Indians in the Lower Mississippi Valley*, 35.

50. Périer au Ministre, May 14, 1732, ANOM, C13 A14, reel 22, fols. 144, 145–147; DuVal, *Native Ground*, 95–96; Marchand and St. Ange to Périer, September 15, 1732, *MPA:FD*, 4:124.

51. Usner, *Indians, Settlers, and Slaves*, 72–75.

52. Périer to Ory, November 15, 1730, *MPA:FD*, 4:53.

53. Broutin actually went on to say that it was not the power or military might of the Natchez that should frighten the French, but rather "only the Choctaws were to be feared." Broutin to the Company, August 7, 1730, *MPA:FD*, 1:131.

54. Lettre du P. le Petit, 1730, sur les Sauvages du Mississipi, et en particulier les Natchez, et relation de leur entreprise sur la colonie française, en 1729, July 12, 1730, ANOM, 04DFC 40, 83.

55. Périer to Ory, August 1, 1730, *MPA:FD*, 4:39–40.

56. Caillot, *Company Man*, 125–127; Balvay, *La Révolte des Natchez*, 138.

57. Lusser to Maurepas, March 14, 1730, *MPA:FD*, 1:102–105; Milne, *Natchez Country*, 195; Lettre du P. le Petit, 1730, sur les Sauvages du Mississipi, et en particulier les Natchez, et relation de leur entreprise sur la colonie française, en 1729, July 12, 1730, ANOM, 04DFC 40, 83–84; Périer, Relation de la défaite des Natchez, March 25, 1731, ANOM, C13 A13, reel 21, fols. 35.

58. Lusser to Maurepas, March 8, 1730, *MPA:FD*, 1:96–97; de Laye, Relation du massacre, June 1, 1730, ANOM, 04DFC 38, 66.

59. Goddard et al., "Small Tribes of the Western Southeast," in Fogelson, *Handbook of North American Indians*, 14:186; Swanton, *Indian Tribes of the Lower Mississippi Valley*, 42; Ethridge, *Chicaza to Chickasaw*, 135, 179, 197, 216, 233–235; Pénicaut, *Fleur de Lys and Calumet*, 239; Memoir of François Le Maire, January 15, 1714, in Waggoner, *Le Plus Beau Païs du Monde*, 131; Barnett, *Mississippi's American Indians*, 70, 120; Usner, *American Indians in the Lower Mississippi Valley*, 50; Usner, *Indians, Settlers, and Slaves*, 29; Galloway, *Choctaw Genesis*, 312.

60. Lusser to Maurepas, Journal of Lusser, December 12, 1730 to March 23, 1730, *MPA:FD*, 1:88, 96–102; de Laye, Relation du massacre, June 1, 1730, ANOM, 04DFC 38, 65–67; Périer à Orry, August 1, 1730, ANOM, C13 A12, reel 20, fols. 328, 331.

61. De Laye, Relation du massacre, June 1, 1730, ANOM, 04DFC 38, 65–67; Périer au Ministre, April 19, 1730, ANOM, C13 A12, reel 20, fols. 300, 304; Extrait de la lettre de M. Périer à Le Pelletier, March 18, 1730, ANOM, C13 A12, reel 20, fols. 295, 299; Périer au Ministre, March 15, 1731, ANOM, C13 A12, reel 20, fols. 42; Périer au Ministre, March 25, 1731, ANOM, C13 A12, reel 20, fols. 46, 47; Régis du Roulet à Périer, March 16, 1731, ANOM, C13 A12, reel 20, fols. 187, 194; Périer à Orry, August 1, 1730, ANOM, C13 A12, reel 20, fol. 328, Périer to Maurepas, March 18, 1730, *MPA:FD*, 1:75.

62. Milne, *Natchez Country*, 198; Sophie White, "Massacre, Mardi Gras, and Torture in Early New Orleans," *William and Mary Quarterly* 70, no. 3 (2013): 497, 519–530; Caillot, *Company Man*, 146–148.

63. Pièce non signée et intitulée, Relation abrégée de la dernière attaque que les Français ont faite aux Sauvages Natchez en la province de la Louisiane, au mois de janvier 1731, ANOM, C11 B12, fols. 84–87v, 6; Périer au Ministre, April 16, 1731, ANOM, C13 A13, reel 21, fols. 55, 60–63; Diron d'Artaguiette au Ministre, June 24, 1731, ANOM, C13 A13, reel 21, fols. 145, 147; Diron d'Artaguiette au Contrôleur general, August 20, 1731, ANOM, C13 A13, reel 21, fols. 152, 152–154; Périer au Ministre, April 19, 1732, ANOM, C13 A14, reel 22, fols. 151, 151–153; Périer to Maurepas, December 10, 1731, *MPA:FD*, 4:103–106; Brain, *Tunica Archaeology*, 300; Ellis, "Natchez War Revisited," 466–468.

64. Juzan, Relation de ce qui s'est passé au fort français des Natchez dans la province de la Louisiane, 1731, ANOM, 04DFC 41, 10–19; Milne, *Natchez Country*, 203.

65. Juzan à Périer, December 29, 1731, ANOM, C13 A13, reel 21, fols. 207, 207–208; Saint-Denis à Salmon, November 2, 1731, ANOM, C13 A13, reel 21, fols. 162, 162–166; Périer au Ministre, April 19, 1732, ANOM, C13 A14, reel 22, fols. 151, 152–154.

66. Edward Noel Smyth's recent work provides the most thorough investigation of the many fates of Natchez survivors after the 1729 war. Edward Noel Smyth, "The Natchez Diaspora: A History of Indigenous Displacement and Survival in the Atlantic World" (PhD diss., University of California Santa Cruz, 2016); John A. Green, facs. repr. of "Governor Périer's Expedition Against the Natchez Indians: December, 1730–January, 1731," *Louisiana Historical Quarterly* 19, no. 3 (July 1936): 551; Périer au Ministre, April 16, 1731, ANOM, C13 A13, reel 21, fols. 55, 68; Périer au Ministre, April 6, 1732, ANOM, C13 A14, reel 22, fols. 56, 61; Salmon au Ministre, June 20, 1732, ANOM, C13 A15, reel 23, fols. 149, 149–50; Bienville et Salmon au Ministre, March 13, 1738, ANOM, C13 A23, reel 31, fols. 7, 8–9; Analyse d'une lettre de Marchand, captain aux Natchez, September 15, 1732, ANOM, C13 A15, reel 23, fols. 189, 189–190; Bienville au Ministre, December 20, 1737, ANOM, C13 A22, reel 30, fols. 111, 116–119; Charles de Beauharnois de la Boische au Ministre, Jean-Baptist Benoist de Saint-Clair, October 11, 1740, BAC, Fonds des Colonies, C11 A, box 74, reel F-74, item no. 3068865; Maurepas to Pierre Rigaud, marquis de Vaudreuil, October 27, 1742, LO 23, 7–8, Vaudreuil Papers, 1740–1753, box 1, 1740–1745, 29 MSS, Loudoun Papers: Americana, Huntington Library; Douglas Summers Brown, *The Catawba Indians: The People of the River* (Columbia: University of South Carolina Press, 1966), 223; Vaudreuil to the Court, May 10, 1751, Letterbook, vol. 2, 130–132, Vaudreuil Papers, 1946–47; James Francis to Governor Lyttelton, December 23, 1757, *Colonial Records of South Carolina* (*CRSC*), series 2, Documents relating to Indian Affairs 1754–1765, ed. W. L. McDowell Jr. (Columbia: South Carolina Archives Department, 1970), 425–426; Ludovic Grant to Governor James Glen, July 22, 1754, *CRSC*, 19; Journal of John Evans, October 14, 1755, *CRSC*, 86–87; Salmon au Ministre, September 1, 1736, ANOM, C13 A21, reel 29, fols. 305, 306–307; Alexander Gregg, *History of the Old Cheraws* (Columbia, SC: State Company, 1905), 10–11; William Bartram and Mark Van Doren, *The Travels of William Bartram* (New York: Dover Publications, 1928), 406; James Francis to Governor Lyttelton, December 23, 1757, *CRSC*, 426; Address of William Bull to the House Assembly, March 25, 1738, *The Colonial Records of South Carolina: Journal of the Commons House of Assembly of South Carolina*, November 10, 1736–June 7, 1739, ed. J. H. Easterby (Columbia: Historical Commission of South Carolina, 1951), 565; William Bartram, *Travels* (New Haven, CT: Yale University Press, 1958), 330.

67. Extrait d'une lettre de Crémont, September 4, 1732, ANOM, C13 A15, reel 23, fol. 192.

68. Salmon au Ministre, March 24, 1732, ANOM, C13 A15, reel 23, fols. 44, 51–53; Salmon au Ministre, June 20, 1732, ANOM, C13 A15, reel 23, fols. 149, 149–151; Analyse des passages de lettres de Bienville, May 15, 1733, ANOM, C13 A16, reel 24, fols. 206, 220, 224; Bienville au Ministre, May 18, 1733, ANOM, C3 A16, reel 24, fols. 245, 245–247; Bienville sur les Sauvages, July 26,

1733 and August 10, 1733, ANOM, C13 A16, reel 24, fols. 249, 250–254; Bienville au Ministre, July 26, 1733, ANOM, C13 A16, reel 24, fols. 277, 278; Bienville au Ministre, September 10, 1733, ANOM, C13 A16, reel 24, fol. 294; Salmon au Ministre, February 7, 1736, ANOM, C13 A21, reel 29, fols. 236, 237; Diron d'Artaguette au Ministre, May 19, 1736, ANOM, C13 A21, reel 29, fols. 346, 346–347; Bienville et Salmon au Ministre, March 13, 1738, ANOM, C13 A23, reel 31, fols. 7, 8–9; Analyse partielle d'une lettre de Bienville au Ministre, December 20, 1737, ANOM, C13 A23, reel 31, fols. 102, 104–105; Loubœy to Maurepas, July 18, 1741, *MPA:FD*, 4:187–188.

    69. Giraud, *History of French Louisiana*, 5:428; Pièce non signée et intitulée, Relation abrégée de la dernière attaque que les Français ont faite aux Sauvages Natchez en la province de la Louisiane, au mois de janvier 1731, ANOM, C11 B12, fols. 84–87v, 8; Périer au Ministre, August 1, 1730, ANOM, C13 A12, reel 20, fols. 306, 309.

    70. Bienville au Ministre, January 28, 1733, ANOM, C13 A16, reel 24, fols. 233, 234; Milne, *Natchez Country*, 201.

    71. Juzan à Périer, December 29, 1731, ANOM, C13 A13, reel 21, fols. 207, 207–208.

    72. The archaeologist Bradley Lieb has suggested that the presence of Natchez pottery at the Tunica village across from Pointe Coupée indicates that, in addition to trade, there may have been Natchez women living with the Tunicas during this era. Jeffrey P. Brain, however, has argued that the presence of Natchez pottery at the Tunica site most likely indicates trade rather than the presence of Natchez women. Jeffrey P. Brain, *Tunica Treasure* (Cambridge, MA: Peabody Museum of Archaeology and Ethnology, Harvard University, 1979), 241; Bradley R. Lieb, "The Natchez Indian Diaspora: Ethnohistoric Archaeology of the Eighteenth-Century Natchez Refuge Among the Chickasaws" (PhD diss., University of Alabama, 2008), 165, 336; Juzan à Périer, December 29, 1731, ANOM, C13 A13, reel 21, fols. 207, 207–208.

    73. Procuration by Juchereau de St Denis, to collect payment for 2 Natchez women, March 8, 1738, Superior Council Records, Louisiana Historical Center, New Orleans, no. 1738-03-08-05; Bienville to Maurepas, December 20, 1737, *MPA:FD*, 3:705–706.

    74. Dan Usner estimates that not more than four hundred additional enslaved Africans were trafficked via the transatlantic slave trades to Louisiana between the end of the war and the Louisiana cession in 1763. Hall, *Africans in Colonial Louisiana*, 60, 87–95; Usner, *Indians, Settlers, and Slaves*, 76, 80–81; Vidal, *Caribbean New Orleans*, 120–121, 140; Johnson, *Wicked Flesh*, 115–116; Terrien, *Exiles and Fugitives*, 140–141.

CHAPTER 6

    1. Bienville au Ministre, February 10, 1736, ANOM, C13 A21, reel 29, fols. 122, 130–149.

    2. Usner, *Indians, Settlers, and Slaves*, 78–82; Atkinson, *Splendid Land, Splendid People*, 36–79; Joseph Peyser, "The Chickasaw Wars of 1736 and 1740: French Military Drawings and Plans Document the Struggle for the Lower Mississippi Valley," *Journal of Mississippi History* 44, no. 1 (1982): 1–25; Hamilton, *Colonial Mobile*, 110–114; Ellis, "Natchez War Revisited," 470.

    3. Lee, *Masters of the Middle Waters*, 98–99; Usner, *Indians, Settlers, and Slaves*, 64–65, 78–79; Périer au Ministre, April 19, 1732, ANOM, C13 A14, reel 22, fols. 151, 154; Salmon au Ministre, February 7, 1736, ANOM, C13 A21, reel 29, fols. 236, 237; Crémont au Ministre, May 15, 1732, ANOM, C13 A14, reel 22, fols. 112, 116–118; Lettre de Charles de Beauharnois de la Boische au Ministre, Jean-Baptist Benoist de Saint-Clair, October 11, 1740, BAC, Fonds des Colonies, C11 A, box 74, reel F-74, item no. 3068865, 49; Ann Early, "The Greatest Gathering: The French and Chickasaw War in the Mississippi Valley and the Potential for Archaeology," *French Colonial Ar-*

chaeology in the Southeast and Caribbean, ed. Kenneth Kelly and Meredith Hardy, 81–96 (Tallahassee: University Press of Florida, 2011), 81–84; Bienville to Pontchartrain, October 27, 1711, *MPA:FD*, 3:159–160.

4. Unlike in Lower Louisiana, during the 1700s the 1700s tensions between European settlers and their Indigenous hosts, including French livestock's destruction of Illinois crops, led colonial administrations to develop a policy that forced the separation of European and Indigenous settlements in order to avoid conflict. Rushforth, *Bonds of Alliance*, 54–80, 199–221; Witgen, *Infinity of Nations*, 267–278, 293–297; Morrissey, *Empire by Collaboration*, 11–108, 171–172; Usner, *Indians, Settlers, and Slaves*, 81–82; White, *Voices of the Enslaved*, 108; Lee, *Masters of the Middle Waters*, 61–88.

5. Rushforth, *Bonds of Alliance*, 54–80, 199–221; Witgen, *Infinity of Nations*, 267–278, 293–297; Morrissey, *Empire by Collaboration*, 11–30, 171–72; Usner, *Indians, Settlers, and Slaves*, 81–82; Heerman, *Alchemy of Slavery*, 30.

6. Périer au Ministre, May 14, 1732, ANOM, C13 A14, reel 22, fols. 144, 144–146; Périer au Ministre, April 6, 1732, ANOM, C13 A14, reel 22, fols. 56, 56–62; Extrait d'une lettre de Crémont, September 4, 1732, ANOM, C13 A15, reel 23, fols. 192, 192–193.

7. Périer au Ministre, July 25, 1732, ANOM, C13 A14, reel 22, fols. 68, 71; Salmon au Ministre, March 24, 1732, ANOM, C13 A15, fols. 44, 51–53; Salmon au Ministre, June 20, 1732, ANOM, C13 A15, reel 23, fols. 149, 149–151; Analyse des passages de lettres de Bienville, May 15, 1733, ANOM, C13 A16, reel 24, fols. 206, 220, 224.

8. DuVal, *Native Ground*, 96–97; Périer au Ministre, January 25, 1733, ANOM, C13 A16, reel 24, fols. 178, 184; Bienville sur les Sauvages, March 25, 1734, ANOM, C13 A18, reel 26, fols. 217, 223; Bienville au Ministre, June 15, 1740, ANOM, C13 A24, reel 32, fols. 104, 105–106.

9. Crémont au Ministre, May 15, 1732, ANOM, C13 A14, reel 22, fols. 112, 113–118.

10. Bienville au Ministre, September 30, 1733, ANOM, C13 A16, reel 24, fols. 300, 305; Nicolas Henri, Succession of Antoine Bunel, September 13, 1735, French Colonial Records, 10143–10187, box 2, folder 22, Notarial Archives Research Center, Office of the Clerk of Civil District Court for the Parish of Orleans, State of Louisiana, New Orleans.

11. Vaudreuil au Ministre, June 6, 1748, ANOM, C13 A32, reel 40, fols. 95, 95–96; Bienville sur les Sauvages, March 25, 1734, ANOM, C13 A18, reel 26, fol. 217; Salmon au Ministre, June 20, 1732, ANOM, C13 A15, reel 23, fols. 150–154; Crémont au Ministre, May 15, 1732, ANOM, C13 A14, reel 22, fols. 112, 113–118.

12. The record of this incident of Choctaws threatening the Mobile River nations in 1734 does not list a specific division, town, or Choctaw leader. It is possible that this news was delivered by Mongoulacha Mingo. This Chickasawhay leader had a close relationship with the Tohomes during the 1730s, and by the 1740s had turned firmly against the French and advocated for his people to do so as well. Bienville sur les Sauvages, March 25, 1734, ANOM, C13 A18, reel 26, fols. 217, 218; Analyse de lettres de S. d. Diron, May 22, 1736, ANOM, C13 A20, reel 28, fols. 128, 128–129; Galloway, *Practicing Ethnohistory*, 275.

13. Many Choctaw villages recognized military leaders by the title of "soulouche oumastabé" or "Red Shoe Killer" as this Choctaw term translates to English. Galloway, *Practicing Ethnohistory*, 262.

14. While it does not appear that the Taposas relocated with the Chakchiumas down to the Lower Yazoo River, the Chakchiumas' decision to ally with the French seems to have influenced them to do the same. Thus, the Taposas also conducted raids on behalf of the French during the Chickasaw War. Bienville au Ministre, February 10, 1736, ANOM, C13 A21, reel 29, fols. 122, 130–149; Analyse de correspondences de Bienville et autres, April 14, 1735, ANOM, C13 A20, reel 28,

fols. 133, 136–137; Analyse de lettres de Bienville, September 14, 1735, ANOM, C13 A20, reel 28, fols. 138, 141; Bienville au Ministre, April 14, 1733, ANOM, C13 A20, reel 28, fols. 33, 45; Périer au Ministre, February 22, 1733, ANOM, C13 A16, reel 24, fols. 198, 199; Bienville sur les Sauvages, July 26, 1733, ANOM, C13 A16, reel 24, fols. 249, 253; Bienville au Ministre, September 30, 1733, ANOM, C13 A16, reel 24, fols. 300, 305.

15. Bienville au Ministre, February 10, 1736, ANOM, C13 A21, reel 29, fols. 122, 138; Jacob Lee, "Lines and Circles: Networks and Regions in Early America," paper presented at the New York University Atlantic History Seminar, February 12, 2019 (unpublished, cited with permission of the author), 16–17; Bienville au Ministre, February 10, 1736, ANOM, C13 A21, reel 29, fols. 122, 130–149; Analyse de correspondences de Bienville et autres, April 14, 1735, ANOM, C13 A20, reel 28, fols. 133, 133–136.

16. Although both scholars and contemporary observers have suggested that 1736 marked the end of the Chakchiumas, it is abundantly clear that Chakchiumas survived within the Choctaw and Chickasaw nations long after the 1730s. James Atkinson has suggested that a group of Chakchiumas may have joined Chickasaw towns by 1737 as well. Bienville au Ministre, February 10, 1736, ANOM, C13 A21, reel 29, 122, 130–149; Jacques Nicolas Bellin, *Remarques sur la carte de l'Amérique septentrionale* (Paris, 1755), 117; Atkinson, *Splendid Land, Splendid People*, 16; David H. Dye, introduction to *The Protohistoric Period in the Mid-South: 1500–1700*, Proceedings of the 1983 Mid-South Archaeological Conference, ed. David H. Dye and Ronald C. Brister, xi–xiv (Jackson: Mississippi Department of Archives and History, 1986), xii; Swanton, *Indian Tribes of the Lower Mississippi Valley*, 292–296; Salmon au Ministre, February 7, 1736, ANOM, C13 A21, reel 29, fols. 236, 237; Robin Fabel and R, "The Letters of R: The Lower Mississippi in the Early 1770s," *Louisiana History* 24, no. 4 (1983): 414–415; Sibley, "Historical Sketches of the Several Indian Tribes in Louisiana, South of the Arkansas River, and Between the Mississippi and River Grande," 725; Brain, *Tunica Archaeology*, 30–43, 300–301; Usner, *Indians, Settlers, and Slaves*, 62–63, 85.

17. Galloway, "Confederacy as a Solution to Chiefdom Dissolution," 408.

18. Purchasing these enslaved Chakchiumas cost the Louisiana government about 2,000 francs. Bienville au Ministre, December 20, 1737, ANOM, C13 A22, reel 30, fols. 111, 111–116; Diron d'Artaguiette au Ministre, September 11, 1736, ANOM, C13 A22, reel 30, fol. 354.

19. Diron d'Artaguiette to Maurepas, May 17, 1735, *MPA:FD*, 1:245; Galloway, *Practicing Ethnohistory*, 80; Lee, "Lines and Circles, 16–18, 23; Lee, *Masters of the Middle Waters*, 99–106; Usner, *Indians, Settlers, and Slaves*, 82–83; DuVal, *Native Ground*, 96–97.

20. Louboey au Ministre, November 28, 1738, ANOM, C13 A23, reel 31, fols. 169, 171–174; Mémoire sur l'état de la Colonie de la Louisiane en 1746, ANOM, C13 A30, reel 38, fols. 259–260; Lettre de Charles de Beauharnois au Ministre, Jean-Baptist Benoist de Saint-Clair, October 11, 1740, BAC, Fonds des Colonies, C11 A, box 74, reel F-74, item no. 3068865, 48–49; Bienville et Salmon au Ministre, September 16, 1735, ANOM, C13 A20, reel 28, fols. 126; Bienville au Ministre, February 10, 1736, ANOM, C13 A21, reel 29, fols. 122, 122–130; Edmond Atkin, "The Revolt of the Choctaw Indians in the Late War from the French to the British Alliance and of Their Return to That of the French," January 20, 1753, British Museum, Lanscl. Ms. 809 microfilm, 2–3; Greg O'Brien, "Quieting the Ghosts: How the Choctaws and Chickasaws Stopped Fighting," in *The Native South: New Histories and Enduring Legacies*, ed. Tim Alan Garrison and Greg O'Brien, 47–69 (Lincoln: University of Nebraska Press, 2017), 49.

21. Lee, "Lines and Circles," 18–19; Usner, *Indians, Settlers, and Slaves*, 83–85.

22. Lee, *Masters of the Middle Waters*, 107–109; Lettre de Charles de Beauharnois au Ministre, Jean-Baptist Benoist de Saint-Clair, October 11, 1740, BAC, Fonds des Colonies, C11 A, box

74, reel F-74, item no. 3068865, 49; Vaudreuil letters, October 27, 1742, Compte de Maurepas to the Marquis de Vaudreuil, LO 23, 2–3, 7–8, Pierre de Rigaud, marquis de Vaudreuil Papers, 1740–1753, box 1, 1740–1745, 29 MSS, Loudoun Papers: Americana, Huntington Library (hereafter cited as Vaudreuil Papers); Pierre de Rigaud, Vaudreuil, Parole à Porter aux Tchactas sur la Paix que les Tchikachas demandent, January 15, 1744, LO 517, Marquis de Vaudreuil-Cavagnal, Letterbook, vol. 1, 9, Vaudreuil Papers, 1740–1753 (hereafter cited as Letterbook, Vaudreuil Papers); Vaudreuil to Maurepas, July 29, 1745, Letterbook, vol. 1, 10, Vaudreuil Papers; David Nichols, "Enterprise of War," 40.

23. Richter, *Before the Revolution*, 346–347, 379; Christian Ayne Crouch, *Nobility Lost: French and Canadian Martial Cultures, Indians, and the End of New France* (Ithaca, NY; Cornell University Press, 2014), 6, 16–17; White, *Wild Frenchmen and Frenchified Indians*, 16; Yevan Terrien, "'More of a Danger to the Colony Than the Enemy Himself': Military Desertion, and Imperial Rule in French Louisiana (ca. 1715–1760)," in *A Global History of Runaways: Workers, Mobility, and Capitalism, 1600–1850*, ed. Marcus Rediker, Titas Chakraborty, and Matthias van Rossum, 96–114 (Davis: University of California Press, 2019), 96; Lettre de La Galissonnière au Ministre, September 1, 1748, BAC, Fonds des Colonies, C11 A, reel C-2397, item no. 3071433, 117–123.

24. Atkin, "Revolt of the Choctaw Indians," 3–5, 19, 25; Vaudreuil to Maurepas, November 20, 1746, Letterbook, vol. 1, 88, Vaudreuil Papers; Maurepas to Vaudreuil, April 25, 1746, LO 64, Vaudreuil Papers, 1740–1753, box 2, 1746–1747, 46 MSS.

25. Vaudreuil to Derneville, September 4, 1745, Letterbook, vol. 3, 168–170, Vaudreuil Papers; Galloway, *Practicing Ethnohistory*, 272–273; DuVal, "Indian Intermarriage and Métissage," 297–300; Pensatubbee, *Choctaw Women in a Chaotic World*, 10, 45–48.

26. Galloway primarily attributes the killings to the death of the British trader, while Carson suggests that the killings of the Chickasaws were the root cause of this conflict. Galloway, *Practicing Ethnohistory*, 272–280; Vaudreuil to Maurepas, November 20, 1746, Letterbook, vol. 1, 88, Vaudreuil Papers; Lee, "Lines and Circles," 23–24; Carson, *Searching for the Bright Path*, 31–33; Usner, *Indians, Settlers, and Slaves*, 92–93; Vaudreuil to the Court, March 20, 1748, Letterbook, vol. 2, 41, Vaudreuil Papers; Vaudreuil to Maurepas, March 15, 1747, LO 89, Vaudreuil Papers, 1740–1753, box 2, 1746–1747, 46 MSS; O'Brien, "Quieting the Ghosts," 50; Beauchamps, "1746 Journal of Visit to the Choctaws," in Mereness, *Travels in the American Colonies*, 264–266; LeAnne Howe, *Shell Shaker* (San Francisco: Aunt Lute Books, 2001), 1–16, 127–136, 170–188.

27. Galloway, *Practicing Ethnohistory*, 261, 282–283; Vaudreuil to the Court, March 20, 1748, Letterbook, vol. 2, 42, Vaudreuil Papers; Vaudreuil to the Court, March 6, 1749, Letterbook, vol. 2, 60, Vaudreuil Papers; Vaudreuil au Ministre, November 5, 1748, ANOM, C13 A32, reel 40, fols. 122, 122–130.

28. During this era, the French outpost at Pointe Coupée had only about 100 soldiers, and the fort at Natchez was similarly sparsely staffed by a mere 50 men. These numbers of soldiers are based on a count of the Louisiana troops from 1751, so they represent an estimate rather than concrete numbers for 1748. By comparison, Mobile had 400 soldiers and New Orleans, as the largest urban center, was supported by 800 French troops. Distribution des Troupes de la Louisiane, 1751, LO 270, Vaudreuil Papers, box 6; Vaudreuil au Ministre, November 5, 1748, ANOM, C13 A32, reel 40, fols. 122, 122–130; Vaudreuil to the Court, February 12, 1751, Letterbook, vol. 2, 95, Vaudreuil Papers.

29. Vaudreuil au Ministre, November 5, 1748, ANOM, C13 A32, reel 40, fols. 122, 122–130; Vaudreuil to Maurepas, June 6, 1748, LO 135, Vaudreuil Papers, box 3; Vaudreuil to Rouillé, February 1, 1750, LO 203, Vaudreuil Papers, box 5; Vaudreuil to Antoine Louis Rouillé, September 22,

1749, LO 185, Vaudreuil Papers, box 4; Vaudreuil to Maurepas, November 5, 1748, LO 153, Vaudreuil Papers, box 3; Vaudreuil au Ministre, March 18, 1749, ANOM, C13 A33, reel 40, fols. 12, 13, 27; Vaudreuil to Maurepas, October 30, 1745, Letterbook, vol. 1, 65, Vaudreuil Papers; Indian Harrangues at the Council of War, June 20, 1745, *MPA:FD*, 5:175–176; DuVal, *Native Ground*, 81; Terrien, "'More of a Danger to the Colony Than the Enemy Himself,'" 107–109.

30. During the 1750s, the Tohomes moved back to their homelands on the Mobile River. Beauchamps, "1746 Journal of Visit to the Choctaws," in Mereness, *Travels in the American Colonies*, 266–267; Galloway, *Practicing Ethnohistory*, 279; Louboey au Ministre, February 6, 1748, ANOM, C13 A32, reel 40, fols. 210, 212–213; Vaudreuil to Louboey, February 20, 1745, Letterbook, vol. 3, 155, Vaudreuil Papers; Memoir on Indians by Kerelec, December 12, 1758, *MPA:FD*, 5:223–224.

31. Vaudreuil to La Jonquiere, March 28, 1751, LO 275, 6, Vaudreuil Papers, box 6.

32. Vaudreuil to the Court, February 12, 1751, Letterbook, vol. 2, 92–95, Vaudreuil Papers; Wood, "Changing Population of the Colonial South," 91–99; Usner, *Indians, Settlers, and Slaves*, 94–96.

33. Swanton, *Indian Tribes of the Lower Mississippi Valley*, 292–296.

34. O'Brien, "Quieting the Ghosts," 47–69.

35. Colin G. Calloway, *Indian World of George Washington: The First President, the First Americans, and the Birth of the Nation* (New York: Oxford University Press, 2018), 79–172; Bryan Rindfleisch, *George Galphin's Intimate Empire: The Creek Indians, Family, and Colonialism in Early America* (Tuscaloosa: University of Alabama Press, 2019), 140–143; Brooke M. Bauer, *Being Catawba: The World of Sally New River, 1746–1840* (PhD diss., University of North Carolina at Chapel Hill, 2016), 91–102; Lee, *Masters of the Middle Waters*, 118–121; Natalie Inman, *Brothers and Friends: Kinship in Early America* (Athens: University of Georgia Press, 2017), 21–27; Paul Kelton, "The British and Indian War: Cherokee Power and the Fate of Empire in North America," *William and Mary Quarterly* 69, no. 4 (2012): 763–792; Fred Anderson, *The War That Made America: A Short History of the French and Indian War* (New York: Penguin Books, 2005), 25–52.

CHAPTER 7

1. "Three Speeches Given at an Indian Council Held by the British at Fort Bute," in "Documents Regarding Indian Affairs in the Lower Mississippi Valley, 1771–1772," ed. and trans. David K. Bjork, *Mississippi Valley Historical Review* 13, no. 3 (1926): 409–410; Talk Between Charles Stuart and Small Tribes on the Mississippi, October 17, 1772, fr. 806, vol. 74, reel 6, pt.1, Records of the British Colonial Office, Library of Congress, Washington, DC. (hereafter cited as Records of the British Colonial Office).

2. Brain, *Tunica Archaeology*, 305; Cedula and Orders 286, October 30, 1781, Confidential Dispatches of Don Bernardo de Gálvez, Fourth Spanish Governor of Louisiana, Sent to His Uncle Don José de Gálvez, Secretary of State and Ranking Official of the Council of the Indies, 192, Survey of Federal Archives, Special Collections, Tulane University, New Orleans; Gilbert C. Din, "The First Spanish Instructions for Arkansas Post, November 15, 1769," *Arkansas Historical Quarterly* 53, no. 3 (October 1, 1994): 312–319; Francisco Rendon to Carondelet, May 4, 1795, Dispatches of the Spanish Governors of Louisiana, 1766–1792, Survey of Federal Archives, Louisiana 5:218, Special Collections, Tulane University, New Orleans; Lee, *Masters of the Middle Waters*, 122–124.

3. The Spanish king accepted Louisiana largely because he envisioned the colony serving as a buffer zone for the more prosperous Spanish settlements in Mexico. Through Louisiana and along the northern boundaries of Spanish control in Texas, Spanish officials aimed to resettle Native Americans along the edges of their colonial possessions in hopes that these Native peoples could act as a human fence against Spain's enemies. The rapid expansion of Britain across the North American continent during the eighteenth century worried Spanish officials and they feared that British officials also had their eyes on Louisiana. David Knuth Bjork, "The Establishment of Spanish Rule in the Province of Louisiana" (PhD diss., University of California, 1923), 100; Colin G. Calloway, *The Scratch of a Pen: 1763 and the Transformation of North America* (Oxford: Oxford University Press, 2006), 144; F. Todd Smith, "A Native Response to the Transfer of Louisiana: The Red River Caddos and Spain, 1762–1803," *Louisiana History* 37, no. 2 (1996): 171–175.

4. Jean-Jacques-Blaise d'Abbadie, "The d'Abbadie Journal," in *A Comparative View of French Louisiana, 1699 and 1762: The Journals of Pierre Le Moyne d'Iberville and Jean-Jacques-Blaise d'Abbadie*, ed. and trans. Carl A. Brasseux, 89–138 (Lafayette: University of Southwestern Louisiana, 1981), 107–113, 124, 138; Calloway, *Scratch of a Pen*, 134–138.

5. Gilbert C. Din, "Protecting the 'Barrera': Spain's Defenses in Louisiana, 1763–1779," *Louisiana History* 19, no. 2 (1978): 183–211; Usner, *Indians, Settlers, and Slaves*, 105–107; Bjork, "Establishment of Spanish Rule," 11–12; Taylor, *American Colonies*, 385–386.

6. Brain, *Tunica Archaeology*, 316–317.

7. Talk Between Charles Stuart and the Small Tribes on the Mississippi, October 17, 1772, fr. 806, vol. 74, reel 6, pt. 1, Records of the British Colonial Office.

8. Brain, Roth, and de Reuse, "Tunica, Biloxi, and Ofo," in Fogelson, *Handbook of North American Indians*, 14:139; Usner, *Indians, Settlers, and Slaves*, 108, 113, 279.

9. Kathleen DuVal, "The Education of Fernando de Lebya: Quapaws and Spaniards on the Border of Empires," *Arkansas Historical Quarterly* 60, no.1 (2001): 1–29; Morrissey, *Empire by Collaboration*, 201–207; Gregory Evans Dowd, *War Under Heaven: Pontiac, the Indian Nations and the British Empire* (Baltimore: Johns Hopkins University Press, 2002), 68–89; Fred Anderson, *Crucible of War: The Seven Years' War and the Fate of Empire in British North America* (New York: Knopf, 2000), 530–533; James H. Merrell, *The Indians' New World: Catawbas and their Neighbors from European Contact Through the Era of Removal* (Chapel Hill, NC: 1989), 203–225; Richter, *Before the Revolution*, 406; David H. Corkran, *The Creek Frontier, 1540–1783* (Norman: University of Oklahoma Press, 1967), 252; Calloway, *Scratch of a Pen*, 100–119, 133–138, 142–149; Amy C. Schutt, *Peoples of the River Valleys: The Odyssey of the Delaware Indians* (Philadelphia: University of Pennsylvania Press, 2007), 94–96, 130–131; White, *Middle Ground*, 256–258; James H. Merrell, *Into the American Woods: Negotiators on the Pennsylvania Frontier* (New York: W. W. Norton, 1999), 276–302.

10. Wood, "Changing Population of the Colonial South," 74–79.

11. D'Abbadie, "D'Abbadie Journal," 96.

12. Robert Farmar to the Secretary of War, August 1, 1764, *Mississippi Provincial Archives, English Dominion* (hereafter cited as *MPA:ED*), ed. Dunbar Rowland (Nashville, TN: Press of Brandon Printing, 1911), 1:115.

13. D'Abbadie, "D'Abbadie Journal," 96.

14. Calloway, *Scratch of a Pen*, 67–76.

15. These Chatots and Mobilians also moved across the river into the Rapides Parish of Spanish Louisiana by 1772. Although this mass exodus from the Mobile region has long been attributed to the Mobile Bay Native peoples' hatred for the British, the conflict between the Choctaws

and Creeks was also a very significant factor in driving the Mobile River nations from their homes. Some Chatots also remained in the region near Mobile and exchanged goods with local plantation owners. Browne to Hillsborough, July 6, 1768, Pensacola, *MPA:ED*, 3:94–95; Waselkov and Gums, *Plantation Archaeology*, 17, 36–38, 215–216; John Stuart's Remarks on Lieutenant Governor Durnford's Letters to the Earl of Hillsborough Relating to Indian Affairs, February 18, 1770, vol. 72, class 5, Records of the British Colonial Office.

16. D'Abbadie, "D'Abbadie Journal," 136–137.

17. Brain, *Tunica Archaeology*, 39; Galloway, "'This nation . . . is very brave,'" 30.

18. Marion Bragg, *Historic Names and Places on the Mississippi River* (Vicksburg: Mississippi River Commission, 1977), 202, 246.

19. Pontiac did not make it as far downriver as Pointe Coupée, but his message was spread south by other Native peoples along the river. M. de Villiers to M. Loftus, April 20, 1764, in Alvord and Carter, *Critical Period*, 244–245.

20. Robert R. Rea, "Assault on the Mississippi: The Loftus Expedition, 1764," *Alabama Review* 26 (1973): 179–189.

21. *New York Mercury*, June 11, 1764 (American Antiquarian Society/News Bank), 2; Loftus to Gage, April 9, 1764, in Alvord and Carter, *Critical Period*, 237–239; Gerald Haffner, "Major John Loftus' Journal of the Proceedings of His Majesty's Twenty-Second Regiment up the River Mississippi in 1764," *Louisiana History* 20, no. 3 (1979): 332.

22. Lawrence Kinnaird, ed., *Spain in the Mississippi Valley, 1765–1794* (Washington, DC: U.S. Government Printing Office, 1949), 2:xv; d'Abbadie, "D'Abbadie Journal," 114; Fogelson, *Handbook of North American Indians*, 14:653–654.

23. D'Abbadie, "D'Abbadie Journal," 114.

24. Brain, *Tunica Archaeology*, 320, 326–327; Robin F. Fabel, *Colonial Challenges: Britons, Native Americans, and Caribs, 1759–1775* (Gainesville: University Press of Florida, 2000), 127; Talk Between Charles Stuart and Small Tribes on the Mississippi, October 17, 1772, fr. 806, vol. 74, reel 6, pt.1, Records of the British Colonial Office; DuVal, *Native Ground*, 141–153.

25. D'Abbadie, "D'Abbadie Journal," 139.

26. Bjork, "Establishment of Spanish Rule," 38–42.

27. Campbell to Governor Johnstone, December 12, 1764, *MPA:ED*, 1:266–267; Bjork, "Establishment of Spanish Rule," 38–42, 303; Talk Between Charles Stuart and Small Tribes on the Mississippi, October 17, 1772, fr. 806, vol. 74, reel 6, pt.1, Records of the British Colonial Office; Brain, *Tunica Archaeology*, 39, 42, 303; Charles Stuart, "List of Several Tribes," 1772, fr. 801–802, vol. 74, reel 6, pt. 1, Records of the British Colonial Office; d'Abbadie, "D'Abbadie Journal," 122–124.

28. In 1766 the governor of West Florida complained that he found it "extremely mortifying" to admit that the colony could not muster five hundred British soldiers. George Johnston to Mr. Conway, June 23, 1766, *MPA:ED*, 1:514.

29. Major Robert Farmar to Secretary of War, November 24, 1764, *MPA:ED*, 1:124–125.

30. Major Robert Farmar to Secretary of War, November 24, 1764, *MPA:ED*, 1:124–125; Charles Stuart to Peter Chester, April 16, 1770, vol. 1, class 21.672, Records of the British Colonial Office; Seven Years' War journal of the proceedings of the 35th Regiment of Foot, by a British officer, and illustrated by a military engineer, MS Codex Eng 41, John Carter Brown Library, Providence, 231; Robert R. Rea, "Redcoats and Redskins on the Lower Mississippi, 1763–1776: The Career of Lieutenant John Thomas," *Louisiana History* 11, no.1 (1970): 7.

31. D'Abbadie, "D'Abbadie Journal," 139–140.

32. Ulloa to Grimaldi, August 4, 1768, in Kinnaird, *Spain in the Mississippi Valley*, 2:61.

33. Jack D. L. Holmes, "Juan de la Villebeuvre and Spanish Indian Policy in British West Florida," *Florida Historical Society* 58, no. 4 (1980): 387–388; Usner, *Indians, Settlers, and Slaves*, 130–131.

34. In 1769 the Tunicas received presents from the Spanish amounting to 121 pesos, 6 reales, and 33 maravedis of silver. In 1771 the Tunicas and Avoyelles jointly received 1212 reales and 13 maravedis de plata with the "el jefe en particular" receiving a considerable quantity of ammunition, silk ribbon, a mirror, salt, cloth, scissors, vermillion, and gunpowder. By my calculation, this gift was the equivalent of 152 pesos and 3 reales and therefore represented a roughly 25 percent increase from their gift just two years prior. This was more than twice the next largest gift to any of the Petites Nations. The Tensas, Biloxis, Ouchas, Chaouachas, Bayagoulas, Houmas, Pakanas, Chitimachas, Pascagoulas, Mobilians, and Chatots also received gifts ranging in value from 251 reales and 1 maravedi de plata to the Mobilians to 570 reales and 5 maravedis de plata to the Biloxis. Additionally, the Tensa and Tunica were the only two Petites Nations to receive additional presents specially gifted to their chiefs. Cumulatively, Spanish expenses to preserve the friendship of the Indians in Louisiana more than quintupled in the decade between 1768 and 1778. "Regalos que se deben hacer annualmente a las Naciones de Indios por Reglamento de Estimado Señor Don Alejandro O'Reilly," no. 2, legajo 274, Papeles Procedentes de Cuba, Library of Congress, Washington DC; Statement of Payment for Indian Presents, January 9, 1770, in Kinnaird, *Spain in the Mississippi Valley*, 2:154–155; Carlos Marichal, "El peso o real de a ocho en España y America: Una moneda Universal (siglos XVI–XVIII)," in *El Camino hacia el Euro: El real, el escudo y la pesesta* (Madrid: Banco de España, 2001), 32; Usner, *Indians, Settlers, and Slaves*, 96–100, 130–131; O'Reilly "Record of Gifts That Should Be Given Annually to Indian Nations," 1777, reel 1, 33–81, Papeles Procedentes de Cuba, Library of Congress; Joseph de Crue, "Demonstracion practicada por la contaduria principal de exercito y de la Provincia de la Luiciana . . . ," May 31, 1786, legajo 597, Papeles Procedentes de Cuba, Library of Congress.

35. Fabel, *Colonial Challenges*, 104; Brain, *Tunica Archaeology*, 316.

36. Marc de Villiers du Terrage, *The Last Years of French Louisiana*, ed. Carl Brasseux and Glenn R. Conrad (Lafayette: University of Southwestern Louisiana, 1982), 240.

37. Desmazelliers to d'Abbadie, March 14, 1764, in Alvord and Carter, *Critical Period*, 236.

38. The estimates for the size of the Ofogoulas in 1771 range from seven to "a dozen" warriors. Using those numbers, the total population was likely somewhere between twenty-five and forty-two people. However, all of these estimates come from British sources and, given Perruquier's adamant refusal to work with the British government, it was firmly in the British interest to emphasize that the Ofogoulas were "of no consequence having only seven warriors." John Thomas to Haldimand, December 21, 1771, vol. 1, class 21.672, Records of the British Colonial Office; Gov. Chester to the Earl of Hillsborough, Pensacola, September 28, 1771, in *Peter Chester, Third Governor of the Province of British West Florida Under British Dominion, 1770–1781*, ed. Eron Rowland (Jackson: Mississippi Historical Society, 1925), 97; Thomas Hutchins, *A Historical Narrative and Topographical Description of Louisiana and West Florida* (Philadelphia, 1784), 44–45.

39. This means that the total population of the seven nations near Pointe Coupée and along the Red River was about 1,043 people. With the inclusion of the roughly 105 Tunicas who lived on the eastern side of the river, that puts the Petites Nations population in the region directly along the river between Pointe Coupée and Natchez at 1,148. The 1777 estimates suggest that the total Petites Nations population west of the river was roughly 5,250. For comparison, British officials

estimated that there were 300 regular troops and about 3,000 militiamen who could be called to fight in Spanish Louisiana. Additionally, there were only 200 settlers at Pointe Coupée in 1699, 104 settlers at Natchez in 1771, and no more than 55 soldiers between the two posts. John Thomas to Haldimand, December 21, 1771, vol. 1, class 21.672, Records of the British Colonial Office; John Thomas to John Stuart, December 2, 1771, vol. 1, class 21.672, Records of the British Colonial Office; John Blommart to John Stuart, August 18, 1777, vol. 78, class 5, Records of the British Colonial Office; General Gage, "List of the French or Spanish Posts on the Mississippi from the Missouri to the Sea," January 6, 1769, vol. 87, class 5, Records of the British Colonial Office.

40. It seems that, following the Tunica's assault in 1764, at least some Pacanas decided to join the Tunicas when they returned to their homelands near Point Coupée. This again underscores the centrality of both mobility and multinational settlements to understanding the power of Native nations in this era. John Thomas to John Stuart, December 12, 1771, vol. 1, class 21.672, Records of the British Colonial Office.

41. John Thomas to Haldimand, December 21, 1771, vol. 1, class 21.672, Records of the British Colonial Office.

42. In 1764 Captain Campbell reported that the Tunicas had promised to "bring in the Arkansas" and convince the nation to move across the river and settle in British territory. This is especially remarkable given the Arkansas (Quapaws) were at least four times the size of the Tunica nation in 1763. Captain Campbell to Governor Johnstone, December 12, 1764, *MPA:ED*, 1:267; Ethridge, *Chicaza to Chickasaw*, 132–133.

43. Charles Stuart to John Stuart, December 2, 1772, vol. 74, reel. 6, pt.1, Records of the British Colonial Office.

44. Stuart to Durnford, April 29, 1771, no. 8, vol. 74, class 5, Records of the British Colonial Office.

45. DuVal, "Education of Fernando de Lebya," 1–29; "Three Speeches Given at an Indian Council held by the British at Fort Bute," in Bjork, "Documents Regarding Indian Affairs," 408–410.

46. After Houmas and Alabamas sacked Fort Bute in 1765, it was reoccupied in 1766. However, the forces at the fort remained meager, and it functioned as more of an imperial outpost within Indigenous territory than as a true bastion of imperial control in the region. Villier to Thomas, November 25, 1771, Thomas to Unzaga y Amezaga, December 4, 1771, and Thomas to Villier, December 5, 1771, in Bjork, "Documents Regarding Indian Affairs," 399–408; David Narrett, *Adventurism and Empire: The Struggle for Mastery in the Louisiana-Florida Borderlands, 1762–1803* (Chapel Hill: University of North Carolina Press, 2015), 37–39.

47. John Stuart to William Howe, October 6, 1777, 695–696, Carleton Papers, Library of Congress.

48. Fabel, *Colonial Challenges*, 108, 132.

49. Talk Between Charles Stuart and Small Tribes on the Mississippi, October 17, 1772, fr. 806, vol. 74, reel 6, pt.1, Records of the British Colonial Office.

50. Statement of Payment for Indian Presents, January 9, 1770, in Kinnaird, *Spain in the Mississippi Valley*, 2:154–155; Charles Stuart to John Stuart, December 2, 1772, fr. 793, vol. 74, reel 6, pt. 1, Records of the British Colonial Office; Charles Stuart to John Stuart, November 15, 1772, vol. 74, class 5, Records of the British Colonial Office.

51. Ulloa to Grimaldi, August 4, 1768, in Kinnaird, *Spain in the Mississippi Valley*, 2:61–62; Fabel, *Colonial Challenges*, 121, 128–129.

52. Kinnaird, *Spain in the Mississippi Valley*, 2:xix, xxii–xxiii.

CHAPTER 8

1. Allain to Unzaga y Amezaga, April 17, 20, May 23, September 25, October 27, 1770, and January 4, June 4, 1771; Unzaga y Amezaga to Allain, April 26 and November 14, 1770; all in legajo 188a, reel 1, Papeles Procedentes de Cuba, Library of Congress, Washington, DC.

2. John Stuart to General Haldimand, March 2, 1770, vol. 1, class 21.672, Records of the British Colonial Office, Library of Congress; John Stuart's Remarks on Lieutenant Governor Durnford's Letters to the Earl of Hillsborough Relating to Indian Affairs, February 18, 1770, vol. 72, class 5, Records of the British Colonial Office, Library of Congress; Brain, *Tunica Archaeology*, 30–31; Ethridge, *Chicaza to Chickasaw*, 174–193; Bartram, *Travels*, 248, 277.

3. Usner, *Indians, Settlers, and Slaves*, 108–109; "Segun los padrones del año 1769 en los papeles remitidos por el Estimado Señor O'Reilly..."—Combined Censuses of 1769 and 1777, legajo 2359, Special Collections, Newberry Library, Chicago; Clinton Howard, "Early Settlers in British West Florida," *Florida Historical Quarterly* 24, no. 1 (1945): 45–55; Deborah Bauer, "'... in a strange place...': The Experiences of British Women During the Colonization of East and West Florida," *Florida Historical Quarterly* 89, no. 2 (2010): 152–153; DuVal, *Independence Lost*, 177.

4. The common, and conservative, estimated ratio of warriors to total Indigenous population is 1 warrior for every 3.5 other people within a population. Using a 5x multiplier is probably a more accurate representation of the true populations of Indigenous nations. John Thomas to General Haldimand, December 21, 1771, vol. 1, class 21.672; John Thomas to John Stuart, December 12, 1771, vol. 1, class 21.672; John Blommart to John Stuart, August 18, 1777, vol. 78, class 5; General Gage, "List of the French or Spanish Posts on the Mississippi from the Missouri to the Sea," January 6, 1769, vol. 87, class 5; all in Records of the British Colonial Office, Library of Congress.

5. Allain to Unzaga y Amezaga, April 20, 1770, legajo 188a, reel 1, Papeles Procedentes de Cuba, Library of Congress.

6. Allain to Unzaga y Amezaga, April 17, 20, May 12, 23, September 25, October 27, 1770, and June 4, 1771; Unzaga y Amezaga to Allain, April 26 and November 14, 1770; all in legajo 188a, reel 1, Papeles Procedentes de Cuba, Library of Congress.

7. Daniel Usner has written extensively about the difficulty in interpreting raiding and banditry as acts either of "deliberate protest" or of desperation. While by the 1790s, Choctaws were increasingly threatened by white settlers on their borders and facing shortages in their villages, the pressure in 1770 was decidedly less intense. Certainly, nearby cattle would be a welcome supplement to the food the Tunicas could provide, but the desire for meat does not in and of itself seem to justify the duration of these visits in a single location. Therefore, given that Allain also recorded the extent of their stickball playing, which has clear political messaging, it seems most likely that during this era these raids were part of a concerted political message rather than raids driven primarily by desperation. For a comprehensive analysis of Choctaw banditry in the Natchez region, see Daniel H. Usner, *Indian Work: Language and Livelihood in Native American History* (Cambridge, MA: Harvard University Press, 2009), 48–68.

8. Greg O'Brien, *Choctaws in a Revolutionary Age, 1750–1830* (Lincoln: University of Nebraska Press, 2002), 41.

9. Milne, *Natchez Country*, 176.

10. Allain to Unzaga y Amezaga, October 27, 1770, Unzaga y Amezaga to Allain, November 14, 1770; both in legajo 188a, reel 1, Papeles Procedentes de Cuba, Library of Congress.

11. Gage to Shelbourne, July 24, 1768, vol. 86, class 5, Records of the British Colonial Office, Library of Congress.

12. Citizens' Council at Mobile to Peter Chester, May 1771, vol. 1, class 21.672, Records of the British Colonial Office, Library of Congress; Usner, *Indians, Settlers, and Slaves*, 124–130; Reed to Gage, March 12, 1768, vol. 86, class 5, Records of the British Colonial Office, Library of Congress.

13. John Thomas to John Stuart, December 12, 1771, vol. 1, class 21.672, Records of the British Colonial Office, Library of Congress.

14. John Thomas to John Stuart, March 12, 1772, *Documents of the American Revolution*, ed. Kenneth Gordon Davies (Shannon: Irish University Press, 1974), 5:49–50.

15. Pointe Coupée, which had declared absolutely no slave population in 1769, was listed as having 482 white settlers, 4 free people of color, and 1,035 enslaved Africans. Paul La Chance, "The Louisiana Purchase in the Demographic Perspective of Its Time," in *Empires of the Imagination: Transatlantic Histories of the Louisiana Purchase*, ed. Peter J. Kastor and François Weil, 143–179 (Charlottesville: University of Virginia Press, 2009), 148; Usner, *Indians, Settlers, and Slaves*, 108–109.

16. DuVal, *Independence Lost*, 136–183; Greg O'Brien, "The Conqueror Meets the Unconquered: Negotiating Cultural Boundaries on the Post-Revolutionary Southern Frontier," *Journal of Southern History* 67, no. 1 (2001): 39–72; Articles of a treaty concluded at Hopewell, January 3, 1786, in *Indian Affairs: Laws and Treaties*, ed. Charles Kappler (Washington, DC: U.S. Government Printing Office, 1904), 2:12.

17. Grand Pre to Carondelet, September 27, 1796, in Lawrence Kinnaird and Lucia B. Kinnaird, "The Red River Valley in 1796," *Louisiana History* 24, no. 2 (1983): 187, 192; F. Todd Smith, *From Dominance to Disappearance: The Indians of Texas and the Near Southwest, 1786–1859* (Lincoln: University of Nebraska Press, 2005), 20–24, 60, 64.

18. Lawrence Kinnaird and Lucia Kinnaird, "Choctaws West of the Mississippi, 1766–1800," *Southwestern Historical Quarterly* 83, no. 4 (1980): 349–352; O'Brien, *Choctaws in a Revolutionary Age*, 10, 51–61; Winthrop Sargent to Timothy Pickering, September 18, 1798, *Mississippi Territorial Archives, 1798–1803*, ed. Dunbar Rowland (Nashville, TN: Brandon Printing Company, 1905), 47.

19. Usner, *Indians, Settlers, and Slaves*, 114–115, 280.

20. Browne to Hillsborough, Pensacola, July 6, 1768, *MPA:ED*, 3:94–95; Waselkov and Gums, *Plantation Archaeology*, 17, 36–38, 215–216; Giraud, *History of French Louisiana*, 1:101; John Brice Harris, *From Old Mobile to Fort Assumption* (Nashville, TN: Parthenon Press, 1959), 16; Usner, *Indians, Settlers, and Slaves*, 28; Smith, *From Dominance to Disappearance*, 24, 64.

21. Valentine Layssard to Luis de Unzaga y Amezaga, March 16, 1775, legajo 189-2, Papeles Procedentes de Cuba, Library of Congress, 4–5; Smith, *From Dominance to Disappearance*, 19–20, 65.

22. Donald Hunter, "Their Final Years: The Apalachee and Other Immigrant Tribes on the Red River, 1763–1834," *Florida Anthropologist* 47, no. 1 (1994): 5.

23. Waselkov and Gums, *Plantation Archaeology*, 160; Galloway, *Practicing Ethnohistory*, 245–291; Galloway, "'So Many Little Republics,'" 518.

24. John Stuart's Remarks on Lieutenant Governor Durnford's Letters to the Earl of Hillsborough Relating to Indian Affairs, February 18, 1770, vol. 72, class 5, Records of the British Colonial Office, Library of Congress.

25. Barnett, *Mississippi's American Indians*, 147–148.

26. Ultimately, the Choctaws were forced to cede the lands of the Mobilians and Tohomes, but they stood stalwart on the Petites Nations' land claims west of the Pascagoula River. John Stuart to General Haldimand, March 2, 1770, vol. 1, class 21.672, Records of the British Colonial Office, Library of Congress; John Stuart's Remarks on Lieutenant Governor Durnford's Letters to the Earl of Hillsborough Relating to Indian Affairs, February 18, 1770, vol. 72, class 5, Records of the British Colonial Office, Library of Congress; Gums and Waselkov, *Plantation Archaeology*, 37.

27. It was not uncommon during the eighteenth century for larger and more powerful Native nations to cede lands that they held contested control over. For example, in the 1730s and 1740s Haudenosaunee leaders ceded large tracts of land in Pennsylvania and Virginia to the British. While the Haudenosaunee people claimed control of these territories, in practice they were the homelands of the Lenape, Susquehanna, and Ohio River Valley peoples, and these Native groups refused to accept the validity of these cessions. Richter, *Before the Revolution*, 374–378.

28. John Stuart to Earl of Hillsborough, February 6, 1772, *Documents of the American Revolution*, 5:33; Kathryn E. Holland Braund, "'Like a Stone Wall Never to Be Broke': The British Boundary Line with the Creek Indians, 1763–1773," in *Britain and the American South: From Colonialism to Rock and Roll*, ed. Joseph P. Ward, 42–59 (Jackson: University Press of Mississippi, 2009), 57–59.

29. Higginbotham, *Mobile Indians*, 80.

CHAPTER 9

1. F. J. Crosby, "The Legend of Singing Waters," *Biloxi Daily Herald*, September 6, 1935, 12.
2. Federal Writers Project in Mississippi, *Mississippi Gulf Coast*, American Guide Series, Works Progress Administration (Gulfport, MS: Gulfport Printing, 1939), 95–96; Minnie Walter Myers, *Romance and Realism of the Southern Gulf Coast* (Cincinnati, OH: Robert Clarke, 1898), 108–109; Keith A. Baca, *Native American Place Names in Mississippi* (Jackson: University of Mississippi Press, 2007), 79; Hortence Davis, *Biloxi Daily Herald*, August 4, 1925, 5; Jim Fraiser, *Mississippi River Country Tales: A Celebration of 500 Years of Deep South History* (Gretna, NE: Pelican, 2001), 112–113.
3. Joanne Anderson, "Singing River Indians' 1939 Mural Returns to Pascagoula Post Office," July 11, 2010, *GulfLive*, https://blog.Gulflive.com/mississippi-press-living/2010/07/singing_river _indians_1939_mural_returns_to_pascagoula_post_office.html; Reuben Noah, "Legend of the Singing River," Indians at the Post Office, Native Themes in New Deal–Era Murals, Smithsonian National Postal Museum, accessed September 1, 2021, https://postalmuseum.si.edu/indiansat thepostoffice/mural27.html; "Pascagoula River," Deep South USA, accessed September 1, 2021, https://www.deep-south-usa.com/mississippi/family-fun/pascagoula-river; "Urban Legends of South Mississippi," WLOX, November 2, 2016, http://www.wlox.com/story/33615753/urban-legends -of-south-mississippi/; "History of Pascagoula," City of Pascagoula, accessed September 1, 2021, https://www.cityofpascagoula.com/255/History-of-Pascagoula.
4. Edmund Boudreaux, *Legends and Lore of the Mississippi Gulf Coast* (Charleston, SC: History Press, 2013), 50–55; Laura F. Hinsdale, *Legends and Lyrics of the Gulf Coast* (Biloxi, MS: Herald Press, 1896), 3–7, 33–35; Thomas J. Carruth, *Tales of Old Louisiana* (Lafayette: University of Southwestern Louisiana, 1979), 60–61; Jim Fraiser, *Mississippi River Country Tales* (Gretna, NE: Pelican, 2001), 65–66, 75–77; Robert Lowery and William McCardle, *A History of Mississippi from the Discovery of the Great River by Hernando DeSoto Including the Earliest Settlement Made by*

the French Under Iberville to the Death of Jefferson Davis (Jackson, MS: R. H. Henry, 1891), 254–258; J. F. H. Claiborne, *Mississippi as Territory, Province and State* (Jackson, MS: Power and Barksdale, 1880), 1:485, 504; George C. Smith, "The Vanishing Race," *Indian School Journal* (Chilocco, OK: Indian Print Shop, 1906), 25.

5. O'Brien, *Firsting and Lasting*, 105–145; Philip J. Deloria, *Indians in Unexpected Places* (Lawrence: University Press of Kansas, 2004), 3–15; Les W. Field, "Mapping Erasure: The Power of Nominative Cartography in the Past and Present of the Muwekma Ohlones of the San Francisco Bay Area," in *Recognition, Sovereignty Struggles, and Indigenous Rights in the United States*, ed. Amy E. Den Ouden and Jean M. O'Brien, 287–309 (Chapel Hill: University of North Carolina Press, 2013), 287–303.

6. Robert Lee, "Accounting for Conquest: The Price of the Louisiana Purchase of Indian Country," *Journal of American History* 103, no. 4 (2017): 921–924, 941–942; Usner, *Indians, Settlers, and Slaves*, 114–115, 280; Usner, *American Indians in the Lower Mississippi Valley*, 108; Tim Alan Garrison, *The Legal Ideology of Removal: The Southern Judiciary and the Sovereignty of Native American Nations* (Athens: University of Georgia Press, 2002), 13–33; Robert A. Williams, *Like a Loaded Weapon: The Rehnquist Court, Indian Rights, and the Legal History of Racism in America* (Minneapolis: University of Minnesota Press, 2005), 47–70; Theda Perdue and Michael D. Green, *The Columbia Guide to American Indians of the Southeast* (New York: Columbia University Press, 2001), 87–97.

7. The British government had forbidden settlement west of the Appalachian Mountains with the Proclamation Line of 1763. This order meant that elite land speculators—like Patrick Henry, Thomas Jefferson, Richard Henry Lee, George Mason, and George Washington—were unable to collect on their investments in the trans-Appalachian West; these Founding Fathers had personal financial motives in overthrowing the British government so they could collect on these ventures. Woody Holton, "The Ohio Indians and the Coming of the American Revolution in Virginia," *Journal of Southern History* 60, no. 3 (1994): 453–478; Calloway, *Indian World of George Washington*, 6–13, 104–106, 289–300; Gary Nash, *The Unknown Revolution: The Unruly Birth of Democracy and the Struggle to Create America* (New York: Penguin Books, 2005), 130, 169.

8. Calloway, *Indian World of George Washington*, 385–400, 423–450; Michael F. Conlin and Robert M. Owens, "Bigger Than Little Bighorn: Nomenclature, Memory, and the Greatest Native American Victory over the United States," *Ohio Valley History* 12, no. 2 (2012): 3–11.

9. Military resistance in the Southeast continued beyond the 1810s. Seminole people in particular continued to defend their lands and community against state and federal forces through the 1850s. Natalie Inman, "'A Dark and Bloody Ground': American Indian Responses to Expansion During the American Revolution," *Tennessee Historical Quarterly* 70, no. 1 (2011): 258–275; Perdue and Green, *Columbia Guide to American Indians of the Southeast*, 80–86; Mikaëla M. Adams, "Race, Kinship, and Belonging Among the Florida Seminoles, in *The Native South*, 144–161, 144; Perdue, *Cherokee Women*, 115–134; Garrison, *Legal Ideology of Removal*, 34–58.

10. Perdue and Green, *Columbia Guide to American Indians of the Southeast*, 86–97; Francis Paul Prucha, *The Great Father: The United States Government and the American Indians*, abridged ed. (Lincoln: University of Nebraska Press, 1986), 68–87; Garrison, *Legal Ideology of Removal*, 1–33; Circe Sturm, *Blood Politics: Race, Culture, and Identity in the Cherokee Nation of Oklahoma* (Berkeley: University of California Press, 2002), 52–81; Katherine Osburn, "Tribal 'Remnants' or State Citizens: Mississippi Choctaws in the Post-Removal South," *American Nineteenth Century History* 17, no. 2 (2016): 201.

11. Sturm, *Blood Politics*; Mikaëla Morgan Adams, *Who Belongs: Race, Resources, and Tribal Citizenship in the Native South* (New York: Oxford University Press, 2016), 7–8, 96–131; David A.

Chang, *The Color of the Land: Race, Nation, and the Politics of Landownership in Oklahoma, 1832–1929* (Chapel Hill: University of North Carolina Press, 2010), 79–89; Angela Gonzales, Judy Kertész, and Gabrielle Tayac, "Eugenics as Indian Removal: Sociohistorical Processes and the De(con)struction of American Indians in the Southeast," *Public Historian* 29, no. 3 (2007): 53–67; Kim Tallbear, *Native American DNA: Tribal Belonging and the False Promise of Genetic Science* (Minneapolis: University of Minnesota Press, 2013), 2–10, 45–61, 53–67; Robert A. Williams, *Like a Loaded Weapon*, 71–83; Kevin Bruyneel, *The Third Space of Sovereignty: The Postcolonial Politics of U.S.-Indigenous Relations* (Minneapolis: University of Minnesota Press, 2007), 1–26; John Rockwell Snowden, Wayne Tyndall, and David Smith, "American Indian Sovereignty and Naturalization: It's a Race Thing," *Nebraska Law Review* 80, no. 2 (2001): 175–205.

12. Jodi Byrd, *The Transit of Empire: Indigenous Critiques of Colonialism* (Minneapolis: University of Minnesota Press, 2011), xv–xxvi; Barker, *Native Acts*, 32–34, 81–97; Patrick Wolfe, "Settler Colonialism and the Elimination of the Native," *Journal of Genocide Research* 8, no. 4 (2006): 387–409; Eve Tuck and K. Wayne Yang, *Decolonization: Indigeneity, Education and Society* 1, no. 1 (2012): 4–9; St. George Tucker, *Reflections on the Cession of Louisiana to the United States* (Washington, DC, 1803), 24–26; Lorenzo Veracini, *Settler Colonialism: A Theoretical Overview* (London: Palgrave Macmillan, 2010), 2–12.

13. Lowery, *Lumbee Indians in the Jim Crow South*, 1–17.

14. John Sibley to General Henry Dearborn, "Historical Sketches of the Several Indian Tribes in Louisiana South of the Arkansas River and Between the Mississippi and River Grande," April 5, 1805, in *Message from the President of the United States Communicating Discoveries Made in Exploring the Missouri, Red River, and Washita by Captain Lewis and Clark, Doctor Sibley, and Mr. Dunbar; With a Statistical Account of the Countries Adjacent* (Washington, DC: 1806), 67–82; Bates, *Basket Diplomacy*, xv–xvii.

15. MSS 79, June 18, 1802, Spanish Land Grant Papers, Historic New Orleans Collection, New Orleans; B. Lafon, "Floride Occidental et une Portion du Territoire du Mississippi," 1805, reel 12, pt. 6, Vicente Sebastián Pintado Papers, Library of Congress; J. Gibson, "A Map of the New Governments of East and West Florida," *Gentlemen's Magazine* (London, 1763); Bernard Romans, "A General Map of the British Colonies in America," map detail (London, 1776); Emma Willard, "Eighth Map: 1789," in *A Series of Maps to Willard's History of the United States, or Republic of America: Designed for Schools and Private Libraries, 1828* (New York: Gallagher and White, 1828); Johann Baptist Homann, Amplissima regionis Mississipi seu provinciæ Ludovicianæ â R.P. Ludovico Hennepin Francisc Miss. in America septentrionali anno 1687, no. 15534700, Beinecke Library, Yale University.

16. Paul Alliot to Thomas Jefferson, "Reflexions historiques et politiques sur la Louysiane," April 13, 1804, trans. James Robertson, in *Louisiana Under the Rule of Spain, France, and the United States, 1785–1807*, ed. James Robertson (Freeport, NY: Books for Libraries Press, 1969), 1:81–85, 102–105; Daniel H. Usner, *American Indians in Early New Orleans: From Calumet to Raquette* (Baton Rouge: Louisiana State University, 2018), 50–75; *Notice sur l'état actuel de la mission de la Louisiane* (Paris: Adrien Le Clerc, 1820), 43–45.

17. Alliot to Jefferson, "Reflexions historiques et politiques sur la Louysiane," April 13, 1804, 1:105; Julia Lewandoski, *Small Victories: Indigenous Proprietors Across Empires in North America, 1763–1891* (PhD diss., University of California, Berkeley, 2019), 84–86; Erbig, *Where Caciques and Mapmakers Met*, 102.

18. Berquin-Duvallon, *Travels in Louisiana and the Floridas, in the Year 1802: Giving a Correct Picture of Those Countries*, trans. and ed. John Davis (New York, 1806), 103–104.

19. Hutchins, *Historical Narrative and Topographical Description*, 39.

20. Daniel Clark, An Account of the Indian Tribes in Louisiana, Enclosed in letter to James Madison, September 29, 1803, *The Territorial Papers of the United States*, ed. Clarence Edwin Carter (Washington, DC: U.S. Government Printing Office, 1934), 9:62–64; Brian Klopotek, "The Tunicas and Biloxis Navigate the American Era," in Klopotek et al., *The Tunica-Biloxi Tribe*, 21.

21. Smith, *From Dominance to Disappearance*, xv.

22. Brain, *Tunica Archaeology*, 206–208; Carl A. Brasseaux, *The Founding of New Acadia: The Beginnings of Acadian Life in Louisiana* (Baton Rouge: Louisiana State University Press, 1997), 182–183; Galloway, "'This nation . . . is very brave,'" 20; D. Davis, "Case of Identity," 478; Swanton, *Indian Tribes of the Lower Mississippi Valley*, 314.

23. Gerald Vizenor, "Aesthetics of Survivance: Literary Theory and Practice," in *Survivance: Narrative of Native Presence*, ed. Gerald Vizenor, 12–35 (Lincoln: University of Nebraska Press, 2008), 17–20.

24. Testimony of R. Lee Fleming, director, Office of Federal Acknowledgement, For the Hearing Before the Committee on Indian Affairs, United States Senate on the Federal Acknowledgement Process, May 11, 2005, U.S. Department of the Interior, Office of Congressional and Legislative Affairs, https://www.doi.gov/ocl/federal-acknowledgement; Federal Acknowledgment of American Indian Tribes, A Rule by Indian Affairs Bureau, July 1, 2015, *Federal Register*, 80 FR 37861, no. 2015-16193, https://www.federalregister.gov/documents/2015/07/01/2015-16193/federal-acknowledgment-of-american-indian-tribes; Testimony of Bryan Newland, senior policy advisor, Office of the Assistant Secretary for Indian Affairs, United States Department of the Interior to the Committee on Indian Affairs, United States Senate Oversight Hearing on Federal Acknowledgment: Political and Legal Relationship Between Governments, July 12, 2012, U.S. Department of the Interior, Office of Congressional and Legislative Affairs, https://www.doi.gov/ocl/hearings/112/FederalTribalRecognition_071212; "Summary Under the Criteria and Evidence for Amended Proposed Finding Against Federal Acknowledgment of the Pointe-au-Chien Indian Tribe," May 22, 2008, Proposed Finding, PACIT (#56b)—Proposed Finding, Bureau of Indian Affairs, United States Department of the Interior, 1–11.

25. Haas, *Tunica Texts*, 9.

26. These translations are a bit awkward in English because I have transcribed them exactly as they appeared in Mary Haas's field notes. Haas recorded the phonetic Tunica as spoken and then the direct English translations of the words. Haas's aim was to analyze the Tunica language, so she was more interested in preserving the syntax and structure than in creating sentences that would sound graceful to modern English-language speakers. Mary Haas, informant "Sam Young," Mss.Ms.Coll.94, Mary Rosamond Haas Papers, series 2, subseries Tunica, box 40, notebook 3, 101, American Philosophical Society, Philadelphia (hereafter cited as APS).

27. Haas, "Sam Young," Mss.Ms.Coll.94, Haas Papers, series 2, subseries Tunica, box 40, notebook 3, 109, APS.

28. Haas, "Sam Young," Mss.Ms.Coll.94, Haas Papers, series 2, subseries Tunica, box 40, notebook 3, 123, APS.

29. Haas, "Sam Young," Mss.Ms.Coll.94, Haas Papers, series 2, subseries Tunica, box 40, notebook 3, 113, 115, APS.

30. Personal correspondence with John Barbry, director of the Language and Culture Revitalization Program at Tunica Biloxi, September 28, 2019.

31. Pénicaut records the presence of a group on the Red River called the Toux Enongogoula, which he says means "Nation of Stones." In Margry's account of Iberville's voyage, this nation appears as the Tassengoula or Tassénocogoula as the name of the river. Swanton traced the Choctaw etymology of this name to suggest that it means "people of the flint," and says that La Harpe

recorded that this group was also sometimes called the Anoy, which he sees as the origins of the Avoyelle name. Swanton also suggested that Avoyelle may be a French rendering of the same term in Natchez for "people of the stone." Bienville to Maurepas, August 10, 1733, *MPA:FD*, 3:624–625; Louboey to Maurepas, November 18, 1738, *MPA:FD*, 4:156–157; Pénicaut, *Fleur de Lys and Calumet*, 147; Margry, *Découvertes*, 4:121, 178; Swanton, *Indian Tribes of the Lower Mississippi Valley*, 24–26.

32. Perrier to Maurepas, November 28, 1729, *MPA:FD*, 1:67; Bienville to Maurepas, August 10, 1733, *MPA:FD*, 3:624–625; Crémont to Maurepas, February 21, 1737, *MPA:FD*, 4:141; Louboey to Maurepas, November 18, 1738, *MPA:FD*, 4:156–157; Louboey to Maurepas, July 8, 1741, *MPA:FD*, 4:188; Bienville, "Louisiana, On the Indians," August 25, 1733, *MPA:FD*, 1:203; Périer, Relations du Massacre des Natchez, March 18, 1730, ANOM, C13 A12-1, reel 19, fols. 47, 44; Louboey au Ministre, November 28, 1738, ANOM, C13 A23, reel 31, fols. 169, 171–174; Louboey au Ministre, January, 14, 1739, ANOM, C13 A24, reel 32, fols. 188, 190–191; personal correspondence with John Barbry, director of the Language and Culture Revitalization Program at Tunica-Biloxi, September 28, 2019.

33. Louis Kerlérec, "Memoir on Indians," December 2, 1758, *MPA:FD*, 5:213.

34. Allain to Unzaga, April 20, 1770, legajo 188a, reel 1, Papeles Procedentes de Cuba, Library of Congress.

35. Bernardo de Gálvez to José de Gálvez, September 15, 1777, and King's approbation of the Same, December 23, 1777, reel 1, doc 16, ledger 1, 197, Mississippi Provincial Archives: Spanish Dominion, John C. Pace Library, University of West Florida, Pensacola; "Regalos que se deben hacer annualmente a las Naciones de Indios por Reglamento de Estimado Señor Don Alejandro O'Reilly," no. 2, legajo 274, Papeles Procedentes de Cuba, Library of Congress; Statement of Payment for Indian Presents, January 9, 1770, in Kinnaird, *Spain in the Mississippi Valley*, 154–155.

36. Emphasis mine. Haas, *Tunica Texts*, 9; Fuentes, *Dispossessed Lives*, 1–8.

37. Swanton, *Indian Tribes of the Lower Mississippi Valley*, 274; Haas, "Sam Young," Mss.Ms .Coll.94, Mary Rosamond Haas Papers, series 2, subseries Tunica, box 40, notebook 3, 101–125, APS.

38. Mary Haas, "Sam Young," Mss.Ms.Coll.94, Mary Rosamond Haas Papers, series 2, subseries Tunica, box 41, notebook 6, 35–51, APS. Quote from pages 35–37.

39. The dangerous spirit is described as a snake with horns. This seems to be an archetypal creature similar to the underwater panther or horned serpent. These creatures have Mississippian origins in Southeastern belief systems. They typically reside in dangerous waterways and can serve to connect our world to the underworld. F. Kent Reilly, "People of Earth, People of Sky: Visualizing the Sacred in Native American Art of the Mississippian Period," in *Hero, Hawk, and Open Hand: American Indian Art of the Ancient Midwest and South*, ed. Richard Townsend, 125–138 (New Haven, CT: Yale University Press, 2004), 127–131; Haas, "Sam Young," Mss.Ms.Coll.94, Haas Papers, series 2, subseries Tunica, box 41, notebook 6, 37, APS; William A. Lovis, "Clay Effigy Representations of the Bear and Mishipishu: Algonquian Iconography from the Late Woodland and Johnson Site, Northern Lower Michigan," *Midcontinental Journal of Archaeology* 26, no. 1 (2002): 116; James E. Maus, "The Horned Water Serpent Bowls," *Central States Archaeological Journal* 62, no. 1 (2015): 31–34; Amy Dahlstrom, "Warrior Powers from an Underwater Spirit: Cultural and Linguistic Aspects of an Illustrated Meskwaki Text," *Anthropological Linguistics* 45, no. 1 (2003): 2–5.

40. Elizabeth A. Fenn, *Pox Americana: The Great Smallpox Epidemic of 1775–82* (New York: Hill and Wang, 2001), 137.

41. John Sibley to the Secretary of War, "Louisiana Indian Condition Numbers of the Louisiana Indians, 1800," April 5, 1805, Secretary of War, Letters Rec'd., 1805, Records of the Bureau of Indian Affairs, Record Group 75, Letters sent/received by the Secretary of War Relating to Indian Affairs, 1800–1824, U.S. National Archives (Washington, DC), 9,12.

42. Haas, "Sam Young," Mss.Ms.Coll.94, Haas Papers, series 2, subseries Tunica, box 41, notebook 6, 35–51, APS; Cain Burdeau, "Native Americans in Bayou Seek Federal Recognition," *Washington Times*, November 25, 2015; Barry Yeoman, "Reclaiming Native Ground: Can Louisiana's Tribes Restore Their Traditional Diets as Waters Rise?," *Lens*, February 9, 2017; Scott, *Art of Not Being Governed*, 127–131, 176–199; J. Daniel d'Oney, *A Kingdom of Water: Adaptation and Survival in the Houma Nation* (Lincoln: University of Nebraska Press, 2020), 39–145; Usner, *American Indians in Early New Orleans*, 132–134.

43. Klopotek, *Recognition Odysseys*, 42–43; Klopotek, "Tunicas and Biloxis Navigate the American Era," 21.

44. F. Smith, *From Dominance to Disappearance*, 30; Usner, *American Indians in the Lower Mississippi Valley*, 111–127; Usner, *Indians, Settlers, and Slaves*, 168–171; Stephanie May de Montigny, "The Alabama-Coushattas," in *The New Encyclopedia of Southern Culture*, vol. 6, ed. Celeste Ray, 94–96 (Chapel Hill: University of North Carolina Press, 2007), 95; Paul Alliot to Thomas Jefferson, "Reflexions historiques et politiques sur la Louysiane, April 13, 1804," trans. James Robertson, in *Louisiana Under the Rule of Spain, France, and the United States, 1785–1807*, ed. James Robertson (Freeport, NY: Books for Libraries Press, 1969), 1:102–105; Usner, *American Indians in Early New Orleans*, 43–75.

45. Brain, *Tunica Archaeology*, 304–308; Hall, *Africans in Colonial Louisiana*, 246, 344–368; Brasseaux, *Founding of New Acadia*, 183; Déposition de Françoise Sauvagess, Pointe Coupée Parish Records, Original Acts, fols. 13–18, box 11, 13–15, Gwendolyn Midlo Hall Papers, Amistad Center, Tulane University, New Orleans; Déposition de Madelaine Sauvagess, Pointe Coupée Parish Records, Original Acts, fols. 13–18, box 11, 15–17, Gwendolyn Midlo Hall Papers, Amistad Center, Tulane University, New Orleans.

46. Berquin-Duvallon, *Travels in Louisiana and the Floridas*, 102; Lewandoski, *Small Victories*, 76–92.

47. De Montigny, "Alabama-Coushattas," 95.

48. Governor Claiborne to the Secretary of War, July 25, 1807, *Territorial Papers of the United States*, 9:756–757; Ford, *Settler Sovereignty*, 1–42; Bates, *Basket Diplomacy*, xv–xvii.

49. Klopotek, *Recognition Odysseys*, 43.

50. Klopotek, "Tunica and Biloxis Navigate the American Era," 23.

51. Presumably, these nations also all spoke French, although Haas does not mention this. Mary R. Haas, *Tunica* (New York: J. J. Augustin, 1940), 9.

52. Barker, *Native Acts*, 27–40; Elizabeth A. Povinelli, "The State of Shame: Australian Multiculturalism and the Crisis of Indigenous Citizenship," *Critical Inquiry* 24, no. 2 (1998): 587–591.

53. Klopotek, *Recognition Odysseys*, 77; Brian Klopotek, "Of Shadows and Doubts: White Supremacy, Decolonization, and Black-Indian Relations," in *Sovereign Acts: Contesting Colonialism Across Indigenous Nations and Latinx America*, 230–253 (Tucson: University of Arizona Press, 2017), 239, 246–247; Arlinda Locklear, "Land, Acknowledgment, and Patrimony: The Tunica-Biloxi Tribe's Leadership in Shaping Federal Indian Law," in Klopotek et al., *Tunica-Biloxi Tribe*, 31–33.

54. John. D. Barbry, "'Tayoroni-Halayihku Hihchi Ɔnta!' The Tunica-Biloxis remain here!," in Klopotek et al., *Tunica-Biloxi Tribe*, 35.

55. Lex Talamo, "POW WOW!! Tunica Biloxi Tribe Hosts 22nd Gathering," May 22, 2017, *Shreveport Times*, accessed September 1, 2021, https://www.shreveporttimes.com/story/news/2017/05/22/pow-wow-tunica-biloxi-tribe-hosts-22nd-gathering/102007162/.

AFTERWORD

1. Dan Copp, "'It's Critically Important': Port Fourchon Rushes to Recover After Hurricane Ida," *Houma Today*, September 4, 2021, https://www.houmatoday.com/story/news/2021/09/04/port-fourchon-recovering-after-hurricane-ida-gulf-mexico-oilfield/5715711001/; Sarah Ravits, "'It's Everyone's Disaster': Isolated Louisiana Tribal Communities Suffer Ida's Devastation," *Gambit*, September 10, 2021, https://www.nola.com/gambit/news/the_latest/article_f96d9aa0-11d1-11ec-ba5e-1fe255de627f.html; Trevor Hughes, "'Nothing You Can Do but Wait': In New Orleans, Frustrations Rise over Hurricane Ida Outages: Death Toll Rises," *USA Today*, September 7, 2021, https://www.usatoday.com/story/news/nation/2021/09/07/hurricane-power-outages-ida-leave-new-orleans-residents-hot-miserable/5751977001/.

2. Robby Chavez, "Why Some Indigenous Tribes Are Being Left Behind in Louisiana's Ida Recovery," *PBS New Hour*, October 20, 2021, https://www.pbs.org/newshour/nation/why-some-indigenous-tribes-are-being-left-behind-in-louisianas-ida-recovery; Kezia Setywan, "Pointe-au-Chien Tribe Members Take Recovery into Their Own Hands," *Houma Today*, September 6, 2021, https://www.houmatoday.com/story/news/2021/09/06/pointe-au-chien-tribe-members-take-recovery-efforts-into-their-own-hands/5723958001/; Oliver Laughland, "'Ida Is Not the End': Indigenous Residents Face the Future on Louisiana's Coast," *Guardian*, September 12, 2021, https://www.theguardian.com/us-news/2021/sep/12/hurricane-ida-louisiana-pointe-aux-chenes-isle-de-jean-charles; LBJ, "Pointe-aux-Chênes Fights for Survival Following Hurricane Ida," *WGNO*, September 28, 2021, https://wgno.com/news/louisiana/terrebonne-parish/pointe-aux-chenes-fights-for-survival-following-hurricane-ida/.

3. Many of these demolished homes are along Highway 665. Chavez, "Why Some Indigenous Tribes Are Being Left Behind in Louisiana's Ida Recovery"; "Hurricane Ida Relief Efforts," accessed September 21, 2021, Pointe-au-Chien Indian Tribe, https://www.pactribe.com/about-3.

INDEX

d'Abbadie, Jean-Jacques-Blaise, 201, 204–5
Abenaki, 19, 193
Abhikas, 31, 64, 68, 109, 110–11, 191. *See also* Upper Creeks
Ackia (Chickasaw village), 183
Acolapissas, 47, 70, 124, 133, 155, 156–57, 205, 244
adoption, 14–15, 52, 73, 83–86, 92, 103, 192, 241. *See also* naturalization; social reproduction
Africans: enslaved 77–78, 98, 109, 116, 118, 128, 143, 145, 148–49, 248, 280n3, 280n5; free, 129–30, 154
agriculture, 116
Alabamas, 31, 43, 64, 67–68, 82, 109, 110–11, 191, 211, 216, 225, 235, 237
Alabama-Coushattas, 253
alcohol, 237
Allain, Jean-François, 214, 217–18, 222, 244
alliances, 54, 62, 198, 211–12, 216–22, 243, 252
alligator, 100–101
Alliot, Paul, 236–37
ambassador, 52
American Indian, 11
American Revolution, 194, 215, 217, 221, 232, 253
Amite River, 202–3
Amylcou, 50
Anishinaabeg, 173, 176–77, 187–88, 193, 198, 202, 232
anthropophagy 36–37. *See also* slave raids
Antobiscania (Bayagoula leader), 56–57
Apalachees, 65–66, 82, 110, 180, 184, 215, 222–25, 234
archeology, 60
Arkansas River Valley, 27
assassination, 189
Atakapa, 8, 216. *See also* Ishak/Atakapas

autonomy, 38, 249, 252
authenticity, 12
Avoyelles, 203–4, 205, 240–45, 247

baptism, 79, 82, 87–89, 92–93
Barbry, Earl, 251–52
Bayacchytos, 50
Bayagoulas, 51–52, 69–70, 73, 96, 110, 122, 133–34, 148, 155, 244; French dependency on, 56,
Bayou Lafourche, 94, 97
Bayou LaFourche Band of Biloxi-Chitimacha Indians, 11, 246, 253, 255, 257
beads, 49
Berquin-Duvallon, Pierre-Louis, 237
Biloxi (colonial settlement), 9, 109, 111, 128
Biloxis, 4, 9, 14, 42, 65, 73, 77, 96, 110, 118, 123–24, 185, 191, 211 216, 223, 225, 234, 239, 245–47, 251–53; early relationship with French, 45–47, 50–52. *See also* Mathaah Cush
blood quantum, 234, 262n22
borderland, 6, 7, 21, 41, 117, 160, 215, 249
borders, 198–99, 236
Bossu, Jean Bernard, 57–58
Bride-les-Boeufs (Tunica leader), 162, 165, 203–5
Broutin, Ignace-François, 157
Bureau of Indian Affairs, 12, 239

Cadillac, Antoine de la Mothe, Sieur de, 80
Caddoan nations, 71, 164
Cahokia, 23
Cahokias, 176
Cahura-Joligo (Tunica leader), 63, 162, 163, 165
calumet ceremony, 28–9, 29fig4, 49, 50, 54, 59, 62, 86, 94–95, 99fig7, 132, 153, 163–64

Canty, Mr., 219–20
Capinans, 45–52, 63, 65–66, 70, 72, 124–27, 185, 285n53
Cap Français, 167
captives, 26–27, 50, 69–74, 80–81, 83–86, 94–95, 100, 153, 168–69, 175, 178, 202; Chakchiuma, 183; Tensa, 87–93; Natchez, 162, 164
Caribbean: French, 167
Carlos III (Spanish king), 198–99
Carolina, 31–32, 164, 193. *See also* South Carolina
Catawbas, 15, 97, 194
Catholicism, 47, 62–63, 89, 223–24
cattle, 218
cession, 200–201, 225–26, 311n26, 311n27
Chahta. *See* Choctaws
Chakchiumas, 10, 123, 160–61, 164–66, 170 172, 174, 181–83, 186–87, 189–93, 195, 302n16
Chaouachas, 35, 96, 106, 124, 131, 133, 154–55, 244, 297n38
Charli, Nicolas, 87–88
Charli, Sieur, 87–88
Charles II (king of Spain), 52
Charleston, 32, 97; slave trade in, 31, 33, 73, 76, 155, 202
Charlevoix, Pierre, 121–22
Chatots, 65–66, 110, 180, 184, 202, 208, 216, 223, 225
Chepart, Sieur de, 140–41, 143, 146–48
Cherokees, 193, 233, 235
Chesapeake, 32
Chicaza, 38. *See also* Chickasaws
Chickasaw Wars, 10, 172–73, 175, 182–87
Chickasaws, 6, 17, 19, 21–22, 31, 36, 38, 40–41, 64, 67, 72, 82, 191, 233, 238; alliance with the English, 33–35; alliance with the French, 95; and the Chakchiumas, 179–80, 183; relationship with Yazoos, 43; raids by, 109, 179–80, 187. *See also* Chicaza
Chika (Tunica woman), 248
Chitimachas, 4, 10, 75–110, 122, 128, 239, 246, 247, 253; alliance with Natchez, 95; enslavement of, 93–108; resistance to French, 127–39
Chitimacha War, 96–97, 101–2, 105, 106–7, 109, 122, 131, 164
Choctaw Civil War, 10, 173, 186–95, 225
Choctaws, 6, 8–11, 21–22, 33, 38–39, 40–41, 64–68, 97, 111, 119, 202, 233, 235, 238–39,

251–53; alliance with the French, 95, 136; and the American Revolution, 221; at Pointe Coupée, 214–17; attacks on Chickasaws, 184; Chickasawhay, 3, 67, 137–38, 155, 180, 184, 190–91, 202, 225, 226; diplomacy, 218; dissatisfaction with French gifts, 120–21; divisions among, 184–85; French fear of, 120–21; gifts to, 137; in West Florida, 219–20; Sixtown 39, 190, 193, 219, 226; Eastern 39, 155, 156, 185, 187, 189–91, 192, 225; Western, 39, 155, 156, 183–84, 187, 189–90, 192; Natchez War and, 149–50, 153–55 159–61, 170; Chickasaw Wars and the, 181, 184; treaty with Spain, 221–22; Yowani, 223. *See also* Coëchitto; Concha
Citizens' Council of Mobile, 219
citizenship, 5–6
Claiborne, William, 251
cloth: European, 19, 20, 26, 47, 56; Limbourg, 119
clothing, 56–57, 59–60, 63, 275n36
clubs: marked, 179
Code Noir, 79, 80, 116–17
Coëchitto, 181, 183–84, 186–89
colonialism, 121, 176, 212, 214, 216, 220, 221, 233–34, 243, 253
colonies, 21; expansion of, 123
colonizers, 17, 21, 24–25, 66, 81, 109
Comanches, 82
community, 8, 13, 14, 20
Company of the Indies, 115–16, 118, 138–39, 167, 291n22
Concha, 64, 215
contamination, 79
Coosa (Creek town), 64
corn, 49, 54, 59
coureurs de bois, 77, 80
Coushattas, 235, 250–51
covering the dead, 27, 101, 189, 219, 250–51, 266n18. *See also* vengeance
Coweta (Creek town), 191
Creeks, 6, 8, 9, 21, 22, 38, 215, 223–24, 233, 238; Confederacy, 204, 235; Upper: 32, 40, 43, 63–64, 67–68, 202; Lower 40; towns, 40–1. *See also* Coosa; Coweta
Crenay, Baron de, 163–64
Crozat, Antoine, 115
Cusabo, 32

dancing, 71
Davion, Father, 62–63

Davion's Bluff, 203–4
decline, 11, 16, 110, 124, 235–39
deerskins, 32
Delawares, 232. *See also* Lenape
Derbanne, François Guyon des Prés, 105
destruction, 121, 127, 133, 237
Diderot, Denis, 7–8
diplomacy, 24, 28, 47, 85, 109, 119, 139, 174, 194, 199–200, 211–12, 238, 241; gender and, 53–63; French, 81, 117; shifts in, 110–15. *See also* calumet; gifts; paint
diplomats, 21, 75, 90, 111; Chickasaw, 189; Choctaw, 185; French, 119
Diron d'Artaguiette, Bernard, 120–21, 156
disappearance, 11, 13, 229–31, 243, 247, 252
disease, 58–59, 84, 124, 246, 279n67. *See also* epidemics; smallpox
dispossession, 4, 122, 220, 228, 231, 233, 235, 238, 251, 253
Dominique (Tunica leader), 162, 167–69
Duclos, Sieur, 92
Dumont de Montigny, Jean-François-Benjamin, 61, 90–92
Dutch, 26

ecology, 1–2, 133
economy: plantation, 128, 232
Elizabeth I (English queen), 58
emergence, 19
empire, 9, 14, 27; American, 227, 231, 249; British, 194, 198, 244; French 51, 97, 109, 170–71, 179, 194; Spanish, 194
English, 17, 19, 34, 53; merchants 97
English Crown, 67, 205
enslavement, 17, 32, 77–83, 75–108, 141, 147, 169, 182, 281n6, 282n16, 282n19, 286n63; of children, 79–81; regulation of, 80. *See also* Africans, enslaved; slavery; slave trade
epidemics, 20, 117, 125
erasure, 122, 231–36, 238–39
ethnogenesis, 38
Europeans, 17, 25, 43. *See also* colonizers
execution, 101–2

Falkland Islands, 210
famine, 109
Farmar, Robert, 201
farming, 59–60
Father Le Maire, 126f
FEMA, 256
femmes, 61–62

Florida: Spanish, 66, 206
Flour Village (Natchez town), 113–15, 129–31, 141, 144–45, 162–64, 167–69
food, 50, 65, 153; scarcity, 117
Fort Bute, 196, 209–11, 308n46
Fort Rosalie, 156
Fort St. Pierre, 152–53, 181
Fort Toulouse, 111
Fox Wars. *See* Meskwaki Wars
Framboise (Chitimacha leader), 131–35
Françoise (Tunica woman), 248–49
French, 9–10, 13, 20, 26, 34, 42, 43–44; dependency, 158; diplomatic relationships with Petites Nations, 45–69, 73–74; immigrants 53–54; treatment of Native women, 55–56, 76–80
French Crown, 46, 49–50 80, 98, 116, 194
French Language, 47
French and Indian War. *See* Seven Years' War

Gravier, Jacques, 59, 89
gender: and diplomacy 53–63; non-binary, 60. *See also* clothing
gender roles, 27, 54–62, 77, 90, 120
gender ratios, 58
German Coast, 190–91, 194
gifts, 119–20, 136–37, 207–8, 219, 244–45, 307n34. *See also* diplomacy
Grand Caillou/Dulac Band of Biloxi-Chitimacha-Choctaw, 11, 246, 253, 255, 257
Grand Village (Natchez town), 24, 115, 128–32, 141–45. *See also* Natchez
The Grand Tohome (Tohome leader), 191
Great Lakes, 19, 26, 176, 198, 202, 233
Grigras, 25, 33, 35, 58, 62, 112–13, 128, 130, 131, 143
Guale, 32
Gulf Coast, 15–16
de la Grande Terre, Jeanne, 105–6
de la Grande Terre, Marie Therese, 106
Grandes Nations, 37–44. *See also* Chickasaws; Choctaws; Creeks

Haas, Mary, 36, 240, 245
Haudenosaunee, 9, 14, 17, 19, 21, 26–27, 31–32, 176, 184, 193–94
hierarchy, 24
Hitchiti, 32
hospitality, 43, 54–55, 135, 207, 214, 218
Houmas, 47, 55, 69, 133, 148, 155, 156–57, 191, 237, 239, 246, 247; female leader of, 58–59

human trafficking. *See* slave trade
humor, 100–101
Hurricane Ida, 255–58
Hutchins, Thomas, 237
Huvé, Alexander, 105

Ibitoupas, 160–61
Illinois, 19, 23, 178, 216
Illinois Confederacy, 173, 175, 176–77, 184, 186, 187–88, 198
indentured laborers, 116
Indian, 263n25, 267n27
Indians: real, 16
Indian Health Service, 12
Indian removal, 231–36, 251
Indian Territory, 233
Indigenous, 263n25
integration. *See* naturalization
intelligence, 179–81, 248–49
interdependency, 42, 47, 127, 181
Iroquois. *See* Haudenosaunee
Isle de Jean Charles Band of the Biloxi-Chitimacha-Choctaw Tribe, 11, 246, 253, 255, 257
Ishak/Atakapas, 4, 57, 94, 164, 239, 247–48, 285n59

Jenzenaque (Natchez town), 113–15, 132–33, 155, 162

Kaskaskias, 176
Kerlérec, Louis, 243–44
Kickapoos, 200, 232
kinship, 8, 69–74, 88, 101–4
Koroas, 23, 25, 30, 33–35, 82, 142; and the Natchez War, 149, 152–53, 161–62, 170

labor, 32, 46, 59, 76–82, 90–92, 98, 102, 115–16. *See also* slave trade; gender roles
LaCour, Widow, 248
Lake Pontchartrain, 70
Lake St. Joseph, 83
La Salle, sieur de (René-Robert Cavelier), 35
Lattanash (Tunica leader), 162, 168, 196, 199, 203–5, 210–11, 213–14, 218–19, 227, 240, 244, 249
de Laudun, Vallette, 61–62, 108–9
Law, John, 115. *See also* Company of the Indies
de Lay (French officer), 148–49
Layssard, Valentine, 224

LeBlanc, Monsieur, 146
LeBoeuf, Pierre-René, 88–89
Lenape, 198
Loftus, Maj. Arthur, 203–6
Louis XIV (king of France), 115
Louis XV (king of France), 52, 196–97
Louisiana: French, 9–10, 21, 43–52, 75–108, 113–15, 171, 175, 196–97, 213; Spanish, 11, 196–98, 204, 206, 210, 213–14, 216, 248, 305n3; Indigenous history of, 11, 13; territory, 231
Louisiana Purchase, 232, 235, 249
Lumbees, 15, 16
de Lusser, Jean-Christophe, 158
de La Maire, François, 60–61

Madeleine (Tunica woman), 248–49
man-eater, 94. *See also* anthropophagy
maps, 126, 236
marginalization, 213–28
marriage, 79, 81, 88–89, 105
Marguerite (Tensa woman), 88–89
Masclary, Jean-Paul, 108–9, 121
Mashpee-Wampanoags, 15
matrilines, 90
Mathaah Cush (Biloxi leader), 209
medicine, 119
merchants: French, 111
Meskwakis, 176–77
Meskwaki Wars, 173, 176
Miamis, 193, 232
Middle Ages, 9
migrants, 4–5, 9, 17, 21–22, 24, 27–28, 30, 37–40, 42–3, 47, 66, 70–72, 84, 113, 115–16, 118, 121, 128, 129, 131, 155, 203, 216, 221, 231, 246
migration, 19, 21–22, 38, 66, 117–18, 125–26, 145, 202, 234–35, 247
Mingo Tallaija (Tunica leader), 199
Miona (mythical Biloxi princess), 229
missionaries, 62, 277n47
missions, 206
Mississippi River, 17, 49
Mississippi Territory, 232, 245, 249
Mississippian cultures, 22–22
Mobile (colonial settlement), 9, 36, 47, 63–69, 70, 76–79, 86, 109, 111, 119, 128, 191, 194, 215, 219 222–28, 271n3; British arrival, 201–2
Mobile Bay, 40, 63–69, 111, 126, 215
Mobile River, 64, 180

Mobilian (trade language), 18, 252, 272n7
Mobilians, 4–5, 47, 63–68, 70, 73, 77, 122, 136–38, 173, 179, 184, 202, 208, 212, 215–16, 223, 225, 227; Choctaw-aligned, 66; resistance to French, 127–39. *See also* Tonty
Moncacht-Apé (Yazoo intellectual), 17–27, 30–34, 38, 42, 43–44, 161. *See also* Yazoos
Mongoulacha Mingo (Chickasawhay leader), 191
monogamy, 89–90
morality, 79
Moreau, Celestin, 251
Mosopeleas, 9, 10, 21, 27–28, 30, 32, 33–35. *See also* Ofogoulas
mounds, 23–24, 83–84, 241. *See also Nanih Waiya*
Moundville, 23, 39
de Montigny, François, 58–59, 84–85
Le Moyne de Bienville, Jean-Baptiste, 60, 65, 67–68, 70, 76–77, 79–81, 88, 94–96, 98, 113–14, 120, 123, 167, 172, 279n63; 1723 expedition against Natchez, 129–36; and the Natchez War, 181–84
Le Moyne d'Iberville, Pierre, 49–52, 54–55, 70, 85
Mugulashas, 42, 50, 51–52, 70, 148, 272n7
Muskogee. *See* Creeks
muskets, 19, 26, 34, 101, 101, 153
Muskogean languages, 39
multinational settlements, 5, 13, 19, 24, 25, 30, 33, 42–43, 50, 63–66, 69–74, 86–87, 124, 128, 136, 192, 195, 209, 215, 223–24, 227, 241, 243, 245; French living in, 46–47; Natchez, 141–42; Yazoo, 160–61
myth, 235

Nairne, Thomas, 86
Naniabas, 63–68, 70, 126–27, 180, 215–16, 223, 225–27; Choctaw-aligned, 66
Nanih Waiya, 39
Nassitoches, 70–73, 82, 96, 109, 164
Natchez (nation), 10, 11, 22–25, 34–35, 50, 58, 60, 85, 104, 109, 127–39, 297n41; French relationship with, 113–15, 142–44, 293n47; resistance 140–171. *See also* Flour Village; Grand Village; White Apple
Natchez (colonial settlement), 102, 112, 191, 194, 202
Natchez War (1729), 10, 140–71, 172–86
Natchitoches, 72, 105, 109, 128, 164, 167, 182, 194, 216

Native American, 263n25
nation building, 38–41
nations, 7–8; Native, 3–4, 12–13; dependent, 65; rebuilding, 69
nationhood, 7–8, 13
nation-states, 41, 238
naturalization 8, 15–16, 22, 26–27, 30, 37, 45–47, 52, 69–70, 84, 93, 148–49, 167–69, 223, 225, 241, 243, 245, 247, 285n53. *See also* adoption
natural resources, 41–42
New Orleans, 13, 35, 47, 70, 109, 117, 119, 154, 178, 182, 191, 197, 200–201, 205, 215, 219, 236, 237
nonbinary people, 47, 279n15. *See also* two-spirit
norms, 142, 150
North Carolina, 200
Noucache (Avoyelle leader), 244
Le Nouveau Mercure, 100, 123, 125

obligation, 7, 260n7, 42
Ocaneechis, 32
Odawas, 176, 198, 232
Office of Federal Recognition, 258
Ofogoulas, 84, 142, 147, 153–54, 161, 164–66, 170, 173, 179, 190, 203–4, 207–9, 212, 215, 216, 245, 247, 307n38. *See also* Mosopeleas; Perruquier
Ohio River Valley, 26–27, 32, 45, 153, 200, 232
Ojibwe, 176. *See also* Anishinaabeg
Oklahoma, 15, 232
Olustee (mythical Pascagoula prince), 229
Opelousass, 216
optimism, 109
O'Reilly, Alejandro, 207
Osages, 14, 207
Ouachas, 54, 106, 131, 133, 244
Ouachitas, 82, 84
Ouilchil (Nassitoches woman), 71–72
Oulchogonime (Nassitoches woman), 71–72

Pacific world, 20
Le Page du Pratz, Antoine-Simon, 21, 100–105, 128, 144–45, 147
paint, 45, 48, 52. *See also* diplomacy
Pakanas, 204–5, 212, 216, 223, 225, 227
Pamunkeys, 15
Paniouachas, 82
Paris, Messieurs, 122
Pascagoula, MS, 230

Pascagoula River, 126, 229–31, 254
Pascagoulas, 50, 64, 118, 124, 173, 185, 191, 208, 211, 223, 225, 229–31, 235, 247
Paul (Tunica leader), 62–63
peace accords, 191–93
Peace of Paris, 198
Pearl River, 125
Peedees, 164
Pénicaut, André, 70–72, 85
Périer, Étienne, 118–19, 154–55, 161–63, 169, 171, 172, 178–79
Perruquier (Ofogoula leader), 203, 205, 207–9, 240, 243
Pensacolas, 65–66
Peorias, 15, 176, 200
peripheries, 16, 27
Petites Nations, 7–14; origins of, 22–31; creating 37–44
Piniscas, 64. *See also* Upper Creeks
Pittman, Philip, 205, 207
place names, 230–31
Plaquemines, 23, 25, 39
Pointe-au-Chien Indian Tribe of Louisiana, 1–6, 11–13, 14, 16, 239, 246, 253, 255–57
Pointe Coupée, 166, 179 ,181, 191, 194, 202, 208–10, 213, 216–22, 225, 227, 237, 240, 243, 245–47, 253, 303n28
du Poisson (Jesuit missionary), 133–35
Pontiac (Odawa leader), 198, 202, 203–4
population, 47, 77–78, 83–84, 94–95, 106, 112, 115–18, 120, 136, 188, 192, 199–200, 216–17, 221, 224, 232, 307n39; density, 25–26; decline, 35–36, 109–10, 121–25; French, 142, 273n14
polities: autonomous: 51; Native, 7–10, 14; Mississippian, 22–26, 37–38
Potawatomi, 176, 232
power: colonial, 14, 64, 66, 78, 101, 115, 136, 142, 170, 194, 221, 232, 249; Indigenous, 4–5, 7, 9, 11,14, 26–27, 31, 36, 37–41, 83–84, 89, 103, 109–10, 112, 114, 117–27, 131, 181, 189, 196–212, 214–15, 218–19, 221–24, 226–28, 235, 238–39, 248–49, 251, 253, 308n40; political, 8, 15, 24, 32, 53–51, 72–76, 236
preservation, 69
propaganda, 108–39
prisoners. *See* captives

Quapaws, 27–28, 83, 134, 157, 161, 179, 183, 200, 207

Quitachoulabenaky (Ishak/Atakapa leader), 57–58
Quinipissas, 42
Quiz Quiz, 24, 25, 265n13

race, 7, 150–51, 233, 254, 267n27
raid, 20, 67, 110, 166, 173, 176, 219, 222, 309n7; slave raid, 21, 32, 33, 35, 49, 62, 64, 69, 73, 76, 154, 223
rape, 78, 80, 105, 188–89
Rapides Parish, 247
recognition, 238; federal, 262n22, 11–12, 14–15, 236, 239, 249, 251, 256, 257; state: 3, 11
Red River, 71, 202, 205, 224, 234, 243, 245
Red Shoe (Choctaw leader), 181, 183–90
refugees, 63–69, 84–5, 133, 150, 163, 164–66, 174, 183, 190, 192, 195, 235
resistance: 76,110, 112, 124, 127–39, 141, 147, 162, 166, 169–70, 198, 204, 212, 226, 233, 249, 312n9
Rochon, Marie, 88
Rochon, Sieur, 88
du Roullet, Régis, 136–38

Saint André (Avoyelle leader), 244
de St. Cosme, Jean-François Buisson, 95–96 101, 133, 286n64, 286n65
St. Cosme (Natchez man), 167
de St. Denis, Jucherau, 94–96, 164, 168–69
St. Domingue, 167
St. Louis, 216
sanctuary, 9, 15, 16, 70, 132, 164, 167–68, 173–74, 181, 190, 195, 204, 212, 235
Sauvole, Sieur de, 56–57, 64–65
Savannahs, 32
Serpent Piqué. *See* Tattooed Serpent
settlement Indians, 65
Seven Years' War, 11, 187–88, 192, 194, 217
sex, 90–92
sexuality, 60–62, 78–79
sharing, 6–7
ships, 20
Shawnees, 14, 19, 43, 193 198
Sibley, John, 246, 250
slavery, 76–77, 80, 89, 92, 101, 103–5, 124, 141, 143, 145–49, 169–70, 249. *See also* Africans, enslaved; enslavement
slave revolt, 248–49
slave trade, 126; Indian, 10, 22, 26, 30–37, 38, 46, 73, 97, 173, 268n37. *See also* Charleston
small nations. *See* Petite Nations

smallpox, 51, 62, 208, 237
social reproduction, 52; 69–70, 72
de Soto, Hernando, 24, 38
South Carolina, 86, 97, 200
Southerners: Native, 22
Spanish, 66
Spiro, 23
Soulier Rouge. *See* Red Shoe (Choctaw leader)
sovereignty, 6–7, 12, 41 215, 221, 233, 236, 248–49
statelessness, 238
stickball, 218, 251–52
Stuart, Charles, 196, 209–11
Stuart, John, 226–27
supplies, 53, 63, 108–9, 118–19, 154, 190, 278n53

Tamaroas, 176
Taposas, 160, 185
Texas, 206
Thomas, John, 208, 210, 219–20
Tohomes, 63–68, 70, 73, 77, 124–25, 136–38, 180, 184–85, 191, 202, 215–16, 223, 225–27. *See also* The Grand Tohome
Tonti, Henri de, 84
Tallapoosas, 31, 64, 68, 110–11, 191. *See also* Upper Creeks
Tale of the Fighting Eagles, 36–37
Tanaghrisson (Seneca/Mingo leader), 193
Tattooed Serpent (Natchez leader), 129–30, 131, 144–45
tattoos, 57, 71, 205
Tawasas, 65–66, 82, 92, 110
Tayoroni. *See* Tunicas
temple, 51, 59, 83–85
theocracy, 83
tobacco, 49, 128, 140–41
Tioux, 25, 33, 35, 58, 62, 112–13, 128, 131, 142, 143, 145, 149–50, 170
Tensas, 9, 10, 25, 27–28, 30, 75–108, 222, 223, 225; gender and sexuality, 89–90
Tomatly Mingo (Choctaw leader), 226
Tombigbee River, 38, 215
Tonty (Mobilian leader), 137 180–81
towns, 17–44
Treaty of Hopewell, 221
troops, 68, 141, 201, 295n4, 297n49
two-spirit, 60–62, 276n39, 277n44
trade, 16, 24, 32, 45, 49, 65, 111–12, 153, 159–60, 182, 201, 248; shortages, 186
traders: British, 172, 191–92
transition, 201

Tunica-Biloxis, 4–6, 16, 243, 245, 252–54
Tunicas, 8–11, 18, 24–25, 30, 33, 47, 58, 65, 69, 73, 83, 89–90, 142, 148, 191, 237, 283n33; female leader of, 59–60; alliances, 62–63, 137, 173, 196, 205, 213, 215, 218–20, 245, 255; villages of, 83–84; and the Natchez War, 151–52, 156, 162–66, 170, 179; and the Seven Years' War, 196–212. *See also* Youchigant, Sesotrie

de Ulloa, Antonio, 206–7
United Houma Nation, 11, 16, 255, 257
United States of America, 15, 221, 245; civilization program of, 233, 234

de Vaudreuil, Pierre de Rigaud, marquis, 188, 190–91
vengeance, 266n18, 33, 34, 72, 95, 150, 163, 182
La Vente, Henri Roulleaux de, 78–79, 88
de Villier, Balthazar, 210
violence, 67, 69–74, 78, 76, 79, 96, 109, 125, 129, 148, 187, 218; colonial, 22, 37
Vincent (French settler), 224
Virginia, 21, 32, 193, 200

War of the Spanish Succession, 46, 52, 67, 109, 112
War of the Austrian Succession, 186, 187
warriors, 48, 68, 309n4
Washington, George, 193
weapons, 17, 19
Wea, 193
West Florida, 196–99, 204, 206, 210, 214, 217
Westos, 32
White Apple (Natchez town), 113–15, 129–32, 140–48, 155, 162
wives, 87–93
"Woman Chief" (Natchez leader), 129
women, 47, 54, 77–78; as leaders, 57–58, 145, 273n15, 276n37. *See also* wives

Yakni-Chitos, 106–7, 289n98
Yamasees, 32, 97
Yamasee War, 97, 109–12, 175, 202, 287n71
Yazoo River, 6, 17, 32, 33, 181
Yazoo River Valley, 10
Yazoos, 9, 18–22, 24–25, 30, 31, 33–35, 37, 43, 142; and the Natchez War, 149, 152–53, 160–62, 170. *See also* Moncacht-Apé
Yellow Canes, 158–59
Youchigant, Sesotrie, 36, 240–43, 245–47

ACKNOWLEDGMENTS

This book would not have been possible without the incredible support of a huge number of people and institutions. The ideas and stories that fill these pages are drawn from years of conversations with friends, colleagues, and many generous Native Southerners who have taught me so much about the Gulf Coast.

More than fifteen years ago, Laura D. Kelley and Patty Ferguson first brought me down to Terrebonne Parish and introduced me to Pointe-au-Chien community members and to the story of the tribe's long fight for federal acknowledgment. Working with Patty and Laura to help collect historical material for Pointe-au-Chien's federal recognition petition led me to some of the core historical questions that would come to shape the research for this book. I am so grateful to Patty Ferguson and to Donald and Theresa Dardar for sharing their cooking and their expertise with me, and to the Pointe-au-Chien tribal council for granting me access to tribal oral histories. Since we first met in her undergraduate history class in 2006, Laura has mentored me and supported my work in all its forms. Were it not for her guidance and encouragement, it would never have occurred to me to apply to graduate school or attempt to pursue a career as an academic historian. Over the years, both Laura and her partner Thomas Bayer have hosted me in their home while I was on research trips back to New Orleans, read and edited drafts of my chapters, and offered critical feedback on my work. I am immensely indebted to them both.

I had the great fortune to work with Kathryn Burns, Kathleen DuVal, Wayne Lee, Malinda Maynor Lowery, Theda Perdue, and Vin Steponaitis at the University of North Carolina at Chapel Hill. Kathleen's generous and patient advising made this research project possible. Each of these scholars critically shaped this book and their criticism, guidance, and research advice have continued to guide my work. Equally as important, the warmth and generosity of this wonderful group taught me much about the critical connections between research and daily praxis. Wayne and Kathleen have continued to read much of my work, and to be invaluable friends and mentors. Both have offered essential research guidance—

sometimes presented on the backs of cocktail napkins and sometimes at a safe social distance across a backyard—in the years since I graduated.

At UNC, I was also exceptionally lucky to learn from my wonderful cohort in the History Department and from the amazing community of Native American and Indigenous Studies scholars. Brooke Bauer, Courtney Lewis, Meredith McCoy, Jami Powell, and Julie Reed kept me grounded with their searing humor and Indigenous feminist sensibilities. These scholars continue to inspire me and to remind me of the importance of community in academic research. Brooke Bauer is the big sister I never had. Jenny Tone-Pah-Hote, Keith Richotte, Malinda Maynor Lowery, and Randi Byrd mentored me with immense kindness and made me believe in the importance of my work. Stephen Riegg, Amanda Bellows, Matt Dougherty, Warren Milteer, Garrett Wright, Jeanine Navarrete, Nora Doyle, Sam Finesurry, and Jessie Wilkerson all helped me write my dissertation and filled my time in North Carolina with happy memories. In meeting Sarah McNamara in graduate school, I found my other half, albeit a half that loves floral prints and romantic comedies. Sarah has read and offered feedback on almost every version of this book since I began working on it in 2010. She is my late-night email hero and I do not know what I would do without her.

The generous support of a Barra Post-Doctoral Fellowship at the McNeil Center for Early American Studies at the University of Pennsylvania provided me with the time and intellectual community that enabled me to revise my dissertation and transform this work. Dan Richter's tremendous generosity, critical eye, and insistence that I figure out how to write about the "whoosh-whoosh" of migration among Native communities helped me develop the central arguments of this book. Max Dagenais, Rachel Walker, Dan Couch, Al Zuercher Reichart, Sarah Gronningsater, Nancy Gallman, Lauren DuVal, Don James McLaughlin, and Nora Slonimsky gave me essential help with revisions and their support and friendship sustained me through the darkest moments of 2016–17. I am also deeply grateful for the wealth of critical feedback that I received at my McNeil Center manuscript review workshop. Christina Snyder and Josh Piker's feedback helped me reshape my central arguments about Native nation-building and connect my book more fully to scholarship on the Native South. James Hill, Bill Carter, Meg Kassabaum, Laura Spero, David Silverman, Chris Bilodeau, Michelle LeMaster, and Sarah Gronningsater, provided essential revision advice and led me to expand the temporal breadth of this book. The terrific editorial team at Penn Press, including Karen Carroll, Bob Lockhart, and Lily Palladino, as well as my own amazing Choctaw copyeditor, David Emanuel, all offered invaluable guidance and revision help as I finished up this manuscript.

ACKNOWLEDGMENTS

I feel very fortunate to be surrounded by a brilliant group of scholars at New York University. Many of my current and former colleagues have deeply influenced my work over the past five years. Becky Goetz, Andrew Needham, Monica Kim, and Susanah Shaw Romney all read parts of this manuscript and offered critical feedback and revision help. Niki Eustace, Karen Kupperman, Emilie Connolly, Hayley Negrin, Kevin Kenny, and Steve Hahn have helped me workshop chapters, and my colleague Dean Saranillio has provided me with unwavering support and the theoretical grounding to support my third chapter.

I am also deeply indebted to a broader community of scholars who have significantly influenced my work. Jeani O'Brien and Coll Thrush have both mentored me with incredible kindness and generosity and provided me with so much of the NAIS foundation that has come to profoundly shape this book. Both Jeani and Dan User read the entirety of the manuscript and offered thoughtful and essential feedback that has strengthened my analysis and helped me figure out how to bring this project together. Dan Usner's continual support over the years, both in the form of feedback on my work and through his sharing of materials, has fundamentally shaped this book. My fellow Louisiana historian, Yevan Terrien, has also had an immense influence on this work. Over the years, he has shared sources, suggestions, and criticism and my work is much better for Yevan's generosity. Both he and Max Dagenais provided vital help with French translations when I struggled with faded ink and early eighteenth-century grammar. John Barbry and Jeffrey Darensbourg have also offered essential guidance for interpreting Tunica and Ishak language and history. Over the years, both John and Jeffrey have offered feedback on my written work, shared their expertise and scholarship on Tunica-Biloxi and Ishak history and culture, and put up with my mountain of foolish outsider's questions. Patty Ferguson and Bruce Duthu helped me figure out how to write the introduction and conclusion for this book, and they have both provided generous and essential critical feedback on my writing. I am so grateful to them both for the wisdom and perspectives they have shared with me. I am also deeply appreciative of all the guidance that Christian Crouch, Alejandra Dubcovsky, Robbie Ethridge, Jacob Lee, and Christina Snyder have offered on my work over the years, and I am indebted to George Milne for his generosity in sharing sources and research with me. Julia Lewandoski, Allison Powers Useche, Emilie Connolly, Nora Slonimsky, Rachel Walker, Brooke Bauer, and Hayley Negrin are the most brilliant collection of writing group partners I could have asked for, and all of their feedback has dramatically improved this book.

Over the years I have published several articles and chapters that were derived from research that I conducted for this book. Michael Martin and the reviewers at *Louisiana History* provided feedback and criticism that helped me strengthen much of the material that appears in chapter 7. Josh Piker and the reviewers of the *William and Mary Quarterly* offered vital critiques of my article on the Natchez War that enabled me to rethink my fifth chapter. Ignacio Gallup Diaz provided essential guidance for an article I wrote on resistance and revolts in early Louisiana for *The World of Colonial America: An Atlantic Handbook*, which helped me strengthen my second chapter. I was also honored to have the opportunity to collaborate with Brian Klopotek, John Barbry, Donna Pierite, and Elizabeth Pierite-Mora for the second edition of their edited volume, *The Tunica-Biloxi Tribe: Its Culture and People*. I am tremendously grateful for the feedback I received from John Barbry and Brian Klopotek as part of this work.

The support of numerous grants and institutions has made this book possible. Financial support from the Peoria Tribe of Indians of Oklahoma helped pay for my graduate education. Research and writing grants and fellowships from the University of North Carolina, the Woodrow Wilson Foundation, the McNeil Center for Early American Studies, the New Orleans Center for the Study of the Gulf South, the Huntington Library, the American Council of Learned Societies, and the Newberry Library all supported this work.

Finally, I am deeply grateful to be surrounded by a loving family that has supported my work for decades. My brilliant parents, Pat Truscelli and Bud Ellis, encouraged me every step of the way, and my brother Ethan's irreverent and witty black humor keeps me going. My grandparents are my inspirations. My grandfather Bud Ellis taught me to be proud to be Peoria and that American Indian stories and histories matter, and both he and my grandmother Barbara pushed me to pursue my education. My grandmother Edythe Truscelli has always believed in me more than I have believed in myself, and for the last five years, she has routinely offered to help me finish this book. I really should have taken her up on that. Finally, I am so grateful to my partner, Ben, for his love and support, and for putting up with being stuck with me in a tiny apartment in New York City while I finished this book in the midst of a global pandemic.

www.ingramcontent.com/pod-product-compliance
Lightning Source LLC
Chambersburg PA
CBHW021849230426

43671CB00006B/317